Modern Sport: The Global Obsession

Sport has become more than a simple physical expression or game – it now pervades all societies at all levels and has become bound up in nationalism, entertainment, patriotism and culture. Now a global obsession, sport has infiltrated into all areas of modern life and despite noble ideals that sport stands above politics, religion, class, gender and ideology, the reality is often very different.

These essays by leading academics and rising new talent consider the phenomenon of modern sport and its massive influence over global society. Together, this collection is also a tribute to the pioneering and inspirational work of Professor J.A. Mangan on the political, religious, class and gender-based aspects of modern sport, from academics greatly influenced by him and his writing.

This book was previously published as a special issue of *The International Journal of the History of Sport*.

Boria Majumdar is a Research Fellow at Latrobe University, Melbourne. He is also Deputy Executive Academic Editor of The International Journal of the History of Sport, Executive Academic Editor of Sport in Society and Co-Editor of the Sport in the Global Society Series.

Fan Hong is the Director of the Irish National Institute of Chinese Studies at University College, Cork in Ireland.

Sport in the Global Society

General Editors: J.A. Mangan and Boria Majumdar

Modern Sport: The Global Obsession
Politics, Religion, Class, Gender
Essays in Honour of J.A. Mangan

Sport in the Global Society
General Editors: J.A. Mangan and Boria Majumdar

The interest in sports studies around the world is growing and will continue to do so. This unique series combines aspects of the expanding study of *Sport in the Global Society*, providing comprehensiveness and comparison under one editorial umbrella. It is particularly timely, with studies in the aesthetic elements of sport proliferating in institutions of higher education.

Eric Hobsbawm once called sport one of the most significant practices of the late nineteenth century. Its significance was even more marked in the late twentieth century and will continue to grow in importance into the new millennium as the world develops into a 'global village' sharing the English language, technology and sport.

Other Titles in the Series

Modern Sport: The Global Obsession

Politics, Religion, Class, Gender
Essays in Honour of J.A. Mangan

Edited by Boria Majumdar and Fan Hong

LONDON AND NEW YORK

First published 2007 by Routledge
2 Park Square, Milton Park, Abingdon, Oxon OX14 4RN

Simultaneously published in the USA and Canada
by Routledge
270 Madison Ave, New York, NY 10016

Routledge is an imprint of the Taylor & Francis Group, an informa business

© 2007 Taylor & Francis

Typeset in Minion by KnowledgeWorks Global Limited, Southampton, Hampshire, UK
Printed and bound in Great Britain by MPG Books Ltd, Bodmin, Cornwall

All rights reserved. No part of this book may be reprinted or reproduced or utilised in any
form or by any electronic, mechanical, or other means, now known or hereafter invented,
including photocopying and recording, or in any information storage or retrieval system,
without permission in writing from the publishers.

British Library Cataloguing in Publication Data
A catalogue record for this book is available from the British Library

Library of Congress Cataloguing in Publication Data
A catalogue record for this book has been requested

ISBN 10: 0-415-39054-0
ISBN 13: 978-0-415-39054-5

AUGUSTANA LIBRARY
UNIVERSITY OF ALBERTA

Contents

Series Editor's Foreword

Boria Majumdar

'The growth of sports studies in the past 20 years has been considerable. ... Most of [the] intelligent research in the public domain has been published ... under the aegis of Professor Mangan ... and social historians everywhere have reason to be grateful ... for [his] tenacity in seeking out this new field.' [1]

Suffice to say that the marriage between sport and nationalism, entertainment and patriotism, culture and passion is a global phenomenon, more global on occasion than even the war against terror. In fact, 'sport' is now the foremost global obsession. This obsession embraces all aspects of contemporary life, yet the naïve still cling to the belief that sport stands above politics, religion, class, gender and ideology in all its forms. The reality could not be more different. Consider this: nowhere is the residual animosity towards England as a nation more aggressively expressed than at Murrayfield, the Scottish national rugby stadium, and in the passionate rendering of the now official anthem of the Scottish Rugby Union, 'The Flower of Scotland' – a lament for lost nationhood. The dirge recalls a rare victory on the battlefield of the Scots over the English:

> O flower of Scotland
> When will we see your like again
> That fought and died for
> Your wee bit hill and glen
> And stood against him
> Proud Edward's army
> And sent him homeward
> Tae think again.
> The hills are bare now
> And autumn leaves lie thick and still
> O'er land that is lost now
> Which those so dearly held
> And stood against him
> Proud Edward's army
> And sent him homeward
> Tae think again.
> Those days are passed now
> And in the past they must remain
> But we can still rise now

And be the nation again
And stand against him
Proud Edward's army
And send him homeward
Tae think again.

Sport, evidently, has infiltrated the politics of all; nations, rich and poor, the religions of West and East, gender struggles throughout the world, radical and reactionary, and ideologies everywhere, pragmatic and idealistic.

This collection of original writings by leading academics and future leading academics interested in the contemporary global impact of sport in society considers the phenomenon of modern sport and its massive impact on the recent and present 'global village'. As such the work stands on its own but, in addition, it is a tribute to the pioneering and inspirational work of Professor J.A. Mangan on the political, religious, class and gender aspects of modern sport, by academics greatly influenced by him and his writing. In evaluating Tony Mangan's impact on critical scholarship on sport, I can't resist the temptation to quote here what we have written in our appraisal of his work:

> One of the main values of an academic oeuvre is, we believe, the degree to which it in a sense encourages its own overcoming – the degree to which future research goes beyond the distance traversed by the oeuvre in question – and it is thus that we make bold to suggest some of the ways in which the considerable genius and erudition of Mangan's oeuvre may be taken further. But just as no matter how many centuries a batsman scores, there will never be another Bradman, just as no matter how many copies a sports journalist manages to sell, there will never be another Cardus, so do we think no matter how far we historians of sports go from here, there will hardly be another Tony Mangan. [2]

Modern Sport – the Global Obsession has aimed to cover a broad geographical canvas: Africa, America, Asia and Europe. It confronts a too often unacknowledged fact: modern sport is a necessary addiction, often for very different reasons, for politicians, ideologues, radicals and reactionaries in the twenty-first century.

Notes

[1] For details see Robert Hands, *The Times*, 22 March 2003.
[2] Boria Majumdar and Projit B Mukharji, 'A Man for the Future', the first essay of this volume, p.508.

Prologue: Transcending National Boundaries

Boria Majumdar

> I am always amazed when I hear people saying that sport creates goodwill between the nations, and that if only the common peoples of the world could meet one another at football or cricket, they would have no inclination to meet on the battlefield, Even if one didn't know from concrete examples (the 1936 Olympic Games, for instance) that international sporting contests lead to orgies of hatred, one could deduce it from general principles. ...
>
> At the international level sport is frankly mimic warfare. But the significant thing is not the behaviour of the players but the attitude of the spectators: and, behind the spectators, of the nations who work themselves into furies over these absurd contests, and seriously believe – at any rate for short periods – that running, jumping and kicking a ball are tests of national virtue. [1]

For the naive, sport is simply another forum for entertainment – for others it serves far more important functions. In the modern global village, it is promoted as an opportunity to bridge cultural gaps and facilitate peace, as seen most prominently with the Olympics. Even then, an undercurrent of nationalism is ever-present in international sporting events. For India and Pakistan, the political arena shifts onto the cricket field, providing symbolic battlegrounds for national supremacy. For England, whose first imperial territories were Ireland, Scotland and Wales, her local empire has produced sporting ripples across, and beneath, the surface of the relationship of the Irish, Scots and Welsh to the English on modern sports fields.

Commentators on modern sport often claim it is a fundamental component of twenty-first century society. Witness Australian journalist Greg Bearne on India-Pakistan cricket clashes and on the threat of cancellation on the eve of the February 2004 tour:

> Pakistan is a country that has never lacked great drama, in the past few months alone its President was nearly blown up twice, its nuclear scientists were exposed as having sold more atomic secrets than Gerry Harvey has sold televisions, and then, Osama was spotted in the hills on the border. But all these events come to nothing compared with the drama of a series against the Indians. [2]

Is this merely amusing journalistic logorrhoea?

Martin Rees in *Our Final Hour* considers the threat of unpredictable science and bolting technology. 'Humanity is more at risk,' he argues, 'than at any earlier phase of its history' – from dangers present and possible: the N-bomb, terrorism, lethal engineered airborne viruses, character-changing drugs and experimental science. He reviews the hazards of human error, ideological terror and environmental catastrophe, and comes to the pessimistic conclusion that humankind has only a 50–50 chance of surviving this century. [3]

Robert Cooper in *The Breaking of Nations* sees the strong possibility in this century of a steady descent into global political chaos: 'The new century risks being overrun by both anarchy and technology,' he writes. 'The two great destroyers of history may reinforce one another.' [4] Thus, in the next 100 years, it could be that only two options are available to the human race: global annihilation and political anarchy.

Cooper attempts to be positive and sees a way ahead. There is, hopefully, a linear progression in human affairs: 'Chaos is tamed by empire: empires are broken by nationalism; and nationalism gives way, we must hope, to internationalism. At the end of the process is the freedom of the individual; first protected by the state and later protected from the state.' [5] How realistic is this? His first condition of survival is that nations make peace with one another. A tall order! Sport is frequently promoted as a medium for peace on earth. The IOC, in particular, takes this line. The 2004 Indian tour of Pakistan was touted as the 'Friendship Series'. [6] So can sport help ensure human survival? An equally tall order! As George Orwell put it, 'Serious sport has nothing to do with fair play. It is bound up with hatred, jealousy, boastfulness [and] disregard of all rules' [7] and nationalistic sport is the most serious of all sport.

It is a truism that India v Pakistan cricketing confrontations are a barometer of Indian and Pakistani political relations. Two ancillary points may be made here: cricket, once viewed as an imperial cement, is now perceived as national mortar; and sport, while hardly fundamental to global survival, has been a not insignificant element in imperial and post-imperial nationalistic assertion and denial. Experiences of turbulence and instability in Indian politics and the rising heat of Indo-Pak foreign relations over Kashmir may readily convert an Indo-Pak cricket match into a test of national superiority.

Immediately after India's victory on 1 March 2003, in a World Cup encounter at Centurion, South Africa, the streets and lanes of Calcutta reverberated with sounds of blowing conches, bursting crackers and the chanting of slogans. At Kalighat, the city's premier religious shrine, many were seen waving national flags with pictures of Sachin Tendulkar stuck in the middle of the Ashoka Chakra, the national emblem. Gujarat, on the other hand, witnessed incidents of Muslims being stopped from celebrating. There were rioting, injuries and also a death in Ahmedabad. Violence also erupted in Bangalore. In all these places, prohibitory orders were imposed and security tightened. The reactions of Indian politicians to the victory also require attention. Army chief N.C. Vij congratulated the team on their win over the phone. It no longer mattered whether India made it to the 'super six', semis or final.

This extreme communalization and politicization of sport is not a phenomenon unique to Indian and Pakistani cricket. Experience suggests that this is not a state of affairs peculiar to the East. Rather these relational complexities between sport and politics in an era of hyper-nationalism seem all-pervasive. English imperialism, it is sometimes overlooked, was local before it was global. In sport, the resonances have been loud and long-lasting. Rugby football will serve here as merely one occidental political barometer. For all the intensity of the rivalry between the Celtic nations, England, for them, is the nation to defeat, and if possible, humble. Sport, as in the subcontinent, has helped sustain local resentments, insecurities and inferiorities. In fact, if the Scots obtain independence again, they could have only a 50–50 chance of survival as a nation to the year 3000. Contrastingly, if the partition of 1947 could be reversed, the Australian hegemony in modern cricket might never have been a thing to reckon with.

Modern Sport – the Global Obsession attempts to deal with all of the themes highlighted above and aims to 'illustrate the conceptual, empirical and analytical subtlety of studies of modern sport'. [8] It is one of the first attempts to geographically span the entire sporting world, drawing inspiration from the work of Tony Mangan, a scholar who has done so with sophistication and rigour. Thus an array of articles which view critical issues of nationalism, religion, class and gender through the lens of sport are made available in this volume.

It was said of Henry Bradley, philologist, lexicographer and senior editor of the *Oxford English Dictionary* that many owed their reputation to his guidance and direction. Thus when required to make a formal statement on his published work, he appended the remark 'that much of his best work was in other men's books'. [9] The same surely can be said of J.A. Mangan. Apropos of this, *The Oxford Book of Literary Anecdotes* records that on the occasion of the savaging of a certain scholar by an academic detractor, who, nevertheless seeking to be fair added that a man could not be a complete fool who had provided such a brilliant contribution to the collection, Bradley, for once allowing honesty to prevail over charity stated bluntly: 'To tell you the truth, I sent him that'. [10]

That Tony Mangan can be prevented from saying so after reading this collection makes it a satisfying tribute!

Notes

[1] George Orwell: 'The Sporting Spirit', first published in *Tribune* (London), 14 Dec. 1945.
[2] *Sydney Morning Herald*, 28 February 2004.
[3] For details, see Martin Rees, *Our Final Hour: A Scientist's Warning: How Terror, Error, and Environmental Disaster Threaten Humankind's Future in This Century – On Earth and Beyond* (London: Basic Books, 2004).
[4] See Robert Cooper, *The Breaking of Nations: Order and Chaos in the Twenty-First Century* (New York: Atlantic Monthly Press, 2004).

[5] Ibid.

[6] The 2005 tour has been billed as the 'Goodwill Tour'.

[7] Orwell, 'The Sporting Spirit'.

[8] 'Series Editor's Foreword' in J.A. Mangan and Fan Hong (eds.), *Sport in Asian Society – Past and Present* (London: Frank Cass, 2003), p.5.

[9] James Sutherland (ed.), *The Oxford Book of Literary Anecdotes* (Oxford: Clarendon Press, 1975), p.290.

[10] Ibid.

A Man for the Future

Boria Majumdar and Projit B. Mukharji

There used to be a happier epoch for reviewers attempting the seemingly impossible task of reviewing the oeuvre of a pioneer in a particular field of academic knowledge. S/he would start with a list of all that the pioneer had written on the subject, briefly outlining each project and then proceed to conclude with a sketched map of the impact the oeuvre had had on the discipline itself.

Unfortunately such a time is no longer at hand. The Internet has quite literally placed chronological lists of books and their brief summaries at the fingertips of any interested reader. At the same time, the immense explosion in publishing brought about by modern technological revolutions has doomed all attempts to exhaustively map influences to being forever inchoate. The new reviewer thus needs rethink his project if the assignment is to retain its cogency and at least a modicum of relevance. The approach we attempt to adapt in the course of this essay to achieve our end, somewhat in keeping with the modern trend, is to 're-read' Tony Mangan's oeuvre as post-colonial subjects.

One of the most delightful (the use of an openly non-academic, playful and personalized adjective here is, we may as well underline, quite deliberate) aspects of Mangan's work is the centrality he affords to the Empire in workwhat is essentially, at least initially, a story of the construction of British Metropolitan culture. When Edward Said wrote his classic work, *Orientalism*, he had lamented the lack of attention paid to the 'Other of Europe' in its constitutive role for the formation of the European self. Tony Mangan's *Games Ethic* is not in itself a story set in the Empire, it Is a story that maps the socialization, in metropolitan Britain, of future administrators and conquerors of the Empire. [1] He eruditely brings to light the centrality that visions and images of the Empire played in the very heart of the Empire to constitute it, socially and culturally. In certain ways, one feels that this re-visiting of the 'other' in Europe has remained central to Tony Mangan's work. Why else should he, as early as 1992, write these perceptive words in his prologue to *The Cultural Bond: Sport, Empire, Society*:

It is wise to appreciate that there was no culturally monolithic response to attempts to utilize sport as an imperial bond. A major problem that the analyst of ideological proselytism and its cultural consequences should confront is the nature of interpretation, assimilation and adaptation and the extent of resistance and rejection by the proselytised – in a phrase, the extent and form of ideological implementation. [2]

He added: 'Any analyst worth his salt should be aware of cultural discontinuities as well as continuities. The unanticipated consequences of stated intentions are neither unusual nor unreal.' He then stated further: 'The inclusion within our consideration of the nature of sport as an imperial bond of cultural encounters between dominant and subordinate groups certainly provides the opportunity "to place the grand and theatrical discourses of colonial knowledge and control in the context of their often partial and ironic realizations".' Finally, he remarked:

It has been claimed that cultural analysis 'breaks up into a disconnected yet coherent sequence of broader sorties with studies building on other studies, not in the sense that they take up where others leave off but in the sense that, stimulated by earlier stumbling, better informed and better conceptualized, they penetrate deeper into the same things. [3]

Through later publications, not only books but a stupendous volume of collaborative work done through the pages of journals such as the *International Journal of the History of Sport, Sport in Society* [4] and *Soccer and Society*, he has been trying to tie up the pieces of his earlier work, exploring on the one hand the foundational dynamics of the 'games ethic', while on the other hand trying to map its variegated patterns of implementation in those other climes ranging from the wind-swept prairies of Canada to the dry plains of central India. This is clear from the following description in *The Games Ethic and Imperialism*:

The Indian public school was created out of a hotchpotch of Victorian motives – imperial calculation, ethnocentric self-confidence and well meaning benevolence. ... Even in its more socially restricted form, however, the early Indian public school system provides a fascinating illustration of the cultural diffusion of an educational ethic arising out of imperial conquest. And, in only gently modified form, it has survived the imperialist. [5]

In a recent piece on Indian sport, 'Soccer as Moral Training: Missionary Intentions and Imperial Legacies', [6] he offers a purposive account of the introduction of football in Kashmir and the North-West Frontier Province (NWFP) in the 1890s. Mangan sees football as a powerful means to an imperial end, i.e. as a moral tool to strengthen the foundations of the British Empire in India. This focus is a continuation of his earlier work, 'Eton in India' [7] and is a key to understanding the inception of colonial sports in the subcontinent. In his words, 'The game was considered by the colonizers to carry with it a series of moral lessons, regarding hard work and perseverance, about team loyalty and obedience to authority and indeed, involving concepts of correct physical development and "manliness".' [8] He illustrates his argument by narrating the experiences of Leighton Pennell in NWFP and Tyndale Biscoe in Kashmir, who, he argues, used soccer as a seductive weapon to win over local populations. [9] This is one side of the story, also revealed of course in his essay 'Eton in India', which undertakes to bring to light the heterogeneity within the broader imperial administrative project. The other side is the need to record and understand the complexity of interpreting indigenous responses to such projects, also a fundamental requirement for Mangan. Too many existing studies have looked upon histories of the origin of British sport in the colonies from a limited perspective, as part of the colonial strategy of a civilizing mission, where sport was simply used as a tool of empire. That Mangan is concerned with what happened to the 'games ethic' in subsequent stages is clear when he declares that 'the legacy of the game in the region hints at a more complex story once the game has been adapted and adopted by Indian groups'. [10] Mangan acknowledges that any assessment of the impact of the intentions and programmes of the colonizers as distinct from their purposes 'is a different matter altogether'. Turning the colonial ideology on its head, resistance and subversion were often dominant in the second phase of the histories of British games in the colonies, especially cricket and soccer. It is in understanding the process of subversion of the 'games ethic' that vernacular literature on sport plays a key role, a point raised by Mangan in his 'Series Editor's Foreword' to *Soccer in South Asia*. [11] Mangan's assertion highlights a need for subtlety that should point the way for future scholars. He thus stands out as not being an ethnocentric Westerner, as some who write South Asian sports history are, and as recognizing the importance of encouraging scholars from the region to comment on the realities of sport in Asia. This is apparent in his foreword to *Soccer in South Asia*, a book, which, he rightly says, is a mere 'stepping stone' to the future. He also, incidentally, mentions the need for a greater number of Asian collection editors and monograph authors in order that the voices of Asia are heard in all its manifestations – political, cultural, social and emotional. Later 'stepping stones', he rightly states, will be put in place by those closer to the cultures, vernaculars and sources, independently and in conjunction with others. [12] To his credit, his studies cater not only for enthusiasts interested in the history of sport in South Asia but also to those who might be uninterested in sport itself but are interested in the broader themes of South Asian history such as colonialism, nationalism and communalism. His work should be viewed as part of the growing concern advanced emphatically, for example, in the series *Sport in the Global Society* (of which he is the founding and general editor) to locate sport within the broader socio-economic processes that shaped colonial and post-colonial societies, a genre of historical scholarship pioneered initially by scholars such as Peter Mandle and then subsequently by Tony Mangan himself.

In a sense he has thus gone back with the diligence of a good scrum-half and patrolled the back-lines of the foundation years to blow up the long established myth that 'muscular Christianity' as it came to be called was the brainchild of Thomas Arnold. Working within the solidly British tradition of social history, he has contextualized the birth of the ethic in the early years of the nineteenth century. Rescuing school history from the clutches of the 'kings and battles' paradigm of history writing, where innovation is forever chained to the chariot-wheels of individual Caesars, the games ethic was a generalized response to what was seen to be a general problem and thus was simultaneously developed, if not in its final form at least in its general tenor, by a host of broadly contemporary masters at a host of different public schools.

Having thus started with a narrative of socialization in British public schools, [13] Mangan has come back and investigated the very provenance of this ethic in the institutional matrix of its birth. Looking forward then, he sought to chart the course of the idea as it changed and adapted in different settings and the ways in which the urge to be different was fostered by a proximate possibility of uniformity. In a sense his works on athleticism in British public schools and on cricketing cultures [14] or indeed 'Europe, Sport, World' [15] are two poles, with his work on the games ethic remaining the defining moment. *Athleticism* is the answer to the question 'where did it come from and why?' while *Cricketing Cultures* answers the query 'what happened to it?'

Thus the entire thrust of his oeuvre seems to be to write '[history] ... as a more inclusive story and one with fewer determining narratives'. He remains constant, almost to the point of determination, in his refusal to view ideas as stable, immutable commodities that may travel across the globe without losing their colour or texture.

A whole host of postcolonials brought up on a diet of British sports and the games ethic had for generations been troubled by what in our contexts had been almost a perverse, guilty love for a tool of the Empire. By staunchly and assiduously asserting the possibility of mutation and the agency of the colonized in adapting, appropriating and refashioning the idea, Mangan remains worthy of deep gratitude from all such who sought a worthier name for their perverse loves.

The question then turns as to how, in the course of this 'reading' of J.A. Mangan's oeuvre, to express that gratitude. Only the intellectually lost would do so by waxing eloquent on the sheer breadth of his achievements. A worthier project, we would like to submit, would be to delineate areas for further scrutiny, now that the spadework has already been done. Both within and without the boundaries of Britain an agenda for further research in the wake of Mangan's oeuvre and along some of the lines implicit in his writings needs to be explored.

One of the first points to which we would like to draw attention is the 'consumption' of the games ethic. Not in the institutional matrix of their transplantation and re-articulation in the colonies, but at a more microanalytical level, i.e. at the level beneath that of institutions and ideologies. Perhaps an example, and a somewhat dramatic one, would make the point better. The 'games ethic', as it was articulated by the likes of Welldon, Sclater and others, kept asserting that 'in the first place, we would rather lose the game, than win it unfairly'; yet the worst perfidy against the noble spirit of the game was committed by Douglas Jardine, a former public schoolboy. Ironically, though, not only the boy from Bowral, Sir Don, but in a sense even Harold Larwood, a product of the social underbelly of England, kept up the ethic when they continued to play the game and Larwood refused to question his Captain's decision. [16] Across the Atlantic, while one public-school alumnus, Cyril Lionel Robert James, lived his entire life by the games ethic, [17] another West Indian (though he seldom thought of himself as being one), Sir Pelham Warner, even attempted to keep the mercurially talented Prince Ranjitsinghji out of the English Test side! [18] At issue here are two perhaps not unrelated points: first, how did the discourse on the games ethic interact with other discourses, such as race; and second, how did individual boys attending these schools understand or interpret what they were being told? Why did Bowes refuse to bowl bodyline, and the Nawab of Pataudi Senior quit an ashes team, while Jardine continued to inflict grievous bodily harm on the Australian players? And why did no one stop him, when later on Roy Gilchrist's international career [19] would end forever, for much the same fault? Why did Warner and his cronies not only discriminate against Ranji, but later on were instrumental in the inhumanity of apartheid in South African sports, despite the obvious talent and inculcation of the games ethic in many of the coloured players? No, the games ethic must now be understood as being read and interpreted by individual public-school products through its cross-hatchings with other discourses.

To belabour the point a little further, one may as well ask why should we not turn on its head the old dictum of seeing the games ethic as an attempt at unity by the diverse imperium and see it rather as a metaphor of difference, at least in some limited contexts? Why was the moral investment in, say, New Zealand such that cricket emerged as an almost solely *Pakeha* (white settler) game, and unfortunately continues to largely remain so, while rugby has truly become an All Black sport?

With the rising tide of globalization and its relationship with sports culture being accentuated through what we call the 'sports-media complex', other dimensions of further investigation begin to emerge. Not only in its contemporary context of big-money media capital and its relation to games, but even earlier. How was the games ethic re-presented and read within a larger social milieu through the print media first and later through the radio and then eventually the moving image? Did the games ethic ever really jump over the walls of the public schools or was it forever an elite ideology? If so, why did Larwood, as we have already seen, exhibit at least the rudiments of it? The ideologies of social control, though of course fostered in their infancy in the institutional matrix of elite public schools, had to then percolate down the social scale if they were to have any effect at all.

Another interesting, if even more challenging, aspect of research might be to move away from the roughly 'culturalist' underpinnings of the adaptation narratives of the games ethic. To look at for instance how the brass tacks of environmental factors affected the ways in which the games ethic was adapted in different regions. How for instance the substantial discourse on 'tropical heat' and its effects on gender and character that evolved in imperial India interacted with the notions of masculinity that lay at the heart of some of the formulations of muscular Christianity and the games ethic. We have, for instance, in earlier work tried to show how the Land

Reclamation project in Imperial Bombay was at least in part responsible for the greater success of cricket in that region of the Raj than in other corners of the subcontinent. To put it down to merely the coincidental presence of Lord Harris as governor of the province [20] alone would not do, just as Mangan showed us that it wasn't merely the genius of Arnold that could explain the games ethic in the public schools themselves.

Actually much of what we have been saying thus far is also an appeal to a more interdisciplinary approach to the history of sports. Mangan himself has been a consistent partisan for such a position. In fact his early work is largely influenced by anthropological work of a slightly earlier era, when it was the norm to study child socialization in order to understand the social dynamics of societies. Although by the time Mangan worked on it, the move was already away from such an approach within anthropology in favour of the study of the social structures and political typologies, Mangan had unabashedly acknowledged the debt in *Making Imperial Mentalities*. [21]

Later still, in his work through journals such as this one, we have increasingly seen an engagement with cultural studies and sociology. Though from a strictly historical point of view, these studies may have been improved upon, the very fact that Mangan provided a forum in his journals and books for the study of sports carried out in completely different disciplinal trajectories to interact and lie side by side has been a clarion call for the sort of interdisciplinary broadening of the horizons that we have been advocating through the issues raised above.

Yet this interaction is not without its pitfalls, and it would be wrong to call for further such interactions without at least attempting to signal some of the obstacles that litter the path to a successful interaction. Mangan's own work, as well as work done in his shadow, has encouraged studies of the relationship, especially in contemporary societies, between the trans-national dimension and nationalisms. Yet there has been little attempt to arrive at a consensual position on this rather complicated and definitely multi-dimensional relationship. While the plethora of understandings have enriched the field of the history of sports, one cannot deny that at times a rather simplistic understanding of the two terms has handicapped the corpus in general. Unlike colonial and anti-colonial nationalisms, the postcolonial nationalisms are much more Janus-faced, and often a sporting rivalry may or may not translate into a structural opposition. For example, just because an Indian roots for her team in the Olympics against the US team does not mean that she does not eventually aspire towards an American passport; or in contrast a cricket enthusiast, just because he wants India to trounce Pakistan, may not stop doting on Shoaib Akhtar. The point we are trying to make is that studying the impact of sports on postcolonial nationalisms and its deployment by modern-day imperialisms requires a far more complex understanding of 'nationalism' and 'imperialism' than has so far been witnessed. In this sense perhaps the problem might also lie with the fact that most of the professional historians whose peculiar business it has long been to study the relationship between nationalism and colonialism have tended to avoid the more recent years in favour of the distant past – thus leaving the study of the relationship between national and trans-national categories largely to those whose disciplinal backgrounds impel them to analyse categories rather than the contexts of their imbrications. Mark Dyreson's very interesting interrogation of the role of modern sport in world history in the pages of this journal, [22] for example, is typical of this rather easy and often antagonistic understanding of globalization and nationalism. The immensity of the scope of a topic as large as this one also probably compels its analytical categories to function at the level of universal applicability rather than as contextual displacements of these universals. For after all to argue that 'the globalization of sport had not transformed Uruguay into a cultural colony of the United States or Great Britain. Instead, Uruguayans employed the social technology of sport in the same way that the Americans and the British had – as a language of defining nationhood' is possibly a classic case of revelling in the questionable virtues of overstatement. As C.L.R. James once rhetorically asked about cricket, 'What do they know of cricket, who only cricket know?' [23] Similarly to compare the role of football in Uruguayan national life and British or American games, is to turn sports history into an arcane discipline that ignores the very real institutional baggage that sustains the differential roles that sports plays in these societies, i.e. the extremely different sociopolitical and economic realities of Uruguay and the USA. Taking the point further to its logical conclusion, we may safely add that the mere media-facilitated instant patriotism at a football game does not always and easily translate into a cultural resistance to American financial imperialism in Latin America.

Another concept, like the nationalism/imperialism dichotomy that probably requires a concerted definition in this journal is that of 'modernity'. Contemporary social science in general, and not just sports history, has been plagued by the catch-all banality of this word, and the problem should perhaps be seen in that light rather than as being specific to *The International Journal of the History of Sport*. Yet indubitably a problem there is. A legacy of the fancy purveyors of fashionable literary criticisms, the term in literature is largely used as mode of articulation, a way of denying continuities and asserting truth-claims, but if one is to use it in a historical context, one must remember that 'modernity' is not merely an idea any longer but also a material set of conditions. Conditions such as increased demographic mobility, made possible by mass engine-powered transport, better roads and so on; the increased flux of standardized ideas by means of print culture and mass transportation once again; the expansion of the literary base of societies and so on. Yet to cite but one example, Hugh Dauncey and Geoff Hare in their introductory article to the volume on the centenary of the Tour de France [24] call the Tour a 'pre-modern contest in a postmodern context'. Now even if we ignore the questions that might be raised about the postmodernity of the French countryside, we wonder how do we agree to call a cycling contest, which depends largely on the very conditions of modernity, started in 1902 – by which time, mind you, even the pneumatic tyre had come into vogue – a 'pre-modern contest'. Further the warnings of scholars such as Dipesh Chakrabarty against the tendency to see the trajectory of modernity/capital as an unitary and single narrative are cogent reminders in this regard. [25] We can hardly forget that the drive of global capital is premised on such an uniform trajectory of capital and modernity, and any subscription to such a trajectory is liable to run counter to the academic virtue of critical distance from contemporary trends in society.

These definitional aporias are not so much problems as they are concepts crying out for extensive debate and clarification in their own right, outside the particular case studies in which they are deployed. The multi-disciplinarity that has been one of the major strengths of Mangan's work, has actually resulted in a number of concepts being exported from various disciplinal specializations, but unless a concerted effort is now made to creatively fashion them into a powerful analytical tool-box, there remains the risk of these concepts just being different streams flowing in one channel, without their waters mixing, thus detracting from the overall analytic potential of the discipline as such.

One of the main values of an academic oeuvre is, we believe, the degree to which it in a sense encourages its own overcoming – the degree to which future research goes beyond the distance traversed by the oeuvre in question – and it is thus that we make bold to suggest some of the ways in which the considerable genius and erudition of Mangan's oeuvre may be taken further. But just as no matter how many centuries a batsman scores, there will never be another Bradman, just as no matter how many copies a sports journalist manages to sell, there will never be another Cardus, so do we think no matter how far we historians of sports go from here, there will hardly be another Tony Mangan.

Notes

[1] For details of this exposition, see J.A. Mangan (ed.), *The Games Ethic and Imperialism: Aspects of the Diffusion of an Ideal* (London and Portland, OR: Frank Cass, 1998).

[2] J.A. Mangan (ed.), *The Cultural Bond: Sport, Empire, Society* (London and Portland, OR: Frank Cass, 1992), p.8.

[3] Ibid.

[4] Formerly *Culture, Sport, Society*, published by Frank Cass.

[5] See the Chapter 'Eton in India' in Mangan, *The Games Ethic and Imperialism*.

[6] For an instructive discussion on soccer as a means to an imperial end, see J.A. Mangan, 'Soccer as Moral Training: Missionary Intentions and Imperial Legacies', in Paul Dimeo and James Mills (eds.), *Soccer in South Asia: Empire, Nation and Diaspora* (London and Portland, OR: Frank Cass, 2001), pp.41–56.

[7] Chapter in Mangan, *The Games Ethic and Imperialism* (London: Frank Cass, 1998).

[8] Mangan, 'Soccer as Moral Training', p.41.

[9] For details, see Mangan, *The Games Ethic and Imperialism*, p.187.

[10] For details, see Mangan, 'Soccer as Moral Training'.

[11] 'Series Editor's Foreword' in Dimeo and Mills (eds.), *Soccer in South Asia*.

[12] Ibid.

[13] The accepted definitive study of public school games as moral training is J.A. Mangan's *Athleticism in the Victorian and Edwardian Public School* (Cambridge: Cambridge University Press, 1981, repr. with new introduction, London and Portland, OR: Frank Cass, 2000).

[14] Boria Majumdar and J.A. Mangan (eds.), *Cricketing Cultures in Conflict: World Cup 2003* (London: Routledge, 2004).

[15] J.A. Mangan (ed.), *Europe, Sport, World: Shaping Global Society* (*European Sports History Review*, Vol.3) (London and Portland, OR: Frank Cass, 2001).

[16] The 'bodyline' controversy of the 1930s was one of the most defining moments in cricket's history. For a definitive account of the controversy see David Frith, *Bodyline Autopsy* (Melbourne: ABC Books, 2003).

[17] Perhaps the most influential book on sport ever written is C.L.R. James, *Beyond a Boundary* (London: Stanley Paul, 1963).

[18] For an impressive biography of Prince Ranjitsinhji, see Mario Rodrigues, *Batting for the Empire: A Political Biography of Ranjitsinhji* (New Delhi: Penguin, 2003).

[19] One of the most feared West Indian fast bowlers of the 1950s. His career ended when he tried to unfairly bounce out Prince Charanjit Singh and was sent back from India by the West Indian captain Gerry Alexander on disciplinary grounds in 1957/8.

[20] Lord Harris served as Governor of Bombay between 1890 and 1895.

[21] J. A. Mangan (ed.), *Making Imperial Mentalities: Socialisation and British Imperialism* (*Studies in Imperialism*) (Manchester: Manchester University Press, 1990).

[22] Mark Dyerson, 'Globalizing the Nation-Making Process: Modern Sport in World History', *The International Journal of the History of Sport*, 20, 1 (2003), 90–106.

[23] For details see James, *Beyond a Boundary*.

[24] Hugh Dauncey and Geoff Hare (eds.), *The Tour De France, 1903–2003: A Century of Sporting Structures, Meanings and Values* (*Sport in the Global Society*) (London and Portland, OR: Frank Cass, 2003).

[25] For details see Dipesh Chakrabarty, *Provincializing Europe* (Princeton, NJ: Princeton University Press, 2000). Also see Dipesh Chakrabarty, *Habitations of Modernity: Essays in the Wake of Subaltern Studies* (Chicago, IL: Chicago University Press, 2002).

Beijing Ambitions: An Analysis of the Chinese Elite Sports System and its Olympic Strategy for the 2008 Olympic Games

Fan Hong, Ping Wu and Huan Xiong

The 28th Olympic Games in Athens was yet another success: the USA finished top of the gold-medal table for the third consecutive time. The games also pleased the Greeks. As host nation, Greece achieved the largest medal haul in its history. However, arguably it was the Chinese who stole the limelight: 407 Chinese competed in 203 events and won 32 gold, 17 silver and 14 bronze medals. Their 32 gold medals put China above the Russians and second to the USA. With 63 medals in total, China came third in the overall medal rankings after the USA and Russia. Furthermore, six new world records were established by Chinese athletes, and they beat Olympic records 21 times. After their triumph in Athens, Chinese senior sports officials claimed triumphantly that China, together with the USA and Russia, had become one of the three superpowers in the summer Olympics. [1] The moment the Athens Olympics ended, the world media turned their attention to Beijing, where the next

Olympics will take place and where the whole world will eagerly watch the next gold medal confrontation between China and the USA.

Victory in Athens

The extent of the Chinese success in Athens came totally out of the blue. Neither Chinese sports officials nor their foreign counterparts had expected it. The strategy prepared in Beijing before the games was to maintain China's fourth place and try to reach third in the gold-medal table. On 25 June 2004, only 50 days before the opening of the Athens Olympics, Li Furong, deputy minister of the China General Administration of Sport and deputy *chef de mission* of the Chinese Sports Delegation to the Athens Olympics, informed the news media: 'We can see few possibilities for our delegation to overcome Russia and the USA on both the gold-medal count and the overall medal ranking in Athens. ... Germany will be our principal rival in the competition for the third place in the gold-medal count.' [2] Chinese athletes were expected to achieve 20 to 27 gold medals at the games. [3] The media in China agreed with the sports officials. There were few opportunities left for Chinese to earn more medals in their usual 'stronghold' events: table tennis, badminton, diving, gymnastics, shooting, weightlifting and judo, which ensured 26 of the 28 gold medals that China won in Sydney. [4]

However, the Chinese athletes surprised the world with their excellent performances. During the first five days of the games, China overtook the USA, Russia and Germany and led the medal ranking. Encouraged by this the Chinese sports officials now had a 'dream target' for the athletes: to achieve second in the gold-medal table. [5] China and Russia competed for seven gold medals in the last four days and Chinese athletes finally beat the Russians and won six of them to make China's dream came true. [6] In total, China won 32 gold medals in Athens: six in diving, five in weightlifting, four in shooting, three in table tennis, three in badminton, two in athletics and two in taekwondo. The other seven came in women's volleyball, canoeing, wrestling, gymnastics, tennis, swimming and judo.

Moving up in World Record Speed

China amazed the world not only with its performance in Athens, but also with its incredible speed in catching up with Western sports powers. In 1984, China re-emerged on the Olympic stage after an absence of 32 years, won 15 gold medals and came fourth. Although the victory in Los Angeles was partly attributed to the absence of the Soviet Union and the Democratic Republic of Germany, nevertheless it excited virtually every Chinese from government officials to ordinary citizens. 'Develop elite sport and make China a superpower in the world' became both a slogan and a dream for the Chinese.

However, the dream became an incubus. For the Chinese, the 1988 Seoul Olympics were a nightmare. When the two superpowers, the Soviet Union and the Democratic

Republic of Germany, returned to the Olympics, China's gold-medal tally shrank to five. China had slipped painfully from fourth to eleventh in the gold-medal table.

In 1992, China fought back at the Barcelona Olympics. Although the Soviet Union had split into several countries, it still took part in as a unit under the name of the Commonwealth of Independent States (CIS). Germany had reunited and was even more powerful than before. However, China won 16 gold medals and returned to fourth in the gold-medal count.

The Atlanta Olympics in 1996 did not please the Chinese, for they again won 16 gold medals and remained fourth on the gold-medal table. No progress was not acceptable.

Four years later China achieved 'a historical breakthrough' at the 27th Olympics in Sydney in 2000. It increased its gold medals to 28 and came third. However, some sports officials argued that this result was not a reliable measure of an improvement in Chinese sports' strength, since five of the gold medals came from the newly-added events: synchronized diving and women's weightlifting.

As already mentioned, in 2004 the Chinese athletes achieved notable success in Athens: four of the gold medals came in traditional Western 'fortress' areas: track and field, swimming, rowing and canoeing. On 30 August 2004, just after the closing ceremony of the Athens Olympics, CNN commented: 'In the six Olympic Games they have competed in, China has moved up the medal tally in world record time.' [7] China is now second in the gold-medal table and intends to make it to the top.

The Chinese Elite Sports System

The modern triumph of Chinese sport is deeply rooted in the Chinese elite sports system, which learned from the Soviet Union in the 1950s but developed its own character in the 1980s. It is called *Juguo tizhi* in Chinese and translates as 'whole-country support for the elite sport system'. This system channelled all sports resources in the country into elite sport and effectively produced hundreds of thousands of young elite athletes in a short time in pursuit of ideological superiority and national status. Its main characteristics are centralized management and administration and guaranteed financial and human resources from the whole country to ensure it maximum support. [8]

This 'whole-country support for the elite sport system' was officially acknowledged in the 1980s when China adopted the 'open-door' policy and competition was advocated as the spirit of the new era. In 1980, Wang Meng, the Sports Minister, stated at the National Sports Conference that forging a relationship between sport and the socialist economy was crucial to the development of Chinese elite sport. On the one hand, China was still a poor country and was restricted in the amount of money it could invest in sport. On the other hand, elite sport was an effective way to boost China's new image on the international stage. Therefore, the solution was to bring elite sport into the existing planned economy and administrative system, which could assist in the distribution of the limited resources of the whole nation to medal-winning sports. [9] The international success of Chinese athletes would, in return, bring to the nation pride and hope, which were badly needed in the new era of transformation. [10]

However, the concept of *Juguo tizhi* (whole-country support for the elite sport system) provoked intense debate in China in the late 1980s. Some intellectuals and administrators in sport began to question the government's policy on elite sport and the relationship between gold medals and mass physical exercise and recreation. Many thought that the government's sports policy was at odds with the essential Olympic spirit – peace, freedom, independence and fair play. [11] It was not until the 2000 Olympic Games, when China achieved extraordinary success that the term *Juguo tizhi* began to appear regularly in Chinese official statements to explain why Chinese sport had achieved so much in such a short time. When Jiang Zemin, the General Secretary of the Communist Party, claimed in 2000 that 'The success of American sport depends on its economic power; the success of Russian sport depends on its rich resources and experience of training elite athletes; the success of Chinese sport depends on *Juguo tizhi*' [12] the concept was approved at the highest political level.

Yuan Weimin, the Sports Minister, officially defined the term in 2001 at the All State Sports Ministers' Conference. He stated that the meaning of *Juguo tizhi* was that the central and local governments used their power to channel adequate financial and human resources available throughout the country to support elite sport in order to win glory for the nation. [13] The distinguishing characteristics of *Juguo tizhi* include the fact that its policy embodies China's political objects; that its administrative and management system is centralized; and that it functions only to improve the level of elite sport through a special selection and training system.

Sports Policy

In the late 1970s and early 1980s, China initiated profound economic reform and made a great effort to integrate with the world economy. The national ambition was to catch up with the Western capitalist world through modernization. Chinese sport played an important part in stimulating the nation's enthusiasm and motivating people to modernity. [14] In 1979, China renewed its membership of the IOC and subsequently other international sports organizations. Many international competitions were now open to the Chinese. The success of the Chinese athletes at the 1979 World Volleyball Championships, the 1982 Asia Games and, in particular, the 1984 Olympic Games, raised hopes that China would become a great country again in the near future. Attending the Olympics and other international competitions and performing well became the symbolic means of catching up with and even beating the Western powers.

In 1985 the Society of Strategic Research for the Development of Physical Education and Sport (*Tiyu fazhan zhanlue yanjiu hui*) produced the Olympic Strategy (*Aoyun zhanlue*) for the Sports Ministry. This strategy clearly stated that 'elite sport is the priority'. It aimed to use the nation's limited sports resources to develop elite sport to ensure that China was a leading sports power by the end of the twentieth century. The strategy was the blueprint for Chinese sport in the 1980s and 1990s while the target was primarily the Olympics. Wu Shaozu, the Minister of Sport from 1990 to 2000, declared: 'The highest aim of Chinese sport is success in the Olympic Games. We must concentrate our resources on it. To raise the flag at the Olympics is our major responsibility.' [15]

In the 1990s, the government, under the pressure of rising demands for grassroots sports participation, began to advocate that the Olympic Strategy and the National Fitness Programme initiated in 1995 should advance simultaneously. However, China's 1993 and 2001 bids to host the Olympic Games ensured that elite sport remained the priority. Furthermore, the success of the bid to host the 2008 Olympic Games stimulated a new set of Olympic objectives in China. As Jiang Zemin, the Communist Party General Secretary between 1989 and 2003, stated: 'The success of the bid will advance China's domestic stability and economic prosperity. The Olympics in China has the objectives of raising national morale and strengthening the unity of Chinese people both in the mainland and overseas.' [16]

Sports Administrative System

One of the significant features of the Chinese elite sports system is its centralized administrative and management structure. The national governmental body, the State Physical Education and Sports Commission (the Sports Ministry) was established in 1952. [17] It was in charge of the formulation and implementation of sports policy and the administration of national sports programmes. It liaised closely with other government ministries, including Education and National Defence. Between 1953 and 1954 sports commissions were established at provincial and local county levels to implement the national sports policy and programmes. By the mid-1950s a centralized system of sports administration was in place and it has dominated Chinese sport ever since.

Figure 1 clearly shows that the Chinese Sports Ministry operated directly under the leadership of the central government. The model of the Chinese sports administrative system reflected the wider social system in China: both the Communist Party and state administrations were organized in a vast hierarchy with power flowing down from the top.

Since the 1980s, the Chinese economy has been changing from a planned to a market economy. At the same time, the sports system has been transformed from a centralized system to a multi-level and multi-channel system. [18] In the mid-1990s the Sports Ministry changed its name from the State Physical Education and Sports Commission (*Guojia tiyu yundong weiyuanhui*) to China General Administration of Sport (*Guojia tiyu zhongju*). To manage its training and commercial interests, 20 sports management centres were established. The change in title and structure – see Figure 2 – was both symbolic and pragmatic. The Sports Ministry hoped that Chinese sport would now stand more on its own feet and rely less on government support.

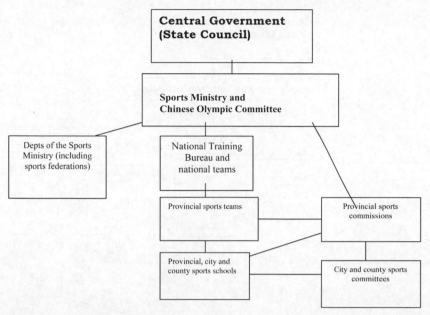

Figure 1 Administrative Structure of Chinese Sport 1952–1996

However, the plain fact is that all the centres except football are far from self-supporting. They still largely depend on the money from central government to survive. With the approach of the Beijing Olympic Games, central government can do nothing but increase its financial support for the games' sake. Therefore the reform of the sports management system is in reality old wine in a new bottle! The traditional centralized system remains and still plays an important role in the Chinese elite sports system.

The Selection and Training System: Resources

As already made clear, in the 1980s, the Olympic Strategy stressed that all available sports resources in China should be concentrated on elite sport. [19] The statistics in Table 1 clearly show that Chinese sport still largely depends on governmental funding. In addition, in the 1980s and 1990s there was special funding for Olympic preparation. For example, to secure success at the Atlanta Olympics in 1996 there was a specific fund for Olympic-related activities of 65 million yuan (US$13 million). [20]

In general, therefore, elite sports teams were major beneficiaries of the government budget. The statistics in Table 2 show the investment by the central government in national elite sports teams from 1991 to 1997. Incidentally, the figures do not include the budget spent on training facilities and equipment, the cost of domestic and international competitions and other activities related to elite sport. [21]

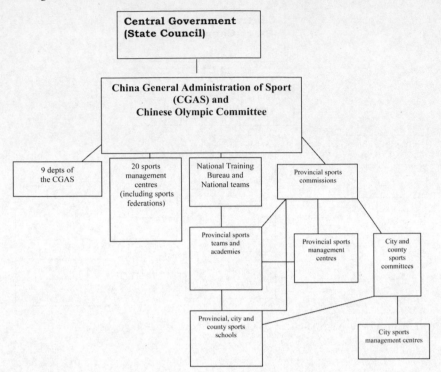

Figure 2 Administrative Structure of Chinese Sport 1997–2005

The Selection and Training System: Athletes

China has one of the most effective systems in the world for systematically selecting and producing sports stars from a very young age. [22] This system was officially created in 1963 when the Sports Ministry issued the 'Regulations of Outstanding Athletes and Team'. On the instructions of the ministry, the selection of talented young athletes took place in every province. [23] Over the years it has developed into a well-organized and tightly structured three-level pyramid – see Figure 3: primary, intermediate and high level. The sports schools at county, city and provincial levels formed the base of the pyramid. After several years' training, about 12 per cent of talented athletes from sports schools were selected to go on to provincial teams and become professional athletes. From there a few lucky ones made it to the top – the national squads and the Olympic teams. The system remains in place today.

In terms of the selection procedure, when boys and girls between ages of six and nine are identified with some talent in a particular sport they will join local sports schools throughout the country. They are trained three hours a day four or five times a week. After a period of hard training, the promising ones will be promoted to semi-professional training: four to five hours' training a day five or six days a week. From there the ones with potential are selected for the provincial sports schools or training

Table 1
Chinese sports budget 1981–96 (in 10 thousand Yuan)

Year	GOVERNMENTAL FUNDING		COMMERCIAL INVESTMENT	
	Central Govt	Local govt	Sponsorship	Commercial profits
1981–5	305,32	226,112	0	0
198690	56,625	543,166	0	0
1991	13,184	153,392	0	0
1992	14,100	172,400	0	0
1993	18,600	190,800	2,192	726,260
1994	15,309	187,045	4,185	67,394
1995	22,567	216,235	3,664	77,820
1996	20,945	263,229	4,737	99,789

Source: *Sports Statistics (1994, 1995–7, 1998)*.
Note: In the 1990s, one US dollar was equivalent to about 5 yuan.

centres. Those young athletes live on campus there and train four to six hours a day five or six days a week. Their aim is to reach the second stage and become professionals in provincial teams and eventually to reach the third stage – becoming members of the national squads and Olympic teams. The selection system is brutal and is the core of the 'whole country support for the elite sports system'. In 2004 there were about 400,000 young boys and girls training at more than 3,000 sports schools throughout China. [24] Only five per cent will be able to reach the top; 95 per cent will leave their sports schools with no formal primary or secondary education qualifications and with broken dreams.

In terms of training methods, the People's Army's methods – 'hard, disciplined, intensive training and practice according to real battle' – were adopted in 1963. In 1964, however, a new training method was invented. It included 'three non-afraids' – not being afraid of hardship, difficulty or injury – and 'five toughnesses': toughness of spirit, body, skill, training and competition. [25] It has become a legendary Chinese sporting method and continues to influence China's training system in the twenty-first century. Nevertheless, since the late 1980s the emphasis has been on more scientific training methods, including coaching techniques, sports science, sports psychology, sports medicine, better facilities and equipment. The number of full-time coaches with a higher education certificate increased from 2,829 in 1979 to 5,926 in 1995, especially for elite sports teams at provincial and national levels. [26] Sports researchers are required to link their research directly to training athletes to win medals. [27]

The Olympic medal-oriented policy, the centralized sports administrative and management system, the selection and training system – in short, the entire Chinese elite sports system – erect a 'human ladder' for a handful of exceptional athletes to win gold medals at the Olympian summit.

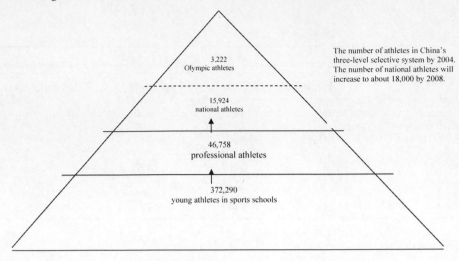

Source: Sports Training Department of China General Administration of Sport

Figure 3 Pyramid of the Selective System

Olympic Gold Medal Fever in China

Why are the Chinese so obsessed by Olympic gold medals? Why are the Chinese so ambitious to be a sports superpower? To understand the obsession and ambition we have to put the Olympic gold medal fever in the context of Chinese politics, history and economics.

First, the government's valuation of Olympic gold medals is based on political objectives. Since the establishment of the People's Republic of China in 1949, sport has always been one of the most powerful weapons in the Chinese Communists' arsenal. It has never escaped from the shadow of politics. In the Maoist era between 1949 and 1978, sport was right at the centre of politics and diplomacy as in other Communist states at that time. China's sporting success demonstrated the fact that socialism was superior to capitalism.

Deng Xiaoping's era followed and was characterized by reform and the famous 'openness'. Since the 1980s, China's sporting success has been regarded not only as evidence of ideological superiority and economic prosperity, but also as a totem of national revival. At the end of the Athens Olympics, an editorial on the front page of the *People's Daily* claimed:

> When a country is powerful, its sport will flourish. Chinese athletes' excellent performance at the Olympic stage is inevitably proof of our great achievements in economic reform and modernization. ... The achievements at the games have showed China's ability to stand proudly and independently among the other nations in the world. ... Chinese athletes will make more contributions to realize our nation's great revival'. [28]

During the Cold War, the government's politicization of sport reflected the confrontation between Communism and capitalism. After the Cold War, the government's politicization of sport reflected the confrontation between nation states. In addition, the Chinese government uses sport as a window to show the world the new image of Communism in the new era – as an ideology to unite the Chinese people in a sporting patriotism as Marxist-Leninist and Maoist ideological beliefs begin to decay and as an opium to distract attention from severe social problems such as corruption and unemployment.

Second, the Olympic gold medal fever among ordinary Chinese people is derived from a mixture of extreme pride and extreme inferiority. China, the so-called 'sleeping giant' with the largest population in the world, cherishes nostalgically the memory of its supremacy at the centre of the world and its glorious prosperity during the Tang Dynasty a millennium ago. It feels painfully about the past 160 years' history of humiliation and inferiority at the hands of the West and Japan. Modern Chinese history is a history of humiliation, struggle and striving to restore national pride and international recognition. Between the 1950s and the 1970s Mao Zedong did however instil a sense of self-worth [29] and made the Chinese mistakenly believe that they were the 'most progressive and advanced force' on earth and that they were responsible for the liberation of all the human beings in the world – especially those living in capitalist societies! [30]

In the 1980s Deng's open-door policy forced open Chinese eyes and they saw clearly that their standard of living as well as their science, technology, military, education and health levels were substantially lower than those of the Western powers. Facing up to this reality was a devastating agony for the Chinese. At this point they shared desperation but also hope with the government. The hope lay in drawing on the spiritual, intellectual and physical powers of the Chinese to create the strength necessary to be a powerful country. In this climate, it is no exaggeration to state that the desire to hold the Olympic Games and to win medals was driven by the powerful requirements of national survival in the face of major internal and external threats to China's political and economic existence. The Olympics are, at the same time, a ritual of cohesion, a battlefield on which to beat the economically advanced nations and a means to restore the confidence of the nation. [31] Competitive sport is war without gunfire. The Chinese, who had lost most of the wars in the recent past, were now longing to becoming winners of any kind of war, including the Olympics.

'A winner is a king, a loser is nothing but a bandit' (*chengzhe wanghou baizhekou*) is an ancient Chinese saying still believed by most Chinese people. The dominant concept for the Chinese is not 'fair play', but winning no matter at what cost. China has a tradition of enduring hardship, of sacrificing individuals' interests for the sake of the nation. Therefore it is only natural that hundreds and thousands of unsung athletes and coaches have been 'built' into the 'human ladder' in the past 55 years to help some 100 Olympic medallists to climb to the top. This brutal system has the enthusiastic support not only of the government but also of most of the people.

Third, the Olympic Games and gold medals will bring economic benefits to Beijing and China. Dick Pound has pointed out that since the Americans made the Los Angeles Games the first ever money-making Olympics two decades ago, hosting the Olympic Games has become a very profitable business. [32] The IOC will provide a billion dollars from television rights and sponsorship to the Beijing organizing committee. Top sponsors such as Coca-Cola, Kodak, Schlumberger-Sema and Swatch quickly renewed their contracts. At the same time, the Beijing Municipal Government is very confident that hosting the games will bring immense business opportunities to the city. On 18–19 April 2004, Beijing hosted a conference called 'Invest in Beijing' to promote the Olympic economy. The conference attracted more than 300 leading foreign and domestic enterprises. The Beijing Municipal Development and Reform Committee announced that the success of the conference had matched its expectation for aggregate demand in both investment and consumer markets in Beijing.

Beijing expects investment to reach more than 3,000 billion yuan (about US$365 billion) by 2008. As for the consumer market, Beijing, a megapolis whose permanent resident population is 14.56 million, had a total volume of retail sales of social consumer goods worth more than 190 billion yuan (about US$23 billion) in 2003, and expects the aggregate demand will increase to be more than 1.5 thousand billion yuan (about US$183 billion) in 2008. The number of new automobiles in Beijing is expected to be more than 2.45 million; the demand for digital products will be worth some 50 billion yuan (about US$6 billion); and for food and clothing 500 to 600 billion yuan (about US$60–73 billion) even before the games start. [33] Beijing has also given a promise to create a national lottery of US$121 million for Olympic projects including structural city development.

The world's top 500 enterprises and domestic industrial and commercial tycoons are ambitious to use this opportunity to grab as much profit as possible in the largest consumer market on earth. Unsurprisingly, He Zhenliang, IOC Executive Board member and former vice-president of the China Olympic Committee, claimed:

> Indeed, the 2008 Olympic Games will serve as a catalyst for furthering reform and the liberalization process in China. Coupled with the far-reaching impact of China's access to the World Trade Organization, China's economy will become more closely linked internationally; ... it will be a milestone in world development. ... The Beijing Games will unquestionably promote elite sport in China. [34]

Elite Sport System Critique

Although the elite sports system has been supported by the might of the state, critical voices emerged as early as the late 1980s. In 1988 Zhao Yu's two sensational reports, *Dreaming to Be A Superpower* (*Qiang Guo Meng*) and *The Defeat in Seoul* (*Bing Bai Hancheng*), revealed the dark inside of China's elite sport and criticized the 'whole-country support for the elite sport system'. [35] In 1989, at the height of the pro-democracy movement (the 'Tiananmen Event') there was an intense debate as to whether millions should be spent on the pursuit of Olympic medals or on improving people's physical exercise and health at the grassroots level. However, discussion came to a sudden end when the pro-democracy movement failed. [36]

The debate reopened, however, with the Chinese bid for the Olympic Games in 1993. Books and articles were published and conferences held. In 1998 an essay entitled 'The Olympic Movement in China: Ideals, Realities and Ambitions' was published in *Culture, Sport, Society*. It reviewed the development of the Olympic movement in China from the 1910s to the 1990s and analysed the problems of the Chinese Olympic movement in which the elite sport system played a major part. [37]

In September 2003, the Xinhua News Agency reported on the unemployment and poor living conditions of the majority of retired professional athletes in China. It pointed out critically that these tragedies were caused by the Olympic strategy implemented by the government at all levels in Chinese society. The elite sports system had not only damaged athletes' bodies but also reduced their opportunities for formal schooling. [38] In August 2004, a report published in *Looking East Weekly* criticized the elite sports system for gravely alienating Chinese sportsmen and women. Its over-consumption of resources, the report asserted, had serious adverse effects on mass sport and the National Fitness Programme. [39] Simultaneously an essay entitled 'Innocence Lost: Child Athletes in China' appeared in the journal *Sport in Society*. It critically analysed the elite sport system and examined the relationship between child athletes and human rights in the context of culture and politics in contemporary China. [40] In addition, more critics emerged on the Internet, where people could express their opinions even more freely.

Despite all the criticism, the Chinese are not likely to give up the elite sports system, especially with the 2008 Beijing Olympic Games approaching. John MacAloon has stated that 'To be a nation, recognized by others and realistic to themselves, a people must march in the opening ceremony's procession. To march in those ceremonies, a people enter into communication and conformity with the requirements of universalizing Olympic organizations.' [41] For the Chinese, however, participation in the Olympics is not only to obtain a measure of recognition but also to win. Medals will bring Chinese people new satisfaction, new inspiration and a revival of national pride. Victory in the Olympic Games symbolizes, above all, the ascension of the Chinese nation to the rank of a world sports power.

The Strategy of Winning Olympic Medals in 2008

The well-developed 'whole country support for the elite sport system' matches China's Olympic medal ambitions. In July 2002 the Communist Party and the central government issued a document on 'Strengthening and Progressing Sport in the New Era' (*Zhonggongzhongyang guowyyuan guanyu jinyibu jiaoqiang he gaijin xinshiqi tiyu dongzuo de yijian*). [42] It emphasized that hosting the 2008 Olympic Games was the priority not only for Beijing but for the whole country; China must grasp this opportunity to display itself to the world and to make the Beijing 2008 the best Olympic Games ever. The Sports Ministry immediately drew up two important internal documents: 'The Outline Strategy for the Winning Olympic Medals 2001–2010' (*Aoyun zhengguang gangyao 2001–2010*) and 'The Strategic Plan for Winning Olympic Medals in 2008' (*2008 Aoyun zhengguang jihua*). These two documents comprise an action plan to ensure the Chinese achieve the victory they expect. The following actions have been the outcome.

Olympic Sports Selection

In 2004 China participated in 26 Summer Olympic sports and 203 events in Athens: 18 key events were targeted for medals and these received most of the support in the elite sports system. In order to gain more medals in 2008, China is now preparing to participate in all 29 Olympic sports. China has carefully analysed its strengths and weaknesses and divided its Olympic sports into four categories:

1. Traditional Olympic sports, in which China is guaranteed to win gold medals, such as table tennis, badminton and diving. There are gold medals in these three sports and China won in 2000. China believes that it will maintain its dominant position in these areas.
2. Capable Olympic sports, in which China has the present ability to gain some gold medals, such as gymnastics, weightlifting, shooting and judo. China will try its best to win more gold medals in these areas.
3. Potential Olympic sports, in which China has the future potential to gain more medals, such as athletics, swimming and water sports. There are gold medals in these areas. China only won one gold in athletics and one gold in swimming in 2004. They are the areas in which China will attempt to gain more medals in order to beat the USA.
4. Weak Olympic sports, in which China lags behind, such as boxing, horsemanship, men's soccer, men's volleyball and baseball. These are the areas in which China will work harder than ever to reach the qualifying standard and then try to win medals. [43]

Training Olympic Athletes

In order to train more athletes for the 2008 Olympic Games the size of the national team is expanding. The national teams consist of experienced team managers, head coaches and coaches who are appointed by the Sports Ministry and sports management centres, and elite athletes who are selected from every provincial sports teams throughout China. According to China's sports custom, when it prepares for international competitions there are two teams for each event: the national team and the resource team. However, for the Beijing 2008 games, in order to ensure the victory, 'The Strategic Plan for Winning Olympic Medals in 2008' (*2008 Aoyun zhengguang jihua*) requires that the number of teams should be expanded. Therefore some key events have three teams: the national team, the youth team and the resource team. All the elite athletes in China whose ages are suitable for the 2008 games are selected and allocated to different teams according to their present ability and future potential.

Each national team will be given the specific medal numbers it is expected to get; no team effort is being spared to ensure success. [44] Managers, coaches and athletes are working under enormous pressure. One head coach of a national team has revealed that he feels as if he has a sword hanging over his head every day. National teams and youth teams train in their national training centres. The resource teams train in provincial sports commission training centres and at those universities that have better training facilities. In 2002 China had 1,316 full-time Olympic athletes in national teams. In 2004 an additional 706 athletes joined national teams and 1,200 joined youth teams. In total, by the end of 2004 there were 3,222 full-time elite athletes training for the 2008 Olympic Games, plus others training in resource teams. [45]

Increasing Olympic Resources

The strategy for the 2008 Olympics provides for increased financial support from the government – in particular, for those sports where Chinese athletes have the potential to win gold medals. [46] Wu Shouzhang, vice-president of the China Olympic Committee, has provided the reason: 'Our aim is to get more gold medals at the Olympics and everything we do is for this goal.' [47] Liu Fuming, deputy head of the Sports Ministry's Department of Finance, confirmed that the Sports Ministry received a budget from the central government of 16 billion yuan (about US$1.95 billion) in 2000. From 2001, the first year of implementation of 'The Outline Strategy for Winning Olympic Medals 2001–2010' (*Aoyun zhengguang gangyao 2001–2010*), the central government increased the budget. Liu has made this quite clear: 'From 2001 we received more than 16 billion yuan from the central government and the figure is increasing every year as 2008 approaches.' [48] The Sports Ministry's Department of Finance has stated that between 2001 and 2004 the central government is augmenting its budget by 1 billion yuan (about US$122 million) every year and between 2005 and 2008 the figure will be 2 billion yuan (about US$244 million) each year, exclusively for the 2008 Olympic Games. Therefore, in 2008 the Sports Ministry will receive 27 billion yuan (about US$3.29billion) in total. This does not include additional special funding for particular programmes related to Olympic preparation. Liu has confirmed that the total figure will reach more than 40 billion yuan (about US$4.88billion) in 2008. [49]

It has been estimated that 90 per cent of the funds are, and will be, used to pay the wages of athletes and coaches, improve existing training centres, build more advanced training centres and provide state-of-the-art equipment. Needless to say, the best coaches in China are selected to train Olympic athletes and others will be brought in from abroad. The best qualified sports scientists will work closely with the national, youth and resource teams to improve the athletic ability of athletes.

Preparation for Olympic Competition

In order to give athletes maximum experience of competition and prepare them physically and mentally for the 2008 Olympics, national competitions have been restructured. The Fifth City Games in China in 2004 added ten more Olympic sports to its traditional 16 sports and concentration was on the events that China expects to win in 2008. The rules and regulations mirrored those of the Olympic Games. The National Games in 2005 and other national championships will follow this model. The slogan is 'Let the national competitions serve the Olympics' (*bian quanyun wei aoyun*) and 'Training the athletes in Chinese competitions and preparing them to fight for China at international games' (*guonei lianbing, yizhiduiwai*). In addition, the Chinese General Administration of Sport plans to send young athletes who have the potential to win gold medals in 2008 to the Asian Games, the East Asian Games and the *Universate* (the World Student Games) in 2006 to prepare them for the Beijing Olympics. [50]

In short, China has increasingly exploited its 'whole-country support for the elite sports system' to systematically produce more Olympic athletes in order to maintain and advance its position in the gold medal table in 2008.

Beijing's Ambition: Number One in 2008

As soon as the Olympics ended in Athens, the USA media predicted that China would top the gold-medal count at the Beijing Olympics. CNN asserted in a report on 30 August 2004 that 'Undoubtedly China wants the top spot in Beijing 2008 and China has enough money, people and pride to achieve this incredible task'. [51] *USA Today* commented that Chinese athletes showed in Athens that they were primed to pump up host-country passions and they were likely to be out front in Beijing in 2008. [52] The Athens Olympics is regarded by *The Times of Asia* as a 'dress rehearsal' for China's future triumphant display in Beijing 2008: Chinese young athletes will use their Athens experience to thrash the rest of the world in 2008 by challenging the Americans and becoming the global athletic superpower. [53]

However, Yuan Weimin, the minister for China's General Administration of Sport, recently admitted frankly that there was still a considerable gap between China and the USA and Russia. He explained: 'We are still comparatively weak in track and field and swimming, the two premier sports at the Olympic Games.' [54] Yuan has never stated openly that China's target in the Beijing Olympics 2008 was to overtake the USA: however, he has admitted publicly that one of the things he is thinking about every day is what China should do to challenge the USA's dominant position in 2008. [55]

In contrast to the cautious Yuan, most Chinese senior sports officials feel absolutely confident about their ability to become the new premier sports superpower in 2008. Wei Jizhong, executive member of the Beijing Organizing Committee for the 2008 Olympic Games, told *Titan Sports Weekly* (*Titan zhoubao*), the most influential sports newspaper in China, that China's target in 2008 Olympics was to overtake the USA. He argued: 'I cannot see any reason why we should doubt our ability to overtake the USA in 2008. In general, the host of the Olympic Games will have a 30 per cent home advantage, and I do not think the gap between us and the USA at present is as big as 30 per cent.' [56] Yang Shu An, deputy president of the China Olympic Committee, informed the Xinhua News Agency that he believed it would be very difficult for Russia to return to the second place in 2008, 'therefore, our task in the Beijing Olympics is to challenge the USA'. [57]

Last Celebration of the Elite Sport System

China's thirst for more gold medals in the 2008 Beijing Olympics has resulted in the further strengthening of its elite sports system. However, the future of the whole-country support system looks uncertain after the games. Some scholars have argued that the China General Administration of Sport (the Chinese Sports Ministry) and its numerous subsidiaries will be dissolved after 2008. [58] The reasons are: firstly, the central government has poured, and will keep pouring, huge sums of money into the 2008 games because, for political purposes, the games must be supported, but it will not be able to maintain such a huge investment in elite sport after 2008. The central government will start again to 'push sport to the market' (*tiyu shichanghua tiyu shangyehua*) with determination. He Zhengliang has pointed out that after the Olympics China will pay more attention to promoting sport throughout the nation at grassroots level and bringing healthy sporting activity into the lives of many ordinary people. [59]

Secondly, local governments, especially the local administrations of sport, have suffered, and, will continue to suffer, from the 'Olympic drainage', which is a unique system within the elite sport system. The provincial and local sports teams and commissions have the responsibility to nurture *and* train elite athletes for the national teams and reward them when they win medals. Therefore, when the Olympic Games or international competitions finish athletes return to their home teams and their provincial sports commissions have to reward the winners with huge amounts of money. For those who are not lucky enough to win medals the local sports authority has the responsibility of looking after them and paying them wages and pensions. Therefore local sports authorities are constantly short of money for sport, for they have already spent most of their budget on training and have nothing left to pay the rewards, wages, pensions and other costs. For example, in Liaoning Province, where athletes won more medals than any other province in China, the local sports commission is financially heavily burdened with the large amounts of reward money it has to give to current Olympic and world champions and the wages and pensions it has to pay to those ex-Olympic-gold-medallists and ex-world-champions. 'Able to produce gold medallists but unable to reward and feed them' (*duo de qi jinpai, yang bu qi guanjun*) is the harsh reality facing the local sports governing bodies. [60]

Thirdly, China's Olympic medal fever will break. As an old Chinese saying goes, the thing is valued when it is rare (*wuyixiweigui*). To become the winner of the Olympics has been the dream for generation after generation of Chinese. Once their dream comes true it will cease to be a dream. The Chinese will move to more practical and urgent social and economic issues and will be more interested in their living standards and working conditions. Sporting patriotism will lose its important position in Chinese people's lives. Cui Dalin, deputy minister of the China General Administration of Sport, has predicted that the 2008 Beijing Olympics will be the watershed of Chinese sports history. He explains:

> Before the Beijing Olympics elite sport has got mighty support from both the state and people. They work together enthusiastically towards 2008. After the games the situation will change. The government will speed up the process of the commercialization of sport and will require elite sport to stand on its own feet. [61]

Simultaneously, Chinese people's abnormal enthusiasm for elite sport will cool down as a result of increasing economic success and a growing subscription to mature and liberal political views. When the Chinese no longer believe Olympic gold medals mean everything to them, the 'whole-country support for the elite sport system' (*Juguo tizhi*) will come to an end. Therefore, to some extent, the coming three years may be regarded as the last celebration of the unique Chinese elite sports system that has played such an important role in China's political life in the form of gold-medal ambition.

Acknowledgements

The authors wish to thank Professor Xiong Xiaozheng of Beijing Sport University for providing some statistics and Craig Gill for his proofreading.

Notes

A great deal, of course, can be, and will be, written about the forthcoming Beijing Olympics. In complementary approaches my colleagues and myself take a general view and Dr. Dong Jinxia later takes a specific view.

[1] 'Yuan Weimin zai xinwen fabuhui shang de jianghua' [Yuan Weimin's Speech on the Press Conference in Athens, August 30, 2004], online at http://www.olympic.cn/athens/daibiao-tuanxinxi/2004-08-30/299251.html (www.olympic.cn is the official website of the Chinese Olympic Committee.)

[2] 'Li Furong zai beizhan yadian aoyun xinwen tongqihui shang de jianghua' [Li Furong's Speech on the Press Conference in Beijing, 25 June 2004.], online at http://www.olympic.cn/athens/china/2004-06-25/214369.html

[3] 'Zhengzhan yadian aoyun mianlin zhuduo kunnian, zhongguo juntuan jinpai yuce 27 Mei' ['Sport Official Predicts 27 Gold Medals at Best for China'], online at http://olympic.people.com.cn/GB/22181/22201/2582171.html. www.people.com.cn is the official website of the *People's Daily* (*Renmin ribao*), the most authoritative newspaper in China, being the organ of the Central Committee of the Chinese Communist Party.

[4] 'Zhongguo aoyun bingtuan jiang zai yadian xianqi jinpai chongji zhan' ['China Fights for Gold Medals in Athens'], online at http://news.xinhuanet.com/sports/2004-07/22/content_1630585.htm; 'Chaoyue deguo!' ['Overcome Germany!'], *Titan zhoubao* [*Titan Sports Weekly*], 25 June 2004, A.01. www.xinhuanet.com is the official website of the Xinhua News Agency (*Xinhua she*), the most authoritative news agency in China; *Titan zhoubao* is the most influential sports newspaper in China. Also see 'Li Furong's Speech, 25 June 2004'.

[5] 'Zheng yi zheng er' ['China and Russia Fighting for No.2'], *Titan zhoubao*, 19 Aug. 2004.

[6] 'Gongxiang aolinpike de guangrong yu mengxiang: Yuan Weimin zai di 28 jie aoyunhui zhongguo tiyu daibiaotuan baogaohui zhang de jianghua' ['Sharing the Glory and Dream of the Olympics: Yuan Weimin's Speech on the Public Lecture Held in Beijing, 14 Sept. 2004'], online at http://www.sport.gov.cn/show_info.php?n_id = 7636. www.sports.gov.cn is the official website of China General Administration of Sport [*Guojia tiyu zhongju*].

[7] 'China Takes the Olympic Limelight', http://edition.cnn.com/2004/SPORT/08/30/athens.games/

[8] Qin, Hao, 'Lun zhongguo tiyu 'Juguo tizhi' de gainian,tedian yu gongneng' [The Definition, Characteristics and Functions of the Chinese Elite Sports System], *Tiyu* [Physical Education], 2004 (3), 15–19.

[9] Meng, Wang, 'Wangmeng tongzhi zai 1980 nian quanguo tiyu gongzuo huiyi shang de gongzuo baogao' [The Report of Comrade Wang Meng in National Sports Conference in 1980], in Zhengyanshi (ed.), *Tiyu yundong wenjian xuanbian (1949–1981)* ['Collection of Chinese Sports Documents 1949–1981'] (Beijing: Renmin tiyu chuban she, 1982), p.150.

[10] Gaotang, Rong, et al. (eds.), *Dangdai Zhongguo tiyu* ['Contemporary Chinese Sports'] (Beijing: Zhongguo shehui kexue chubanshe [Chinese social science press], 1987); Fan Hong, 'The Olympic Movement in China: Ideals, Realities and Ambitions', *Culture, Sport, Society*, 1 (1998), 156.

[11] Fan Hong, 'The Olympic Movement', 162.

[12] Li Furong, 'Li Furong tan ruhe nuli chengwei yi ming youxiu jiaolianyuan' ['Li Furong's Speech on How to Become an Outstanding Coach'], *Zhongguo tiyu bao* [China Sports Daily], 4 Dec. 2002, 2.

[13] Yuan Weimin, 'Yuan Weimin tongzhi zai 2001 nian quanguo tiyu juzhang huiyi huiyi shang de jianghua' ['Comrade Yuan Weimin's Speech at the Conference of All-state Sports Ministers'], *Zhanlue jueze-2001 nian quanguo tiyu fazhan zhailue yantao hui wenji* ['Strategic Plan – A Collection of the Symposium of the National Sports Development Strategy in 2001'] (Beijing: Guojia tiwei zhengfa si bian, 2001), p.364.

[14] Tong Yilai, 'Zhaozhui jiehe dian, liqiu duchuanxin' ['The Combination of the West and the East'], *Lunwe ji*, 8 (1989), 114–17.

[15] Wu Shaozu, *Zhonghua renmin gongheguo tiyu shi (zonghe juan)* ['Sports History in the PRC'] (Beijing: Zhongguo shuji chubanshe, 1999), pp.402–4.

[16] Xu Qi, 'A New Height in Beijing', *China Sport*, 10 (1992), 36–7.

[17] Wu Shaozu, *Zhonghua renmin gongheguo tiyu shi*, pp.49–51.

[18] Ibid., pp.288–303.

[19] Ibid., p.310.

[20] Zhang Tianbai, 'Di 26 jie aoyunhui ji zhongguo tiyu daibiaotuan cansai qingkuang' ['The Situation of the Chinese Delegation at the 16th Olympic Games'], *Tiyu gongzuo qingkuang* [Sports Affairs], 624–5, 16–17 (1996), p.14.

[21] Guojia tiwei jihua caiwu si [Planning and Finance Department of the NSC], *Tiyu shiue tongji nianjian (neibu ziliao)* ['Statistical Yearbook of Sport (internal information)'] (1994), p.44.

[22] See Fan Hong, 'Innocence Lost: Child Athletes in China', *Sport in Society*, 2004 (3), 338–54.

[23] Zhengyanshi, *Tiyu yundong wenjian xuanbian 1949–1981*, p.102.

[24] Dai Qinting, 'Zhongguo tiyu yexu yige xinshidai' ['Chinese Sport Needs a New Era'], *Xinwen zhoukan* [Chinese News Weekly], 7 Sept. 2004.

[25] Fan Hong, 'Women's Sport in the People's Republic of China: Body, Politics and the Unfinished Revolution', in Iise Hartmannn-Tews and Gertrud Pfister, *Sport and Women: Social Issues in International Perspective* (London: Routledge, 2003), pp.227–8.

[26] Guojia tiwei jihua caiwu si, *Tiyu shiue tongji nianjian*, p.3.

[27] Lu Xianwu and Lin Shuying, 'Outstanding Athletes and Their Coaches', in Howard G. Knuttgen, et al. (eds.), *Sport in China* (Champaign, IL: Human Kinetics, 1990) pp.123–41.

[28] 'Wuxing hongqi wo wei ni jiao'ao: relie zhuhe woguo tiyu jianer zai aoyunhui shang qude youyi chengji' ['I Am Proud of the Five Starred Red Flag: Congratulations for the Victory of Our National Sports Heroes in Athens'], *Renmin ribao*, 30 Aug. 2004, 1.

[29] G.R. Barme, 'To Screw Foreigners Is Patriotic: China's Avant-Garde Nationalist', in J. Unger (ed.), *Chinese Nationalism* (New York and London: M.E. Sharpe, 1996), p.187.

[30] Ibid, p.208.

[31] Fan Hong, 'The Olympic Movement', 158–9.

[32] Richard Pound, *Inside the Olympics* (Ontario, Canada: Wiley, 2004), p.xi.

[33] 'Beijing aoyun touzi he xiaofei shichang zong xuqiu jiang chao 3 wan Yi' ['Investment and Consumer Requirement Caused by the Beijing Olympics More Than 3 Trillion'], *Renmin ribao*, 19 April 2004, 4.

[34] Cited in David Miller, *From Athens to Athens: The Official History of the Olympic Games and the IOC, 1894–2004* (Edinburgh: Mainstream Publishing Company, 2004), p.340.

[35] Zhao Yu, *Qiang Guo Meng* ['Dreaming to Be A Superpower'] (Beijing: Zuojia Press, 1988); Zhao Yu, *Bing Bai Hancheng* ['The Defeat in Seoul'] (Beijing: Chinese Social Sciences Press, 1988).

[36] Fan Hong, 'The Olympic Movement', 162.

[37] Ibid., 160–3.

[38] 'Jinzita xia de beiju: tuiyi yundongyuan chengcun zhuangkuang diaocha' ['Tragedy Under the Pyramid: Investigation of Living Conditions of Retired Players'], http://news.xinhuanet.com/focus/2003-09/11/content_1073593.htm

[39] 'Zhuanxiang xiuxian de wanju: bozu zhongguo tiyu he qu he cong' ['The Changing Face of Chinese Sport: Leisure Sport'], http://news.xinhuanet.com/sports/2004-08/09/content_1742895.htm

[40] Fan Hong, 'Innocence Lost: Child Athletes in China', *Sport in Society*, 2004 (7), 338–54.

[41] John J. MacAloon, 'The Turn of Two Centuries: Sport and the Politics of Intercultural Relations', Opening ceremony address at the International Symposium on Sport: The Third Millennium, Quebec City, Canada, 22 May 1990.

[42] *Renmin ribao*, 22 Aug. 2002, 1.

[43] See 'Ouyu zhengguang gangyao 2001–2010' ['The Outline Strategy for Winning Olympic Medals 2001–2010'] and '2008 Ouyunzhengguang jihua' ['The Strategic Plan for Winning Olympic Medals in 2008'].These documents were issued by the Chinese General Administration of Sport in 2002. See also Yang Su An, 'Woguo jingji tiyu de shili xianzhuang, xingshi, renwu ji duice fengxi' ['The Analysis of our Elite Sport'], *Zhongguo tiyu keji* [Chinese Sports Science], 1 (2002), 3–9. Yang is deputy minister of the Chinese Sports Ministry and the head of the Department of Competitive Sport in the Sports Ministry.

[44] Ibid.

[45] Ibid.

[46] Ibid.

[47] Cited in 'Zhongguo jinpai de chengben' ['The Cost of Gold Medals'], *Quanqiu caijing guanca* [*Observer*], 13 Aug. 2004.

[48] Ibid.

[49] Ibid.

[50] See'Aoyu zhengguang gangyao 2001–2010'and '2008 Aoyunzhengguang jihua'.

[51] 'China Takes the Olympic Limelight'.

[52] 'Young Chinese Team Exerts Its Strength; Head Start on '08: Record 63 medals' *USA Today*, 30 Aug. 2004, D.01.

[53] 'Turning the World Upside down', *The Times of Asia Magazine,* 30 Aug. 2004, online at http://www.time.com/time/asia/magazine/article/0,13673,501040830-686104,00.html

[54] 'Yuan Weimin: women shi jinpai dahu, dan hai bushi jingji tiyu qiangguo' ['Yuan Weimin: We Are A Big Gold-medal Winner, But Not Sports Superpower'], online at http://www.beijing-2008.org/13/37/article211633713.shtml. www.beijing-2008.org is the official website of the Beijing Organizing Committee for the Games of the XXIX Olympiad (BOCOG).

[55] Ibid. See also 'Yuan Weimin zai zhongguo daibiaotuan canjia yadian aoyuanhui zongjie dahui shang de jianghua' ['Yuan Weimin's Speech on the Summing-up Meeting held in Beijing, 3 Sept. 2004'], online at http://www.olympic.cn/athens/daibiaotuanxinxi/2004-08-30/299423.html

[56] 'Ban aoyunhui, jiushi yao rang duoshuo ren manyi' ['Satisfy the Majority by Hosting the Olympics'], *Titan zhoubao*, 6 Sept. 2004, A.16.

[57] 'Aoweihui fu zhuxi yang shu'an cheng zhongguo jijin di yi jituan: Beijing aoyun jiaoban meiguo' ['Challenge the USA in the Beijing Olympics'], online at http://www.xinhuanet.com/chinanews/2004-09/11/content_2849625.htm

[58] 'Zhuanxiang xiuxian de wanju: bozu zhongguo tiyu he qu he cong'. See also 'Lin Siyun: aoyun jinpai yijing biancheng jiqu guojia jinqian caifu de xianjing' ['Olympic Gold Medal: Trap for China's Wealth'], online at http://www.epochtimes.com/b5/4/8/20/n633790.htm

[59] Cited in Miller, *From Athans to Athens*.

[60] 'Liaoning: duo de qi jinpai, yang bu qi guanjun' ['Able to Produce Gold Medallists but Unable to Reward and Feed Them'], *Nanfan tiyu zhoubao* [South China Sports Weekly], 30 Aug. 2004, 8.

[61] 'Zhuanxiang xiuxian de wanju: bozu zhongguo tiyu he qu he cong'.

Women, Nationalism and the Beijing Olympics: Preparing for Glory

Dong Jinxia

When Beijing was awarded the right to host the 2008 Olympic Games in 2001, all the Chinese watching the live telecast of the voting burst into thunderous cheers and applause. A public demonstration of national pride was witnessed on a scale rarely seen in Chinese history.

Arguably, elite sport in contemporary China has been to a large extent motivated by nationalism and it, in turn, has contributed to the further development of sport. The Beijing Games in 2008 will have clear implications for Chinese government policies on international politics, the domestic economy, gender relations and sport. It is well known that Chinese women have made a great contribution to China's quick rise in international sport and won recognition and respect for the country and themselves. Here a question should be asked: what is the possible relationship between women, national identity and the Beijing Games in China? It necessitates an enquiry.

To understand Chinese sporting nationalism, it is necessary to listen to the Chinese expressing their nationalist sentiments. Their voices can help us with the thorny problem of just what 'Chinese nationalism' is. Based on official documents, published articles and books, interviews with Chinese elite athletes and questionnaires to students in Peking University, this article will explore the interconnections of sport, women and national identity, analyse the impact of Beijing's successful bid and preparations for the 2008 Olympic Games on value systems, sports policies, management and competition systems and financial structures, and foresee the future of women's elite sport in China by the end of 2010.

Nationalism and China

Nationalism is of relatively recent historical provenance. It appeared with the emergence of the nation state system in Europe and spread to the rest of the world after non-European countries were brought into the system. [1]

The rise of modern nationalism basically meant the ascendancy of sentiments associated with the particularistic features of the nation over universal principles. The ascendancy of particularism led to the drive by nations to gain political independence and then to acquire and maintain equal status with other nations. In extreme cases, this drive took the form of ultranationalism, with the supremacy of the national will, which led to aggressive behaviour in the modern world. It also gave birth to many fervent and even murderous independence and separatist movements. [2]

Because it is based upon analysis of European history, the definition that nationalism gives rise to when nations seek to become states does not apply very well to China. [3] A nation is defined as a category of persons who, as a result of common history, language, culture and association with territory, regard themselves as a distinct people or ethnic group and who aspire to some form of statehood of their own. According to the PRC constitution, 'the People's Republic of China (PRC) is a unitary multinational state (*tongyi de duo minzu guojia*), created in common by its various nationalities'. This multinational state is composed of 56 ethnic nationalities. The majority of the population is of Han nationality (about 92 per cent in the 1990 census). In this case Chinese nationalism – a collective psychological state that is a necessary condition for the survival of the politico-legal-coercive state – is equivalent to national identity. The Western view of the nation as a uniquely *modern* institution is also problematic in the Chinese context. 'China' has four millennia of documented history, and two millennia of centralized rule. Did it only become a 'nation' in the twentieth century? Some historians have argued that because the pre-modern Chinese shared a common culture, they were the 'first nation'. [4] Other historians disagree, arguing, for example, that local religious practices accentuated regional differences, undermining consciousness of a common 'Chinese' identity. [5]

As a modern concept, nationalism will refer to any behaviour designed to restore, maintain or advance public images of a national community, combining the political notion of territorial self-determination, the cultural notion of national identity and the moral notion of national self-defence in an anarchical world.

Chinese nationalism has derived from the injustices China suffered in more recent history – in particular, China's domination by the Western nations [6] and Japan (1937–45) from the nineteenth century until the end of the Second World War, which China refers to as 'the century of shame and humiliation'. In China, nationalist sentiment is officially expressed as *aiguo*, which in the Chinese language means 'loving the state', or *aiguozhuyi* (patriotism), which is love and support for China, always indistinguishable from the Communist state. As Michael Hunt observes, 'by professing *aiguo*, Chinese usually express loyalty to and a desire to serve the state, either as it was or as it would be in its renovated form. [7] From this perspective, Chinese patriotism can be understood as a state-centric or state-led nationalism.

Nationalism and Sport in Modern China

The bitter recollection of China's suffering at the hands of foreign powers has continued to be a source of Chinese nationalistic sentiment since Mao Zedong announced that 'the Chinese people have stood up' in 1949. When sport is referred to, this sentiment has turned into a driving force to advance to world level in the Olympic Games and to raise China's identity in the world. This is reflected in the slogan 'to win glory for the nation' hung on the wall of every gymnasium across the country.

In the early 1950s, when China and America were dragged into the Korean War, their relationship deteriorated. Matches against Americans and Japanese at the time were often regarded as 'political' and participation in international competitions stirred up an intense patriotism among Chinese athletes. The 1952 Helsinki Olympic Games provided the newly-founded Communist regime with a chance to enter the world competitive arena. A 41-strong delegation, including 24 male basketball and football players and two female swimmers, were sent there. However, only one swimmer took part in the competition due to the late arrival of most participants in Finland – a result of the delayed invitation from the IOC, which was thrown into confusion by the political reality of 'two Chinas' – Taiwan and China. [8] It is clear that from the outset of the PRC, Chinese sport was inextricably entwined with international political struggle. As the United States and its allies opposed the Chinese claim to be the only legitimate representative of China in the International Olympic Committee, China withdrew from the organization and eight other international sports federations in 1958.

Twenty year later, China began to open its door to the West, and its seat on the International Olympic Committee was reoccupied in 1979. Since then technological and cultural exchanges between China and foreign countries have increasingly multiplied. At the same time, the Chinese were astonished by the backwardness of their country and the severity of its problems. A crisis of belief in the Communist Party and the nation resulted. As they struggled to regain their lost dignity, the Chinese people found little scope for hope. As a weapon to counteract public discontent, the government called upon the forces of nationalism.

International sporting success can be an instrument for building up a positive national image, self-esteem and self-confidence. In 1980 the Chinese Diving Team put forward a slogan 'Go beyond Asia and join the advanced world ranks' (*zhouchu yazhou, chongxiang shijie*), which became the goal of Chinese sports people. The

Chinese Women's Volleyball Team (CWVT) took the lead in moving towards the goal. In 1981 the team for the first time defeated Japan and won the World Cup. On the crucial occasion of the last set of the final against Japan, [9] the head coach Yuan Weiming said to his players:

> Think of where you are playing – Japan, the home of Japanese invaders who killed hundreds of thousands of Chinese in the Second World War. You are representing the Chinese nation. People on the motherland need you to risk your life to fight and to win all the rounds. If you don't win this game, you will regret it all your life. [10]

These patriotic words aroused the female players to all-out effort and ultimate victory. Sport gave the Chinese some measure of pride, dignity and confidence. Between 1981 and 1986, the team won five world titles in succession. [11] These victories gave the Chinese a chance to enjoy the experience of international success. A huge wave of patriotism resulted across the whole country. Wild celebrations took place. Thousands of articles, photographs and paintings as well as a televsion series were devoted to these girls. They became hugely popular and greatly admired and were regarded as heroines – models for all. The spirit of the CWVT (*nupai jinsheng*) became a political slogan spurring on millions of Chinese to strive to modernize their country. Chinese political and sports officials openly acknowledged that they viewed sport as an instrument for the promotion of national pride and identity. The projection of successful Chinese athletes, in particular women athletes, shows this statement to be wholly correct. Thus the CWVT was a political tool. [12] Such sporting performances strengthened the cohesion of the Chinese nation, provided it with a new pride and demonstrated a new, confident face of China to the world. The symbolic power of the team was translated into political power. Contemporary competitive sport in China is motivated by nationalism and in turn contributes to the enhancement of patriotism. Seventeen years later, the team reclaimed the world title in the 2003 World Volleyball Championships. Again, it aroused a huge wave of patriotism, in spite of the fact that China had entered the top three sporting powers in the world.

In 1984 the Chinese buried their humiliating 'nil' record in the Olympic gold-medal table once and for all, capturing 15 gold medals at the Los Angeles games. This performance stirred up an intense patriotism among the Chinese and fuelled Chinese ambition to become a world sporting power. This proves that 'apart from war, no other form of bonding serves to unite a nation better than representational sports and nowhere is the sport-place bond more graphically illustrated than in the Olympic Games'. [13]

To further raise the level of Chinese sports, an 'Olympic Strategy' was put forward in 1985. In line with the strategy, the emphasis was shifted to Olympic sports and all available resources in China were concentrated on a few key sports in which athletes had the best opportunities of winning medals in the Olympic Games.

However, the road to world supremacy was full of twists and turns. In 1988 the Chinese suffered an unanticipated blow at the 24th Olympic Games. With the expectation of 15 to 20 gold medals and of becoming one of the top six nations, Chinese athletes won only five gold medals and China was placed eleventh, lagging behind even South Korea. This failure not only disappointed the Chinese but reinforced their determination to become an Olympic power in the near future.

To secure Olympic success, national policies and management on sport were adjusted. First of all, the timing of the National Games was changed from the year before the Olympics to the year after. In addition, only Olympic sports and the traditional Chinese martial arts sports were incorporated into the National Games after 1997. A winning-oriented sports policy dominated the sports community, from athletes to coaches, from researchers to administrators. The consequence of this unswerving pursuit of success was the astonishing achievements of Chinese athletes, women in particular, in the Olympics in the last decade of the twentieth century (see Table 1).

At the Atlanta Olympic Games in 1996, for example, China took 16 gold medals, 22 silver and 12 bronze, ranking fourth both in the gold-medal tally and in the total number of medals won. At the Sydney Olympics in 2000, China became the third sports power after the United States and Russia by collecting 28 gold, 22 silver and 15 bronze medals. More astonishingly, the Chinese even beat the Russians in the 2004 Olympic Games in terms of the number of gold medals won. These astonishing achievements greatly changed the Chinese image in the world and stimulated people from all walks of life to work hard and to help strengthen and modernize the Chinese nation. Competitiveness and success in sport were thus transferred to the whole of society. Consequently, a strong nationalism was once again aroused in all Chinese at home and abroad. [14]

Winning is often equated with prestige, the acceptance of a particular nation's political ideology or a symbol of a country's culture or dignity. As mentioned repeatedly, the century of humiliation by foreign invasion and 'semi-colonization' after 1840 made the Chinese under Communism obsessed with the desire to put behind them the image of the 'sick man of East Asia'. Thus the century of struggle for the improvement of the Chinese image in the world made international success

Table 1
Medals won by chinese in the last four olympics

	Golds	Silvers	Bronzes	Total	Rank
1992	16	22	16	54	4th
1996	16	22	12	50	4th
2000	28	22	15	65	3rd
2004	32	17	14	63	3rd

extremely important. Winning Olympic medals now became a symbol of the rise of China in the world. Motivated by winning honour for the nation, along with the desire for personal success, respect and acclaim, some athletes and coaches, and even officials, regarded drugs as a secret weapon ensuring sporting success as quickly as possible. As a result, drug-taking became a thorny problem in China in the 1990s and brought disgrace and international criticism to the Chinese. It could be argued that the urge to build up a national identity in the world to a considerable extent sowed the seeds of drug-taking in the Chinese sports community.

Women and Sport in Contemporary China

After the PRC came into being in 1949, Chinese women suddenly obtained equal rights with men in law, family and education. They have taken up organized elite sport on a large scale and made crucial contribution to China's advances in world sport. [15] Indeed, 'women hold up more than "half the sky"' in sport. At the Olympic Games between 1992 and 2004, female Chinese participants outnumbered their male counterparts (see Table 2) and played a major part in progressively raising China's position [16] in the medal table (see Figure 1).

The women's prominent performances convinced the Chinese government of their part in building an applauded national identity. As a result, many women's sports obtained special treatment. The 'Olympic Strategy' mentioned earlier greatly favoured women, who were considered more likely than the men to excel in international competitions. [17] Specific support at all levels and in all aspects was given to promising women athletes, including the adoption of 'male sparring partners' (*nan pei nu liang*) – male athletes were summoned to train with women in order to improve their techniques and strength – in a number of women's sports teams. How could men sacrifice their own career prospects for women's success? There might be a number of reasons for this. One of them is the nationalism mentioned time and time again:

> To be a world sporting power – symbolic of a strong nation – has been the ambition of generations of Chinese. ... To win prestige for the country, female athletes and those supporting them, including the male sparring partners made

Table 2
Comparison of Chinese male and female participants in the Olympics

	1992	1996	2000	2004
Females	132	200	188	269
Males	118	110	93	138
Percentage of women in total	52.8	64.5	66.9	66.09

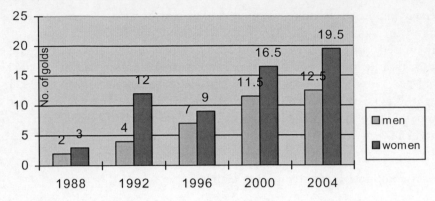

Figure 1 Olympic gold medals: Comparison of Chinese men and women

huge efforts to raise their standards. Given that women are more likely to win world championships, training with them is a need of the nation. As a result, the national interest takes precedence over any lingering male chauvinism. [18]

Olympic victories put women centre stage. They became the heroines of the nation. They won enormous social esteem and prestige. For example, on their return from the Olympic Games, they were warmly received by people from all walks of life, including high-level officials. Women athletes have been awarded all kinds of honorary titles, for example, the Honourable Badge of Sport [19] and the Best Ten Athletes. Since the launch of voting the 'Best Ten Athletes of the Year' across the country in 1978, women have made up 62.3 per cent of those chosen in the 25 years between 1978 and 2003. In 1998, only one of the Best Ten Athletes was a man. [20]

Athletic performance has been the sole criterion for determining the allocation of resources, and the consequent stratification of athletes in the sports community and in society at large has led to huge political, social and financial rewards. These Olympic winners have obtained enviable material rewards. For example, a gold medallist received 80,000 yuan in 1992 and 1996 from the central government. This sum rose to 150,000 yuan in the year 2000. This was topped up by various sponsorships from local governments, enterprises, businessmen and overseas Chinese. Thus, a gold medallist in 1996 could have bonus of about one million yuan. Four years later it was certainly more than this. [21] Deng Yaping, the female double Olympic table tennis gold medallist both in 1992 and 1996, has received a multi-million yuan bonus, becoming the most highly rewarded athlete in China. Women's success in international sport, together with the consequent financial and social benefits, has helped raise sportswomen in the public's esteem and promoted women's social status both in the sports community and society at large. By way of example, there were 44 women among the 93 sports deputies to the fourth, sixth and seventh National People's Congress. [22]

However, sportswomen have not always been positive roles in promoting patriotism among the Chinese. When the female tennis player Hu Na [23] became a political refugee in the United States in 1982, she was immediately accused of being a traitor. This event resulted in an emphasis on patriotism education for athletes. This issue attracted more attention 12 years later when He Zhili , the former Chinese female world table tennis champion, represented Japan and defeated her former team-mates and the hitherto world champions Deng Yaping [24] and Qiao Hong. [25] Her post-competition remark 'It is the happiest moment in my life to defeat the Chinese' added salt to the wounds of defeat [26] and aroused an intense nationwide debate on the issues of patriotism in China.

To ensure the patriotism of athletes, various educational activities are often organized. A number of national teams, such as those for gymnastics and volleyball, went to army barracks for a few days of military training before the Sydney Olympic Games. Through living together with soldiers athletes and coaches experienced the hardship of the military camps and understood their preferential treatment by the state. As the world gymnastic champion Li Xiaopeng said, 'being provided with such wonderful conditions, we have no reasons not to work hard. The state's aegis and people's favour could only be returned by winning medals in the Olympics.' [27]

To further arouse gymnasts' determination to win honour for the nation, the national team established a 'glory board' on which gymnasts who win world championships will have their photos and names listed. There is an official ceremony for this each year. Gymnasts' parents and sporting officials from their hometown are invited to attend the ceremony, where the national anthem is played and the national flag raised. The former world champion Huang Liping once said that

> The most memorable moment is not receiving a gold medal in the World Championships, but the solemn ceremony of listing on the 'glory board'. Listening to the national anthem and seeing my own picture being put on the board under the national flag, tears of emotion ran down my cheeks. [28]

Bidding for the Beijing Games

China's ambition is to become a world power in the foreseeable future. Sport is often used as an effective political instrument. The ability to host a big international sports competition has been a symbol of Chinese political stabilization and economic prosperity. [29] As former President Jiang Zeming once stated: 'The bid was made to further China's domestic stability and economic prosperity. The quest for the Olympics was to raise national morale and strengthen the cohesion of the Chinese people both on the mainland and overseas.' [30]

China's Olympic bid intentions date back to 1908, when the Tianjin Youth magazine asked the questions 'When can China send an athlete to participate in the Olympic Games? When can China send a team to participate in the Olympic Games?

When can China host an Olympic Games?' The first two questions have already been answered, but the last question has to wait until 2008.

At the closing ceremony of the Beijing Asian Games on 7 October 1990, there appeared in the stands a huge banner that read: 'With the success of the Asiad, we look forward to hosting the Olympic Games.' The successful hosting of the Asian Games in 1990 stimulated Chinese enthusiasm for organizing a larger-scale international event – the Olympic Games. A year later Beijing declared its intention to host the 2000 Olympic Games. Various activities [31] were organized and infrastructure was greatly improved, [32] but Beijing lost by two votes to Sydney. This failure dealt a heavy blow to Chinese morale.

However, China did not simply give up. Beijing made its second bid for the Olympic Games in 1999. By then China had achieved social stability and economic prosperity through reform, opening up to the outside world and modernization, and its national strength had increased greatly. Beijing as the capital had also shown great potential for economic growth, with its gross domestic product surging to US$2.4 billion in 1999, registering a per capita GDP of more than US$2,000. In the context of social and economic reforms, the motto of Beijing's bid was 'New Beijing, Great Olympics', meaning that reform and opening up to the outside world had brought about great changes in Beijing, a city with a 3,000-year history. This state of affairs proves that sport does not occur in a social vacuum. It is an integral part of social life. [33] It reflects, and is affected by, the dominant social structures and values of the society in which it exists. [34]

Virtually all of China, from the government to its citizens, pledged all-out support for Beijing's bid to host the 2008 Olympic Games. According to a poll conducted by the Gallup Research Co Ltd. (China), 98.7 per cent of its citizens support Beijing's effort to hold the games. [35]

Through sport China made a political statement. It is noticeable that women played an essential part in the bid. To ensure a successful bid, seven Chinese celebrities, six of whom were women, were officially appointed as endorsers of the Beijing Games to sway IOC voters. (The only male endorser was Jackie Chan, the internationally well-known martial-arts film star.) This once again shows women's popularity in the country.

When the former IOC President Juan Antonio Samaranch declared Beijing as the host for the 2008 Olympic Games, Beijing and China as a whole exploded. 'Smiles Everywhere, Joy Ignites' – newspaper headlines matched the delirious mood of the population. Many Beijing residents poured into the city centre to join the celebrations of national pride. Even Chinese President Jiang Zemin made an unannounced appearance and gave the exuberant crowd his 'warmest congratulations.' National identity rose to an unprecedented level.

Here it should be made quite clear that 'sporting nationalism is not a single generic phenomenon; on the contrary, it is a complicated socio-political response to challenges and events, both sportive and non-sportive, that must be understood in terms of the varying national contexts in which it appears'. [36] China's astonishing achievement in international sport and the successful bid for the 2008 Olympic Games coincided with radical domestic economic and social transformations. For the past 25 years China's economy has grown an average of 9.4 per cent annually, making it the world's sixth largest economy. Over the same period real per capita income – both in cities and in rural areas – has multiplied more than five times. As for total trade, China reached $851 billion in 2003, at which point it surpassed Japan as the world's third-largest market. [37] Sporting success is the reflection of China's rising power in the world.

Along with the growing influence of China in world affairs, by the mid-1990s Chinese nationalism began to surge. Out of the concern over international pressure following the end of the Cold War, popular nationalism emerged in the country. The book *China Can Say No* [38] and *China Can Still Say No* [39] in 1996 symbolized this tendency. The 1999 American bombing of the Chinese embassy in Belgrade and the 2001 spy plane collision over the South China Sea further fuelled this rising nationalism, which saw anti-US demonstrations and the resultant harsh criticism of 'Western values'. As Chinese nationalism is still further powered by feelings of national humiliation and pride, [40] the suspicion of foreign powers, opposition to any implication of inferior status and a desire to reassert sovereignty and independence could reinforce Chinese nationalism. This is true in the case of Beijing's bid for the 2008 Olympic Games. Western opposition to the Chinese bid because of China's human right records did not frighten the Chinese, but to some extent strengthened Chinese determination – at home and abroad – to fight and win. As a result, the comfortable win by 56 votes, a large margin, over other rival cities effectively consolidated a sense of the national identity of China.

Towards the Beijing Games

Due to the contemporary global significance of the Olympic Games, to become an Olympic power has been the persistent and ultimate dream of China. The Beijing Games in 2008 will provide a golden chance of fulfilling this dream.

First, preparations for the Olympics, particularly when coupled with WTO accession, will mean more inflow of funds and new ideas from the West. China can fully interact with the Western world. The unprecedented global attention on China and investment funds going the country's way will provide a major economic boost to China's economy. Billions of dollars of infrastructure building and related activities are expected to boost China's annual GDP by 0.3 per cent. All this will buttress the Chinese determination to build a 'China century'.

Second, staging the 2008 Olympic Games will provide Beijing with a chance to showcase to the world a new, vigorous image of an open, modernized, civilized and well-developed metropolis. Between $20 and $30 billion will be spent to modernize Beijing's airport and other infrastructure, building the required 35 competition venues and cleaning up its pollution and environmental hazards. [41] The National Stadium, known as 'the bird's nest' because of its giant latticework structure of irregularly angled metal girders, will cost about 2.267 billion yuan. All this will provide a material basis for the coming games.

Third, by delivering a 'green Olympics', a 'high-tech Olympics' and a 'people's Olympics', Beijing will turn into a truly international city with its own characteristics. It is worth mentioning that an overwhelming majority of Chinese feel proud of China's long historical heritage. Thus Chinese traditional culture should be presented through the symbols of the Beijing Games. Indeed, the emblem, entitled 'Chinese Seal-Dancing Beijing', features a single Chinese character on a traditional red Chinese seal with the words 'Beijing 2008' written in an eastern-style brush stroke. The IOC president Jacques Rogge commented: 'In this emblem, I saw the promise and potential of a New Beijing and a Great Olympics.'

Finally, hosting the Olympic Games will have broader social and political impacts. Society, culture and lifestyle in China will become more pluralistic, which will engender more pressure on political reform as the year 2008 draws closer.

It is widely claimed that if successful, the Beijing Games can help restore China's national grandeur [42] by bringing to an end the century of humiliation and subordination to the West and Japan. To this end, the Chinese are making concerted effort to ensure the Beijing games are the best ever one in Olympic history.

First, China's central government and Beijing's municipal government have promised to guarantee the funding of any shortfall, the construction of infrastructure and venues and working capital for the games' organizing committee.

In addition, the Beijing games have received promised support from the public. A survey showed that about 82 per cent of respondents promise to help make the games a success by doing their own work well; over 60 per cent of college and middle-school students and retirees wish to do active publicity work to ensure the success of the games; around 60 per cent of college and middle-school students would volunteer their services for the Olympic Games; and 30 per cent of Beijing residents said they would donate contributions for the Olympiad. [43] My own investigation in 2004 of 43 Peking University students reveals over 90 per cent (39) of respondents want to volunteer for the Beijing games.

Chinese athletic performance in the games will be an important indicator for judging if the Beijing Games are successful or not. It has been stated that 'all kinds of government, representing every type of political ideology, have endorsed international sporting competition as a testing ground for nation or for a political system', [44] and the Chinese government is no exception. To ensure Chinese accomplishment in 2008, the 'Plan to Win Glory in the 2008 Olympics' was drafted in 2002. According to the plan, Chinese athletes will participate in all 28 sports competitions and obtain more medals in more events than in past games, aiming to be one of the top three powers at least. Specifically, the Chinese wish to capture 180 medals from the 298 events. [45]

Again, women will play a major part in achieving this goal. Over 80 per cent of medals are to be won by women. Can this promise be fulfilled? The answer lies in the following factors. First, Chinese women have harvested a crop of gold medals in gymnastics, diving, badminton, table tennis, shooting, volleyball, weight lifting, wrestling, long-distance running, race walking and swimming in recent years. [46] They are quite likely to maintain their advantages in these sports until 2008. In addition, Chinese women have once achieved, and will again achieve, great performances in team sports such as volleyball, football, basketball, handball and hockey. They qualified for the 2004 Athens games in these sports. To win medals in team sports will surely be women's task. To maintain women's dominance in the Olympic sports, favourable policies and treatments for women, which have been adopted since the early 1990s, will certainly continue.

As Wang Xiaodong suggests, 'nationalism is indispensable and a rational choice to advance the national interests of China', [47] and China will utilize this sentiment to win popular support for organizing the 2008 games and to stimulate athletes to win medals for the nation. The 2008 games will clearly have the potential to raise the national identity of China. As a table tennis player gushed: 'Having the Olympics here will let foreigners see what a great and powerful country this is.' [48] In contrast to this positive attitude, some foreigners have voiced their fears that Chinese victory could exacerbate growing nationalism on the mainland. [49]

However, nationalism is a double-edged sword. Its destructive effects may set a limit on the utility of nationalism to Chinese leaders. While nationalism may be used by the regime to stimulate people's enthusiasm for the Olympics, it may also cause a serious backlash and place the government in difficulty. If the Olympics are not satisfactory or if Chinese athletes do not perform well, negative consequences – for example, violence against rivals and criticism of the government – could result. Furthermore, nationalism is inherently unstable. The apparent unity forged around the Olympics may be a strictly temporary phenomenon.

Summary

Nationalism can be the means by which a nation gains political respect and acquires and maintains equal status with other nations. Chinese nationalism has been linked with its century of shame and humiliation by the Western powers prior to the founding of the People's Republic of China.

International sporting success can be an instrument for creating and asserting nationalism. Beijing won the right to stage the 2008 Olympic Games in 2001 in the face of worldwide concern about China's human rights record. This victory greatly boosted Chinese nationalism.

To stage the 2008 Olympic games will be a great opportunity for China to showcase itself as a modern nation. It is widely assumed in the world that the twenty-first century will witness China's take-off. The Beijing games will accelerate this process. In the run-up to the games, China has attracted and will further attract the world's attention. China will exert a tremendous impact on world affairs in the future.

Finally, Olympic victories have put Chinese women centre stage. Successful sportswomen have become the heroines of the nation [48] and won enormous social esteem and prestige. Due to their potential to capture Olympic medals, Chinese women will continue to play a major part in promoting a positive image of China, the 2008 Olympics and beyond. Sport has advanced Chinese women and Chinese sportswomen have advanced China.

Notes

As stated earlier, this is a specific consideration of Chinese women athletes and national ambitions for them in the forthcoming Beijing Olympics. It thus complements the earlier contribution on these Olympics.

[1] Ernest Gellner, *Nations and Nationalism* (Ithaca, NY: Cornell University Press, 19(83); Eric J. Hobsbam, *Nations and Nationalism since 1780* (Cambridge: Cambridge University Press, 1990).

[2] Fong-ching Chen, 'Chinese Nationalism: A New Global Perspective,' *Stockholm Journal of East Asian Studies*, 6 (1995), 4.

[3] Gellner, *Nations and Nationalism*.

[4] Prasenjit Duara, 'Superscribing Symbols: The Myth of Guandi, Chinese God of War,' *Journal of Asian Studies*, 47, 4 (1988), 778–95; James L. Watson, 'Standardizing the Gods: The Promotion of Tíien Hou ("Empress of Heaven") Along the South China Coast, 960–1960', in David Johnson et. al. (eds.), *Popular Culture in Late Imperial China* (Berkeley, CA: University of California Press, 1985), pp.292–324.

[5] Michael A Szonyi, 'The Illusion of Standardizing the Gods: The Cult of the Five Emperors in Late Imperial China', *Journal of Asian Studies*, 56, 1 (Feb. 1997), 113–35.

[6] The First Opium War erupted in 1840. China lost the war; subsequently, Britain and other Western powers, including the United States, forcibly occupied 'concessions' and gained special commercial privileges. Hong Kong was ceded to Britain in 1842 under the Treaty of Nanking, and in 1898, when the Opium Wars finally ended, Britain negotiated a 99-year lease of the New Territories, significantly expanding the size of the Hong Kong colony.

[7] Michael Hunt, 'Chinese National Identity and the Strong State: The Late Qing-Republican Crisis', in Lowell Dittmer and Samuel S. Kim (eds.), *China's Quest for National Identity* (Ithaca, NY: Cornell University Press, 1994), p. 63.

[8] For further details, see Jonathan Kolatch, *Sport, Politics, and Ideology in China* (New York: Jonathon David, 1972), pp.171–4.

[9] The final game was between China and Japan. China would be the World Cup champion providing it won two sets, no matter whether it defeated Japan or not. The Chinese girls won the first two sets of the game, becoming too excited to concentrate on the remaining part of the game. As a result, they lost two sets in a row, which put them in a crucial position.

[10] Rong Gaotang (ed.), *Dandai zhongguo tiyu* ['Contemporary Chinese Sport'] (Beijing: zhongguo shehui kexue chuban she, 1984), p.198.

[11] They include the 1981 and 1985 World Cup, the 1984 Olympics, and the 1982 and 1986 World Championships.

[12] Zhao Yu, 'Bingbai hancheng' ['Defeat in Seoul'], in *Zhao Yu Tie Wenti baogao wenxue ji* ['Collection of Zhao Yu and Tie Wenti Reportage'] (Beijing: Zhongguo shehui kexue chuban she, 1988), p.10.

[13] John Bale and Joe Sang, *Kenyan Running: Movement Culture, Geography and Global Change* (London and Portland, OR: Frank Cass, 1996), p.39.

[14] Susan Brownell, *Training the Body for China: Sports in the Moral Order of the People's Republic* (Chicago and London: University of Chicago Press, 1995).

[15] They won 16.5 gold meals in table tennis between 1979 and 1987 (men won only one) and 25 and 14 world titles respectively in badminton and diving. They also created world records in walking, shooting and weight lifting as well as judo, fencing, basketball and football. In 1987 the nation's 'Best Ten Athletes' in athletics were all women.

[16] China's rank in the Olympics progressed from eighth in 1988 to fourth in 1992 and 1996, and then to third in 2000.

[17] Three reasons contribute to this judgement. First, many sports have been introduced to women only recently. Second, women's inequality is pervasive in the world, which leads to less investment in women's sport in many other countries. Finally, Chinese women have the historical heritage of hard work and obedience.

[18] Dong Jinxia, *Women, Sport and Society in Modern China: Holding Up More than Half the Sky* (London and Portland, OR: Frank Cass, 2003), p.200.

[19] This honorary title, established by the National Sports Commission, is presented to eminent athletes and coaches.

[20] Yuan Honghen, 'Benjie 'shijia' pingxuan, huojianzhe nannu bili wei 1:9: zhongguo tiyu yinsheng yangshuai toushi' ['The Ratio of "The Best Ten" Athletes Selected This Year Was 1:9: Exploration of the Female Blossoming and the Male Withering in China's Sport'], *Beijing wanbao* [Beijing Evening Daily], 9 April 1999.

[21] 'Zhongguo aoyun guanjun jiangjin da jiemi' ['Disclosing the Situation of Olympians' Bonuses in China'], *Beijing qingnian bao* [Beijing Youth Daily], 7 Nov. 2000.

[22] Zhang Caizhen, 'Zhongguo funiu tiyu fazhang huimou yu zhangwang' ['A Review of and a Plan for the Development of Chinese Women's Sport'], *Tiyu wenshi* [Sport History], 4 (1995), 5–8.

[23] Hu Na was the first Chinese tennis player to win the International Tennis White House Cup in Mexico in January 1982. She was given the honorary title of 'New Long-March Fighting Worker' and became a leading member of Communist Youth League. Her picture appeared on the cover of the magazine *New Sport*. Three months later she sought political refuge in America.

[24] Deng Yaping began playing table tennis at five. By 1997 she had already won 18 world titles. As the first seed, she won the 1992 and 1996 Olympic championships in both single and double women's events. She defended her title at the 1997 National Games. Thereafter, she entered the famous Qinghua University to study, and specialized in economic management. In early 1998 she was sent to Cambridge University to study English.

[25] Qiao Hong was the playing partner of Deng Yaping. They won the women's doubles titles at the 1992 and 1996 Olympic Games and at various world championships.

[26] Long Xiong, 'Dandai zhongguo titan da jiaodian renwu' ['Focused Sports Figures in Contemporary China'], *Haishang wentan* [Haishang Literary Circle], 4 (1996), 4–11.

[27] Qian Kui, 'Zhongguo ticao changsheng bushuai de mijue' ['"The Secret of Chinese Gymnastics Dominates the World'], speech at coaching seminar in Hong Kong in 2002.

[28] Ibid.

[29] Nicholos D. Kristof and Shery Wudunn, *China Wakes - the Struggle for the Soul of a Rising Power* (London: Nicholas Brealey Publishing, 1994), p.54; Zheng Fa, 'Deep Effects of the Beijing Asian Games', *China Sports*, 5 (1992), 35.

[30] Xu Qi, 'A New Height in Beijing', *China Sports*, 10 (1992), 36–7.

[31] For example, under the theme of 'Bid to host the 2000 Olympics', June 1992 was named 'Sports Month' in Beijing. Over 30,000 participants were attracted to 123 activities, including Olympic knowledge contests and marathon running. In addition, a special TV programme documented Olympic history and the measures that Beijing had taken to ensure the success of its bid for the 27th Olympic Games. An exhibition entitled 'A More Open China Looks

Forward to the 2000 Olympics' was held at the China Sports Museum. Moreover, the Chinese edition of the Olympic Charter was published in Beijing.

[32] An overall scheme for the 2000 Beijing Olympics was designed, which included four sports centres, an Olympic village occupying an area of 60 hectares, a press centre covering an area of 100,000 square metres and many other projects. An expressway from the airport to the city and a large railway station were also newly established (Chang Luya (ed.), *Shiji qing – zhongguo yu aolinpike yundong* ['A Century of Contact – China and the Olympics'] (Renmin tiyu chuban she, 1993), p.204).

[33] Peter Hain, 'The Politics of Sport and Apartheid', in Jennifer Hargreaves (ed.), *Sport, Culture and Ideology* (London: Routledge &Kegan Paul, 1982), p.233.

[34] Gunther Lushen, 'The Interdependence of Sport and Culture', *International Review of Sport Sociology*, 2 (1967), 127–39.

[35] 'Poll on Support Rate of Olympic Bid', 19 November 2002, official website of Preparatory Office Organizing Committee of the 2008 Olympic Games.

[36] John Hoberman, 'Sport and Ideology in the Post-Communist Age', in Lincoln Allison (ed.), *The Changing Politics of Sport* (Manchester: Manchester University Press, 1993), p.18.

[37] Ernesto Zedillo, 'Current Events: On China's Rise', 24 May 2004, online at http://www.forbes.com/columnists/free_forbes/2004/0524/043.html

[38] Song Qiang, Zhang Zangzang and Qiao Bian, *Zhongguo Keyi Shuo Bu* ['China Can say No'] (Beijing: Zhonghua Gongshang Lianhe Chubanshe, 1996).

[39] Song Qiang, Zhang Zangzang, Qiao Bian, Tang Zhengyu and Gu Qingsheng, *Zhongguo He Shi Leng Shuo Bu* ['China Still Can Say No'] (Beijing: Zhongguo Wenlian Chuban Gongshi, 1996).

[40] Andrew J. Nathan and Robert S. Ross, *The Great Wall and the Empty Fortress: China's Search for Security* (New York: W.W. Norton, 1997), p.34.

[41] Daniel Covell (ed.), *Managing Sports Organizations: Responsibility for Performance* (Thomson, GA: South-western, 2003), p.296.

[42] John W. Garver, *Foreign Policy of the People's Republic of China* (Englewood Cliffs, NJ: Prentice Hall, 1993), p.20.

[43] Feng Xiuying, Zhou Yang, 'Jiucheng shimin dui banhao aoyun hen you xinxin' ['90 per cent of citizens are confidant in successfully hosting the Olympic Games'], *Beijing Xiandai Shanbao* [Beijing Modern Commerical Daily], no. 580, 10 June 2004.

[44] Hoberman, 'Sport and Ideology', p.17.

[45] Guojia tiyu zongju jingji tiyu si [Department of Competitive Sport in the National Sports Administration], 'Ge sheng zizhiqu zhixia shi beizhan 2004 nian 2008 nian aoyunhui diaoyan qingkuang baogao' ['Survey Report on the Preparation of Provinces, Autonomous Regions and Municipalities for the 2004 and 2008 Olympic Games'], in 'Quangguo jingji tiyu gongzuo huiyi canyuan cailiao zhiyi' ['Reference Materials for the National Work Conference of Competitive Sport'], 2003.

[46] See Jim Riordan and Jinxia Dong, 'Chinese Women and Sports Success, Sexuality and Suspicion', *China Quarterly*, 145 (March 1996), 130–52.

[47] Shi Zhong, 'Weilai de Chongtu' ['Future Conflicts'], *Zhanlie yu Guanli*, 1 (1993), 46–50; also 'Zhongguo xiandaihua mianlin de tiaozhao' ['The Challenges to China's Modernization'], *Zhanlie yu Guanli*, 1 (1994).

[48] Covell, *Managing Sports Organizations*, p.296.

[49] John Derbyshire, 'An Outsider Inside: More Notes from China', http://www.nationalreview.com/derbyshire/derbyshire072301.shtml; 'Beijing Games win divides world opinion', http://archives.cnn.com/2001/WORLD/asiapcf/east/07/13/beijing.win

[50] Xinhua she guonei xinxi bu [Domestic Information Department of the Xinhua News Agency] (ed.), *Zhonghua Renming Gongheguo dashi ji (1985–1988)* ['Documents of Major Events of the PRC, 1985–8] (Xinhua chuban she, 1989), p.361.

'Sadly Neglected' – Hunting and Gendered Identities: A Study in Gender Construction

Callum Mckenzie

J.A. Mangan's considerable academic reputation rests, among other things, on his work on the relationship between society and masculinity. [1] His publishing profile in this area will surely be enhanced by the forthcoming publication of *Blooding the Male: Hunting, Masculinity, Militarism and the Imperial Officer* (Routledge, spring 2006) However, despite Professor Mangan's efforts, the historical profession remains 'highly resistant to problematizing the masculinity of its male subjects' to the extent that we 'still do not understand the historical relationship between masculinity and sport well enough'. [2]

The reluctance of historians to adequately explore the masculine imperatives associated with hunting is attributable, according to John Mackenzie, to the liberal intellectual tradition in the twentieth century, which has generally found the 'suspected assault upon, and destruction of, animals in the recent past thoroughly repugnant and that aversion has tended to induce a certain amount of scholarly silence'. [3] This is a view shared by John Reiger, who has asserted that 'historians have been guilty of a compulsion to remove the stain of "bloodsports"'. [4] Scholastic silence, according to Timothy Smout, is accentuated by the curiously erroneous assumption, reinforced by the historical profession, that the nineteenth century rural world 'lived by farming alone'. [5] The exclusion of field sports analysis from sociological analyses, according to other scholars, is testimony to the fact that sociology cannot be value-free but can be biased in its choice of research topics, regardless of their potential yield. [6]

The availability and significance of money, time and space, states John Lowerson, is not enough to explain the upsurge in sport during the autumn of Victoria's reign; to do this, it is necessary to *identify the values* ascribed to it. [7] Taking up the cause of academics of the history of ideas and adopting a wider view, Mangan has warned against overlooking the influence of *morality* in the evolution of modern European sport. [8] Others too have argued for the deeper probing of the values associated with sport. [9] This article is a response to both advocacy and caveat and will examine how the moral values associated with hunting – a form of period masculinization – were transmitted and assimilated by Victorian and Edwardian middle-class men and in turn, shaped the attitudes and responses of Edwardian women. This is the thrust of the essay.

Transmission and assimilation, it was maintained, had to begin early. Subscription to field sports, it was argued, had to be achieved during the receptive stage of childhood – conveniently known as the 'hunting stage' by exponents – since in later life, so the argument went, the urge to kill wildlife receded. [10] As noted by one Rugby schoolmaster who took pupils on annual shooting trips attracted by a 'keenness of youth' that, in his view, was rarely found in the middle aged, 'it is a melancholy fact that as we get older, we lose much of the thrill we got out of shooting as a boy'. [11]

Ritual indoctrination is a global staple of formal integration into groups. The Edwardian hunting community had its own esoteric practices that 'bonded' the novice to the veteran. These were as revered as those of the public schools from which many, if not most, of the hunting set were recruited.

Mangan, of course, was one of the first to draw on concepts from social anthropology in the analysis of Victorian and Edwardian middle-class educational mores. As the title of the relevant chapter in his *Athleticism in the Victorian and Edwardian Public School* makes clear, the ritual relationship between hunting field and playing field was close. This is hardly surprising as both were locations for the making of period middle-class masculinity! The contention here is that these linked stories are invaluable for those who wish to consider late-nineteenth-century field sports and their relationship to masculinity.

The 'blood' was the iconic superman of the late nineteenth century. 'Blooding' – the ritual celebration of 'kill' by daubing the quarry's blood on to the face of the young hunter – was invested with the same moral significance. One receptee declared that as a small boy he was 'delighted to have been "blooded" since he was now a fox hunter'. He added that 'many gillies "blood" those who have not shot a stag before. It is also the custom with some keepers to "blood" a young sportsman on the occasion of the first grouse or pheasant he shoots.' He was in no doubt that it 'was a very *necessary* custom' which he hoped would survive as 'long as the world goes round'. 'The abolition of a custom like this', he explained, 'would add another nail in the coffin of Great Britain's hardihood. The nation as a whole is getting much too soft, and will quickly get worse if ideas like abolishing "blooding" are encouraged.' [12]

He had clearly got the point of ritualistic practice. He made the link between masculinity and hunting, and in doing so, he spoke for many. 'Blooding' was first and foremost a hallmark of sterling masculinity. Unsurprisingly, therefore, in *Letters to Young Sportsmen*, (1920), Lieutenant-Colonel John Mackillop and Major Kenneth Dawson both argued for the earliest introduction to this rite of passage which familiarized the boy with 'the struggles' of life and death. Indeed, for this reason, there was nothing inappropriate in 'blooding' infant boys as young as 18 months in their perambulators. This rite, Dawson asserted, 'was considered almost sacred in some families'. [13]

In fact, the 'first kill' was an important event at any stage of life. In 1893, Ewart Scott Grogan crossed Africa from the 'Cape to Cairo'. [14] He found a 'solid satisfaction about grappling with death and sitting on one's first elephant or shaking the paw of one's first lion, thus, basking in the warm glow of vigorous manhood'. [15] In this way, he acquired his male caste mark. It was for this reason too that Henry Seton-Karr, Frank Wallace, Alfred Pease and Lord Ormathwaite declared that their first 'kills' gave them more satisfaction than any other. [16]

In the absence of a bloody mammal, a less bloody fish would do. Even the 'gentle' art of angling was imbued with masculine moral virtue. The significance of the boy's 'first' salmon was described by one young 'nimrod' as an 'indelible experience which fully tested his knowledge and manly skill. ... My father was a fisherman. What a triumph if I should kill a fish larger than he had! With what pride should I display my prize and afterwards narrate my prowess! Moreover, *would I no longer be considered a boy*?' [17]

In 1923, *The Field* lamented the dearth of boys coming through to run and organize shoots under their father's guidance. To remedy this, it offered some hopeful advice: lessons at shooting schools had to be supplemented by wood lore and the keen observance of things that 'he and his father's friends are out to kill'. [18] Educating the boy sportsmen, the periodical concluded with due gravity, meant expertise in such matters as differentiating between dead and wounded birds during covert shooting, the despatching of wounded rabbits and the carrying distance of shot. Even for the boy who had not yet started to shoot, carrying the adult's gun represented an early and appropriate initiation into manhood. *The Field* concluded, without the slightest hint of irony, that a 'boy's mind' was open and retentive and if he is 'shown and told the right things it will make him a knowledgeable shot with a love and understanding of woods and birds and the things he shoots'. [19]

Advocacy of field sports as a preparation for future 'male' responsibilities then reflected the importance of killing wildlife as moral instruction. Killing was far from being the whole of it. Field sports *prepared* the boy for his life's journey which would require stoicism, peseverence and robustness. 'Who would not sometimes be soaked?', asked one sportsman:

> It is then you may feel a little of the elemental man in you. And how, if you always were to run away from the elements and keep dry indoors, could you grow hardy

and seasoned? It is part of the business of the British boy to lay in such a store of hardiness as shall serve him well in later life. It is not the least thing that can be said for shooting that when taken up early in life, it does in many cases help to give a man the toughness and endurance which may be called a virtue. [20]

What all this amounted to was that killing wildlife for sport in all its aspects was considered by many to be a practical, sensible and 'normal' way of inculcating character – a prized period trait only to be 'taught by men and not those who are half men, half women'. [21]

But what of women? Where did they stand in all this emphasis on maleness through hunting? In a phrase: as outsiders. Shooting wildlife was essentially an introduction into, and a demonstration of, masculinity. Although the *Encyclopaedia of Sport* (1911) suggested that there were not many sports from which women were now excluded, it insisted that sports such as cycling and lawn-tennis were more *appropriate* for ladies than shooting. Big-game hunting therefore – particularly its more dangerous forms such as alligator shooting – and other 'unfeminine practices' such as badger-digging were properly undertaken by men. [22] They masculinized men; they unfeminized women. Indeed, *The Field* piously questioned whether women should be allowed to 'draw blood' from sentient life. [23] Compromise was possible. One commentator allowed that the presence of women at the covert side could be tolerated – provided they took no active part in the killing. [24] For many, women spilling animal 'blood' or taking 'risks' at the covert demeaned women's essential femininity. *The Field* candidly confessed to an honest prejudice against 'ladies armed in the stubble or turnip field'. Frederick George Aflalo provided the reason: shooting differed from both fishing and fox-hunting because of its greater cruelty and bloodshed. [25] It was not for the 'gentle sex'. Shooting, it was pointed out, could unnerve even '*strong men*, and the cries of wounded game, especially rabbits and hares, was incompatible with female sensibilities'. [26] Male sensibilities too were not to be overlooked. If women were to persist with the gun, another patronizing gentleman suggested, they should practice despatching wounded game without 'shuddering about it'. [27] For Anglo-Saxon Annie Oakleys, not only was femininity at risk but also matrimony *and* domesticity:

> A young lady firing small shot at partridges rather deters than attracts serious suitors. The cool handling of even a semi-toy gun suggests a *strong force of character* which future domestic contingencies might render uncomfortable to the accredited head of the house. If ladies desire to test their accuracy of eye and aim, is there not archery, with its absence of saltpetre, its attractive costumes, its leisurely ways, its imposing, engaging attitudes, and its bloodless results?' [28]

This self-interested male point of view caught the patronizing patriarchalism of the period perfectly.

Convention is seldom totally inflexible and women are seldom totally submissive to it. Against all the odds, with the support of some men, some women did make their mark with the sporting gun. Barbara Hughes was a case in point. In 1897, she determined to shoot pig in Albania, despite 'wounding the finer susceptibilities of disapproving men', and found the experience – horror of period horrors – 'edifying.' It made 'life worth living'. [29] Kate Martelli also described her shooting experiences in 'male' terms, asserting that her tiger-shooting experiences were useful for endurance, judgement and self-reliance, while Catherine Ninna Jenkin's *Sport and Travel in Both Tibets* (1909) and Agnes Herbert's *Two Dianas in Somaliland* (1908) made it quite clear that big game hunting in remote locations was not to be considered an entirely a male prerogative.

Despite the considerable discouragement faced by aspiring female 'shots', the allure of both target and game shooting continued to attract their interest. [30] Winifred Louisa Leale's performance at the Bisley Meet of 1891, for example, stimulated correspondence in the national press from other women anxious to learn the secret of her success against the best male 'shots' in Britain. [31] This upstart woman was too much of a challenge to traditional male chivalry. Not surprisingly, in the dismissive climate of the times, Leale's performance was ungraciously regarded by some as well beyond the capacity of the 'normal female shot'. [32] In short, she was a freak of nature! Leale's success, however, was not an isolated phenomenon. Pat Strutt (1895–1999) on her Kingairloch Estate on the Morvern Peninsula shot her first stag in 1912 at the age of 17, before killing another 2,000 deer in her career as a 'sportswoman'. [33] Her lust to kill remained with her all her life: she climbed the Kingairloch Hills up to her 85th year without assistance, in order to shoot deer. [34] The Duchess of Bedford, in 1923, was described by *Baily's Magazine* as a bold rider to hounds and an expert angler with, in addition, the enviable record of shooting almost 4,000 head of game in one season. [35] Predictably, however, some attempted to place such achievements in an unchivalrous perspective; the mysogynostic Frederick George Aflalo, mentioned earlier, for example, ungenerously declared that only 12 lady 'shots' in the whole of England in 1903 could attain the criteria required of a proper 'marksman'. [36]

Some women wrote about their hunting experiences to advocate and promote an independent 'feminist-hunting' culture. Isabel Savory was one who endorsed independence for 'Diana'. She wrote her *Sportswoman in India* (1900) in an effort to encourage lady shots. [37] Her sporting accounts represented a departure from the male-dominated hunting literature which with its emphasis on killing was, in Savory's provocative view, excessive and repetitive. [38] She killed sparingly but effectively – a 'selective' rather than 'non-selective' killer!

Always carefully within the bounds of conventional etiquette, Savory challenged the hegemony of the masculine heroic hunting stereotype which occupied a prominent place in the masculine imagination through the works of Robert Ballantyne, Rudyard Kipling, George Henty and their ilk. This literary world, where male comradeship and male hierarchies found their fullest scope, free from feminine ties, was also, according to Savory, a perfectly legitimate aspiration for the female. [39]

To make her point, Savory travelled unaccompanied to and through the Indian and African continents in search of sport and adventure. In India, she enjoyed tiger-shooting in the Deccan, the thrill of which had 'not been worked' from a woman's perspective. [40] Her description of her 'calculated long-shot' to save the life of a stricken army captain as he was about to be mauled by a tiger departed pointedly from the stereotypical cool and expert male 'defender' universally portrayed in the genre. [41] Her enthusiastic independence of action was also illustrated by hunting with the Peshawar Hunt, with dogs specifically brought over from England every year by Lady Harvey. Savory would get up for a hunt at 4.0 a.m. to hunt with 'the best pack in India'. [42] She broke the male mould. Within a few years, a number of ladies were also hunting with dogs, shooting elephants and rhino and displaying 'true nerve, determination, physical endurance and skill' in the process. [43]

Sporting women confronted head on the myth of 'tender' female sensibilities. They made it quite clear that the emotional distress caused by hunting, shooting or fishing could be handled by women as well as men. [44] Lady Boynton, an enthusiastic shooter, mocked the notion that woman's sensibilities were unsuitable for killing wildlife. [45] She insisted that feminine charm, refinement or grace was *not* compromised by their participation in field sports. Her only regret was that she had never shot a stag. [46]

Women eventually had their male admirers. Indeed, women hunting game were eventually welcomed in some quarters. As early as the 1890s, Colonel T.S. Sinclair for one, sang the praises of both sportsmen *and* sportswomen, asserting that

> the sporting instinct is generally planted in every British lad … and the ladies too! In these days of sexual equality are they less sporting than the youths? Certainly not. Depend upon it, our prestige among the nations of the world will never diminish so long as our wives and daughters maintain their present high standard of devotion to duty and honour and their participation in healthy open air exercises.' [47]

Here was an old argument going back to the time of Sparta: strong mothers made strong sons. Others declared magnanimously that manliness was not threatened nor femininity diminished by women with guns. White women were to be found travelling alone in every quarter of the globe, explained The Field, because colonial lands explored by the likes of Helen Caddick and Violet Markham had 'already been explored, hunted, mapped and recorded by earlier imperialists and celebrated hunter-naturalists, such as Sir Alfred Sharpe and Harry H. Johnston'. In similar vein, another 'shot' argued, a little later, that the dangers and difficulties involved in hunting overseas had diminished with easier travel and better rifles, to such an extent that 'women could do well now'. [48] In short, times were now less dangerous. Women could cope with the now safer conditions.

Women, of course, despite those well disposed to them, were at a clear disadvantage when it came to familiarity with guns, opportunities for using them and *acceptable* immersion in the whole culture of hunting. There was little or no training in firearms for girls and women. 'The first thing a *boy* does when he gets home for his holidays,' claimed someone who clearly knew,

> is to rush off to his den to see if his fishing rod, gun, butterflies or stuffed birds are all right: then, off he goes to the kennel to see his spaniel and ferrets. His first question will be whether there are lots of rabbits or trout about, and whether any rats have come back to the hayloft since he left home.

The same boy, he continued, in his

> spare time will pore over books of sport and travel and it will be his dearest wish to visit the countries he has read so much about, when he is a man. All night, his dreams will be about shooting elephants and lions, or getting to a country where no man has been. He will not give a thought to towns in foreign countries, but only of the mountains, forests and plains where big-game exists. When he goes to the library, he will make for *The Field* and *Country Life*, and whenever the opportunity comes, he will be off to obtain trophies of his own. [49]

This was a perfect description of, among others, Wilfried Thesiger. [50]

Women who wanted to shoot certainly recognized that a sound training in firearms use at an early age was essential. [51] Recognition was one thing; achievement was another. A vast hiatus divided the training of boys and girls. The numerous 'instructional' books for young men emphasized shooting for character-building. Juvenile sporting literature for boys such as *Woodlore for Young Sportsmen* (1922) by Harry Mortimer Batten, FZS, and *Horses, Guns and Dogs* (1903), by the established 'shots', J. Otho-Paget, G.A.B. Dewar and A. Innes Shand, praised field sports as superb character training for *boys*. Their books were part of the 'The Young England Library', which included *The Road to Manhood* by W. Beach Thomas, *British Soldiers in the Field* by Herbert Maxwell, *The Open Air Boy* by the Reverend G. Hewitt and *Sea Fights and Adventures* by J.Knox Laughton. Such men wrote at length of, and for, the aspiring young male 'gun'.

In stark contrast, there were very few practical, technical or inspirational books for girls. [52] In their efforts to compete with male shooters, therefore, women shooters were disadvantaged from childhood by custom, literature, training and opportunity.

In summary, upper-class society made it hard for women to learn to shoot. 'Within the education of the family,' according to one early-twentieth-century observer,

> boys both cost and are allowed more, and the opportunities of girls are more cramped, so that whilst men can indulge in the more expensive, the women have to be content with the less exciting occupations. The woman can play tennis, golf and croquet, which are comparatively cheap, but she does not get asked, as her brothers are, to go shooting, fishing and hunting. Take the case of a man with money and a sporting estate; he will entertain his male friends and give them of his best. But a woman with like advantages never thinks of having her house full of women ... she

is much more likely to get married and surrender the sporting capabilities to her husband!' [53]

Shooting, in this view, was part of a cohesive 'bourgeois hegemony' which illustrated how gender relations intersected with specific forms of capitalisim and 'patriarch-alism'. [54] It defined womanhood in terms of opportunity, biology and destiny.

The hiatus, mentioned earlier, was bluntly and brutally reinforced in F.A.M. Webster's laconic *Splendid Stories for Boys* (n.d.) which instructed its youthful readers how to hunt lion and bear, and included a chapter entitled 'Girls don't Count'! [55]

Shooting as a male activity helped confirm the proper relationships between the sexes and between 'ruler' and 'ruled'. [56] Colonel Alexander Kinloch for one stridently condemned those liberal humanitarians who would put an end to shooting as 'men would then become effeminate'. [57] Without a hint of irony, he declared that he 'loved his hunting rifle as much as his wife', who dutifully followed him from hunting camp to hunting camp. Her protected presence served to demonstrate how, he suggested, 'the fair sex' could overcome the challenges of the jungle and 'enjoy a little adventure'. [58] Of course, a woman had to be good walker and rider and 'possessed of the "pluck' in which English ladies seldom fail'. [59] Mrs Kinloch clearly possessed all these attributes. She crossed

some of the highest passes in the Himalayas by riding a Yak and, in the lower hills, when she did not walk, she travelled in a dandy, a small hammock carried by four men [and] saw nearly every species of game in the wild state, and witnessed her husband shoot Ovis Hodgsonii, Thibetian Antelope, Ibex and Bear. [60]

Appropriately, in his view, she herself never shot anything.

The ideal of the female chaperoned by the hunter was an enduring one. The colonial administrator E.P. Stebbing advised as late as the 1920s that when shooting with women, even from the security of *machans*, [61] in the interests of safety the 'ladies should be escorted by respective husbands or fathers, or with a senior male member of the party'. [62] A subordinate role, at least in the company of men, was part of the scheme of 'imperial' things. Certainly, in *Roughing it in Southern India*, published in 1911, Mrs Mavis Handley thought so. She encouraged and supported her Forest Officer husband in his sport, 'which every energetic Englishman, if inclined to outdoor pursuits, would revel in'. [63] He for his part was always the considerate chaperone. On one occasion, when her husband caught a record specimen of Mahseer [64] weighing over 96 pounds on a local river, Mrs Handley was sent to the opposite bank for safety with her books and a chair. [65] Frances Swayne, sister of the noted hunter-soldier Lt. Col. Henry G.C. Swayne of the Uganda Rifles, was fascinated by big game hunting, a sport she described in her book, *A Woman's Pleasure Trip in Somaliland* (1907). [66] But she did not participate in it. It was men's work. She was on 'holiday' while her brother did the 'real' work of surveying and mapping and hunting in Somaliland. [67]

Shooting's contribution to 'separate' spheres, however, is only part of the story of gender division determined by hunting. There is evidence that points to an androgynous sport of the privileged – that of hunting on horseback. But as will be seen shortly, too much should not be made of this. Riding to hounds was deemed more suitable for women than shooting because the rider could distance herself from the actual killing. The difference between the various 'killing' sports was explained by Alfred Edward Pease, who stated that

> fisherman may weary of flogging the unresponding waters; the best shot may feel sated with killing, grow disgusted at the shrieks of dying hares and have moments when he asks in vain for a logical defence of pleasure derived at the expense of wholesale slaughter and mutilation. There is no sport without blood, but there is no field sport with so little bloodshed about it as hunting. [68]

By the late Victorian period, women were chasing the fox in some numbers in established hunts. [69] What were the reasons for change? Arguably, it reflected wider social changes in gender relationships influenced by an upsurge in female confidence due to increased opportunities for education and employment. [70] An ancillary reason was the unprecedented interest in natural history field clubs and the study of natural history by women. The educational opportunities they offered for self-improvement and raised self-esteem was one manifestation of feminist progress. [71] Despite the gradual appearance of women at the larger hunts after the 1850s, Victorian men's attitudes towards women's fox-hunting remained mostly negative. Interestingly, in contrast, during the eighteenth century, women killing foxes produced little or no complaint from sportsmen; indeed, upper-class women killing foxes without male disapproval is well-documented. [72]

Confident intrusion into the male world of the Victorian hunt, therefore, was not plain sailing. [73] There remained a masculine cultural, psychological and symbolic importance in riding to hounds and hunting in general. In upper-class male circles, rather ambitiously and certainly fancifully, it was asked of the ideal MFH that he demonstrated the

> boldness of a lion, the cunning of a fox, the shrewdness of an excise man, the calculation of a general, the decision of a judge, the purse of Squire Plutus, the regularity of a railway, the punctuality of a time piece, the liberality of a sailor, the patience of Job, the tact of an MP, the wiliness of a diplomatist, the politeness of a lord, the coolness of a crocodile

– but all these would be to no avail unless the master also had '"that indescribable quality" of being a *gentleman*'. [74] The tone was set even if the ambition was impossible to realize. Thus, it was not surprising that in 1859, *The Field*, in response to an increasing demand by women for participation in field sports, adopted a cautious approach towards women on the hunting field. However, the weekly gave circumscribed encouragement: 'Consideration should be given to the participation of young ladies in fieldsports – so long as they are not led to adopt the slang in which too many sportsmen indulge. We desire greatly to see the fair sex in the coursing field or even with hounds to a certain extent.' [75] Britain's national reputation for 'bodily strength' was dependent on the 'health of the mothers'. [76]

The rationalization was a familiar one. Negativism was still to be found. The Revd Andrew Clark contributed to *Baily's Magazine* on hunting matters from 1861 to 1887. [77] He held strong views against womens' encroachment onto the Victorian hunting field. Women who hunted, he suggested, *were not women*: 'There is nothing so disagreeable, nothing so distasteful to men, especially hard-riding men, or true sportsmen, as a horsey female. How far is woman fulfilling her mission by adopting the attributes of the other sex?' [78] His hostility towards the emasculation of the chase was certainly shared by others. Another uncharitable male rider to hounds claimed that women who ventured onto the hunting field were 'rather masculine' while even the more unchivalrous pointed to the deleterious physical effect of hunting on the faces of the 'fair sex'. This was meant as a dire warning to ambitious 'Dianas'. [79]

Damage to their complexions was not the only physical liability women faced. The 'delicacy' of the female body was seen as an impediment to riding to hounds. They faced risk to their weaker physique. A 'first-rate horsewoman', according to *Baily's Magazine* in the 1890s, could never equal a first-class horseman; she lacked the necessary muscular power. [80] It was a widely held view. If women persisted in their desire to *compete* in the field, argued one elitist, they would be better served with 'powerful bits' and easily controlled horses. [81] That even 'superior' equestrian skills might compensate for the inferior physical abilities of women was generally rejected. Even 'school-taught' female-riders, it was believed, were physically ill-equipped to deal with the rigours of difficult hunting country. To add insult to possible injury, they lacked the strength of personality to control volatile packs. [82] Even the most generous conceded that 'only a few women' reached the physical standards demanded by experienced riders-to hounds'. [83]

All in all, many concluded that the more women were allowed access to the emotional stress inseparable from the aggressive lifestyle of men, the more they lost gentleness of nature and tenderness of expression and became hard and lined in feature – weather-beaten from exposure to the air, and stamped with the strained look that comes from exchanging the placidity of uncompetitive home life for the strenuous challenge of competition.

Criticism did not end there. Female hunting, so the argument went, contributed to 'unfeminine mediocrity in the hunting field' perpetrated by 'pretty women' with inadequate horsemanship as well as to fading looks coupled with the loss of feminine innocence and 'natural, trusting confidence'. [84] Inappropriate imitation 'hardened women and made them more like men'. [85] Lady riders to hounds were 'less womanly in the old way in which women used to be appreciated: they are talked about with less consideration, men are less deferential towards them'. Regrettably, hunting 'made women more assertive and less sex-concious'. [86] And it might be added, so the argument went, that exposure to coarseness of language and the cruelty of killing destroyed the gentility and sensitivity that were *innate* qualities of the fair sex:

> The presence of a father, brother or even a husband cannot prevent the fair amazon from hearing language, and seeing sights that are not fit for her to expose herself to. And I am sure that no lady ought to derive enjoyment from the cries of a hare in the fangs of a greyhound, or the sight of a fox torn to pieces by Foxhounds after the animal has been hunted till he succumbs to his fate from inability to run any further. Let ladies avoid the coursing and hunting field, and only grace with their presence those scenes where their presence is undoubtedly in accordance with feminine modesty and humanity. [87]

These were the views of the late-nineteenth-century 'sage', Old 'Meltonian'. He had other anxieties. He was a 'fervent admirer of the Real English Lady', he declared, but he too was fearful of possible immodesty: 'If females must hunt and accompany men in their sports, they must adapt their costume as much as possible to ours. I advise Diana to consult her father or brothers on the subject of underclothing'. [88]

Male bias against the lady hunter lingered on into the twentieth century, when fox-hunting was described by yet another disgruntled male as an 'unseemly' sport for ladies – and indeed an unnecessary one, since

> they have so many resources which beautify and embellish life, that no lady should follow hounds. It is a pretty sight to see ladies at a meet but when the chase begins, let them go home and, having had their morning exercise, return to their social duties and elegant amusements, leaving the excitement of the chase to that sort to whom dirt and disarray, red faces and noses are not unbecoming. The best runs are on moist days when a female looks limp and uncomfortable in the saddle. Could the lady hear the remarks of the sex she seeks to emulate on ladies hunting, she would turn to cultivation of the mind and accomplishment, by which she becomes a real magnet to us, and obtains the love, sympathy and respect of our sex. [89]

To make matters worse, some complained, those women who insisted on hunting often ignored the seriousness of the hunt and were thus more likely to flippantly disturb the Master at inappropriate times. [90] And there were yet more disadvantages to their presence.

Some women developed thick skins and exuded self-belief. By the late nineteenth century, 'feminist' horsewomen such as Frances Slaughter, Violet Greville and Mabel Howard, flouted convention confidently and pushed for full and proper recognition for female hunting skills since, in their view, most women matched men for 'nerve' in the saddle and also, in their view, had stronger equestrian skills. [91] Such women gave their full support to the hunting fraternity against those who would abolish the sport – entirely for reasons of self-interest. 'For ladies especially,' declared Mabel Howard, the cessation of hunting would be a severe blow. It is the only sport they can really take part in to any great extent. A few have gone in for shooting, some fish with fair success and some try to play the game of cricket, but in hunting alone are they really successful and can equal and even surpass men, in spite of pommels and a one-sided balance. [92]

Women's morale was doubtless boosted by the tone of 'The Rights of Women to Sport' in an editorial in *The Field* of 1885. It took note of women's' advances in education, and cautiously supported

feminine ambition to aspire to what have hitherto been masculine sports – so long as they can be followed by the weaker sex with due regard to that delicacy of taste which should be the watchword of a woman. One great merit of sport is that it inculcates instincts of fair play and of generosity to an opponent. A true sportsman is never cruel at heart and has far more feeling of mercy for the brute creation than the vulpecide and those of suchlike sympathies; and the same doctrine will apply to the newly-expanding class of sportswomen. [93]

Thus early and later arguments about the inappropriate callousness of field sports were turned on their head. Dianaphiles went even further than Francis Slaughter and as far as to suggest that some dedicated huntresses were in better physical and mental shape for hunting than many male hunters. [94]

Enthusiastic huntresses agreed. One clear indication of the growing presence of women at the hunt was fashion advertisements. 'Every new season,' according to *Baily's Magazine* in 1899, 'heralded fresh advertisements of skirts, saddles and stirrups, each firm trying to out-do the other with suggestions and inventions; and there is no doubt that all this has considerably improved the conditions of ladies hunting.' [95] Alys Serrell hunted otters in the 1890s and chased carted deer at Baron Wolverton in Blackmore Vale wearing the green habit worn by women members of Mr Garth's hounds of the South Berks and the pink and scarlet outfit of the Vine. [96]

Contributions to period sporting literature by women writers illustrated women's improved standing in the hunting field. The eminent Grafton and Bicester Hunt, for example, was documented by Lady Sophie Scott in her *Hunting Diaries* between 1894 and 1936, thus breaking the tradition of male-dominated hunting narratives in this premier hunting county. [97] The number of 'serious' contributions to women's sporting historiography increased significantly during the 1890s, reflecting women's involvement as practitioners of the 'chase'. Some women made especially significant contributions to this genre. Hunting observations by the likes of Lady Violet Greville (*The Gentlewoman's Book of Sports*, 1892, *The Gentlewoman in Society*, 1892, *Ladies in the Field*, 1899 and *The Greville Memoirs*, 1899), Alice M. Hayes (*The Horsewoman*, 1893), and F.E. Slaughter, editor of *The Sportswoman's Library* (two volumes, 1898) were followed by Francis Alys Serrell (*With Hounds and Terrier*, 1904), Amy C. Menzies, (*Women in the Hunting Field*, 1913), Maud Isabel Harvey (*Hunting on Foot with Some Yorkshire Packs*, 1913) and Beverly Robinson (*From Start to Finish, Fifty*

Galloping Years, 1919). Later, Lady Diana Maud Nina Shedden's *To Whom the Goddess, Hunting and Riding for Women* (1932) and Frances Pitt's *Hounds, Horses and Hunting* (1948) consolidated 'feminine' presence on the hunting field. The *Hunting Recollections* (1911) of Miss Augusta Samaurez Tawk (1865–1949) affirmed her reputation as the '*hardest riding* woman in the Essex Union Country', while Violet Bullock-Webster's *The Sport of the Past and the Future* (1929) and the *Sporting Reminiscences* (1920) by Dorothy Conyer (1873–1957) contributed to an autonomous 'nostalgic femininity' which enabled female riders to be remembered in same way as their male counterparts. [98] 'Women,' Frances Slaughter advised, 'should take more opportunities to understand the art of venery and the work of the hounds'. [99] She maintained that such books as the above provided women with the inspiration, information and assistance that they were not likely to find in books written from a man's point of view, although women's reading should not exclude the 'great body of sportsmen who so far have held almost undisputed sway in the realm of sporting literature'. [100]

The historiography of sport, recreation and leisure as sources of pleasure, instruments of control or symbols of emancipation have focused on the nineteenth century for one very good reason. It was the nineteenth century's social, industrial and technological changes, and accompanying ideological ferment, that gave much to modern sports. [101] One aspect of the sports revolution was the persistence of a dominant assumption about the 'inferiority' of the female sex and the unwillingness on the part of women to be completely constrained by dominant social norms. Sport has had a large part to play in maintaining and sustaining a patriarchal social order in Western society. To overlook this is to fail to recognize the potent influence of sport not only in terms of class but also of gender. However, it is as well to recognize that both reality and society are complex. Male domination is far from the truth. Individual and group assertiveness even in the heyday of patriarchy – the Victorian era – 'stimulated diversity in the midst of apparent uniformity'. [102]

John Lowerson in his nicely named chapter, 'Lesser Breeds', in *Sport and the English Middle Classes, 1870–1914,* has an excellent section entitled simply 'Women' in which he refers to Hobsbawm's characterization of the emergence of women in sport in the late nineteenth century as a celebration of their public individuality and as questions of separation from their domestically focused subjection to men. [103] Hobsbawm's statement is perhaps a little too emphatic, but contains a certain amount of truth. In his chapter on women, Lowerson was concerned with locating such associated matters as public and private gender identities, female economic independence and the striving for political and intellectual enfranchisement in 'the context of a male-dominated agenda of middle class self-realization'. [104]

This consideration of women and hunting has the same preoccupation. The consequence of male domination was social tension – a tension articulated publicly mostly by men. [105] They had a greater freedom from adverse consequences and they took full advantage of this. Tense outspokenness typified the response of most men to the efforts of women to share the pleasures of hunting fields and grounds.

Many men were critical; far fewer were complimentary. On grounds of male appropriateness and female inappropriateness, women hunters were given a hard time by the majority of men. The issue was essentially one of appropriate social training for adulthood. In the opinion of many men and not a few women, hunting served boys well and girls badly.

Nevertheless, up to a point, hunting was subject to changing times, new female assertion, ideological argument and simply determined women. Within the world of sport, hunting was a microcosm of a macrocosm – it faithfully reflected a broader reality. In the final analysis, hunting was at one with other sports in that it remained a place of social containment, gradually extending rather than radically challenging restrictive boundaries. [106]

In his foreword to *Soccer, Women, Sexual Liberation: Kicking off a New Era*, on the subject of women's stubborn insistence on sharing in the pleasure of playing football, which many men tried to keep for themselves, Mangan aptly quotes the playwright Ben Johnson: 'If women have a will they do it against all the watches of the right'. [107] In another sports setting at much the same time, as this chapter hopefully demonstrates, some women pointed up the appropriateness of the quotation.

Finally, in another foreword, this time to *Freeing the Female Body: Inspirational Icons*, Mangan wrote: '*Freeing the Female Body* aims not only to enlighten its audience but to advance reflection on female emancipation, the body and power.' He points out that the book considers 'iconic figures who have challenged prejudice, denied the validity of custom and pushed aside the barriers to progress'. [108] This article, on a less ambitious scale, has precisely the same aim.

Notes

[1] J.A. Mangan, *Athleticism in the Victorian and Edwardian Public School* (Cambridge: Cambridge University Press, 1981, repr. with new introduction, London and Portland, OR: Frank Cass, 2000); see in particular Chapter 7, ' Fez, "Blood' and Hunting Crop: the Symbols and Rituals of a Spartan Culture', pp.141–78. Mangan, incidentally, has also explored the militarism associated with English, imperial and European masculinity in a series of studies including (with R. Holt and P. Lanfranchi) *European Heroes: Myth, Identity and Sport* (London and Portland, OR: Frank Cass, 1996). See also his *Making European Masculinities: Sport, Europe, Gender* (London and Portland, OR: Frank Cass, 2000); *Shaping the Superman: Fascist Body as Political Icon* (London and Portland, OR: Frank Cass, 1999); also *The Imperial Curriculum: Racial Images and Education in the British Colonial Experience* (London: Routledge, 1993). The latter contains an important chapter on militarism and symbolism as mechanisms for ensuring imperial self-confidence – 'Images for Confident Control: Stereotypes in Imperial Discourse', pp.6–22.

[2] G. Whannel, *Media Sports Stars, Masculinities and Moralities* (London: Routledge, 2002), p.252; M. Roper and J. Tosh (eds.), *Manful Assertions: Masculinities in Britain since 1800* (London: Routledge, 1991), p.2.

[3] J. Mackenzie, *The Empire of Nature* (Manchester: Manchester University Press, 1988), p.1.

[4] J. Reiger, *American Sportsmen and the Origins of Conservation* (Corvallis, OR: Oregon State University Press, 2001), p.194.

[5] Timothy Smout, Edinburgh University, letter to author, November 1992.

[6] R. Hummel, *Hunting, Fishing and Shooting for Sport* (Bowling Green, OH: Bowling Green Press, 1998), Ch.1.

[7] J. Lowerson, *Sport and the English Middle Classes* (Manchester: Manchester University Press, 1988), p.171.

[8] J.A. Mangan, 'The History of Modern Sport as a History of Modern Ideas', *European Sports History Review*, 4 (2002), 255.

[9] J. Nauright and T. Chandler, *Making Men: Rugby and Masculine Identity* (London and Portland, OR: Frank Cass, 1996), p.1.

[10] Andrew Clark, 'School Life; its Sports and Pastimes', *Baily's Magazine*, 1 (April 1861), 370; A. Lang, 'The Old Sportsman', *Badminton Magazine*, 1 (1895), 370–5.

[11] D.J. Watkin-Pitchford, *Tide's Ending* (London: Joseph, 1950), p.18.

[12] Quoted in H. Salt, *The Company I have Kept* (London, 1930), pp.168–9.

[13] J. Mackillop, H. Hutchinson, K. Dawson, *Letters to Young Sportsmen* (London: Country Life, 1920), p.3.

[14] E.S. Grogan and A. Sharpe, *From the Cape to Cairo* (London: Hurst and Blackett, 1900), p.172.

[15] Ibid.

[16] Sir H. Seton-Karr, *My Sporting Holidays* (London: Edward Arnold, 1904), p.6; H.F. Wallace, *Hunting Winds* (London: Eyre and Spottiswoode, 1949), Ch.5; A.E. Pease, *Hunting Reminiscences* (London: W. Thaker and Co., 1898), pp.159–60; The Lord Ormathwaite, 'My First Stag', *Badminton Magazine*, 6 (June 1897), 119–32.

[17] Parker Gilmore (pseud. 'Ubique'), *Accessible Field Sports* (London, 1871), p.11 (emphasis added).

[18] 'Boys and Shooting', *The Field*, 143 (January 1924), 97.

[19] Ibid.

[20] J. Otho-Paget, G.A. Dewer, A.B Portman and A.I. Shand, *Horses, Guns, and Dogs* (London, 1903), p.121.

[21] R.S. Baden-Powell, *Scouting for Boys* (London: C. Arthur Pearson, 1908), p.226; Sir Henry Newbolt, *The Book of Good Hunting* (London: Longmans and Co., 1922), pp.22–3. See also J. Hearn, *Men in the Public Eye* (London: Routledge, 1992), p.109, and J. Hearn, 'Reviewing Men and Masculinities – or Mostly Boys' Own Papers', *Theory, Culture and Society*, 6 (1989), 18–20.

[22] Lord Suffolk and Lord Berkshire (eds.), *The Encyclopaedia of Sport* (4 vols), Vol.1 (London: William Heinemann, 1911), preface. Alligator-hunting seems have aroused contrasting emotions in hunters and non-hunters, owing perhaps to its aggressive nature and 'prehistoric' physical characteristics. For a criticism of the persecution which these animals suffered at the hands of imperial hunters, see G.S. Sandilands, *Atalanta or the Future of Sport* (London: Kigan Paul and Co., 1928), pp.9–10.

[23] 'Sport and Matrimony', *The Field*, 39 (January 1872), 49; A. Haig-Brown, 'Women and Sport', *Baily's Magazine*, 83 (1905), pp. 25–6.

[24] 'Woman and Sport'.

[25] Ibid.

[26] Pease, *Hunting Reminiscences*, pp.159–60.

[27] Ibid.

[28] 'Sport and Matrimony', 49.

[29] 'Pig-shooting in Albania', *Badminton Magazine*, 4 (1897), 239–41.

[30] Amy C. Menzies, 'Skirts and Guns', *Badminton Magazine*, 5 (1899), 761.

[31] W.L. Leale, 'Rifle-Shooting', in Greville (ed.), *Ladies in the Field* (London: Beatrice, Violet Ward and Downey, 1899), pp.159–72.

[32] *Daily Telegraph*, 26th July 2000, 33. I am grateful to Professor J.A. Mangan for this reference. See also *Badminton Magazine*, 4 (June 1897), 238–41.

[33] Ibid.

[34] Ibid.

[35] *Baily's Magazine*, 120 (November 1923), p.223.

[36] F.G. Aflalo, 'The Sports Woman', *Fortnightly Review*, n.s., 77 (May 1905), 891–9.

[37] I. Savory, *Sportswomen in India* (London, 1900), p.3.

[38] Ibid., p.255.

[39] Ibid., p.267.

[40] Ibid., pp.47, 255, 262–7.

[41] Ibid., p.267.

[42] Ibid., p.47.

[43] R.B. Cunningham, 'A Lady's Experience of Elephant and Rhino Hunting', *Badminton Magazine*, 26 (1908), 503–515, 512.

[44] Lady Boynton, 'Shooting', in Greville, *Ladies in the Field*, pp.199–200, 230.

[45] Ibid.

[46] Ibid.

[47] T.S. St Clair, 'The Subaltern in India', *Baily's Magazine*, 48 (1888), 97–105.

[48] Review of *White Woman in Central Africa* by Helen Caddick (London: Fisher Unwin, 1903), in *The Field*, 95 (August 1903), 256; Lord Cranworth, *Profit and Sport in British East Africa* (London: MacMillan, 1919), p.321.

[49] C. Stigand and D. Lyell, *Hunting the Elephant in Africa* (New York: MacMillan Co, 1913), p.4.

[50] M. Asher, *Thesiger* (London: Viking, 1994).

[51] A. Menzies, 'Skirts and Guns', *Badminton Magazine*, 5 (May 1899), 759–68.

[52] Ibid.

[53] T. Claye-Shaw, 'Women in Sport', *Baily's Magazine*, 40 (June 1913), 408.

[54] J. Hargreaves, quoted in C. Rojeck (ed.), *Leisure for Leisure: Critical Essays* (New York: Macmillan, 1990), p.134; A.M. Hall, *Feminism and Sporting Bodies* (Champaign, IL: A.M. Hall, 1996), preface, pp.23–6; and, 'Where's the Virtue, Where's the Grace', *Theory, Culture, and Society*, 3 (1986), 108–9.

[55] F.A.M. Webster, *Splendid Stories for Boys* (London: J.F. Shaw and Co., 1932), pp.19–29. See also Edward, Duke of Windsor, *A King's Story, The Memoirs of the Duke of Windsor* (New York, 1947), p.87.

[56] A.A.A. Kinloch, *Large Game Shooting in Tibet, Himalayas and Central India* (Calcutta, 1885), Introduction, p.4.

[57] Ibid.

[58] Ibid.

[59] Ibid.

[60] Ibid.

[61] A machan was a safe area built into a tree top where the sportsman could see and from which he could shoot his quarry.

[62] E.P. Stebbing, *The Diary of a Sportsman Naturalist in India* (London: John Lane, 1920), pp.30–50.

[63] Ibid.

[64] Mahseer is a salmon-like fish hunted for sport and food.

[65] Mrs M. Handley, *Roughing it in Southern India* (London: Edward Arnold, 1911), pp.3–38.

[66] F. Swayne, *A Woman's Pleasure Trip in Somaliland* (Bristol: John Wright and Co., 1907), preface.

[67] Ibid., pp.1–3.

[68] Pease, *Hunting Reminiscences*, p.160.

[69] See D. Itzkowitz, *Peculiar Privilege; A Social History of English Foxhunting, 1753–1885*, (Hassocks: Harvester Press, 1977), pp.48–9.

[70] 'Impecunious', 'Ladies and Field Sports', *The Field*, 105 (January 1905), 43–4.

[71] 'The Progress of Sport in Scotland', *Baily's Magazine*, 70 (December 1888), 157.

[72] *The Field*, 10 (December 1857), 180. See also J. Strutt, *The Sports and Pastimes of the People of England*, 3rd edn (London: Thomas Tegg, 1838), p.13; R. Longrigg, *The History of Foxhunting* (London: Macmillan, 1975), p.30; T. Wright, *A History of Domestic Manners and Sentiments in England During the Middle Ages* (London: Chapman and Hall, 1862), pp.305–10; S. Shahar, *The Fourth Estate*, trans. Chaya Galai (London: Methuen, 1983), p.152; A. Guttman, *Women's Sports* (London, 1992), p.18. For female hunting prowess in the classical world, see E.T. Vermeule, *Greece in the Bronze Age* (Chicago, 1964), p.194, and R. Dawkins, *Artemis Orthia* (London, 1929), pp.150–1.

[73] 'Foxhunter', *The Field*, 10 (October 1857), p.251.

[74] R.S. Surtees, *Analysis of the Hunting Field* (London: R. Ackermann, 1846), pp.4 and 21; E.C. Wingfield-Stratford, *The Victorian Sunset* (London: Routledge, 1932), p.76; G. Maxwell, *The House of Elrig* (London: Longmans, 1965), pp.138–40; G. Kitson Clark, *The Making of Victorian England* (London: Methuen, 1962), p.255.

[75] Quoted in *The Field*, 301 (January 2003), 38–9.

[76] Ibid.

[77] Andrew Clark (pseudonym), 'The Gentleman in Black', worked for *Baily's Magazine* from 1861 until the 1870s.

[78] Women and their Habits', *Baily's Magazine*, 4 (February 1862), 163.

[79] *The Field*, 10 (December 1857), 180; 'The Progress of Sport in Scotland', *Baily's Magazine*, 50 (December 1888), p.157.

[80] 'Fair Huntresses', *Baily's Magazine*, 46 (January 1896), 33.

[81] *The Field*, 105 (April 1895), 514.

[82] 'Fair Huntresses'; 'Ladies and Field Sports', *The Field*, 105 (January 1905), 44. See also Surtees, *Analysis of the Hunting Field*, p.295, and A. Trollope, *Hunting Sketches* (London: Chapman and Hall, 1865), p.30.

[83] 'Fair Huntresses'.

[84] 'The Gentleman in Black'; 'Women and their Habits', 163.

[85] T. Shaw-Claye, 'Women', *Baily's Magazine*, 40 (June 1913), 407.

[86] F. Slaughter (ed.), *The Sportswoman's Library*, 2 volumes (London, 1898), Vol.1, pp.6, 30–1; Shaw-Claye, 'Women'.

[87] 'Ladies Hunting', *The Field*, 8 (September 1857), 180, 196; (October 1857), 251.

[88] Ibid.

[89] Ibid.

[90] 'Ladies and Field Sports', *The Field*, 105 (January 1905), p.44.

[91] See Violet Greville, *The Greville Memoirs* (London: Longmans, Green and Co., 1899); *The Gentlewoman's Book of Sports* (London, 1892); *The Gentlewoman in Society* (London, 1892); Alice M. Hayes, *The Horsewoman* (London: W. Thacker and Co., 1893); Slaughter, *The Sportswoman's Library*; F. Alys Serrell, *With Hounds and Terrier in the Field* (Edinburgh, 1904); Amy C. Menzies, *Women in the Hunting Field* (London, 1913); Maud Isabel Harvey, *Hunting on Foot with Some Yorkshire Packs* (Monkton, 1913). See also Jennifer Hargreaves quoted in E. Dunning, J. Maguire and R. Pearlon (eds.), *The Sports Process* (Champaign, IL: Leeds, 1993), p.80.

[92] Mabel Howard, 'Ladies in the Hunting Field', *Badminton Magazine*, 4 (1897), 110–20.

[93] 'The Rights of Women to Sport', *The Field*, 65 (September 1885), 449–50.

[94] 'Borderer', *Baily's Magazine*, 86 (November 1906), 354. 'Borderer', was the pseudonym of Sir Richard Dansey Greene-Price (1862–1909). See also 'Hunting From a Woman's Point of View', in A.E.T. Watson (ed.), *English Sport* (London: MacMillan and Co., 1903), p.33; 'Borderer', *Baily's Magazine*, 86 (November 1906), 354; M. Wynter and C.M. Creswell,

'Hunting Ladies', *Baily's Magazine*, 85 (March 1906), 234–7; C. Cordley, 'Women in the Hunting Field', *Baily's Magazine*, 80 (April 1900), 269–72.

[95] 'Fair Huntresses' and 'The Fashions of Hunting', both *Baily's Magazine*, 65 (March 1896), 33–40 and 163–166 respectively; 'Hunting Dress, Ancient and Modern', *The* Field, 73 (January 1900), 19–23; 'Women and their Dress', *The Field*, 99 (March 1902), 452.

[96] Serrell, *With Hounds and Terrier*, pp.39, 111–12.

[97] Northampton Record Office: MS Hunting Diaries: Lady Sophie Scott's Hunting Diaries, 1894–1936, YZ 8773–7; The Pytchley, The Hunting Diaries of Charles King, 1800–18; William Scarth-Dixon, ZA 7791, c.1900; Diaries of William Wilson, 1833–76, ZA 3801; The Fitzwilliam Hunt, Diaries of V.H.Sykes, c.1900, ZB 772; The Grafton Hunt, Lord Euston, c.1860s, G 3947-6.

[98] Miss Augusta Samaurez Tawk, *Hunting Recollections* (Essex: printed privately, 1911); V. Bullock Webster (Mrs Armel O'Connor), *The Sport of the Past and the Future* (Ludlow, 1929).

[99] Slaughter, *The Sportswoman's Library*, Vol.2, preface and p.145.

[100] Ibid.

[101] J.A. Mangan and Roberta J. Park, *From Fair Sex to Feminism: Sport and the Socialization of Women in the Industrial Post Industrial Era* (London and Portland, OR: Frank Cass, 1987), p.3.

[102] Ibid.

[103] Lowerson, *Sport and the English Middle Classes*, Ch.7, p.203.

[104] Ibid., p.204.

[105] Ibid.

[106] Ibid.

[107] Fan Hong and J.A. Mangan (eds.), Foreword, in *Soccer, Women, Sexual Liberation: Kicking Off a New Era* (London and Portland, OR: Frank Cass, 2004), p.xi.

[108] J.A. Mangan, Foreword to J.A. Mangan and Fan Hong (eds.), *Freeing the Female Body: Inspirational Icons* (London and Portland, OR: Frank: Cass, 2001), p.ix.

Amateur World Champion, 1893: The International Cycling Career of American Arthur Augustus Zimmerman, 1888–1896

Andrew Ritchie

If the biographies of individual champion athletes are one of the most significant and revealing means of examining and understanding the history of sport, then within the emergence and development of each sport certain personalities occupy key positions. They are notable, and worthy of critical examination, not only for their outstanding athletic abilities but also for the nature and character of the historical moment at which they excelled. Such athletes may set new standards by breaking world records, they may overcome racial or political boundaries or they may introduce new techniques or embrace new technologies. But whatever they achieved was inevitably within and as a result of the specific conditions which determined and affected their lives. They stood at a critical moment of history, redefining excellence and interacting with a variety of specific social, cultural and technological factors, which determined and defined the terms of their success.

Of the many prominent careers well documented in the press during the competitive and recreational cycling boom of the 1890s in Britain, France and America, that of Arthur Augustus Zimmerman (1869–1936) was one of the most dramatic and meteoric, and it is also one of the least explored. In the early 1890s, Zimmerman was rapidly elevated to international 'star' status, arguably one of the first athletes in the newly emerging international bicycle racing scene to have been thus honoured and have thus risen to fame. His short and fascinating career was expressive of the sporting preoccupations and controversies at the highest level of the sport at the time, particularly those concerned with the moral values attached to amateurism and the inevitability of professionalism, and the ongoing debate in the press about the nature of sponsorship and commercialism within a sport that had close links with the rapidly developing bicycle manufacturing industry.

Zimmerman's active racing career lasted only from 1888 to about 1896, but this was a period of rapid expansion and intense change within the sport and the bicycle industry, and Zimmerman's winning of the first official amateur world championship title in 1893 in Chicago (recognized by the newly created International Cyclists' Association) gives the opportunity for an examination of the career of an international cycling star of the period, particularly as it touches the rising surge of professionalism within cycling in the mid-1890s. At the same time, there is something enigmatic and mysterious about the personality of Zimmerman, a 'star' whom no one really seemed to know very well, who lived in the spotlight of public adulation in America and Europe for a short time, was turned into a media personality and then was just as suddenly gone. His career may, perhaps, be defined as modern, not merely because cycling was then a young sport but because his fame was to a large extent created by the press, hungry for an outsized personality. Sport thus became the avenue to and realm of sudden stardom, and of instant oblivion. Because he was so much 'hyped', Zimmerman's actual achievements thus become more difficult to evaluate.

Before discussing Zimmerman further, it is essential to give a brief background to the history of bicycle racing in the United States in the previous 20 years (from 1868 to about 1890), for this was the athletic and technological context within which his career was shaped and formed. A brief surge of activity in the period 1868–70, which saw the arrival in America of the French bicycle first designed and manufactured in Paris by Pierre Lallement, Pierre and Ernest Michaux and RenéOlivier, and the emergence of a short-lived but energetic American bicycle industry in the same period, resulted in a recreational and sporting 'fad'. Racing was held outdoors but also indoors, where it featured as a substantial component of professional entertainment. Following a decline in the sport in the mid-1870s, the arrival on the East Coast of examples of the English high-wheel bicycle stimulated a renewal of interest in bicycling in and around the Boston area, and the initially imported English bicycles were soon being manufactured by the Pope Manufacturing Co. and other companies. From 1877 onwards, American cycling clubs were formed, riders explored the roads of New England, New York and Pennsylvania, the first journal devoted to the sport and recreation was published (*The American Bicycling Journal*) and the League of American Wheelmen – the governing body of American cycling – was founded in Boston. [1]

As the sport expanded, at first based mostly in the larger East Coast and Midwestern cities, road and track racing became increasingly organized. National championships were held over short distances on the track, longer distances were covered on the challenging roads of the time and larger-scale meetings celebrating the sport, drawing principally on amateur club members but also including professional riders, were promoted at Springfield, Massachusetts and other East Coast locations. A quasi-military discipline required club members on the road to present a responsible, respectable image of cycling to the general public. A strong link with collegiate athletic activities was established and colleges such as Harvard and Yale fielded expert cycling teams, with the cycling events at first included as a component of track and field activities – until the popularity of the sport and the consequent need for dedicated cycling facilities led to investment in tracks, or 'paths' as they were known. The League of American Wheelmen initiated the 'Good Roads' movement, lobbying city, state and federal governments for improvement in the nation's neglected roads.

Technologically speaking, in the second half of the 1880s, the solid-tyred high-wheel bicycle was quickly outmoded from about 1886 onwards, first by the solid-tyred 'safety' bicycle (with two wheels of the same size), and then from about 1890 onwards by the pneumatic-tyred 'safety', which originated with John Boyd Dunlop's invention of a tyre to overcome the negative effects of vibration on rutted and stony roads, but which was quickly also experienced as faster and smoother than the solid tyre. Zimmerman's competitive career thus coincided precisely with this moment of revolutionary technological change and heightened development within the sport as it was emerging from the high-wheel phase and being transformed. With such crucial structural changes occurring, the sport was linked symbiotically and economically with the development of the industry, which leaned heavily on competitive and touring riders for feedback on the design and quality of the bicycles and other products that it introduced into the marketplace. As a technology-dependent sport, cycling inevitably turned all its devotees into consumers of the tools of the sport – the bicycle, its paraphernalia and its accessories. In this sense, cycling can be said to have been expressive of modernity, of modern patterns of consumption and of modern modes of presenting a dynamic, exciting, technology-based sport to a general public hungry for novelty, sensation and speed. The sport encouraged extensive publicity in the press and with posters, the creation of the velodrome (an arena within which competitive struggle could take place and be watched) and the systematic commercial sponsorship (for advertising purposes) of individual riders and teams.

Zimmerman began his cycling exploits on the high-wheel bicycle as an amateur within the active club life of the East Coast, and his outstanding initial successes led quickly to national champion status, world records and international professional stardom. His athletic qualities and status were extravagantly rated at the time. In 1893, the *Wheelmen's Gazette* called him 'the greatest cycle racer of the time'; *The Wheel* stated that he occupied 'the most exalted position ever held by an athlete'; and writer Gregory Bowden later called him 'one of the most extraordinary superstars of the sport the world has known'. [2] His well-compensated sponsorship arrangements with two of the largest bicycle equipment manufacturing companies, Raleigh and Dunlop, were typical of the expanding commercial interconnectedness of the sport and the bicycle-manufacturing industry, and demonstrated how a top amateur tended to be drawn inevitably into professionalism. In Zimmerman's case, it appears to have been almost against his own wishes. If the qualities demonstrated by a dedicated amateur were an almost casual attitude towards his sport and an effortless indulgence in his mastery and physical superiority, then Zimmerman appears to have been temperamentally more suited to amateurism. Once he had taken the leap into full professionalism, his career did not last very long.

Arthur Zimmerman was born in 1869 in Camden, New Jersey, the son of a wealthy real-estate owner, and as a teenager attending the Freehold Institute and the Military School was headed towards business and the law. From an early age, however, he 'showed great proficiency in athletic sports, in which he was ever encouraged and assisted by his father and his brother-in-law, Joseph McDermott, both thorough sportsmen'. In 1888 and 1889, 'Arthur was the best jumper in his County, carrying off first prizes for standing long, standing high and three jumps' – i.e., long jump, high jump and hop, step and jump). McDermott, according to Bowden, 'has had for Zimmy more than the affection of a brother … and has encouraged and trained Zimmy from the first in all his great encounters, and has neither spared time nor money to aid Zimmerman in attaining success'. [3] McDermott accompanied Zimmerman on his European trips as trainer and manager. In 1889, Zimmerman began to ride the high-wheel bicycle, his chosen machine being the transitional solid-tyred 'Star' high-wheeler, driven by an unusual lever action with the small wheel at the front. By the end of the 1890 season, as a member of the New Jersey Athletic Club and Freehold Cyclers, he had won 45 first prizes, including a victory over Willie Windle, the reigning American sprint champion. For the 1891 season, as a member of the New York Athletic Club, Zimmerman made the transition from the high bicycle to the newly introduced pneumatic 'safety' bicycle, and by the end of the season had amassed 52 first places, won the League of American Wheelmen national half-mile championship and established several short-distance world records. [4] He had thus climbed quickly, in three seasons, to championship level in amateur bicycle racing.

Exchange visits between British and American cyclists had been a regular occurrence through the later 1880s, and early in 1892 Zimmerman announced his intention of racing in England. An invitation was extended to him by the prominent cycling figure George Lacy Hillier to become a member of Hillier's own club, the newly formed London County Cycling and Athletic Club, and to train at Herne Hill track in South London, of which Hillier was the director. It is hardly possible to overestimate the importance of George Lacy Hilllier in British cycling in the 1880s and 1890s, both in the recreational and competitive sport. A fierce propagator and defender of ideological amateurism and denigrator of commercialism and professionalism – which he thought were the enemies of the true sporting spirit in cycling – Hillier was an ex-high-wheel national champion, a member of the Racing Committee of the National Cyclists' Union, the editor of an influential cycling newspaper, *Bicycling News* (for which he wrote acerbic and verbose editorial articles), a promoter of and well-respected judge at race meetings, and a tireless and outspoken critic of those with whom he disagreed, which was almost everyone! Two of his most provocative campaigns were, firstly, to publicly question the legitimacy of various world records established on American tracks (they were inaccurately measured, he claimed, and American time-keepers did not understand how to stop and start their watches properly relative to the starter's gun) and, secondly, to assert against all the evidence to the contrary that pneumatic tyres would not last and were not an improvement over the solid tyre. Later, he mounted an editorial campaign claiming that wooden track surfaces were superior to cement or asphalt. An 1889 publication said of Hillier that

> he is passionately fond of judging races, and was amateur champion of bicycle and tricycle at all distances in 1881. He is good at running, walking and swimming, a fluent and able speaker and ready writer, holding strong views, and a stronger will to back them up ... an able and energetic man. [5]

As soon as he arrived in England, Zimmerman was invited to Nottingham and presented with a state-of-the-art lightweight Raleigh bicycle and other material support by Frank Bowden, the chairman of the large and prosperous Raleigh company, whose bicycles already held many national and international championships and records. Zimmerman had already begun to ride a Raleigh in America that year, and although his amateur status had been questioned by the League of American Wheelmen, the league's 'Class B' amateur rules did in fact allow him to accept a certain amount of material assistance. [6] 'One of the main reasons for the tremendous demand for Raleigh bicycles in the 1890s was that they were so very successful in racing all over the world', asserts a history of the company:

> This was yet another aspect of Frank Bowden's business genius; from the moment he became chairman of the firm, he began to approach leading cycle champions of every nationality and encourage them to race on Raleighs. The combination of his infectious enthusiasm and the excellence of his machines proved irresistable and by 1892 Raleigh was leading the world in cycle sport successes. [7]

Bowden's approach was exactly the kind of tactic that helped to blur the distinction between the true amateur and the sponsored professional. A prominent rider claiming to be an amateur was inevitably a *de facto* advertisement for the manufacturer of the bicycle he rode. Even black tape or the removal of manufacturer's lettering did not prevent recognition of a bicycle's maker.

In the early stages of his training in England in 1892, Zimmerman 'was winning golden opinions everywhere by his unassuming manners, and the good tempered way in which he bore defeat with the same quiet smile as when afterwards victorious'. [8] His amateur status, however, was further questioned by *British Sport*, which, 'without mincing its words about the matter, plainly demands that the NCU should make inquiry into Zimmerman's financial resources. ... In justice to the English riders, it should be ascertained who pays the piper for the Yankee.' [9] The situation was confused by the existence of the League of American Wheelmen's two-tier amateur class, 'Class A' and 'Class B', where 'Class B' amateurs could accept certain expenses from promoters and some equipment from makers, and by the fact that Zimmerman had previously been disqualified by the LAW for a technical violation of the amateur rule and then reinstated. A letter attesting to his amateur status was sent to the National Cyclists' Union by the LAW and read in committee. [10] As a member of the London County C and AC, and a registered LAW amateur, Zimmerman was eligible to compete in all four of the English amateur national championships, and was thus, as a member of Hillier's own club, in a provocative position likely to attract publicity. In the 25-mile race 'he fell through the crowded condition of the track', but in the one-mile and five-mile events,he 'made common hacks of the best in England', while in the 50-mile race he beat Frank Shorland, one of England's best distance riders. [11] Zimmerman's performances in the two short-distance races in Leeds, reported the *Irish Cyclist*, marked him as

> a champion of champions ... we never saw a man sprint as Zimmerman sprints, and sweep by men with such supreme ease. His pluck and quiet determination have excited our liveliest admiration from the first. ... In Zimmerman, the Americans really have a rider to be proud of, one possessing the best qualities of a MAN first and of a racing crack afterwards. [12]

Zimmerman's business relationship with Raleigh made him, in effect, the most prominent of the controversial category of semi-professional cyclists, the 'maker's amateurs'. As an amateur, he was not supposed to be fully sponsored by a manufacturer. Bowden, of course, knew this, as did Lacy Hillier, whose own club's promotions profited from the large gates that Zimmerman's presence generated. As an aggressive proponent of amateurism, Lacy Hillier had created a conflict of interest situation, in which his own club benefited from the attractions of the questionably 'amateur' star. The 1892 European tour was a resounding success. Zimmerman did not meet F.J. Osmond, England's best long-distance rider, but there was good sportsmanship on all sides, and Zimmerman was a popular star. The *American Cyclist* thought that 'nothing could have been more graceful than the Englishmen's acknowledgement of the American representative's prowess'. [13] *Wheeling* concluded that 'There is probably no man racing in England today more popular personally than Zimmerman'. [14] His behaviour was exemplary, his athletic feats outstanding and he made good copy for the press.

Zimmerman's victories in the 1892 English championships made him an even greater celebrity in the United States, where the press was effusive with its patriotism. 'The American champion's visit to England excited greater attention and interest than any previous happening in the history of all cycledom', reported *The American Cyclist*:

> He went abroad to meet the English racing men solely from motives of personal curiosity and pleasure. He did not in any sense posture as a representative of America against England. But nothing on the face of the earth could have prevented the international aspect of the events in which he competed while on the other side. All American wheelmen have expanded with pride over Zimmerman's success with the English. They have appropriated everything connected therewith and have made Zimmerman's personal cause a cause of America *versus* England. The American eagle has flapped his wings and screamed himself hoarse. The champion was received back with such an ovation as was never before accorded to any living cyclist. [13]

At home in the United States, Zimmerman broke a world record at the Springfield Tournament, for which he won a carriage and a pair of horses worth $1,000, and took the New York state championship. The sum total of his 1892 season was, out of 100 starts, 75 first, ten second and five third places, for a total value of $8,800. He was reported, during the season, to have won '29 bicycles, several horses and carriages, half a dozen pianos, a house and a lot, household furniture of all descriptions, and enough silver plate, medals and jewelery to stock a jewelery store'. [14] Zimmerman's successful competitive technique was based on both his strength and his speed, and his thorough understanding of the principles of 'drafting' behind other riders. Manager McDermott told a reporter from the *New York Times* that:

> No matter how fast the other men go he stays within hailing distance and wins his race in the last spurt. Generally Zimmerman allows the other men to cut out the pace. He follows in their wake, and when within a quarter of a mile from the finish he begins to hit 'er up a bit. Then all hands get to sprinting. For 200 yards all go at a rapid pace, straining every nerve, and apparently they are all tired out. When within about a furlong from the tape Zimmerman again increases the pace, and this generally kills off the other men. Zimmerman has one big advantage. He can stay in a race and go fast without pumping himself out, and then when the final effort comes he is faster than anybody. ... Zimmerman is not a rider, but one of the wonders of the age. [17]

In spite of this international success, Zimmerman was still officially an amateur on his second visit to England in 1893, where he intended to contest the English championships again. He raced and won in Ireland and France. But in June 1893 the racing committee of the NCU stirred up international cycling relations by this time refusing to recognize his amateur status. He was also, reported the *New York Times*, 'without having been given a proper hearing, told to change his wheel [i.e. his make of bicycle, which was a Raleigh]; this he declined to do unless he was given time to get an American make of wheel. ... Zimmerman said that he considered his treatment exceedingly unsportsmanlike and contrary to a spirit of fairness.' [18] Later, challenged to reveal why it had acted in such a severe fashion towards the American star, the NCU officials alleged that he had received shares of Raleigh stock, that he had published a book endorsing Raleigh, that Bowden had given him diamonds and that he continued to have a business relationship with the Raleigh company, all of which confirmed that he was indeed a professional. Evidently, to combat the systematic, ongoing, high-profile sullying of the amateur ranks, the NCU had decided to make a prominent example of Zimmerman. [19] But a further exacerbating factor may well have been Zimmerman's refusal, on this second visit, to be contractually bound to appear exclusively in meetings organized by Lacy Hillier and the London County Cycling and Athletic Club, and Lacy Hillier's consequent determination as a powerful official within the NCU to exclude him from amateur competition completely if he could not have Zimmerman's crowd-pulling power in the palm of his hand, working to his own financial advantage.

Upon his return to America, Zimmerman outlined the above explanation of the controversy to the *New York Times*, telling a reporter:

> It is not difficult to understand the position of Hillier's Association. Here they were in the position of standing by and seeing their championships go over the water again. I do not think I exaggerate when I say things looked that way. I had won the first twenty races I had started in, and the men whom the Englishmen had counted on to beat me were not track possibilities, having been protested off the track. Unless some charge was trumped up against me, what hope had they for their championships! [20]

This interview gives further revelations of the hypocrisy and double-dealing within the power structures of English 'shamateurism', and is particularly interesting on the role of George Lacy Hillier and Zimmerman's reactions to him:

> Lacy Hillier, one of the cycling editors of the metropolis, has become quite an autocrat on racing matters. The first year I went over I placed myself under his guidance. He took me everywhere and got some credit, I can fairly say, out of my victories. Of course, when the season was nearly over, lovers of racing in various parts of the United Kingdom expressed themselves with some bitterness to me. They argued that I had no right to slight their cities, that I was a drawing card, that they had always been friends of mine, and that I had hurt honest sport by continuing my work to the limits set by Hillier. You see, most of my racing had been done under the direction of the London County Association, a limited company which gives athletic tournaments [in fact, the London County Cycling

and Athletic Club]. Mr Hillier is financially interested in it. My presence at their meetings always meant a big gate for them, and of course they were interested in keeping me as much as possible under their wing. I don't boast when I talk thus of big gate receipts, for that was a fact based on the international character that I would give a meet. ... I see all this more clearly now than I did then. I didn't appreciate then that I had made a mistake in not taking in the Irish and Scotch championships instead of confining myself so largely to London events.

This year when I went over I decided that I would do a little of my own directing and race all over the kingdom. It is not going too far to say that this was not agreeable to the Hillier crowd, who would thus lose the monopoly of what was formerly a source of revenue and more or less reputation. I went to Scotland and to Paris on my own hook and won my races as before. I suppose that if I had allowed my name to be used for the exclusive advantage of the London County Association Limited, I might not have encountered such fierce opposition and found my amateur standing so bitterly protested. I believe that the Scotch and Irish racing men stand by me, as do those who are outside of London and are not under the influence of the London Association.

It is clear from this account the extent to which Hillier, as a proponent of the amateur ideal, was nonetheless dependent on his 'amateur' star to ensure a good take at the box office for his promotions. *Véloce-Sport*, the leading French cycling journal, understood the attitude of the National Cyclists' Union, but criticized it heavily:

It is logical, but it is also profoundly regrettable. Once more, we in France condemn this idiotic business of classifying riders, which deprives international competition of really good matches by excluding men of the same level. Above all, the English should at least be as strict with their own maker's amateurs as they are with Zimmerman. [21]

The American press exploded with impatience, hardly stopping to remind itself that Zimmerman's amateurism had also been questioned at home. The *New York Times* reported the affair with intense interest. *Bearings* called the NCU's actions 'uncalled for and disgraceful ... not only unsportsmanlike, but cowardly and dishonorable'. [22] An editorial, 'The Treatment of Zimmerman', in the Indianapolis *Wheelmen's Gazette*, protested at the 'insular pride and prejudice' of the NCU:

There is no doubt that in matters of sport England is exceedingly unfair. When the English think they are going to see something superior, they shut their eyes – and don't see it. ... If the American is a second-class performer he is welcomed, if he is first-class and threatens to wrest a prize away from Britain's sons he is given the cold cut. ... The action of the National Cycling Union of England in withholding a licence from Zimmerman is a particularly aggravating instance of this British peculiarity. ... The action was due to a determination to prevent Zimmerman from reaping the benefit of his pluck and skill. He won the championship events last year and there was every reason to believe that he would repeat the achievement this year. So the wily Britons ruled him out. [23]

The NCU's actions raised the possibility that the LAW and even the International Cyclists' Association might also rule against him, and that he might have trouble qualifying as an amateur for the World Championships to be held in Chicago in August 1893. But the NCU, with all its power and influence, could still not claim jurisdiction over him in America. Having been excluded from NCU competition in England, Zimmerman returned to America to win the first official amateur World Championships, at one mile and ten miles, in August 1893. [24] These championship races were also ridden on a Raleigh, and Zimmerman subsequently appeared as 'Champion of the World' on an internationally distributed advertising poster for the Raleigh company (now frequently reproduced) where his image and fame were used to endorse and advertise the company's product in no uncertain terms. No sooner had an 'amateur' world cycling champion been enthroned than his name and image were immediately coopted by the maker of the bicycle he rode. A new and modern kind of advertising had been created. [25] The same commercial dynamic, hugely expanded, still exists today, not only in cycling, but in all sports – a fact of life in the social and economic dynamic of modern sport. Yet, in 1893, such a selling technique was hardly known outside cycling, and was only at that moment coming into focus as a way of mass-marketing both sport and utility cycling to the consuming public.

Zimmerman, in spite of his prominent success, was reported to have been a reluctant and reticent 'star'. In Indianapolis, in August 1893, where the African-American teenager Major Taylor watched as Zimmerman won a gold cup worth $1,000 and set a new one-mile world record, Zimmerman

> shot by the grandstand like a stone from a catapult. ... He then dismounted and walked back with that awkward, gawky gait of his, looking neither to the right nor the left, as the cheers rent the air and hundreds of handkerchiefs were waved. ... He received an ovation which would have caused most any man to have swelled visibly, but he paid no attention to it, and ambled along to his dressing room like some green, country boy who never seems to know where to put his hands. ... When he is called upon to make a speech or respond to an address of presentation, he blushes and stammers and gets as nervous as a school girl, and yet he can go out on the track and whip the world riding. [26]

By the end of 1893, Zimmerman was a de facto Raleigh professional except that he still had official amateur status. An American commentator confirmed that his amateurism was merely titular:

> Those near him admit and even boast that the smiling Jersey-man has turned his racing abilities to more practical account than any other man on the path, either amateur or professional. But Zimmie never broke the rules blatantly. If he bartered his speed for coin of the realm, it was most diplomatically done. [27]

Full, formal professionalism appeared inevitable, and Zimmerman took out his professional licence at the beginning of the 1894 season. The editor of *The Wheel* expected Zimmerman to be 'as smooth, level, impeturbable and honest' as a professional as he had been as an amateur, and 'to prove that a man may be a professional crack-a-jack and continue to advance in those graces, talents and attributes which settle upon the right men as they grow into manhood'. [28] Zimmerman went on to bring 'glory, delight and prosperity to Raleigh by winning a total of 100 races that year in England, France, Germany and Ireland' against all the leading European riders. [29]

The specific instigation to turn professional were guarantees proffered by Baduel, the director of the Velodrome Buffalo in Paris. Zimmerman's manager, Willis B. Troy, went to Paris and negotiated a contract worth about $10,000 in cash, 30 per cent of gate receipts and any prizes he won. [30] The press generally approved of his move. 'Nothing has awakened so much interest in a long time as the desertion of the amateur ranks by Zimmerman', commented *Bearings*:

> It has been almost the sole topic of cyclists and the cycling press for the past few weeks. ... What does it all mean? It means that we are coming nearer an era of professionalism; that, before long, professional bicycle racing will be as well established as horse racing. That time has already come in France, and it is bound to come in this country. The fact that the great Zimmerman has led the way will make it all the easier for others to follow.

Outing thought that

> in these days of big purses for pugilists and expensive prizes for amateurs, the successful athlete despises the simple prizes which were given in the olden days when amateurs were really amateurs. The king of amateurs will become the king of professionals. ... It is a question, however, whether Zimmerman can last longer than a season or two more. [31]

Others were tempted by generous offers from Raleigh, and Harry Wheeler (East Orange), George Banker (Pittsburgh) and Austin Crooks (Buffalo) also joined the professional ranks to make up a Raleigh team in Europe, with Willis Troy as 'diplomat, general manager, cashier and treasurer' and Harry Rue as trainer – not the first American cycling team to cross the Atlantic, but probably the most accomplished ever. [32] Troy was another representative, like the prominent ex-high-wheel racer H.O. Duncan (a central figure in French bicycle racing), of a new kind of figure in the world of sport, the promoter/manager/trainer/agent, who began to play an increasingly important role in cycling in the mid-1890s: in effect, a liaison between the industry and the sport. It was reported that Zimmerman expected to make as much as $30,000 during his trip. [33] J.-M. Erwin, a newspaper reporter who followed Zimmerman and Wheeler in Europe during the 1894 season, wrote of 'the triumph of professionalism in Europe'. The professionals were everywhere; only England held out as an amateur country, with its 'severe and tortured' amateur definition. France was 'a sort of apostle of the revolutionary professional movement', with its attractive velodromes and rich prizes. Belgium was a hybrid of professionalism and amateurism. Switzerland was much like France, and Italy went further still, with organized betting at its tracks. [34] Erwin was convinced that 'next year will see professional racing in the ascendancy in England. The hide-bound sticklers for amateurism still hold out against it … but the public wants the professional racing, and that means they will have it.' [35]

Zimmerman himself was of the opinion that the amateur sport had been eclipsed by the high quality of the new professionals:

> In Europe, amateurs who one could really call racers are now in such a minority that when they appear at race meetings it is an occasion for curiosity and amusement. This is true above all in France and Italy, where the racing is at such a high level that the other countries go there to take lessons. [36]

The word 'professional' increasingly took on its modern meaning, being equated with serious, full-time athletic commitment, with equipment and training support and financial sponsorship, with which the old-style amateurs could simply not hope to compete. But, after his experiences in Europe in 1894, Zimmerman was less sure of the future of professionalism in America, where he suggested the old pejorative significance of the word might still apply. He complained of the readiness of American audiences to criticize and slur athletes' performances, suspecting them of dishonest practices, of 'throwing' a race for financial reasons:

> Europeans take naturally to professional cycling. It is the style they have been mostly educated to like, and they accept defeats of idols philosophically, not with murky glances and whispered slurs. The outlook for professional racing in this country for this season is not bright. The very best men will be continually driven to the other side by these unjust criticisms. [37]

Zimmerman's 1894 season in Europe lasted from May to November. As a visiting American star, he was obsessively pursued by the press as he competed in 34 race meetings in France, England, Switzerland, Italy and Belgium. He was first 27 times, second twice and fourth once. In Paris, he stayed at the best hotels and made the rounds of his training and racing at the famous Buffalo and Seine velodromes wearing a top hat and dress suit. Representing Raleigh necessitated a serious public relations stance. In Belgium, he was beaten by Belgian champion, Houben, and in England, he raced in London, Birmingham, Leicester and Newcastle. In Newcastle, 'the boys who sold programmes on the street had "Zimmerman" in large letters on their hats, and "Zimmerman, Champion of Champions" could be seen on tram-cars and omnibuses', while promoters Troy, Baduel and H.O. Duncan 'watched the people pass through the gates, and the click of the turnstiles was sweet music to their ears'. But the crowd was not happy at the doubling of the price of admission from the customary sixpence to one shilling, and Troy was called 'a damned thieving Frenchman'. In Leicester, Zimmerman made the mistake of throwing a few pennies to the street urchins, and quickly 'boys in various stages of dirt or rags sprang up from the pavement. ... They fought and rolled over in the dirt for every coin that jingled on the stones, and the people came in swarms to watch the fun.' [38] These vignettes of commercial activity are evidence of the new intensity of sport promotion in the mid-1890s, as professionalism expanded and bicycle racing was marketed to an enthusiastic public.

'Why do Zimmerman, Wheeler, Lehr, and a host of other famous riders, prefer the Raleigh?' demanded the Raleigh Cycle Co. in an advertisement in *Cycling*: 'Because they know it to be the Fastest Machine built. The Fastest Machine is that which is The Easiest-Running. This is what YOU want!' [39] 'Zimmerman, Wheeler, Banker, the Great American Professionals who are beating all the European cracks, all ride the wonderful Dunlop Racing Tire. And that wonderful Dunlop Racing Tire Holds all World's Records from 110 to 460 miles,' trumpeted the American Dunlop Tire Company. [40] Interviewed by the press when he returned to the United States, Zimmerman was effusive in his praise of the European racing scene. 'To the European the idea of amateur racing for clocks, prizes etc is ridiculous. The poor and the wealthy riders alike wish to race for money,' he told *The Wheel*. [41] And for the *New York Times*, he painted a glowing picture of Paris. He had, he said:

> never seen such splendid tracks as the Buffalo Velodrome in Paris and the track in Bordeaux. They are about perfect. ... There were about 12,000 people at the Seine track, in Paris, one day when I was there. The French enjoy themselves at these races in great style. The events are twenty minutes to half an hour apart, and during these intervals the people sit around the grounds, drinking, smoking, and discussing the last race. In Paris the tracks, or rather the grounds about them, resembled a picnic. They do not have classes, as we do. All their racing men are professionals, and ride to advertise the firms whose wheels they use. Such clubs as we have are unknown, the men being unattached. ... Paris is the best place in the world for bicycling. Nothing surprised me more at first than the great number of wheels [i.e. bicycles] used in Paris. [42]

Zimmerman's athletic decline after 1894 was rapid, for reasons which are not absolutely clear, because he was still only in his mid-twenties. Scheduled to cross again to France in 1895, financial negotiations evidently proved difficult. Even at home, Zimmerman's high appearance fee may have dampened the enthusiasm of promoters and those who wanted to challenge him. He visited Australia in the winter of 1895/6, had a successful tour (27,000 people were reported at the opening meeting in Sydney), [43] but announced his retirement soon after. He attempted a comeback in both 1897 and 1899, but his racing consisted of little more than a few 'exhibitions'. At the races of the Quill Club Wheelmen in Manhattan Beach in 1897, Zimmerman 'was surrounded by old-timers, but from the new field of racing men he attracted no attention. The champion of the world of but a couple of seasons ago passed in front of the grandstand and not a cheer was heard from the people. Such was fame.' [44] He invested in a short-lived company manufacturing the 'Zimmy' bicycle, wrote a column for a New York newspaper and talked briefly of becoming an actor. He prevaricated as to whether or not to return to France in 1896, but did not finally return until 1902, by then merely a symbol of his past excellence, well past his athletic prime. [45] Mostly he appears to have concentrated on his business career, becoming a hotel owner in Freehold, New Jersey.

Yet Zimmerman's short career was highly significant in the context of the emergence of mass-spectator bicycle racing in the late 1880s and 1890s. One of a handful of pioneer international champion cyclists, he participated at the highest level in taking the sport from the solid-tyred, high-wheel bicycle period into the era of the pneumatic safety; from a somewhat limited athletic coterie out into the mass-market, where he became a star with enormous public appeal. In the 1890s, bicycle racing on the track became a significant mass-spectator sport, where modern sporting heroes were created and promoted. In a review of the 1893 bicycle racing season, the Indianapolis *Wheelmen's Gazette* spoke of

> an exceedingly profitable season, both for race meet promoters and the racers themselves. ... The racing cracks have thriven wonderfully the past season. They have been the idols of the land, and the whole cycling world has bent knee to do them homage. Rival cycling clubs have fallen over themselves in their frantic efforts to secure the attendance of the stars.

Zimmerman had been the biggest attraction, 'the ideal racer. He has yet to meet his superior on the cycle track. He is certainly the greatest cycle racer of the time and bids fair to remain so. He is an honest and gentlemanly athlete; as much cannot truthfully be said of some of his rivals.' In a similar review the following year, the same publication concluded that:

> There is no question but that the cycle racing season of 1894 outshone in brilliancy all preceding seasons. Public interest in the sport took on an even more enthusiastic tinge than ever before. Many more meets were held than in 1893, and the love of the American people for this phenomenally popular youthful sport was largely increased. ... The progress of racing is dumbfounding the false prophets. This comparatively new rival of the diamond and the turf is shaking the hold of both on the public heart. [46]

A revealing editorial from *The Wheel* spoke of the 'enlightened folk of the nineteenth century, who love football, the prize ring and the race track', many of whom

> have come to look upon the cycle and its lithe and sinewy rider as the best exponents of the modern idea of clean, enjoyable athletics. ... We turn to the cyclist as the coming man. The season just ended has proved beyond a doubt that man has at last secured for himself the one thing for which he has longed so many centuries, namely, a self-driven vehicle which will bear him further and faster in a given time than any animal-drawn conveyance. [48]

In a relatively short career, Zimmerman had made the transition from amateur to professional during a period of tremendous growth and change in the institutional organization and the economy of the sport; he became a 'modern' professional athlete, his celebrity created not only by his own athletic ability, but also by the commercial interests that promoted him and profited from his success. Zimmerman was one of the most prominent of those cyclists who carried bicycle racing from a national to an international level, and was one of the first cycling champions to become a media celebrity both inside and outside his own country. His three tours in Europe (1892, 1893 and 1894), as well as his amateur World Championship in Chicago in 1893, put the United States firmly among the world's foremost cycling nations.

Although Zimmerman had only a short career as a professional, his decision to become a full professional was a demonstration of the inevitability and feasibility of a professional class in the United States, sponsored by the bicycle industry, and organized outside the pervasive amateurism of the League of American Wheelmen. In reaction to the difficulties the LAW had coping with its administration of the newly professionalizing sport, a new professional organization, the National Cycling Association, came into existence in 1893. Zimmerman's gentlemanly sporting conduct and demeanour as a professional challenged the entrenched idea that only amateurs could uphold high standards of behaviour. Going to Europe to take on the European champions, he set a trend and paved the way for other American cyclists, such as Major Taylor and Jack Kramer, in the future. With Zimmerman's visit, Paris became firmly established as the Mecca of international bicycle racing where, at a growing number of important promotions, foreign champions had to educate themselves and establish their athletic skill and global credibility.

As with other biographies in this rich period of sport activity, much remains to be uncovered and understood in Zimmerman's life and career. His family and educational background and his relatively privileged social class appear to have been the basis of his athletic success, possibly predisposing him negatively towards a career in professional sport. Certainly, he does not seem to have taken advantage of his extraordinary reputation to prolong his career. Further research in contemporary newspapers and the cycling press will give further shape and meaning to the life of one of the most important international cyclists of the mid-1890s period, the first amateur world champion, Arthur Zimmerman.

Biographical Notes

Biographical summary: Arthur Augustus Zimmerman (1869–1936)

1869:   born in Camden, New Jersey.

1886:   began to train in real estate law.

1888/89:   early athletic talent; prizes in running and jumping.

1889:   first appearance as a racing cyclist, first prize on Long Island.

1889/90:   45 first, 18 second and three third prizes in competition riding a solid-tired Star bicycle, geared to 54 inches. In fall 1890 beat reigning US champion Willie Windle. Member of New Jersey Athletic Club and Freehold Wheelers.

1891:   during season made transition from Star to pneumatic safety, racing on both styles of bicycle. In September won half-mile safety LAW championship setting a world record for quarter-mile, and then set a new half-mile world record. 1892 total was 52 first, ten first and three third places and a number of world records. Became American sprint champion. Became member of New York Athletic Club.

1892:   February–July, first visit to England. Invited by Lacy Hillier to base himself at Herne Hill track in South London as member of London County Cycling and Athletic Club (LCAC). Approached by Frank Bowden, Chairman of Raleigh, to ride a Raleigh bicycle, which he agreed to do, although still an amateur. After slow start to season, entered and won NCU English championships at one, five and 50 miles. 'He made common hacks of the best in England'. During the trip he beat all the best riders in England. Later in year, having returned to US, broke world records at Springfield, where he won carriage and pair of horses worth $1,000. Total for season was 75 first, ten second and five third places, worth nearly $9,000.

1893:   crossed to England again. Declared a professional by the NCU. American press outraged. Raced in Ireland and Continent, then returned to US. Published his book, *Training Points for Cyclists*. In August, won first official amateur world sprint championship (sponsored by International Cyclists' Association) in Chicago. A week later, in Indianapolis, met 14-year-old Major Taylor at Munger's house and made a deep impression on him. Season total was 111 races, of which he won 101.

1894:   turned professional. European tour from April to November, together with seven other US cyclists. Indicative of the rise of true professionalism. Competed in 34 events in France, England, Switzerland, Italy and Belgium: 27 first, two second places and one third. 'Friendship, politeness and a great sporting spirit'.

1895/96: visited Australia, where he appears to have contracted malaria. Unsuccessful trip. Began to produce bicycles back in US, but evidently not successful.

1899:   brief comeback.

1902:   sentimental return to Paris, but no racing successes.
         Post-cycling career: owned hotel in Point Pleasant, New Jersey.

1936:   death in Atlanta at the age of 67 (obituary in *New York Times*, 22 October 1936).

Notes

[1] The key text of the early sport is Charles Pratt, *The American Bicycler*, first published in 1878, with a second revised edition in 1880 (Boston: privately printed, 1880). Pratt was attorney to the Pope Manufacturing Company, founder of the Boston Bicycle Club, and founder-member

of the League of American Wheelmen. Another key research resource of the early period is *The American Bicycling Journal* (published 1877 to 1879), which was succeeded by *Bicycling World* in 1880.

[2] *Wheelmen's Gazette*, Nov. 1893; *The Wheel*, 4 Jan. 1895; Gregory Houston Bowden, *The Story of the Raleigh Bicycle* (London: W.H. Allen, 1975).

[3] Quoted from the Introduction by Frank Bowden in A.A. Zimmerman, *Points for Cyclists with Training* (London: F.W.S. Clarke, 1893), p.5.

[4] Zimmerman's amateur career, within the New Jersey Athletic Club, Freehold Cyclers and New York Athletic Club is certainly worthy of further research, particularly in original archival sources if these are available.

[5] *The Cyclist Christmas Number* for 1889, quoted in Zimmerman, *Points for Cyclists*, p.11.

[6] The division of LAW amateurs into Class A and Class B was intended to distinguish between those amateurs who were true amateurs and accepted no money, equipment or assistance from any manufacturer and those who did receive a certain amount of support or compensation, but were nevertheless not paid a salary or fully sponsored by a manufacturer.

[7] Bowden, in Zimmerman, *Points for Cyclists*.

[8] Ibid.

[9] *British Sport*, quoted in *American Cyclist*, April 1892.

[10] Modern Records Centre, University of Warwick: Mss. 328/B, 'LAW re Zimmerman', Minutes of General Committee of NCU, 29 April 1892.

[11] Bowden, in Zimmerman, *Points for Cyclists*.

[12] *Irish Cyclist*, quoted in *American Cyclist*, Aug. 1892.

[13] 'Zimmerman's Latest', *American Cyclist*, Sept. 1892.

[14] *Wheeling*, quoted in *American Cyclist*, Aug. 1892.

[15] 'Zimmerman's Latest'.

[16] Bowden, in Zimmerman, *Points for Cyclists*; *New York Times*, 30 June 1893.

[17] *New York Times*, 30 June 1893.

[18] 'Zimmerman Treated Unfairly', *New York Times*, 25 June 1893.

[19] A revealing insight into attitudes within the National Cyclists' Union following Zimmerman's victories in the 1892 championships is given in the report of a committee meeting of 17 Dec. 1892 (reported in *NCU Review and Official Record*, March 1893). E.B. Turner proposed the motion, which was seconded by Hillier, that 'In the opinion of this Council the time has now arrived when it is advisable that no person connected with the· trade of making, selling, or letting on hire cycles or their essential parts, should be eligible to act as a representative ... on the Council or on the Appeals or General Committees of the Union'. The proposal was voted down, 31 for, 39 against. E.B. Turner addressed the meeting: his proposal was 'a first step towards the purification of the sport', which 'was being dragged in the mire by those men who were suborned by the makers. The Union was being held up to derision by foreign countries. ... It was a prostitution of a most noble sport. ... They must keep the sport free from any trade influence whatever. The moment that pounds, shillings and pence came in at the door, amateur sport flew out at the window.'

[20] Interview with Zimmerman, *New York Times*, 12 July 1893.

[21] *Véloce-Sport* (Paris), 15 June 1893 (author's translation). The French attitude towards the amateur/professional distinction was much less polarized than the British approach. French riders were separated according to levels of proven ability, and cash was routinely given for prizes. Amateurism was less valued or insisted upon and much less based in class considerations – the very concept of the 'amateur' had less resonance in France.

[22] Quoted in 'American Comments on the Zimmerman Incident', editorial in *Cycling*, 8 July 1893.

[23] *New York Times*, 14, 25 and 26 June; 12 and 29 July 1893; *Wheelmen's Gazette* (Indianapolis), July 1893.

[24] These championships were held under the auspices of the recently constituted International Cyclists' Association, which had been formed in London in 1892 to attempt to give international form and order to the growing practice of international championships. International exchanges between British, American, French, German and Belgian cyclists had been occurring with increasing frequency in the decade of the 1880s and sport continued to become increasingly internationalized in the 1890s. It is worth noting that the creation of the ICA took place only three years before the first modern Olympic Games in 1896. See 'Formation of an International Cycling Association', *Scottish Cyclist*, 30 Nov. 1892; 'World's Champions', *Cycling*, 3 Dec. 1892; 'Plans for International Races', *Bearings*, 3 March 1893; 'The International Championships', *Bearings*, 4 Aug. 1892; and extensive coverage of the actual event in *Chicago Tribune*, *New York Times* and other leading newspapers, Aug. 1893.

[25] This poster is published in various places, most accessibly in Jack Rennert, *100 Years of Bicycle Posters* (New York: Harper and Row, 1973). The art for the poster was drawn by George Moore, the doyen of late nineteenth-century commercial artists working in cycling in Britain, and the copy in Rennert advertises the Paris agency of the Raleigh company.

[26] *Indianapolis Sentinel*, 25 Aug. 1893. Another interesting description of Zimmerman was published in *Véloce-Sport*, 15 June 1893: 'His head is somewhat small, his clear, grey eyes attractive and big, his mouth well-shaped and full of excellent teeth, and his nose prominent. His hair is brown at its roots, but becomes almost yellow-coloured in front and on top, which makes him look as if he is wearing a badly coloured and combed wig. He speaks quietly and seldom, and has a soft and sympathetic smile. Both on and away from the track, he is completely nonchalant about his appearance, and certainly isn't a dandy.

'He walks slowly about town, with his hands in his pockets, seeming to be quite indifferent to everything he encounters. Thoroughbred race horses also have this same kind of nonchalance. 'On the track, he dresses all in black. He wears socks, but lets them fall around his ankles. His shorts don't fit him well. His jersey, which has a wing embroidered in colour on the front, like a coat of arms, not only is not fresh but seems even to be dirty. This is the jersey in which the champion won all his races last year, and it is said that it has never been washed and never will be. Zimmerman thinks of it as a lucky charm and is perhaps afraid his luck will run out if it is washed. Zimmerman is big, but quite light, weighing only 72 kg. His body and arms are somewhat thin, but his legs are strong and powerful and extraordinarily supple. He never travels without his brother-in-law, MacDermott, and his own personal trainer, who he consults before doing anything and who is never far away. His bicycle weighs about 11 kilos, and has a gear of 66/67". He doesn't want a lighter bicycle since he feels that he loses in rigidity what he gains in lightness, or a bigger gear reasoning that more force results in less speed.

'In riding, Zimmerman is very interesting to study, especially since he has a style and a position completely different from our best riders. When he is going slowly, he is balanced on his machine with a side-to-side movement of his shoulders, although his hips are completely still. But when the pace picks up, all his body movement stops as it is an obstacle to speed. Our best riders tend to bend their arms, to arch their backs, to move their head and shoulders, but Zimmerman simply pedals faster, without any visible sign of effort. Rather than lowering his head, like the others, he stretches it forwards, looking straight in front of him, his nose in the air, rather like a hare or a thoroughbred horse. He doesn't bend his arms, but holds them close to his body, while his legs rotate with absolute regularity like the pistons of a locomotive. His ankles are extraordinarily supple, and you have the impression that his feet press the pedals with a smooth and continuous motion, such a difficult perfection to achieve. When he begins his sprint, it is not sudden, and you can't tell when it begins, and you have the impression that it is just his normal style, and not exceptionally fast. He is certainly the best rider at the moment, perhaps the best ever. Everyone who has seen him agrees that it is a new experience, that he deserves to be called the king of the track'.

[27] Editorial, *Wheel and Cycling Trade Review*, 6 April 1894.

[28] Zimmie', *Wheel and Cycling Trade Review*, 6 April 1894.

[29] Bowden, in Zimmerman, *Points for Cyclists*.

[30] *Wheel and Cycling Trade Review*, 6 April 1894.

[31] *Bearings*, 27 April 1894; *Outing*, May 1894.

[32] *The Wheel*, 13 April 1894.

[33] *Cycling Life*, 19 April 1894.

[34] Information quoted from J.-M. Erwin and A.A. Zimmerman, *Conseils d'Entrainement par Zimmerman et Relation de son Voyage en Europe* (Paris: Librarie du Vélo, 1894).

[35] *The Wheel*, 31 Aug. 1894.

[36] Quoted from Erwin and Zimmerman, *Conseils d'Entrainement* (author's translation).

[37] Interview published in *Chicago Evening Post*, date unknown, quoted in *The Wheel*, 18 Jan. 1895.

[38] *The Wheel*, 7 Sept. 1894.

[39] *Cycling*, 18 Aug. 1894.

[40] *The Wheel*, 7 Sept. 1894.

[41] Interview published in *Chicago Evening Post*, date unknown, quoted in *The Wheel*, 18 Jan. 1895.

[42] *New York Times*, 13 Nov. 1894.

[43] *New York Times*, 18 Feb 1896.

[44] *Bearings*, 27 May 1897.

[45] See 'Zimmerman et Elkes à Paris', *L'Auto-Vélo*, 12 Sept. 1902. Another account of Zimmerman's life in 1900 can be found in Robert Coquelle, 'Une visite à Zimmerman', *La Vie au Grand Air*, 23 Dec. 1900.

[46] See 'The Cycle Racing of 1893', *Wheelmen's Gazette*, Nov. 1893 and 'A Resume of the Racing Season', *Wheelmen's Gazette*, Nov. 1894.

[47] 'The Men of the Year', *The Wheel*, 4 Jan. 1895.

An Imperial Legacy – British by Inclination: Socialization, Education and a Gibraltarian Sense of Identity

E. G. Archer

Throughout years of difficulty the Gibraltarian people have had no standing in the sovereignty dispute between Britain and Spain. In his day Franco dismissed them thus: 'The Gibraltarians are almost entirely Spanish although they enjoy British citizenship. The rest are Jews and foreigners and they live under one flag as much as under another.' [1] Something like this view also prevailed in the United Nations, to the chagrin of the Gibraltarians, who have all along seen themselves as like other colonial people seeking self-determination, but who were not properly treated as such. The United Nations saw its responsibilities primarily in terms of a sovereignty issue to be left to the two major powers concerned.

Of late, matters have begun to change, for several reasons. Firstly, for many years Spain had been urged by some observers to soften its wholly legalistic and unproductive stance and to accept that the inhabitants of Gibraltar could not be ignored and perhaps this view was being heeded. Then, in 2003, a second referendum in Gibraltar replicated the findings of the one held in 1967: the people again overwhelmingly rejected any deal which involved ceding even the smallest degree of sovereignty to Spain. This would have left Gibraltar's neighbour in no doubt as to the political realities. Perhaps the most important factor of all, however, has been the able presentation of Gibraltar's case through the media and on various international platforms by its political leaders, notably Chief Minister Peter Caruana and Leader of the Opposition Joe Bossano. By 2004 something of a new climate was beginning to prevail, with Spanish endorsement of ideas involving cross-border cooperation at local level and talks at higher levels involving three voices – Spain, the United Kingdom and Gibraltar. This change was also reflected in resolutions at the United Nations which now appear to offer more room for manoeuvre.

Nevertheless, as regards the fundamental issue over sovereignty, and any matters interpreted as having bearing on sovereignty, it is unlikely that there will be dramatic outcomes to any future talks. Even if sovereignty somehow gains a place on the agenda for any new forum, the Gibraltarian people will not give one inch of ground, literally and metaphorically. Anyone thinking otherwise should pause to consider the socialization processes which for 300 years have made the Gibraltarian people what they are. The words of J.A. Mangan are highly illuminating in this respect when he defines political socialization as 'tuition, formal and informal, planned and unplanned, explicit and implicit, involved in the adoption of appropriate political perceptions, the acquisition of associated cultural beliefs and the learning of related social attitudes'. [2] Furthermore, within this 'tuition' education has played a major part. Other important factors have been at work. These include geographical factors, the ethnic origins of the people, economic and political factors, religion and the churches and language as well as a host of informal cultural influences, [3] including games and recreations, the media, the press and the arts. [4] A word about some of these will provide the larger picture before proceeding to a more detailed examination of educational influences.

Regarding geography, having a homeland and a territory is often important to a sense of identity and the Gibraltarians' affinity with the Rock is deeply felt and strongly expressed. The years of wartime evacuation [5] were a heavy burden to bear and never again would such a separation be entertained. The actual physical geography of a place also influences its people and Gibraltar's small size, lack of natural resources and general vulnerability to outside threats and influences have helped to create a resilient and enterprising population.

Who in fact are the people? What is their ethnic make-up? When British and Dutch forces took the Rock in 1704, all but a handful of the Spanish inhabitants left. As regards the population a new start was made. The raw material of the Gibraltarian 'nation' came from elsewhere. Initially the arrivals were largely Genoese in search of a new life and North African Jews whose motivation was largely commercial. Subsequent incomers, of course, included the British, who added noticeably to the population of traders and merchants over the years. They were regularly encouraged by the authorities who favoured the establishment of a core of reliable and loyal British residents. Others who came to Gibraltar were Portuguese and Maltese, who brought much-needed skills. The Spanish element was largely represented by women from nearby Spain who became the wives of Gibraltarian men. There were others, too, and the true Gibraltarians emerged as the children born on the Rock of the various immigrants who settled there. All have mingled together to form a homogeneous population, largely mindful only of their roots as Gibraltarians. Thus, a distinctive population was created and, in the words of a past Governor,

> it is very clear that the Gibraltarian is certainly not a Spaniard. He has naturally developed characteristics of his own derived from his forbears and it is not too much to say that the Gibraltarian race is unique and very proud of its British citizenship. The synthesis of blood is still going on. [6]

Ethnic factors have been closely linked to the economic as various immigrants came looking for new opportunities for work and enterprise. They provided some of the skills and the labour that the garrison, the city and the port always needed, not forgetting that a substantial part of the unskilled labour force for long periods was provided by workers crossing daily from Spain. The native Gibraltarians, through their energy and resourcefulness, survived the ups and downs of an economy that was always sensitive to outside changes and influences. With the reduction of the garrison after the Second World War and the subsequent closure of HM Dockyard, Gibraltar appears to have made a successful transition to an economy which is no longer dependent on Britain. A well-educated Gibraltarian population today has control over a 'new economy' that is largely based on tourism and financial services.

Political influences have gone hand-in-hand with the economic and they have been of two sorts. On the one hand there have been the political impositions of the Gibraltarians' erstwhile colonial masters, the British. These have conveyed clear ideas of rank, status and class to Gibraltar as throughout the empire. On the other hand there have been those processes whereby Gibraltar gradually acquired its own political structures and institutions, albeit based on British models and examples. Gibraltar today, with its own distinctive people, its own parliament and legal system, is substantially in charge of its own affairs in its own territory. As is reflected in the proposals for a revised constitution, [7] the degree of autonomy achieved so far is seen as the springboard for further advance and the achievement of full self-determination.

If political and economic influences have often been determined by the British presence, those associated with religion and the churches present a different aspect. Here too there has been British input, through the 'official' Anglican church and through Methodism and the Church of Scotland. Although these churches have been more preoccupied with the needs of the garrison and the expatriate establishment, they have left their mark on society as a whole. However, for most of the native population the Roman Catholic Church has held sway, which is not surprising given that most incomers, apart from the Jews, came from Roman Catholic countries.

A further point is that Gibraltar's 'particular' church, with its links direct to Rome, has reinforced Gibraltar's distinctiveness and separate identity.

Linguistic influences on the Gibraltarian sense of identity provide a similarly interesting story. Spanish as the lingua franca of the area, and the language of Gibraltar's neighbour was likely to assume a significant role. In addition, frequent marriages of Gibraltarian males to Spanish brides helped to make it the language of the home and the nursery. At the same time, English was greatly encouraged by the British establishment and was unchallenged as the official language of the colony. English became the language of political and intellectual discourse. All along, therefore, there has been a significant role for both languages. Furthermore, a third emerged: the two languages became mixed in everyday speech to form 'Llanito' and dual coding is still very much a characteristic of the language heard in Gibraltar's Main Street. Thus Gibraltarians have their own language and when they speak English or Spanish they do so with a distinctive Gibraltarian accent.

Place, ethnicity, politics, economics, religion and language – each of these throws light on the making of a particular people or nation. Some of these are linked to or have implications for education, a major formative factor to which we now direct our attention. [8]

Early Years

The first hundred years of British rule in Gibraltar saw various sieges as the Spanish and their allies tried to re-take the Rock. Given the difficulties caused by hostilities, and other problems as major epidemics took their toll on the population, educational activity was likely to have been limited. There is little written evidence of education for that period although there are indications of a degree of public interest, on the one hand through *escuelas de enseñanza* ('schools of the municipality') of which Cornwell wrote that 'even up to 1840 a few schools of this class were in operation'. [9] In addition to these vestiges of a Spanish past, the two censuses of 1777 and 1791 list a few individuals who were teachers, and they were almost certain to have run the small private schools operating in Gibraltar for those willing and able to pay for instruction.

Then the early decades of the nineteenth century saw the appearance of the military strand, alongside the civil – mutually beneficial parallel systems which to some extent still survive today. Undoubtedly Gibraltar benefited from pioneering developments within an enlightened military sector. As N.T. St John Williams explains, the British army recognized the need for a literate and numerate cadre of non-commissioned officers, linking the command structure and the fighting soldiers. It was also accepted that education could 'contribute to morale and to a soldier's personal and social well-being and that a regiment benefits from both'. [10] To start with, therefore, the emphasis was on schooling for military personnel. The education of the children of the military was only possible when time and resources were available. Even then, the objective was 'to implant in the children's minds early habits of Morality, Obedience and Industry and to give them that portion of learning which might qualify them for NCOs'. [11] The education of civilian children, when there was inadequate local provision, was a low priority and then only when there were places to spare.

Army schools in Gibraltar were advantaged by this thinking in a number of ways, both pedagogical and organizational. Dr Andrew Bell had developed his ideas for the monitorial system of education in Madras and these were practised later at the Royal Military Asylum in Chelsea. The army saw Bell's system as the preferred model of teaching, 'through the agency of the scholars themselves', and some of Bell's Chelsea-trained teachers went overseas, among the first being 'Thomas Alcock and James McLeod who were sent in September 1815 to Gibraltar to superintend a School upon the Madras system'. [12]

The ground in Gibraltar was ripe for such developments because army schools there were among the first to be established. This growth of schooling had been encouraged by the governor and

> towards the end of 1802 or the beginning of 1803 ... it was approved that a school should be formed in each regiment stationed in Gibraltar and that soldiers and their children should attend classes conducted by one of the sergeants in each regiment – and a sergeant's wife to take charge of the girls. [13]

Later, under Lieutenant-Governor George Don (1814–31), regimental schools were extended and reorganized on an area basis as garrison schools and – something that was of great importance to Gibraltar they became accessible to local children. Nor did Don want poverty to be a barrier: in some cases children were admitted free of charge when their parents could not pay. Albert Traverso argues that Don, by including local children, had 'laid the foundations of a centrally sponsored general education system'. [14]

Church Initiatives

The first grant-aided and non-denominational Gibraltar public school was established in 1832, although this sector had little room for further development at the time. These were the years when the churches – the Methodists, the Anglicans and the Roman Catholics – became seriously involved in education. As Traverso puts it, 'The 1830s saw the beginning of a trend away from centralised community education to separate development on confessional lines which was to be the dominant factor until after the Second World War'. [15] The Methodists led the way as they endeavoured to increase membership through the schools they set up, and this was probably part of a wider strategy to extend their missionary activities into Spain. [16] Through their pioneering efforts, the Methodist Mission quite quickly had four day schools and two evening schools, 'well-established and, we hope, well-taught'. The pupils who attended were regularly from Roman Catholic and other religious backgrounds.

Understandably, the managing body of the Roman Catholic Church in Gibraltar was not pleased by these educational developments and plans were drawn up for the building of a Catholic poor school. Even more significantly, a request was made for the services of teachers from the Order of Irish Christian Brothers to staff this school for what was described as their 'first Colonial adventure'. They remained for only two years, encountering various difficulties. They spoke no Spanish, they found the climate troublesome and unacceptable restrictions were placed upon them by the Roman Catholic authorities. The founder of the order, Brother Edmund Ignatius Rice, was himself disappointed by this first mission overseas. Nevertheless, when the brothers left, ground had been retrieved from the Methodists and the school continued to operate without them.

Catholic education continued to expand and schools were opened on various sites. Then, a few years later, the Catholic cause was strengthened further when nuns from the Institute of the Blessed Virgin Mary, the Loreto sisters, were invited to Gibraltar. They opened a fee-paying school for girls in 1851, beginning a long association which continues today in the surviving Loreto Convent School. In time the nuns came to provide a good deal of the staffing in Gibraltar's primary and girls' schools. The legacy of the labours of the nuns was perhaps as great as that of the brothers, if acknowledged rather less.

One development during the last two decades of the century that cannot be forgotten is the adoption of the Education Code, drawn up along British lines. First introduced in 1880 and revised in 1992, it set out the elementary school curriculum and the regulations for the payment of grants. After some initial reluctance, the Roman Catholic bishop accepted the code and the inspection and the funding that went with it. Attendance and basic standards benefited. Also, through the application of the 'conscience clause' religious rivalries lost some of their intensity.

The Early Twentieth Century

The early years of the twentieth century saw the same mix and similar trends. The government, through the Education Code, continued to set the parameters, although the Roman Catholic element was dominant. Most of the schools receiving grants were in fact Roman Catholic, as were the private Loreto Convent school and Line Wall College, run by the Christian Brothers. There were also ten army schools which enrolled a number of civilian children.

A new if small development was an Anglican initiative. The demand for a non-Catholic school for well-to-do girls had been apparent for some time and one, Bringhurst, had operated for over 12 years. A second, Brympton, also an Anglican foundation, was intended in the first instance as an Anglican alternative to the Loreto Convent School for girls. Brympton made a start during the late 1930s and it continued with some success until the early 1970s. Traverso comments as follows:

It is, perhaps, a reflection of the degree to which expatriate families, serving in Gibraltar up to the end of World War 2, felt a need for separation from the indigenous community, that there was such persistence in pursuing the aim of providing separate schools such as Bringhurst and Brympton which catered mainly for the children of officers and the wealthier anglicised Gibraltarians. [17]

Also during the decades at the turn of the century, the British authorities began to take a more direct interest in educational matters in the colonies. This was prompted by general concerns about education and the future of the British Empire. Economically and militarily, Britain was declining in comparison with its competitors and educational deficiencies were seen as a determining factor. British education needed to improve not only at home but in the colonies too. In Gibraltar, and no doubt everywhere else during those years, there was a steady flow of pamphlets, audio-visual materials, reports and other documents from the Board of Education in London. The board also called for reports from the colonies and a format for reporting was provided. The reports for Gibraltar were compiled by the local inspector of schools. In part these reports were required for the various imperial conferences that were convened.

These were also the years when the non-governmental League of Empire was most active, particularly through the schools. Reflecting this influence, a letter in the *Gibraltar Chronicle* stated that 'the aim of education should be the creation of good citizens equipped and able to take their share of the burden of Empire'. Gibraltar certainly had its place in the imperial network and there is correspondence on file with Lord Meath, the major driving-force behind the Empire Day movement. Leaflets circulated in Gibraltar included an extract from the Earl of Meath's speech on 24 May 1905: 'It is intended that the Empire Day celebration shall be an outward sign of an inner awakening of the Peoples who constitute the British Empire to the serious duties which lie at their door'. Celebrations in Gibraltar seemed to involve most of the civil and military population.

There are also file references to *Chums* magazine, which was available in Gibraltar. Its aims included 'giving young people an idea of the vastness and unity of the British Empire'. The schools were urged to enter competitions, to exchange flags and to form links with others through the School Linking Scheme, thereby promoting enthusiasm for Empire. For a time Gibraltarian schools did all these things, and pupils had a share of the success in competitions.

The Second World War and the Aftermath

The first half of the century raised other questions about the state of education in the colony. One recurring theme , touched on by the local Inspector of Schools, [18] highlighted a continuing problem affecting technical education: 'A boy who reaches 6th Standard considers himself to belong to the educated class and will not follow manual labour. ... The general result of a complete preliminary education in Gibraltar appears to produce clerks and superior shop assistants.' The fact that the curriculum, still based on the Education Code, had remained virtually unchanged since the 1890s, was another concern. Among other identified shortcomings, despite the Compulsory Education Ordinance of 1917, was that of poor attendance, worsened by the economic depression. In addition, there were concerns over the lack of a professionally qualified Gibraltarian teaching force, the long-standing problems of bilingualism and various matters relating to buildings, resources and finance. The visits of inspectors from London had noted all these deficiencies for remedial action when war intervened and all educational activity came to a halt.

The war had far-reaching consequences for the people of Gibraltar. Only the able-bodied men remained in the colony on wartime duties. The women, older men and all the children were evacuated, mostly to London. In one way or another, for all Gibraltarians, their horizons were broadened, their attitudes changed and their aspirations raised. While the evacuees may have begun to think of themselves as more obviously members of the 'British family', the separation deepened their love for the Rock where they were born. Repatriation and reunion with their families came slowly after the war. When life at home was resumed, education was to take on a very different pattern from that which prevailed before 1939.

After the war, British commitment to educational change was undeniable. In Gibraltar the blueprint followed British thinking closely, thinking which led to the epoch-making 1944 Education Act for England and Wales. In Gibraltar the document *A New Educational System for Gibraltar* was prepared by a committee under the chairmanship of a senior British administrator, Colonial Secretary Miles Clifford, and it set out the pattern for the next 30 years or so. After primary education, a tripartite system of secondary education – secondary modern schools, grammar schools and a technical school – was to be put in place. There was to be schooling for all, very much along British lines, followed by higher education in the United Kingdom for those selected. An experienced director of education from the UK was appointed in 1943 [19] to implement the plans. In these, while the needs of Gibraltar were to the fore, the larger British and imperial context was not forgotten: 'Emphasis throughout the whole of school life ... should be on the English language and the Imperial connection', the report stated. [20] This thinking was extended to adult education, the British Council playing an important part. 'The fundamental policy of the British Council in Gibraltar has been to encourage every form of cultural, educational and recreational activities and thereby to strengthen the closest relations between the people of Gibraltar and those of the United Kingdom and the Commonwealth.' The ideas underlining the educational blueprint, therefore, were British and the implementation initially was largely British too. Service personnel, largely from the RAF and the Army Education Corps, provided vital teaching support in the classroom as the system got under way. In due course teachers from the British Isles took their place. Most were the returning Christian Brothers and Loreto nuns, whose credentials were closely vetted by the authorities. The system that they were to return to, although welcoming their teaching expertise, was to be very much a government-controlled system.

It took some time for the system to settle down. By 1949 everything was in place – infant and junior schools, separate grammar and modern schools for the boys and girls, a small commercial school and the Technical and Dockyard School for boys. The structure and administration was confirmed in detail in a major education ordinance in 1950 drafted by colonial officials. While these officials largely held the reins, they were supported by a regular flow of advice from the London establishment, for example in the Ingrams Report of 1949 [21] and those by Gwilliam during the 1950s. While Ingrams was concerned overall with 'the maximum economy of administration costs', he took a broad view, speaking also of the need 'to bring standards and practice as close to those of the United Kingdom as possible'. As regards education, Ingrams approved of the recruitment of expatriate teachers 'to preserve an assimilative policy effectively'. For the first time a close link with an education authority in Britain, preferably in London, was advocated, along with regular inspections by UK inspectors of schools. Pertinently, Ingrams added that 'there may still be a time when the Home Office is a more natural custodian of its affairs than the Colonial Office', suggestive of the closer association with Britain which many thought ought to have occurred and to which they still aspire.

The reviews by Freda Gwilliam, an education adviser to the Secretary of State for the Colonies, naturally focused on the state of education. Generally speaking, she commented favourably on progress made, noting that 'nearly 3,000 local and services children were catered for'. In particular she mentioned the headmaster of the boys' grammar school, Brother Foley, 'an energetic, single-minded, obstinate, critical but loyal Englishman'. His examination results (like those in the girls' grammar school) were good. Furthermore, Foley himself claimed that 'During my nine years as Head ... I had secured recognition from the English public examination boards that Gibraltar be treated on a par with British schools and that we did not take overseas examinations as "colonials" or "foreigners".' Gwilliam concluded that 'To all appearances, the educational system in Gibraltar reflects current thought and experience in this country'. Of the Gibraltarians, she wrote: 'They are more British than the English and their loyalty deserves recognition.'

Towards Comprehensive Education

There can be no better illustration of the closeness of Gibraltar's system of schooling to that of the United Kingdom than the case of the transition to comprehensive secondary education. Thinking in that direction began in the 1960s when comprehensive schools were already being established in Britain. Doubts about selection tests and the selection process in general were at the heart of the debate. The Christian Brother and headmaster Brother Foley was among those who voiced the doubts. He said he had grown to loathe the 11-plus entry system to the Grammar School, as being socially divisive, premature in judgment of natural ability, restricting the curriculum of the junior schools, imposing a fearful trauma on the victim as he/she approached the dreaded day of judgment under the eyes of family, friends and teachers. [22]

In practical terms, change in Gibraltar began with the removal of the technical component of the tripartite system: in 1965 a special committee reported that, among other things, the technical school classes were not attracting able pupils and it recommended that only post-school technical provision be retained.

The overall review of the system was taken very seriously and a Secondary Education Commission of five, all Gibraltarians, was appointed. The commission took evidence widely. Many documents were studied and visits were made to authorities and schools in the UK. Clearly the experience gained by UK schools was going to carry a great deal of weight with members of the commission. The details of the deliberations need not be presented, although one matter dealt with separately, namely co-education, requires mention. The evidence was that teachers and pupils were in favour but that parents and the Roman Catholic Church were not. At the time the views of the latter won the day and co-education at secondary level (not at primary nor middle school level) was at least deferred. [23] The grammar schools and secondary modern schools were to be abolished and replaced by two single-sex comprehensive schools. Various candidates were interviewed for headship and Sister Aoife Hynes became the first head of Westside Secondary School for Girls; Brother Hopkins became head of Bayside Secondary School for Boys.

Although implementation of these changes began in 1972, it took over ten years before the two schools were fully operational in purpose-built buildings. Progress was held up by various construction problems. Everything depended, of course, on UK funding and it was the visit by Minister of Overseas Development Judith Hart in 1978 that resulted in an agreement to fund the building of a new Westside School and the disappearance of the awkward multi-site provision that had existed.

Just as there was reliance on UK funding for all manner of things, particularly during those years from 1969 to 1983 when the frontier was closed by Franco, there was also a continuing dependence on UK expertise. The transition to comprehensive education and a series of other changes in educational practice had obvious implications for in-service training. A teachers' centre was created, following British examples, and advisers from the UK were appointed to work there. Courses were run in Gibraltar and Gibraltarian teachers attended courses in the UK. Matters were further complicated by a stubborn problem of teacher shortage and the recruitment of significant numbers of UK expatriate teachers was necessary until 1978 when parity of salaries with the UK was agreed.

Gibraltar's Modern System of Education

By the time the first Gibraltarian director of education, Julio Alcantara, was appointed, much of Gibraltar's present-day educational system was in place.

The processes of localization had run their course as far as existing legislation permitted and within this context education reflected the high degree of autonomy which Gibraltar had achieved. Although the governor was still the ultimate authority, certainly as regards foreign affairs, education as a 'defined domestic matter' was wholly in Gibraltarian hands. Following British parliamentary practice, an elected House of Assembly controlled most matters. A leader of the opposition and members of opposition parties faced the chief minister and his council of ministers across the floor of the House. Among the ministers was the Minister for Education with responsibility for the matters which that portfolio contained. Day-to-day management was in the hands of the Director of Education and his small team of education officers and advisers, following familiar British practice. He was guided by legislation which, since the Education Ordinance of 1974, had been devised by Gibraltarians and implemented by Gibraltarians. It should be remembered, however, that, despite the process of Gibraltarianization, the evolution of the system remained very close to developments in the United Kingdom.

Gibraltarian directors of education have seen the implementation of important changes. One instance is that of pre-school education. For a long period after the war this had been left to others in the face of uncertainty as to what is best for this age group. As one writer put it, 'Pre-five education is non-statutory and its development has therefore been spasmodic, diverse and variable, and characterized by both government and public ambivalence'. [24]

The Clifford Report of 1943 made no mention of the early years and during the 1950s various individuals took the opportunity to open nursery schools, sometimes in their own homes. One or two of the teacher-owners had relevant experience and all sought help and advice at home and in the UK. By the early 1960s there were about a dozen of these private nursery schools offering a reasonably varied programme based on play, practical activities, music and language development. They appeared to satisfy an obvious need. However, government intervention was not far away, coming firstly through the implementation during the 1960s and 1970s of a three-tier system of schooling – first schools, middle schools and secondary comprehensive schools. With an entry age of four years, at a stroke the first schools deprived the private schools of one year-group. Their clientele was further diminished when two government nursery schools were opened. Later, a new administration which came to power in 1996 took matters further and by 2003 there were seven such schools, creating an excellent foundation for Gibraltar's educational system as a whole.

Gibraltarian politicians and officials are also proud of their achievements in providing for less fortunate children, those with special educational needs. There were some voluntary initiatives taken in the 1930s to help the blind, but the beginnings of today's provision can really be found in the 1950s. Again, one or two individuals got things moving, at first through efforts to support parents who were struggling to cope. Official recognition of the problem came with a colonial adviser's report in 1968, in which he stated that 'steps should be taken to identify all children in need of special educational treatment whether on account of physical or mental handicap, and proper provision made for them'. The government began to take note. Some support was made available although it was the Warnock Report of 1978, entitled *Special Educational Needs*, that was the spur to change. Some Gibraltarian teachers were on special training courses in the UK at the time of Warnock and they came back with the latest ideas. Acquiring finance for the building of the new St Martin's Special School was a crowning event. The building was planned using the expertise of specialists from the City of Leicester College of Education and architects from London. The first head was an expatriate British appointee. Today, however, all involved in special education are Gibraltarian. An adviser in special education oversees the provision across the schools and an assessment panel decides on individual cases as required. Each school has a special needs coordinator (SENCO) so that support as far as possible can be provided in mainstream schools. For the more severely handicapped there is St Martin's School and for those aged over 15 years there is the modernized St Bernadette's Occupational Centre. It can be said that all aspects of the arrangements are British in conception and origin, while their realization owes much to local Gibraltarian initiatives. In fact, special education is a good example of how British and Gibraltarian elements overlap and coalesce.

During this first decade of the twenty-first century, the Gibraltar government can readily claim that the educational system as a whole is performing well. One criterion is economic: with unemployment at less than two per cent, and given that the economy has 'never in the entire history of Gibraltar been more prosperous and successful than it is today', [25] education and training appear to be meeting Gibraltar's skill needs. This is due not only to the efforts of the schools but also to the work of the Gibraltar College of Further Education and other training centres.

The origins of the college are to be found in HM Dockyard, which served the needs of the ships of the Royal Navy. While key positions were occupied by UK expatriates, the large installations, including stores, workshops and dry docks, required a steady flow of local apprentices. The dockyard school was established for that purpose. The range of apprenticeships was later extended to include those in the military and public sectors. The Clifford Report of 1943 argued for this extended role and the school gradually became integrated with the colony's educational system. After it underwent various shifts and changes there was a demand for more local control. The Chief Minister of the time, Sir Joshua Hassan, pressed strongly for 'the eventual complete localization' of what was becoming more like a traditional British further education college. Control passed into Gibraltarian hands in 1985, soon after the re-opening of the frontier following 14 years of closure. By then the base had been much reduced in size and the dockyard had been closed. A 'new economy' was dictating Gibraltar's needs. At the beginning of the twenty-first century there is a small privatized ship repair yard requiring a range of engineering skills, but the main economic priorities now lie in the areas of tourism, financial services and retailing. Although the Gibraltar College of Further Education is, as its name states, Gibraltarian, its British origins and its British characteristics are not forgotten.

From time to time advantage is still taken of UK expertise which the links with Britain facilitate.

Success is similarly claimed for Gibraltar's secondary schools. The grammar schools in their day performed well, at least for the select few, while comprehensive schooling extended this success to others. In 1997 there were celebrations to mark 25 years of comprehensive education in Gibraltar. 'Comprehensivism is a veritable success story in every sense,' said the Minister for Education, Dr Bernard Linares. 'Our public examination results,' he continued, 'have soared from year to year placing our schools among the top in UK league tables.' Almost 50 per cent of school leavers were proceeding to courses of higher education in the United Kingdom. Secondary education, it seems, is producing the highly-educated population that Gibraltar requires if it is retain its present levels of economic success.

Before discussing some of the issues relating to the remaining level of education, namely higher education, it can be noted that home-bred students are joined in university courses by their fellows who have received their secondary schooling in private schools in the UK. Although the numbers attending have been relatively small, the families who have sent their children to these schools have been wealthy and influential; they have represented Gibraltar's 'upper class'. Long ago, before travel to the UK became feasible, they would have been the parents who sent their children to the private schools in Gibraltar, often schools run by the brothers or the nuns. The schools chosen in the UK, perhaps suggested by the nuns or brothers, have tended to be in the south of England, but extending northwards to Stonyhurst College in Lancashire and Ampleforth College in Yorkshire. Almost all are Roman Catholic foundations combining 'the academic standards of the English public school with a distinctly Catholic ethos'. Most are boys' schools. All were/are single-sex schools, although this is changing. Some have preparatory schools on site or separately. All are members of the Headmasters' and Headmistresses' Conference or the Girls' Schools Association. While the numbers of Gibraltarians enjoying this private boarding school education have been comparatively few, and while they have tended to come from a narrow social band, the impact on Gibraltarian society may have been considerable. Certainly, former pupils display a keen sense of allegiance to the school they attended – Stonyhurst College, Prior Park, Worth School and so on. Furthermore, the experience there seems to have enhanced their self-confidence as Gibraltarians and British.

The time spent by Gibraltar's large contingent of post-secondary students in the UK, 'the mother country', cannot but be significant. Reaching the large numbers took time. During the immediate post-war years they were negligible and only partly government-initiated. In 1945, the Director of Education reported that 'A number of scholarships had been given by the Mackintosh Trust, [26] local firms and Government to enable students to study in England'. Numbers increased and by 1950 over 50 students were in receipt of scholarships and grants, most being teacher trainees. Numbers remained in the 30–50 range for some years. In 1974, a points system was introduced based on school examination passes and by 1980 over 90 students were receiving awards. Seeing the points system as discriminating against some students, a Gibraltar Socialist and Labour Party (GSLP) administration, when it came to power in 1988, abolished the system: anyone who had secured a place in a university or college became eligible for means-tested support. By 1996 over 600 students were simultaneously in receipt of awards. Less that one-third of these were attending teacher training courses. Degree courses in accountancy, business and law were among the most popular, reflecting the needs of Gibraltar's 'new economy'. Courses in music, the arts, computing and tourism were not far behind in popularity.

As numbers of students in higher education increased, so did the number and type of institutions attended. At the start colleges and universities near to London were almost always chosen, but this has changed somewhat. In 1998, close to 100 institutions enrolled Gibraltarian students, from Aberdeen University in the north to Plymouth University in the south. Although most received only one or two students, some were much more popular, for example, Cardiff University, Kingston University in London, Nottingham Trent University and Southampton Institute. The newer universities were well-represented but the ancient establishments – Oxford, Cambridge, St Andrews, Aberdeen and Edinburgh – have also admitted Gibraltar students from time to time.

The statistics for higher education speak for themselves: almost half of each generation of secondary school leavers are now involved. The effects on students and on Gibraltar must be considerable. Many return, while others seek employment in the UK or elsewhere. While strengthening their grasp of English whatever courses they may have taken, all will have benefited from first-hand extended experience of life in Britain, their sense of being both Gibraltarian and British probably stronger than ever. They and their fellows who stayed behind in Gibraltar have enjoyed the advantages of a well-structured system, extending from pre-school to higher education and beyond, wholly financed and controlled by the Gibraltar government. Given a lack of natural resources, the reliance on human resources in the form of a well-educated workforce becomes particularly important.

Reflections

As the third millennium gets under way and after modern Gibraltar's 300 years of existence, inevitably there is cause for reflection on the significance of the past, the priorities for the present and a vision for the future. Education has its place in that reflection and the question posed in these pages focuses on the implications for a Gibraltarian sense of identity.

First of all, it may be asked, what is the image or profile of the Gibraltarian as perceived by self and others? Among various attributes, the Gibraltarians have a keen sense of their own 300 years of history; they have a deep psychological attachment to their territory, the Rock; born of their own years of difficulty and adversity, the Gibraltarians are caring and keen to help others; they are proud of their ethnically diverse make-up; they have a business-minded money-making mentality; they are proud of their tolerance of others in a multi-faith society; Gibraltarians are vehemently not Spanish; nor English, but loyally British as other groups are British; they look favourably on Gibraltar's association with the Commonwealth; and they are mildly, not wildly European.

Education has contributed to most if not all these, for example, as follows:

(a)   The agents of imperialism, namely the governors and other officials, have used education as a vehicle for conveying preferred ideas and values, highlighting Gibraltar's place in the British Empire and Commonwealth.

(b)   Throughout the centuries education has stressed the importance of the English language.

(c)   Private schooling, among other things, has exemplified an entrepreneurial spirit through the private nursery, primary and secondary schools operating in the colony.

(d)   A long-standing reluctance to engage in manual labour, perhaps inadvertently encouraged by education, has underpinned a preference for white-collar and business-orientated occupations.

(e)   The emphasis during the past three decades on providing the skills which the 'new economy' demands has added substance to a business-minded ethos.

(f)   Schooling, while for long periods provided along confessional lines, increasingly brought the various sections of the community together, initially because of the Education Code governing organization, curriculum and grants introduced by the British.

(g)   While factors other than education have determined the not-Spanish nature of the people, the educational system, related only to that of Britain, has underlined Gibraltar's credentials as in no sense Spanish.

(h)   Higher education in the UK on a relatively large scale has strongly reinforced Gibraltarian feelings for Britain and for feeling British.

(i)   For Gibraltarian higher education students, rubbing shoulders with students from various parts of Europe has added somewhat to a Gibraltarian sense of being European.

The various levels and sectors of education have been examined and some of the possible consequences for the people identified. Overall, the main message for the Gibraltarians appears to be: 'We are British because the system has formed us thus'. Taking this further, to the implications for the sovereignty dispute, the supplementary message is: 'We simply cannot be given away to a non-British authority just like that. On the contrary, our education and our history say that we should be allowed to move further along the road to self-determination which the British have consistently laid down for us during at least the past 125 years. Further political development towards even greater autonomy, in line with British values and practice, would be a natural progression'.

Finally, this account should end as it began, by reference to what looks like a new climate as regards discourse between the United Kingdom, Spain and Gibraltar, Gibraltar at last having a voice in these affairs. With education and other factors in mind, what does the past say about better relations between Spain and its neighbour, with the immediate Campo area of Spain particularly in mind?

The economic history of the area shows that the Campo developed largely because of Gibraltar as the economic dynamo. [27] The Campo has been, and to some extent still is, Gibraltar's hinterland in a foreign country. Supplying the needs of the garrison was a major preoccupation. This meant goods, fresh food and much more. It also meant supplying labour, largely but not exclusively unskilled labour. Over many years several thousands of workers crossed the frontier from Spain to Gibraltar, as they still do, including today Gibraltarians and foreign nationals who need to take housing in Spain. As a result of all the activity, the villages of the area, especially La Linea, grew as did Campamento, San Roque and Los Barrios. All are in the Province of Cadiz. It is the mayors of these neighbouring municipalities, including Algeciras, who are keen to discuss common concerns with the authorities in Gibraltar. By no means are they all in political accord, neither between themselves nor with Madrid, but they all feel that the time is ripe for as comprehensive a dialogue as possible.

The economy of the area has moved on apace since the earlier days when the mere presence of the garrison was the basis for much economic activity. The Campo, and indeed the whole of Andalucía, has developed an economic momentum of its own. While tourism, including golf tourism, may have been the springboard, this is now far from the whole story. Clearly, the climate and the amenable lifestyle are factors that stimulate growth – the so-called 'cultural capital' of the area – but economic activity is no longer seasonal. There is a vibrant all-the-year-round economy, driven by young entrepreneurs engaged in a wide range of commercial activities. Not surprisingly, with money moving around globally, the participants have a distinctly multinational flavour. With Algeciras, it is said, about to become the largest container port in southern Europe, and with talk of an under-sea tunnel to Morocco, the economic outlook is seen as bright.

This, then, is the area locally with which Gibraltar might have closer relations. With its well-educated English-speaking population, Gibraltar could perhaps have much to offer and much to gain. There have been fruitful cross-border activities before, of course, mostly informal and less by way of formal contacts. Sometimes the formal has been restricted to coolly diplomatic and adversarial exchanges, when queues have been long at the frontier, for example. On the positive side, there has been some inter-school visiting, encouraged by a sympathetic minister for education and his Spanish counterparts. There have also been some joint endeavours in the cultural field.

The one matter that springs to everyone's mind when better cooperation is mentioned is Gibraltar Airport and its potential development in the economic interests of the whole area, Gibraltar and the Campo. In the past Spain has persistently put restrictions on flights to and from Gibraltar. Then, in 1987 a proposed agreement for the joint development of the airport was rejected by Gibraltar because it seemed to imply a loss of sovereignty over part of its territory. The development of Gibraltar Airport is almost certain to be on the agenda for any new talks. Such talks will presumably be at two levels: at local level, involving Gibraltar and the neighbouring municipalities across the border; and, at higher level, between Spanish diplomats, Foreign Office diplomats and the Chief Minister of Gibraltar.

From our discussion of education, positive outcomes to any talks are by no means assured. The Spanish position seems basically unchanged: the main objective is still to gain sovereignty, which is unthinkable for Gibraltar. The Gibraltar position is firm in other respects. Any so-called concessions from Spain may not be perceived as such. Gibraltar wishes to see the end to what have been seen as longstanding and impermissible, even illegal, restrictions on the economic activities of the territory – restrictions on aircraft movements, on cruise ships calling at Gibraltar, on telephone numbers, on frontier delays and so on. Discussions would only begin to break new ground once these restrictions were removed.

If Gibraltar's position seems unbending, a look at the territory's history explains why, as this focus on education illustrates. The Gibraltarians might well say: 'We are British and the British have been instrumental in making us British. We are British in our own territory and any discussions with Spain can only be as between good neighbours.'

Notes

[1] 'Los llanitos son españoles en su casi totalidad, aunque se aprovechen de la ciudadanía inglesa, y el resto, judíos y extranjeros, que lo mismo pueden vivir bajo una bandera que baja otra.' Quoted in F. Tornay (*Gibraltar Y Su Prensa*, Diputación de Cadiz: 1997).

[2] J.A. Mangan (ed.), *Making Imperial Mentalities: Socialization and British Imperialism* (Manchester: Manchester University Press, 1990), p.1.

[3] The informal influences here referred to are not dealt with in this essay. See E.G. Archer, 'imperial Influences: Gibraltarians, Cultural Bonding and Sport', *Culture, Sport and Society*, 6, 1 (Spring 2003).

[4] For a detailed examination of all these factors see E.G. Archer, *Gibraltar, Identity and Empire* (London: Routledge, 2005).

[5] The women, children and older men were evacuated. While some went to Jamaica, Madeira and elsewhere, the majority were sent to London where they experienced the Blitz. Because of housing difficulties the process of repatriation was long drawn out and not completed until the early 1950s.

[6] Sir Kenneth Anderson, in the foreword to H.W. Howes, *The Gibraltarian* (Medsun, 1950).

[7] An all-party committee was convened to review the constitutional position in 2003 and to make recommendations. The unanimous view was that the existing constitution should be revised and not replaced, extending local autonomy further.

[8] Matters to do with education are dealt with more fully, if rather differently, in the following two works: E.G. Archer and A.A. Traverso, *Education in Gibraltar 1704–2004* (Gibraltar Books, 2004), and Archer, *Gibraltar, Identity and Empire*.

[9] G.F. Cornwell, 'The Systems of Education in Gibraltar' in *The Board of Education Special Reports on Educational Subjects,* Vol. 12, Part 1 (1905).

[10] St.John N.T Williams, *Tommy Atkins' Children; The Story of the Education of the Army's Children 1675–1970* (1971), p.3.

[11] War Office Library, General Order and Circular Letter Collection 1811–1833, Folio 592, letter dated 14 Nov. 1811. Quoted by Williams, *Tommy Atkins' Children*, p.34.

[12] Williams, *Tommy Atkins' Children*, p.31.

[13] A.A. Traverso, 'A History of Education in British Gibraltar 1704–1945' (unpublished MA dissertation, University of Southampton, 1980), p.2.

[14] Ibid.

[15] Ibid., p.28.

[16] See Susan Jackson, 'The Methodists in Gibraltar and their Mission in Spain'. (unpublished PhD thesis, University of Durham, 2000).

[17] Traverso, 'A History of Education'.

[18] T.W. Haycraft, *Inspector of Schools Report for 1913*. Copies of School Reports are held in the Gibraltar Government Archive.

[19] Namely one H.W. Howes, who had been principal of Norwich Technical College.

[20] *A New Educational System for Gibraltar*, Report of the Clifford Committee (Miles Clifford, chairman), 1943. A copy of this report can be found in the Gibraltar Government Archives.

[21] See Public Record Office (hereafter PRO), File CO/926/54.

[22] From unpublished correspondence held in the Gibraltar Government Archive.

[23] The issue has lain dormant and at the end of 2004 the Minister for Education, Dr Bernard Linares, stated that the introduction of co-education to comprehensive secondary education would shortly be placed on the agenda again.

[24] Joyce Watt, 'Pre-Five Education', in T.G.K. Bryce and W.M. Humes (eds.), *Scottish Education* (Edinburgh: Edinburgh University Press, 1999).

[25] Chief Minister Peter Caruana's address to the Gibraltar Federation of Small Businesses (GFSB), as reported in *The Gibraltar Chronicle*, 20 Jan. 2005.

[26] The fund administered by the Mackintosh Trust was set up in memory of one of Gibraltar's best-known businessmen and benefactors, John Mackintosh.

[27] A distinguished economist, F.A. Hayek, was invited to Gibraltar to make recommendations as to the best way forward for the Gibraltar economy after the 1939–45 war. See PRO File CO91/522.

Discipline, Character, Health: Ideals and Icons of Nordic Masculinity 1860–1930

Henrik Meinander

I

Central European and British historians and social scientists tend to approach the Nordic countries – in other words Denmark, Finland, Norway, Sweden and Iceland – as a peripheral and backward area of European culture. This is generally speaking perfectly true. Northern Europe was not a part of the Roman Empire, its conversion to Christianity happened as late as during the first three centuries of the second millennium and its societal transformation has ever since then predominantly been a reflection of developments in the Central European and Anglo-American worlds.

Yet in certain fields of society Nordic countries are considered rather advanced. Social welfare is one of these exceptions; education is another. These phenomena correspond clearly with the fact that the Nordic countries have formed the world's most homogeneous area of Protestant faith, which in its Lutheran interpretation has given high priority to a centralized government, the written word and formal schooling. After Germany, the heart of the Lutheran realm and its educational culture, Nordic countries have been in the forefront in terms of state-directed educational centralization.

This is of certain significance as we focus on one sphere of Nordic schooling, physical education for middle- and upper-class boys, and analyse the views and visions of its function and aims put forward by influential Nordic educationists and thinkers between approximately 1860 and 1930. The debate in question should partly be understood in the context of the contemporary consolidation and centralization of the Nordic educational system, which from a European perspective was both early and relatively progressive. As in France or Germany, physical education became an institutionalized part of Nordic secondary education for boys during the second half of the nineteenth century. Thus its introduction was a part of the transformation of the Nordic education system and society in general.

The transformation was by no means uniform in the different Nordic countries, but similar enough to be analysed here from a single North European perspective. The educational and cultural contrasts inside each Nordic country were in fact much bigger than between these nations. Despite all the studies from a national perspective, still dominating Nordic research, it is obvious that the bourgeois cultures in question were in many respects one culture with distinctive North European features. This culture will be the ultimate framework for the discussion in the following pages.

II

Nordic secondary education between 1860 and 1930, like its counterparts in Central Europe and Great Britain, was essentially an institution for the upper and middle classes. Both in absolute and proportional terms pupils were predominantly recruited from these strata, while those who had a different class background were taught to adopt bourgeois values during their years as secondary school pupils. It seems obvious therefore that these schools had an important role in the reproduction of bourgeois culture. [1]

In which ways? The question is by no means irrelevant; neither the concept of bourgeoisie nor culture are easily defined or described. Peter Gay, the distinguished scholar on European bourgeois culture, has pointed how many confusions and paradoxes are linked with the use of the somewhat synonymous concepts of middle classes, *Bürgertum* or bourgeoisie, which all have their roots in different languages as well as in certain political cultures. The plural form 'middle classes' reflects above all the Anglo-American awareness of the heterogeneous circumstances in which these strata of society functioned. The German concept *Bürgertum*, exactly like its Scandinavian equivalent *borgerskap*, again originally stood for the urban estate beneath the aristocracy. [2] The French term *bourgeoisie*, initially meaning the new middle class of entrepreneurs, had in this sense no wider connotations, but became something of a fashionable catch-all word during the last century, which it still is. Its weakness lies naturally in this vagueness. Yet it is paradoxically also its strength, as Gay has shown in his study *The Bourgeois Experience*. In short, it reflects the 'underlying unity' in which the middle classes coexist. [3]

The concept of culture is obviously no less disputable, but if we follow the habits of most historians and social scientists and understand culture 'as a collective noun for the symbolic and learned, non-biological aspects of human life' [4] it is possible to explain the cultural reproduction in question as an education that included training in a range of skills essential for those who wanted to maintain or achieve a lifestyle that corresponded with the dominant culture in the Nordic countries.

Reproduction was a continuous process and happened on many levels simultaneously. One dimension of it was the used and taught language; pupils were trained to use a correct language in speech and in writing in order to master the codes of the dominant communication system. Another dimension was teaching in subjects such as history or science, which, apart from establishing a useful knowledge base, functioned as an implicit indoctrination into the values and world-view of bourgeois culture. It is not difficult to see why history lessons had this double function; the reconstruction of the past is in itself an intellectual exercise that in conservative institutions tends to strengthen existing values and beliefs, [5] and this was certainly the case in European secondary education, which as a successor of the Latin school paid much attention to the classical heritage. But more often it is forgotten that science teaching also had an important function as an instrument of ideological reproduction: it taught pupils the basics of scientific reductionism and, above all, the principles of the logical tradition in Western philosophy, which was another cornerstone of bourgeois culture.

In this context, however, it is of special interest to take a closer look at a third dimension of the Nordic process of cultural reproduction, which could be characterized as the discipline of the body. In contrast to the other dimensions of schooling, this was a process that went on continuously; the development of an appropriate physical demeanour in the pupil went hand in hand with other kinds of education. Pupils were supposed to behave physically in a way that suited the education they were receiving. In this sense it was truly a question of a bourgeois cultivation of the body. Roberta J. Park, who has looked at the same phenomenon in North America, has also made this point: 'The well-ordered body also served as an icon for the ordered society at a time when many middle-class Americans were anxious about social changes they saw all around them.' [6]

Neither should it be forgotten that this cultural reproduction was at the same time a process that formed pupils' gender identity. In addition to their psychological and physical socialization for a bourgeois adulthood, they were also trained to think in terms of a set of ideals regarding their own sexuality, which prepared them for a manhood that was thought to be different from the one that working class or peasant boys of the same age were aiming at. [7] It is not a coincidence, for example, that Nordic physicians showed special concern about the sexual hygiene of secondary-school youth. Their energetic campaign against masturbation was not only caused by the fear of impotence and a dull mind, which many nineteenth-century physicians claimed were the results of onanism, but also very much a question of the moral preparation of bourgeois youth for a 'clean' manhood, which should prevent them from being enticed into any kind of pre- or extra-marital intercourse. [8]

This is not to say that the propagation of extra-marital continence was merely a question of a moral crusade; the second half of the nineteenth century and the first decades of the twentieth century were also times when the spread of venereal diseases reached alarming figures in the Nordic countries. [9] The point is therefore that the campaign was a form of functional moralizing predominantly designed to enlighten bourgeois opinion and create and maintain a strong ruling class. It is not easy to say to what extent Nordic secondary-school boys were explicitly advised to restrain their sexual desires, but it seems plausible to think that the message was brought out in different disguised forms during schooling. The 'secret vice' and the 'fallen woman' were notions that figured heavily in Nordic manuals dealing with manliness and morality. [10]

The stereotype of bourgeois masculinity that was advocated was that of a man who mastered his own sexuality with the same ease and precision that he was supposed to handle a gun. The ideal manhood of the European middle and upper classes of the second half of nineteenth century was a state in which the individual had strict control over his body and mind. [11] Furthermore, it was a state in which he was able to release and transform his potential in order to fulfil all his social and cultural obligations. [12] The philosophical basis for these demands can be found in Christian thinking which – a fact often forgotten – was strongly influenced by classical Stoicism. [13] Yet it is clear that the ideal manhood of the late-nineteenth-century European bourgeoisie had developed a nature of its own; it was not a contradiction of the ideal Christian but implied a new life strategy. It was a capitalistic life strategy. This meant above all that obligations in an increasing degree had to be met by new sets of ideals and action rather than by merely maintaining a traditional order.

It was not only a more individualistic ideal of manhood than previously but also an ideology that paid more attention to gender differentiation. Boys and girls had for ages been brought up differently, but now they were told that their segregation was a crucial part of the cultivation of their gender; [14] it was as if parents and educationists had become conscious of the growing demands of individual freedom and therefore instead tried to introduce more polarized gender identities. This is of course a simplification, but all the same it gives us some idea of one of the most important ideological forces that directed education in institutions such as the Nordic secondary school during the time in question. [15]

III

Let us continue the discussion by investigating the role physical education was understood to have in the process of preparing Nordic youth for a bourgeois manhood. As has been stated, physical education was a subject that step by step during the second half of nineteenth century gained a position in the Nordic secondary school curriculum. The force behind its actual introduction was predominantly militaristic; Nordic advocates of physical education were often eager to point out that it was a form of character building and health promotion, but only few of them were successful in their campaigns before the authorities and political opinion began to understand that exercise could function as a substitute or preparation for national service. It is therefore not surprising that in the 1860s and 1870s many of these educationists, for tactical reasons if nothing else, began to strongly endorse this function.

For example, in 1874 T.J. Hartelius, director of *Gymnastiska Centralinstitutet* (GCI), the gymnastics teachers' college in Stockholm, declared that the military victories of the German forces during the last ten years had been, to a considerable degree, a consequence of the disciplinary preparation which pupils had got in school. He pointed out that German physical education in this sense was a part of the country's national service. Hartelius tried thus to convince his readers that gymnastics and military drill should continue to have a central role in Swedish physical education too. Games should by no means be neglected in teaching, but they could never compensate for the more traditional forms of the cultivation of the body. Hartelius also had a clear idea of the function of military training: 'It strengthens discipline and carriage, it improves the flexibility and vigour of the movements.' [16]

Hartelius's remarks are interesting for many reasons. They show how explicitly the discussion of the need for reforms in physical education was linked to demands for stronger military preparedness. Both educationists and public opinion were aware of the health-promoting effects of regular exercise but seem nevertheless to have paid most attention to their disciplinary purposes. Collective social survival, in other words, was more important than the physical condition of individual. This approach was of course in no sense extraordinary in Nordic secondary education in the nineteenth century; it was based on the educational ideals of formal neo-humanism and followed to a considerable extent the didactic practices of Herbartianism (J.F. Herbart, 1776–1841), which in practice was a method to master and control the collective.

The tradition of discipline and the lack of space for individuality was especially visible in a subject such as physical education which, in addition to the pedagogical frameworks mentioned above, was also directly influenced by the instructional methods of the military. The configurative structures of school gymnastics and military drill were both rooted in the linear tactics of eighteenth-century infantry. The emphasis was on geometrical discipline, which required detailed instructions about the position, function and movement of each participant. Metaphorically speaking, through these detailed instructions the collective exercises would turn into a bodily grammar. The idea was to add one correct performance to another according to a certain formula. In classical Latin this was how grammar was learnt; in gymnastics a choreography was acquired with certain physiological objectives. [17]

It is thus simplistic to think that Hartelius and his Nordic colleagues would have understood physical education merely as a preparation for national service. On the contrary it is obvious that many of them had more ambitious motives in their minds when they advocated sound discipline during lessons. For instance, in 1875 Hartelius wrote that it was necessary for people to remember that physical education was not only a groundwork for war but above all a subject that prepared pupils to fulfil their civic duties during times of peace. [18] The same idea, by the way, was put forward by the Finn Viktor Heikel in 1870, who between 1876 and 1911 was director of the Finnish Gymnastics Teachers' Institution at Helsinki University. In connection with a comparison of the physical education practised in Germany and France – which, most probably as a result of the news from the battlefields of the Franco-German War, ended in favour of the German system – Heikel was keen to add that the exercises developed skills that were patriotic virtues in all conditions. [19]

It is no accident that men such as Hartelius and Heikel understood the virtues of courage, discipline and stamina as qualities most useful to cultivate also in bourgeois youth. As true patriots and energetic promoters of state-building in their own countries, they were both inspired by the widespread belief that it was these virtues that had directed German development in the 1860s and 1870s, which, in short, was an impressive mobilization of the masses as well as an efficient integration of the elites. They saw physical education as a means of preparing the youth of the ruling classes to become obedient, honest and hardworking servants of the state.

Nevertheless, it would be wrong to claim that Nordic educationists would have had their eyes fixed only on Germany in those days. Many of those who praised the disciplinary virtues of the German secondary education system were at the same time ready to point out that the most developed form of physical education was to be found in Great Britain, which, as a consequence of increasing trade and better communications during the second half of the nineteenth century, became recognized also in the Nordic region as the most advanced society in the world. The British system, however, was not admired for its discipline or order but above all as an excellent way to form and strengthen character.

The concept of character was, of course, used among Nordic educationists before they came in close touch with British school culture and its ideological advocates. It was known from classical literature, especially the Stoics, who emphasized the need for a strong character, [20] and also played an important role in Renaissance literature, but it was not especially relevant as long as moral education in schools had a collective end rather than the refinement of individuals. The concept had many connotations, but stood in the first place as a measure of the efforts to master and develop the self for the benefit of the group. In addition, it was a self-control that was supposed to be practised in public and in favour of the dominant culture.

As Warren I. Susman has pointed out, the notion of character in the Anglo-American culture of the nineteenth century was frequently related to a number of terms that could be called key words in the bourgeois vocabulary. Some of the most used combination words, for example citizenship, duty, work and golden deeds, reflected the idea that character-building was a part of state-building, whereas others, such as outdoor life, conquest, reputation and manhood, clearly showed that character should be formed through individual initiatives as well as through actions, and therefore was a process that had personal aims. [21]

These two perspectives were recognized by the Nordic educationists who began to advocate physical education as a form of character building. For example, Viktor Heikel wrote on several occasions during the 1870s and 1880s that he was convinced that the expansion of the British Empire was in large measure a consequence of educational policy in the public schools. Through their harsh outdoor games, boys acquired characters full of self-confidence and ready for action, which made them fit for public service in the expanding empire.

Heikel's images of British athleticism were of course not self-invented; he had visited English and Scottish public schools in 1871 and was ever since then sure that games and competitions were the most efficient means of character formation. In 1891 he defended the roughness of the games, although they caused 'many arm and leg fractures, sometimes even the loss of life', by emphasizing that British education was established on the principle that the individual had to be prepared to give his life or sacrifice a limb in order to increase the physical and moral strength of the nation. Furthermore, Heikel reminded the reader that this attitude was gained above all through sport, without which youth became weak and immoral. [22]

This was by no means an inaccurate interpretation of the ideological message of British athleticism. In fact it is obvious that Heikel was one of the few Nordic educationists during the second half of nineteenth century who had a thorough idea of what the British meant by their muscular Christianity and games ethic. Heikel was a religious man. He was born into a clerical family and began his academic studies as a theology student before he became interested in physical education. During his studies at the GCI in Stockholm in the late 1860s he converted from puritan Lutheranism to the more liberal Baptism. These choices gave a clear direction to his whole life; from then on Heikel seldom failed to point out that the cultivation of the body was an important element of cultural reproduction and that the ultimate goal of physical education was the refinement of the soul. The muscular Christianity of the public schools was in his eyes a proof of that religion and action went hand in hand in British culture and that this was the secret behind Britain's imperial strength. [23]

Heikel was on this point as sincere as many of the most zealous muscular Christians in Great Britain such as Edward Thring or H.H. Almond. [24] It can even be claimed that he, as an active Baptist, tended to overestimate the religious component of the educational policy of the public schools. His visit to the British Isles in 1871 was first of all a religious pilgrimage; he was lodged with local Baptists and spent the most of his time socializing with them and telling them about religious conditions in Finland. It is therefore understandable that his first and long-lasting impression of the ethos of British public schools was a confirmation of what he had picked up earlier on from the educational and religious literature. He saw in that sense what he wanted to see. [25] He was carried away with a myth, which J.A. Mangan describes in these terms: 'Consideration of public school life in Victorian and Edwardian England reveals that the public image seldom mirrored the private morality. Too frequently, there was an ideology for public consumption and an ideology for personal practice; in a phrase muscular Christianity for the consumer, Social Darwinism for the constrained.' [26]

It was this honest, not to say naive, admiration of the moral facade of muscular Christianity that by the turn of the century had made Heikel a sharp critic of the unlimited hunt for records and personal fame that more and more had begun to dominate the modern sports movement. Heikel was still an advocate of outdoor sports, but required that the moral and aesthetic aspects of the cultivation of the body should be more important than the mechanical counting of scores and the exact measurements of bodily performances. [27] This attitude was of course partly a result of the fact that Heikel, as the leading man in Finnish physical education, was eager to maintain a balance between teacher-centred gymnastics and sport, which from a psychological point of view was more emancipating, but was certainly also a consequence of his opposition to Social Darwinian tendencies in the sports movement.

Heikel belonged clearly with those educationists who saw the formation of character first of all as a part of state building. He was critical both of the established tradition in physical education, which paid little attention to individual needs and which in practice emphasized only the need for collective discipline, as well as of the shameless attitude towards winning among those educationists who wanted to strengthen character through competition not only in order to achieve a better society but also as an attempt to increase the mental capacity and happiness of individuals for their own sake.

IV

This qualified outlook on sport as such was not uncommon among Heikel's Nordic colleagues. Most of them were by the turn of the century ready to admit that educational practice was too monotonous and collective, and a lot of them were also convinced that sport could be an excellent way of forming characters if only it was practised in the right way and under the right conditions. However, opinion diverged markedly when the question was discussed on a practical level.

Some of them, such as the Swede L.M. Törngren, Hartelius's successor as director of the GCI in Stockholm, were highly impressed by what they had seen of physical activities in the British public schools but were nevertheless eager to point out that an unchanged British model was not appropriate for the Nordic secondary school system, which had more subjects and much less time and space for outdoor activities. [28] Törngren and his followers were prepared to supplement Swedish physical education with suitable activities but had no intention of reducing the dominant position of their gymnastics system. They admitted that games and other outdoor sports were a most efficient type of character training in physical education as long as competition was not overemphasized and any kind of egotism was excluded. Yet they were equally convinced that the established gymnastics-oriented programme could also have a strengthening impact on the character, if it only was practised properly. [29] According to Törngren the authority and initiative of the teacher was in fact more essential in character building than the choice of exercises. This view was naturally rooted in the strong belief in the efficacy of teacher training at the GCI and in the potential of the Swedish gymnastics system, but was also a consequence of the fact that Törngren, even more sharply than for example Heikel, saw the character-strengthening dimension of physical education as a preparation for respectable citizenship and participation in state building. The teacher, not surprisingly, was given a central role in this notion of character building. It was his authority and instructions that guaranteed that pupils were conditioned to obey orders and fulfil their duties and, above all, were taught to know their hierarchical position in the social order. [30]

Others, however, such as for example Viktor Balck, a teacher at the GCI in Stockholm and leading figure in the Nordic sport movement at the turn of the century, and his kindred spirits, such as the interesting outsider William Hovgaard, were convinced that character education was a process that required the active and independent involvement of pupils and were therefore eager promoters of a more sport-oriented physical education. Balck and Hovgaard had both visited Britain for the first time in the 1880s. And both of them had been fascinated during these visits by the splendid conditions for physical activities in the public schools; they were amazed by the 'enormous' size of the playing fields at Eton and Harrow and could not stop praising the physical well-being and dynamic character of British school youth.

These reactions were of course by no means unique among Nordic educationists who, during the last three decades of nineteenth century, had had the opportunity to visit some of the famous 'great public schools' and other wealthy boarding schools in England and Scotland. As mentioned earlier, Heikel and Törngren had both returned from their British pilgrimages with similar impressions and by the end of last century this distinct form of athleticism had become a well-known and widely admired phenomenon among Nordic educationists with British connections. The words 'It was on the playing fields of Eton that the battle of Waterloo was won', falsely ascribed to Wellington, [31] were repeated on almost every possible occasion, as were many other claims that the superiority of the British empire was due to the moral and physical training the imperial conquerors and administrators had received in the public schools. This not infrequently occurred in form of quotations of quotations; the prize example is a Norwegian translation from 1899 of an Austrian review of the French book *La superiorité des Anglo-Saxons*, in which the reader was once more reminded of the blessings of British playgrounds: 'And what John has done as a boy for his form, his school, and his university, that he will do as a man for his native land out in Africa and Asia: he fights. [32]

Nevertheless, Balck and Hovgaard were more sincere than most of their contemporaries in northern Europe in this admiration of public school athleticism. It was not only that without hesitation they were in favour of this kind of bodily discipline and therefore were ready to replace a considerable part of established gymnastics exercises with games and other sports. Both of them were absorbed by the idea that it was the competitive moment and the open, often aggressive confrontation between the pupils that was the secret behind the character-forming function of sport. Furthermore, neither of them was seriously interested in the religious dimensions of British athleticism, the muscular Christianity which, as we remember, had such a strong impact on more contemplative men such as the Finn Heikel. And this was most probably a consequence of the fact that Balck and Hovgaard were men of action who were strongly attracted by Social Darwinian motives, which could be found beneath the thin layers of Stoic and Christian ideals in British athleticism.

Balck's life is a fascinating chapter in Nordic sport history, which, although thoroughly outlined in Swedish research, [33] is worth recapitulating briefly in this context. We observe how as a school teacher in the 1880s he introduced sports to school youth in Stockholm, how his popular writings were spread to neighbouring Nordic countries during the last two decades of the nineteenth century, and how by the turn of the century he had become the leading figure in the Nordic sports movement. However, it is of special interest to note here that Balck was strongly influenced by his compatriot the physiologist Frithiof Holmgren, who used evolutionary metaphors in his energetic campaign in favour of bodily exercises and outdoor games. [34] The point here is that Balck through Holmgren had become familiar with Social Darwinian thinking before he arrived in Britain and became directly acquainted with sport in the public schools. Balck was mentally prepared to find ideological motives in the brutal side of British sporting culture and was in this sense actually in the same situation as Heikel, who, although as a true Christian had fixed his eyes above all upon the more the idealistic side of athleticism, had seen what he wanted to see. [35]

The Social Darwinian approach played an important role in Balck's thinking throughout his life and seems to have been especially strong in his promotion of sport as a character-forming exercise. He was a true admirer of Anglo-Saxon culture and like most of his Nordic sport-advocating colleagues was convinced by those who claimed that the character-strengthening outdoor life of the public schools was one of the secrets behind the supposed efficiency of the British Empire. As a consequence of this he seldom missed a chance to emphasize the state-building function of the Swedish sports movement. However, he was equally fascinated by the more individualistic motives and desires of the sporting. He defended, on different occasions, matches, competitions and other forms of open confrontation between teams as well as between individuals, and easily found reasons for celebrating prize-winners. According to Balck the British example was the best evidence that competitive sport was an excellent preparation for the inevitable struggles of life. The defeats and victories on the sports fields were not only outstanding lessons in the education of the survival of the fittest; they taught youth that there was no contradiction in playing the game and still nourishing egoistic desires for fame and success. [36]

Interestingly enough, Balck was carried away with the idea that individual sports had an even stronger impact on the character than team games. The team could be a shelter, whereas personal competition forced individuals to take complete responsibility for their own actions. [37] This interpretation of the moral dynamics of sports was in fact not in line with British athleticism, which essentially was a cult of the games ethos; neither was it in line with the principles of most of his Nordic physical education colleagues who, as we remember, were suspicious of the educational value of both limitless competition and individual rewards. It seems therefore often more accurate to understand Balck's notion of the character-forming functions of sport in conjunction with the growing pragmatism and individualism that was characteristic of both the European and North American sport cultures at the turn of the century. [38] He frequently used an idealized interpretation of the British games ethos in his speeches and articles but showed in practice much more interest in result-oriented enterprises such as the Olympic Games and the organizational consolidation of the Swedish sports movement. Put slightly differently, it could be said that Balck's active involvement in the expanding sports movement was both motivated and inspired by the Social Darwinian component of his world-view; he believed in the evolutionary necessity of human selfishness and saw no reason why this force should be neglected in education.

Balck was for these reasons something of an outsider among his Nordic colleagues in the educational field at the turn of the century, but he had many allies in North Europe who had accepted the open competitiveness of the growing sports movement and saw it as an efficient way to strengthen individual characters. One of the most radical representatives of the latter category, which we briefly mentioned earlier, was the Danish submarine constructor William Hovgaard (1857–1950), who after studies in England at the Royal Naval College in Greenwich between 1883 and 1886 [39] returned to Copenhagen and began to promote British sports as a superior form of physical preparation for bourgeois manhood. Like many of his contemporaries, Hovgaard compared healthy and well-behaved British public school youth with secondary school boys in his hometown, whom he accused of being both anaemic and weak characters.

Hovgaard's conclusions were as such not original; he claimed like many others that a too-extensive intellectual curriculum and shortcomings in physical education in the secondary school transformed Danish upper- and middle-class boys into lame civil servants who never would survive in free competition between individuals or as conquerors of colonies 'where no government or family could give a helping hand'. [40] Yet it is apparent that he was one of the few Nordic promoters of the British public school model of physical education who saw sport entirely as a way of strengthening individual characters and not as a function of state building. Hovgaard was thereby more Social Darwinian than Herbert Spencer himself, who often emphasized that cooperation, persuasion and altruism were essential social skills in advanced industrialized societies. [41]

V

The Social Darwinian interpretation of the social function of sports could not apparently play a specially significant role in the debates about physical education in the Nordic countries. It was too unsociable and not in line with the dominant educational outlook among Nordic secondary-school teachers, who were trained to pay attention to the cultivation of pupils' social responsibility and obedience to the state apparatus. Sport was advocated as a character-forming activity by a number of Nordic educationists, especially between 1880 and 1920, but it was only exceptions such as Balck or educational laymen such as Hovgaard who on the practical level promoted sport in schools as a moral and physical preparation for selfish competition between individuals and the harsh struggle for survival.

Most of those who spoke in favour of more sports in the curriculum saw these activities above all as an efficient form of exercise in social interaction and cooperation. [42] This was the case with influential men such as the Swede Carl Svedelius, headmaster and school sport promoter, who from 1910 onwards often emphasized that sport could improve internal solidarity within schools and develop responsible citizens. [43] This was also the case with many other Nordic educationists who during the 1920s and 1930s emphasized the positive function of sports; Tahko Pihkala, a skilful sports organizer famous for his invention of a Finnish variant of American baseball, wrote for example in 1927 that games and other competitive exercises were superior to gymnastics because of their stronger impact on pupils' sense of social responsibility, [44] whereas his Norwegian colleague Hans Hegna in 1931 was eager to point out that juvenile delinquency in Christiania/Oslo had decline markedly since the town had built in the 1910s a number of public playgrounds. [45]

It is also of interest to note that the ideological vocabulary and arguments used in favour of physical education were renewed and acquired new nuances during the inter-war period. For example, the idea of sports as a character-building activity suitable especially for bourgeois youth lost a lot of its credibility when the concept of character began to be over-used within the educational debate and gave way to other educational keywords such as personality, which, in contrast to the concept of character, first and last contained the idea of a self-knowledge and self-fulfilment. [46]

The philosophical notion of personality was by no means new. It had been used already by the Stoics to signify the innermost nature of the individual human and obtained a steady metaphysical foundation in the Christian interpretation of the person as a rational substance, indivisible and individual. [47] It emerged in educational discourse in a more concentrated form during the Age of Enlightenment and had a central position in Wilhelm von Humboldt's neo-humanistic *Bildungsideal* which, as we remember, was the dominant ideological foundation of Nordic secondary education up until the twentieth century. Yet is apparent that the Humboldtian ideal of *Bildung* as a harmonious 'process of self-becoming of the individual' and thereby a fully developed personality [48] played only a minor role in

Nordic educational practice before the First World War. Bourgeois schooling in essence was a form of cultural reproduction and as such emphasized the formal dimension of neo-humanism. As a corollary of this, the concept of personality did not have a very significant function to perform in the Nordic educational vocabulary before the 1920s.

However, from the 1920s onwards the increasing use of the concept of personality in Nordic educational literature and debate was not only a sign of the weakening impact of neo-humanistic formalism. It was also a sign of a more psychological approach to the educational process; most Nordic educationists probably did not open a single book by Freud and yet they were all in one way or another influenced by his theories of the unconscious and the fragile relationship between sexuality and social order.

This trend, the increasing concern among educationists with the different layers of the human psyche, was not surprisingly less explicit in a subject such as physical education, but it is still possible to point to a certain element in professional debates which was indicative of such attitude changes. We mentioned the slackening impact of the argument of sports as a character-forming activity. The argument was at first regularly used by educationists but was more and more overshadowed by medical arguments in favour of physical exercises. [49] It is true that the health aspect always had played an important role in the promotion of physical education and that it was strengthened each time scientists found new evidence for a positive correlation between exercise and health. Yet it is also true that medical discoveries played only a minor role in the Nordic debate about physical education before the third decade of the twentieth century. The professionals did not have the required scientific knowledge and were to a too large extent occupied with disciplinary issues or absorbed by the idea of physical education as a form of character training. However, the situation began to change in all four countries during the 1920s; teacher training became more science-oriented at the same time as the physicians were offered a more central role in the debate. [50]

The growing emphasis on hygienic and physiological questions in fact could been seen as a rational consequence of the social transformation of Western cultures which, to follow Norbert Elias, can be analysed as a civilizing process. [51] In other words, the systematization and modernization of physical education may be interpreted as a move from an emphasis on the external discipline of bourgeois youth, in the form of military drill and collective gymnastics, towards a more refined outlook on the individual cultivation of the body, in which discipline was understood as a physiological and also as a psychological process. [52]

This is not to say that the fundamental motive for physical education for the schoolboys in question changed markedly between 1860 and 1930; the aim throughout the period was to discipline the body and make it a strong and healthy servant of the individual soul, which again was trained to be an obedient citizen and hard-working state builder. However, the point is that an increasingly scientific approach made Nordic educationists aware of the fact that discipline became more efficient and total if outward control was achieved through a self-imposed restraint of the body and the emotions. For example, hygiene campaigns and improvements in schools were not only an attempt to improve pupils' health. They were also an ideological and moral undertaking; the hygienic principle accustomed pupils to think in terms of bodily isolation and individual refinement and was therefore an excellent way to develop their self-control and bourgeois personality. [53]

The application of medical innovations and interpretations led also to the re-evaluation of established justifications for certain exercises in physical education. The most famous example of this development is probably the dispute between the Danes K.A. Knudsen and Johannes Lindhard, which poisoned professional dialogue in Denmark during the 1910s and 1920s. Knudsen, an energetic physical education inspector who had been trained at the GCI in Stockholm, was a sworn advocate of Swedish gymnastics and as such convinced of its rationality and 'scientific' basis. He was therefore almost obliged to stand up and defend Hjalmar Ling's dogmas when they were questioned as untenable by Lindhard, professor of physiology at Copenhagen University between 1917 and 1935, who was responsible for the theoretical training of student teachers in physical education.

The dispute was also rooted in personal antagonism, which in a way explains why it ended in a complicated law suit, but in this context it will be examined entirely as an issue of principle. Lindhard was strongly opposed to Knudsen's claim that the formalism of Swedish gymnastics could be justified from a physiological point of view. He emphasized on many occasions that the 'Swedish system' was nothing but a collection of postures and saw therefore no reason why they should be understood as especially rational or health promoting. For example, Lindhard challenged the very heart of Ling's method by stressing that a straight back and a good carriage were only outward gestures which were by no means healthy as such or physiologically functional. [54] It is not an exaggeration to claim that Lindhard's arguments were more convincing than Knudsen's defensive replies. Lindhard could base his claims on empirical evidence – in contrast to Knudsen, who had only external observations and his Swedish authorities to lean back on – and was an active scientist, up to date with the new and more psychological approaches in contemporary educational thinking. In addition, Lindhard was an eager proponent of physical activities such as rhythmic gymnastics and outdoor sports that were not only less formal and more energy-consuming but also intellectually more stimulating than the 'Swedish system'. [55]

The dispute was not just a quarrel between two strong minds. It was a confrontation between two forceful physical education ideologies. And as such it highlighted some of the main characteristics of the debate that occurred in connection with a move from an emphasis on outward discipline and character training towards a more genuine physiological, health-promoting approach to the cultivation of the body. Firstly, it showed to what extent the image of physical education was dependent on how the notion of bodily discipline and health was defined. Secondly, it illustrated how strongly chosen definitions could dictate and dominate the professional debate. And thirdly, it revealed how little the academic disputes and ideological confrontations were determined by factual problems and circumstances in the gymnasiums and playgrounds.

Knudsen defended not an educational practice but an idealistic principle; physical education in Danish secondary schools was not yet fully organized according to an outspoken didactic system, although Knudsen claimed differently, and was anyhow not in line with his 'Swedish' model. Sports and other less formal activities continued to gain more space in education during the inter-war period and thereby made the whole quarrel over the rationality of the 'Swedish system' somewhat irrelevant at a practical level. [56] Lindhard's arguments were often equally academic; he demanded a physical education based on scientific know-how but did not have the patience to test how this should be carried out in practice.

VI

In essence, it should be emphasized that the arguments used in the propagation of physical education for Nordic secondary-school boys were strongly influenced by the changing values of bourgeois education and an evolving notion of the ideal of manliness. The early emphasis on the disciplinary function of collective gymnastics did not merely have a military basis; throughout the nineteenth century drill was believed to mould bourgeois youth into an obedient and hard-working class of servants of the state. It is clear that the later campaign in favour of school sports as a more efficient way of building character was influenced by the more individualistic and action-oriented manliness ideal of the late nineteenth century. Furthermore, it is apparent that during the twentieth century the move towards a more health- and hygiene-conscious advocacy of physical education should be seen in the context of the growing attention paid to scientific understanding in the bourgeois world-view.

Taken together, it was not so much the need for discipline, character and health as such that inspired Nordic educationists to promote various forms of physical exercise for secondary-school pupils, but above all the belief that these exercises prepared this exclusive youth for its bourgeois manhood and its future obligations as honourable citizens.

Notes

[1] Hartmut Kaelble, *Social Mobility in the 19th and 20th Centuries: Europe and America in Comparative Perspective* (Lemington Spa: Berg Publishers Ltd, 1985), Tables 2.1, 2.2, 2.3, 2.7, 2.8, 2.11. See also following statistics: *Statistisk årsbok för Finland. Ny serie. VIII. Utgiven av statistiska centralbyrån* (Helsingfors, 1910), Table 220; Vagn Skovgaard-Petersen, *Dannelse og demokrati: fra latin- til almenskole: lov om høiere almenskoler 24 april 1903* (København: Gyldendalske-boghandel, 1976), Table VII. Unsurprisingly, the recruitment of children from the established bourgeoisie was especially strong in the Nordic capitals. In Copenhagen, for example, the bourgeois background of secondary-school pupils became more dominant between 1844 and 1899; see Cordt Trap, *Københavnske Skolebørns fordelning efter Skolernes art*

og Forældrernes samfundsstilling (København: Københavns Kommunalbesty-selse, 1900–14), Tables F and G.

[2] The concept of *Bürgertum*, as all historical terms, has its different and contradictory dimensions. For more detail, see Jürgen Kocka, 'Bürgertum und Bürgerlichkeit als Probleme der deutschen Geschichte vom späten 18 Jahrhundert bis 1848/49', in Jürgen Kocka (hg.), *Bürger und Bürgerlichkeit im 19. Jahrhundert* (Göttingen: Vandenhoeck and Rupsecht, 1987), pp.21–63.

[3] Peter Gay, *The Bourgeois Experience*, Volume 1 (New York: Oxford University Press, 1984), pp.18–44.

[4] Nicholas Abercrombie, Stephen Hill and Bryan S. Turner, *The Penguin Dictionary of Sociology* (London: Penguin Books, 1988), p.59.

[5] See for example Håkan Andersson, *Kampen om det förflutna. Studier i historieundervisningens målfrågor i Finland 1843–1917* (Åbo: Åbo Akademi, 1979).

[6] Roberta J. Park, 'Biological Thought, Athletics and the Formation of a "Man of character": 1830–1900', in J.A. Mangan and James Walvin (eds.), *Manliness and Morality: Middle-class Masculinity in Britain and America 1800–1940* (Manchester: Manchester University Press, 1987), p.29.

[7] Jonas Frykman and Orvar Löfgren, *Den kultiverade människan* (Lund: Liber Lärsmedel, 1981), pp.184–98.

[8] Bode Janzon, *Manchettyrken, idrott och hälsa. Studier kring idrottsrörelsen i Sverige, särskilt Göteborg, intill 1900* (Göteborg: Göteborgs universitet, 1978), pp.76–84.

[9] Ibid., pp.78–9.

[10] Ibid., pp.39–51; Frykman and Löfgren, *Den kultiverade människan*, pp.200–4; Henrik Meinander, *Towards a Bourgeois Manhood: Boys' Physical Education in Nordic Secondary Schools 1880–1940* (Helsinki: The Finnish Society of Science and Letters, 1994), pp.216–22.

[11] Gay, *The Bourgeois Experience*, pp.188–97, 328–402.

[12] Hans Bonde, 'Den hurtige mand. Mandsidealer i den tidlige danske sportbevægelse', *Historisk Tidskrift* [Denmark], 1 (1988), 128–51.

[13] Maxwell Staniforth, 'Introduction', in Marcus Aurelius, *Meditations* (Hammondsworth: Penguin Books, 1969), pp.23–7.

[14] Gay, *The Bourgeois Experience*; this motive was apparent also in the education of Nordic upper-class girls during the second half of nineteenth century. See Angela Rundquist, *Blått blod och liljevita händer. En etnologisk studie av aristokratiska kvinnor 1850–1900* (Stockholm: Carlsson, 1989), pp.48–84.

[15] For a valuable analysis of the formation of distinct gender identities in Swedish secondary schools, see Christina Florin and Ulla Johansson, '*Där de härliga lagrarna gro...*'. *Kultur, klass och kön i det svenska läroverket 1850–1914* (Stockholm: Tiden, 1993), pp.105–43.

[16] T.J. Hartelius, 'Kroppsöfningarna såsom ett hufvudsakligt vilkor för helsa, kraft och skönhet', *Tidskrift i Gymnastik*, 1874, 18–21. The original version of the sentence is as follows: 'Den gifver tukt och säkerhet i hållning, spänstighet i kraft och smidighet i rörelsen' (21).

[17] For a more thorough analysis of the theme of bodily grammar, see Meinander, *Towards a Bourgeois Manhood*, pp.147–56.

[18] T.J. Hartelius, 'Gymnastikens betydelse för allmän värnepligt', *Tidskrift i Gymnastik*, 1875, 166.

[19] Viktor Heikel, 'Om kroppsöfningarne i England, ungdomens och karakterernas land', *Hufvudstadsbladet*, 292 (1870).

[20] Seneca, *Letters from a Stoic* (*Epistulae Morales ad Lucilium*), selected and translated with an introduction by Robin Campbell (Hammondsworth: Penguin Books, 1974), letters XXVII and XXVIII.

[21] Warren Susman, '"Personality" and the Making of Twentieth-century Culture', in John Higham and Paul K. Conkin (eds.), *New Directions in American Intellectual History* (Baltimore and London: John Hopkins University Press, 1979), p.214.

[22] Viktor Heikel, 'Manlighet eller veklighet. Svar till Hr R.A. angående "gymnastikens faror"', *Nya Pressen*, 6,6 (1891).

[23] Viktor Heikel, 'Om den engelsk-amerikanska söndagskolan, en frihetens grundpelare', *Helsingfors Dagblad*, 22–23 Jan. 1871.

[24] J.A. Mangan, *Athleticism in the Victorian and Edwardian Public School. The emergence of an Educational Ideology* (Cambridge: Cambridge University Press, 1981), pp.43–58.

[25] See Heikel's diary from this trip and correspondence with his family, 1871: Suomen urheiluarkisto, Helsinki, Viktor Heikels arkiv, kansio I.

[26] J.A. Mangan, 'Social Darwinism and Upper-class Education in Late Victorian and Edwardian England', in J.A. Mangan and James Walvin (eds.), *Manliness and Morality: Middle-class Masculinity in Britain and America 1800–1940* (Manchester: Manchester University Press, 1987), p.139.

[27] Viktor Heikel, 'Idrott men inte rekordjakt! Ett upprop till våra gymnastik- och idrottsföreningar' (Öfvertryck ur *Hufvudstadsbladet*, 1903).

[28] L.M. Törngren, *Fria lekar. Anvisning till skolans tjenst. På offentligt uppdrag* (Stockholm, 1879), pp.1–27; L.M. Törngren, 'Reseberättelse. Några iakttagelser angående den kroppsliga utbildningen i Engelska skolor', *Tidskrift i Gymnastik*, 1890, 145–89.

[29] Many of Törngren's strongest supporters were to be found in Denmark. See K.A. Knudsen, *Om Sport. Indtryk fra en reise i England* (København: I hovedkommission hors J. Frimodt, 1895), pp.40–50; R. Rasmussen and B. Kjølner, *Vor Skolegymnastik kontra Skoleidrætsstævner* (København: [eget förlag], 1903).

[30] Riksarkivet, Stockholm, L.M.Törngrens arkiv, Kapsell 14, LXVIII: Manuskript till sakkunnigeutlåtande till Kungl. Öfverstyrelsen för rikets allmänna läroverk 1908.

[31] David Birley, 'Bonaparte and the Squire: Chauvinism, Virility and Sport in the Period of the French Wars', in J.A. Mangan (ed.), *Pleasure, Profit, Proselytism: British Culture and Sport at Home and Abroad 1700–1914* (London: Frank Cass, 1988), p.28.

[32] Leon Kellner, 'Engelsk ungdom', *Den höiere skole* (Kristiania), 1899, 133–4 (author's translation).

[33] See above all Jan Lindroth, *Idrottens väg till folkrörelse. Studier i svensk idrottsrörelse fram till 1915* (Uppsala: Acta Universitatis Upsaliensis, 1974); Henrik Sandblad, *Olympia och Valhalla, Idéhistoriska aspekter av den moderna idrottsrörelsens framväxt* (Stockholm: Almqvist and Wiksell, 1985).

[34] This influence is profoundly analysed by Sandblad, *Olympia och Valhalla*, pp.159–72, 216–25, 241–3.

[35] For instance, Balck was acquainted with boxing culture England in 1898 and defended it – although he admitted that it was a raw exercise – as one of the most typical British character-building sports: Riksarkivet, Stockholm, V.G. Balcks arkiv, Vol. 1, Sveriges Centralförening för Idrottens befrämjande, Manuskript till texten 'Minnen från Englandsresan 1898'.

[36] Viktor Balck, 'Om idrott och kropppsövningar i uppfostrans tjänst', *Sjunde nordiska skolmötet i Stockholm den 6., 7. och 8. augusti 1895* (Stockholm: Vart Canal, 1896), pp.199–219.

[37] Riksarkivet, Stockholm, V.G. Balcks arkiv, Vol.2, Sveriges Centralförening för Idrottens befrämjande; Två odaterade manuskript till föredraget 'Om kroppsöfningarnas betydelse för karaktersdaningen såsom ett medel att höja folks lifskraft'.

[38] Roberta J. Park, 'Sport, Gender and Society in a Trasatlantic Victorian Perspective', in J.A. Mangan and Roberta J. Park (eds.), *From 'Fair Sex' to Feminism: Sport and Socialization of Women in the Industrial and Post-Industrial Eras* (London: Frank Cass, 1987), p.68.

[39] Hovgaard (1857–1950) eventually made a successful career in the US Navy forces. His submarine and ship construction had a decisive impact with the North American Navy during the First World War.

[40] William Hovgaard, *Sundhed eller Kunskaber. Nogle Bidrag til Spørgsmaalet om Ungdommens Opdragelse* (Kjøbenhavn: [eget förlag] 1886), pp.12–19: the translated quotation is from page 17. See also William Hovgaard, *Sport* (Kjøbenhavn: [eget förlag], 1888), pp.30–4.

[41] Herbert Spencer, *Essays on Education* (London: Menp, 1939), pp.84–152.

[42] See Riksarkivet, Stockholm, Sveriges riksidrottsförbunds arkiv: Gymnastik- och idrottskommitténs protokoll 11.2.1914, ÖIi:3.

[43] Henrik Meinander, 'Karaktärsdaning framförallt! En skiss av Carl Svedelius, pedagog och idrottsideolog av nordiska mått', in *Svenska idrottshistoriska föreningens årsskrift 1991* (Stockholm: Svenska idrottshistoriska Föreningens 1991), pp.85–102.

[44] Lauri Pihkala, 'Mietteitä liikuntakasvatuksesta ja varsinkin voimistelusta biologian valossa', in *Liikuntakasvatuksen työmailta. Voimisteluopettajaliiton julkaisu II* (Porvoo: WSOY, 1927), pp.33–54.

[45] Hans Hegna, 'Lekeplass-spørgsmålet i Oslo', in *VI Nordiska kongressen för skolungdomens fysiska fostran i Stockholm den 12–16 september 1931* (Stockholm: [eget förlag], 1932), pp.46–8.

[46] Susman, '"Personality" and the Making of Twentieth-century Culture', p.220.

[47] Marcel Mauss, 'A Category of Human Mind: The Notion of Person; The Notion of Self', in Michael Carrithers, Steve Collins and Steven Lukes (eds.), *The Category of the Person: Anthropology, Philosophy, History* (Cambridge: Cambridge University Press, 1985), pp.18–20.

[48] Harvey Goldman, *Max Weber and Thomas Mann: Calling and Shaping of the Self* (Berkeley, CA: University of California Press, 1988), pp.125–8.

[49] The change happened naturally slowly and it is therefore difficult to point to specific documents, writings or books that would have functioned as a breakthrough for the new paradigm. However, a glance through Nordic physical education journals and conference reports from the 1910s and 1920s gives an idea of the transformation. See for example *Tidskrift i Gymnastik* (Sweden), *Gymnastisk Tidskrift* (Denmark) and *Koulu ja Kasvatus* (Finland).

[50] Meinander, *Towards a Bourgeois Manhood*, pp.215–16.

[51] Norbert Elias and Eric Dunning, *Quest for Excitement: Sport and Leisure in the Civilizing Process* (Oxford: Blackwell, 1986), pp.126–49.

[52] For a systematic application of Elias's theory of the civilizing process on Nordic material, see Claes Ekenstam, *Kroppens idéhistoria. Disciplinering och karaktärsdaning i Sverige 1700–1950* (Stockholm, 1993).

[53] Lars-Henrik Schmidt and Jens Erik Kristensen, *Lys, luft og renlighed. Den moderne socialhygiejnes fødsel* (Viborg: Akademisk Förlag, 1986), pp.82–115.

[54] Ove Korsgaard, *Kampen om kroppen. Dansk idræts historie gennem 200 år* (København: Gyldendal, 1982), pp.182–6.

[55] Johannes Lindhard, *Den specielle Gymnastikteori* (København: [Tryk som manuskript], 1914).

[56] Meinander, *Towards a Bourgeois Manhood*, pp.166–172, 204.

Closing the Circle: Sponsorship and the Greek Olympic Games from Ancient Times to the Present Day [1]

Penelope Kissoudi

Donors and Games in Ancient Athens and Olympia

Artistic and athletic events were an integral part of life in ancient Greece. Sponsorship (*choregia*), which dates back to the fifth century BC, became essential to the promotion of these cultural activities and increasingly became the sine qua non for the economic and cultural development of the city of Athens. Wealthy citizens of the ten tribes [2] of the city financed dramatic competitions, public festivities and rituals as an indication of active concern for society in general and culture in particular. The *choregia* was one of a number of public responsibilities (*leitourgiai*) which were established and introduced in ancient Athens in the fifth century BC. It took the form of a involuntary direct tax on wealthy citizens, replacing taxes that had been suspended after the Kleisthenes reforms. [3] The *leitourgiai* (which increasingly became indicative of success in the economic reconstruction of Athens) were divided into two categories: the 'ordinary' and 'extraordinary'. The 'ordinary *leitourgiai*' included *choregia* which involved the financing of the chorus that participated in dramatic and lyric contests and financial support for dramatic performances. There were various other taxes. The *gymnasiarchia* involved the financing of the athletes' preparation for competitions, and there was the funding of the meals offered to the members of a tribe at public festivities, which was called *hestiasis*. [4] *Architheoria* covered the payment of the expenses of the Athenian delegation to the cult ceremonies that took place on the island of Delos. The participation of the young in torch races was financed by the *lampadarchia* or *lampadedromia*. The 'extraordinary' public responsibilities included the *trierarchia*, which was concerned with the manning and maintenance of a trireme and was considered the most costly responsibility of all. [5] The sponsors were held in especially high esteem. Their name was inscribed on a marble slab. Those who lavishly financed cultural and athletic events were entitled to erect a monument in commemoration of the winners. It should not be overlooked that not infrequently their enthusiasm for both sport and culture motivated many sponsors to offer considerable amounts of money to finance the events voluntarily. [6]

The sites of the games such as Olympia, Delphi, Nemea and Isthmus became over time the stage where one city displayed its supremacy over the others, and the treaties agreed between two or more cities were officially announced. The sacred pan-Hellenic site at Olympia, to which official embassies and many people came from all over the Greek world every four years, provided opportunities for various activities that had political implications. State documents were not infrequently deposited with the wardens of Olympia and treaties were inscribed in bronze or stone plaques and publicly displayed. The treasure-houses of the early period, and later the statues and endowed buildings, publicized both cities and monarchs. [7] For this reason, kings and the well-to-do chose the sites of the ancient games to flaunt their riches and display personal generosity or political power. [8]

In Athens in the sixth and fifth centuries BC citizens took a keen interest in athletics and education, which were closely linked to each other. In addition, there was a deep-rooted belief that impressive public buildings and utilities characterized the mature city and differentiated it from immature cities. Well-constructed streets, water-works, sewage systems, public libraries, temples and gymnasiums were all seen as indisputable evidence of progress and prosperity. Lycourgos was treasurer of Athens between the years 338 and 337 BC. [9] The descendant of an eminent family of priests, he revered tradition, led an austere life and was relentlessly opposed to those who offended against the moral order. Due to Lycourgos's efforts Athens acquired new defences and was embellished with impressive public buildings. His renovation of the Theatre of Dionysus and the replacement of its wooden seats by stone seats were intended to improve both the site of dramatic performances and the city of Athens. [10]

More significantly, it is believed that he personally provided money for the construction of a stadium in 330/29 BC to hold race contests, which took place at the ancient Agora of Athens during the 'Big Panathenaia' festival. [11] The stadium was on an ideal site between two hills and by the Ilissos river. The field for the construction of the stadium had been granted to Athens by an Athenian called Deinias. Modelled on earlier Greek stadiums, the new stadium, under the name Panathenaikon Stadium, was a plain construction, consisting of the track events field (*dromos*) and stone tiers. [12] Lycourgos was not alone in his generosity. Financial support of the games and lavish donations to their sites of competition frequently attested to the donor's affluence. The more famous the games, the more people saw and admired the donation. Therefore it was no coincidence that many donors offered Olympia money and precious offerings in preference to other sites in an attempt to maximize their social standing. The sites of the games, especially Olympia, clearly benefited and became endowed with imposing buildings and sports facilities. [13]

The earliest donor to Olympia whom the archaeologists have identified with any certainty was Leonidas, [14] a wealthy architect from the isle of Naxos. In about 330 BC, Leonidas financed the 'Leonideion', an edifice with spacious apartments and dining rooms, which was named after its donor and was erected in the western part of Olympia. It had rooms on all four sides facing inwards into a 'peristyle' court with Doric columns. The building was surrounded on the outside by an Ionic colonnade. Initially, the Leonideion was intended to accommodate official guests and distinguished visitors. In the Roman era it was converted into a dwelling for officials. With measurements of approximately 82 by 89 yards, the impressive building, which surpassed in area all the other buildings on the site, provided extremely comfortable accommodation. [15]

Mostly, the demonstration of political power was the motive for beneficence to Olympia. The lavish gifts of the Macedonian kings to the games were typical examples of the desire for the ostentatious display of political power and associated statement of supremacy over other Greek cities. [16] After the Battle of Chaironeia (338 BC), which resulted in subjugation of the Greek cities to Philip II, the powerful Macedonian king, who had already made a vow to Zeus to erect a memorial at Olympia and embellish the site of the games if he was victorious, decided to keep his vow. Two years after the battle, however, Philip II was assassinated. Nonetheless, in 335 BC the intention of the dead king was implemented by his son and successor Alexander the Great. Alexander financed the 'Philippeion', a magnificent circular building, which stood on a marble stepped base (most of which has been preserved) and had a row of Ionic columns around it. The wall of the circular cellar was divided by columns in the Corinthian style and inside it, opposite the door, five statues situated on a semicircular pedestal and made of gold and ivory depicted Alexander between his parents and forefathers. [17] The donation did not simply demonstrate exhibitionism and egocentricity but also ambition. The Macedonian king wished to link his name with the most important athletic event of ancient times and an integral part of the religious and cultural life of the Greeks. [18] Moreover, it is believed that the construction of a colonnade at Olympia was financed by Alexander the Great. [19] There was a hundred-yard-long colonnade, whose foundations and stairs resembled the Philippeion in their decorative aspects. It faced the altar's square and was designed to replace the mound on the western side of the stadium. The new construction, which was intended to improve the spectators' stand, was left uncompleted for many centuries. Possibly administrators of the sanctuary of Olympia urged Alexander to finance it. Work on the colonnade stopped abruptly due to the early death of Alexander. Friction among the heirs that followed his death led to the withdrawal of funds. The construction was finally completed much later by Roman financiers. [20]

In the third century BC, the Ptolemies of Egypt endowed Olympia with impressive buildings and simultaneously supported the games with self-effacing enthusiasm. Although statues of members of the dynasty were placed at Olympia as a token of gratitude for their donations, the Ptolemies as benefactors of the games avoided any public display of exhibitionism and self-glorification. They shunned publicity. Ptolemy II, the 'Benefactor' (285–247 BC) financed a gymnasium in Athens while the 'Palaistra', a magnificent building on the western side of the sanctuary of Olympia, was constructed thanks to the donation of Ptolemy in about 270 BC. [21] The commander of the Ptolemies' fleet was ostensibly the donor. For this reason, he visited Olympia and publicly expressed his reverential devotion by financing a building as a gift to the site of the games. Then, in the second century BC and especially in about 175 BC, Olympia and other Greek cities benefited from the generosity of Antiochus VI (175–164 BC), a perspicacious politician and capable military governor. Antiochus VI not only supported the games, but also provided for the construction of defensive walls, temples, theatres and other public buildings. [22]

Roman Donors and the Games

The Roman occupation of Greece marked the decline of the ancient games. Following the subjection of Greece by the Romans in 146 BC, in the wake of general economic and social decline most of the local games ceased to be held and the pan-Hellenic competitions fell into decay. Nevertheless, two factors contributed to the preservation of sport. The first was the great reputation the pan-Hellenic competitions had gained over the course of time. The second was the preservation of the gymnasium, which had become a cultural institution. After the Roman occupation of Greece, the Greeks continued to meet at gymnasiums and be involved in sport and various cultural activities. [23]

Until the reign of the Roman Emperor Gaius Julius Octavian Augustus (29 BC – AD 14), little interest was taken in sport by the Romans. As a result of the decline of the games, Lucius Cornelius Sulla, the powerful Roman general, was able to plunder the treasures of Olympia to secure money for his campaign against Mithridates during the Second Mithridatian War (83 BC). Furthermore, in 80 BC Sulla transferred the Olympic Games to Rome to celebrate his military triumphs and forced the athletes to compete for the Romans' amusement. [24] The pan-Hellenic games suffered a serious blow: they lost the fame they had gained over the course of time. Games were now held only between regional cities, losing, at least temporarily, the pan-Hellenic character that differentiated them from other athletic events. [25] In time, however, Roman emperors who admired Hellenic civilization, such as Hadrian (AD 117–138) and Antoninus (AD 138–161) ensured the traditional games were once again promoted. [26]

Olympia thus rediscovered its glory. The majestic temple of Zeus and other buildings were restored and the organization of the games was considerably improved. Athletes came eagerly from all over the known world. In addition, Roman emperors and eminent citizens financed gymnasiums and baths in Greek cities and elsewhere, derelict stadiums were renovated and damaged sports facilities were repaired. Simultaneously, new games were established throughout the Roman Empire and many of these were named after the pan-Hellenic Games. For example, the Pythian Games, which traditionally took place at Delphi, moved to Philippopolis in Thrace and in Cilicia (Asia Minor), the Nemean Games, which had been held only in Peloponnese, now occurred in both Achialos in Thrace and Aetna in Sicily. Games under the name 'Olympic' were founded in Cyrene in North Africa and in Smyrna, while the Isthmian Games, which had previously been held only in Corinth in Peloponnese, were established in Ankara and Syracuse. Furthermore, in AD 86 the Emperor Domitianus founded the quadrennial Capitoline Games in Rome while Antoninus Pius established games at Puteoli in the Bay of Naples in AD 138, in honour of the deceased Hadrian. Not all these competitions had the same longevity. Some were held only as long as the emperor in whose honour they were established lived. [27]

The reign of the Roman Emperor Hadrian (AD 117–138) and that of his successor Antoninus Pius (AD 138–161) marked, to an extent, the revival of the ancient games in Greece. Hadrian's munificence demonstrated his interest in Greek cities' religious and cultural traditions. As soon as he assumed the city's highest magistracy *in absentia*, he restored old buildings or completed unfinished edifices on which work had begun long before the Roman occupation of the region. In the wake of this policy, the games at Olympia flourished and Olympia was again flooded with visitors. Athletes and spectators, with their families and trainers, the priesthood and participants in cult ceremonies, again flocked to the most celebrated of athletic locations. The stadium was extended and numerous statues and precious offerings were donated. [28] Hadrian seemed to recognize the important role of sport in the socio-political life of the Roman Empire in general and its contribution to the weaving of an attractive myth around the emperor in particular. For this reason, athletic events took place in many cities of the Roman Empire, such as in Pergamos, Halikarnassos, Sardis and elsewhere without, however, equalling the ancient games in reputation. In addition, the ceremonies that preceded the contests, were relatively insipid spectacles. [29]

Although the competitions seemed to thrive in the Roman era, the newly established games, for various reasons, did not gain the same fame as the games of the classical times. Augustus established the 'Actia Games' at Actium, for example, to commemorate his victory over Anthony. He set a bad precedent. [29] To flatter the Emperor, vassal cities vied with each other to establish competitions named after him. In addition, in the reign of Augustus, the Romanus Sebastinica, Iso-Olympia Games were established in Naples in Italy early in the first century AD and were held every four years. They initially included athletic and equestrian events, but in the course of time embraced musical and dramatic competitions. Several athletic events took place in honour of the Emperor Augustus while the 'Hadrianian Games' were sanctioned in Athens in honour of the Emperor Hadrian. [31] The cities thus established and supported the games only with the aspiration of good relations with the emperor. Cut off from their sacred origins, the newly established competitions symbolized the vassals' obsequiousness. [32]

To focus on Roman donors chronologically, in the reign of Gaius Julius Octavianus Augustus, an extensive restoration of destroyed buildings throughout the Roman Empire was initiated and new constructions were financed to foster and promote culture and sport. King Herod of Judaea in the first century BC financed new gymnasiums in the cities of Tripoles, Damascus and Ptolemaida. Beirut and Tyros saw the creation of temples and market buildings. Theatres were built in Sidon and Damascus, and water-supply reservoirs, baths and decorative fountains and colonnades were constructed in almost every city in the Eastern Mediterranean. [33] Olympia again benefited lavishly from King Herod and Marcus Agrippa I, Augustus's son-in-law and designated successor, who wielded supreme power over the provinces of the Roman Empire jointly with the Emperor. [34] The baths, on the western side of the administrative building at Olympia were financed by Herod of Judaea. In addition, an impressive construction, which surpassed the baths in splendour, dates back to the same imperial years. It seems that the colonnade, which had been left uncompleted by Alexander the Great, was finally finished with Agrippa and Herod's donations. The colonnade, called the 'Echo Portico' or 'Echo Stoa', was quickly embellished with precious offerings. [35] The new construction was modelled on an old building style, the so-called 'stoa', which dominated architectural design in the fourth century BC. It was an oblong edifice of 107 yards long with a wall on one side and a colonnade on the other. [36] The two donors, Herod of Judaea and Agrippa, were no doubt proud to finish an imposing building in honour of the Emperor Augustus, the foundations of which had been laid by Alexander the Great. [37]

Recent excavations at Olympia have unearthed a construction that is believed to have been financed by the Emperor Nero (AD 54–68). [38] The building was discovered to the south-west of Olympia and to the south of the Leonideion. Its role can be determined with some certainty: it was for use by the local athletic union or guild. [39] Guilds of performing artists, the so-called *synodoi* and athletes' unions, had been established early in ancient Greece. The athletic guilds, at first, showed no indication of an overt professionalism. In the Hellenistic era (the third century BC), many sports unions emerged in the cities of the Eastern Mediterranean. They were administered by the director, the secretary, the treasurer and the overseer of the games, the so-called *gymnasiarchos*, a title equal to that of president of an athletic association in modern times. [40]

To return to Nero's building, the conclusion that Nero had financed the building, where members of the local union at Olympia lodged, was drawn from important archaeological finds revealing stylistic similarities to buildings in Rome. [41] It seems likely that Roman builders were sent from Rome to Olympia. On the occasion of Nero's visit to Greece and his involvement in Olympia in the winter of AD 66/7, the wardens of the sanctuary of Olympia suggested that a new sporting building for the athletes' training and accommodation should be constructed for use by the local athletic union. [42] Nero agreed and work began. A little later, a conspiracy to overthrow him broke out in Rome and Nero left Olympia in haste. In June AD 68 he committed suicide. In consequence, the union building was unfinished. [43] Some years later, Lucius Vettulenus Laetus, a man of both Greek and Roman origin, undertook its completion. [44] The name of Emperor Domitian (AD 81–96) as benefactor was written on several fragments of a marble plate of AD 84, which was excavated in the ruins of the building. It seems possible that Lucius Vettulenus Laetus urged the Emperor Domitian to finance the completion of Nero's building. In appreciation, the members of the local sports union honoured Lucius Vettulenus Laetus with a statue. [45]

Roman finds in Athens provide evidence that the city became the centre of the Greco-Roman world thanks to Hadrian's admiration for Hellenic civilization, and his consequent munificence. After becoming emperor in AD 117, Hadrian visited Athens many times, made many benefactions to it and supported its festivities and games. Athens honoured its benefactor by erecting numerous statues of the emperor, including one placed on the altar of the 'eponymous' heroes in the Athenian Agora. [46] Many of Hadrian's lavish donations to Athens have been dated to his third visit in AD 131/2. It was during these years that a league of Greek cities under the name 'Panhellenion', with headquarters in Athens, was established. Hadrian attended the ceremony for the completion of the 'Olympeion', a magnificent temple consecrated to Zeus. The establishment of the 'Penteteric Panhellenian Games' in Athens is associated with the creation of the Panhellenion league. It is believed that Hadrian financed a new gymnasium as well as renovations in the Roman Agora and that he concerned himself with the revival and promotion of the Big Panathenaia festival and competitions. Thus, by the virtue of the creation of the Penteteric Panhellenian and Hadrianian Games and the promotion of the Panathenaia festival and competitions, Athens enjoyed the privilege of staging several 'sacred' games. Furthermore, the emperor re-established a double-length race for boys, a race of 710 metres that had been included in the Nemean Games but had been neglected over the course of time. [47] The fact that Hadrian had linked his name with a relatively large number of competitions clearly indicates that the Emperor was aware of the important role that public spectacle in general and sport in particular played in the Roman world. [48] Moreover, the Romans' interest in the revival of local traditions resulted from their desire to ensure that the emperor was part of the worship of gods and heroes that was typical of the Greeks in general. The games that the emperor patronized evoked both local traditions and the central power of Rome personified by the emperor and his family. In consequence, donations to the games created a bond between the emperor-donor and the local society and symbolized the Emperor's interest in sport. [49]

In the second century AD both Athens and Olympia benefited from the generosity of Herod Atticus (AD 101–177). He was an Athenian and Roman senator and consul, a friend of the Emperor Marcus Aurelius and probably the wealthiest citizen in Greece in the Roman era (see Figure 1). Among his most generous donations were a water-supply system at Olympia and the grandiosely reconstructed stadium in Athens. Herod Atticus spared no expense. Thus, the magnificent edifices he financed in Athens and Olympia still inspire admiration. [50] Herod's ancestors had accumulated a vast fortune and the family's extensive estates in Marathon in Attica, were extremely profitable. He received

Figure 1 Bust of Herod Atticus

a good education at the Philosophical School of Athens and assumed the highest public office in the city of Athens. [51] The appointment of Annia Regila, Herod's wife, as priestess of Demeter in Olympia in about AD 153, [52] stimulated both her and her husband to provide a solution to Olympia's water deficiency. The problem was worst during the summer when the great throngs of people visiting for the games made the shortage insufferable. [53] An enormous aqueduct was financed by Herod and water from a spring to the east of Olympia was channelled through pipes into the imposing 'Nymphaion'. [54] It was a semicircular construction, which had two small circular temples in front of it, one on each side. Their walls were made of baked brick and faced with coloured marble. In the niches on the face of the semicircular wall stood 20 statues, depicting Antoninus Pius and his family and the family of Herod Atticus, with a statue of Zeus prominent in the central niche. Between the two small temples, there were two cisterns on two different levels, one in front of the semicircular wall and one lower down. The water ran into the higher semicircular cistern and from there it ran into the lower rectangular one, from where it was channelled to the whole of the sanctuary by a vast network of conduits. [55]

Herod's generosity was appreciated. In about AD 143/4, he was entrusted with distributing the prizes to the winners at the Big Panathenaia festival and competitions, which were initially held every year in honour of goddess Athena, patroness of the city of Athens. From 566/5 BC, the Big Panathenaia events were scheduled to be held every four years. Ten prosperous Athenian citizens traditionally financed the athletic events, provided the winners' prizes and funded the weaving of Athena's veil on which the battle of the goddess against the giants was magnificently depicted. The Panathenaia festival opened with athletic competitions. The winners were each given an amphora, which depicted Athena on one side and on the other the contest at which the athlete had defeated his challengers. [56] The provision of winners' prizes for the Big Panathenaia was seen as a great honour. In recompense for his momentous distinction, Herod promised to offer Athens a big marble stadium. He kept his promise. The Panathenaikon Stadium, which had been built in the fourth century BC, was reconstructed with white Pentelic marble and was modelled on the Roman stadiums with a semicircular 'sphendone' and slight curvilinear sides. The tiers, divided into two sections, provided seating capacity for 50,000 spectators. Marble steles of Hermes delineated the starting and finishing line of the stadium. A three-arch marble bridge over the Ilissos river provided easy access to the stadium, while a temple was erected on the eastern site in honour of goddess of luck, to whom the donor owed his great wealth. [57]

Regarding the Roman donors who financed sports buildings at Olympia in the second century AD, some impressive buildings to the south and south-east of Olympia were donated by the Roman Emperor Septimus Sevirus (AD 193–211), a keen supporter of the games. The buildings were possibly intended for use by the local athletic union. From the third century AD onwards, however, there was little interest in the games and donors became increasingly fewer. Then in the late third century AD Olympia suffered serious earthquakes. A quake in about AD 290 caused extensive damage and the games were badly affected. Nevertheless, recovery was swift. The damaged buildings were quickly restored. However, the *coup de grace* to the pan-Hellenic games was subsequently delivered by the spread of Christianity and Christian hostility towards them. [58] The Byzantine Emperor Theodosius I (AD 379–395) banned pagan worship by edict in AD 393. The games' sanctuaries were all closed save Olympia. However, recent excavations have revealed evidence that the Games of Olympia continued to be held until the first decades of the fifth century AD. It is likely that the competitions were discontinued by a decree issued by the Byzantine Emperor Theodosius II in AD 426. That was not all. Two disastrous earthquakes in AD 522 and 551 dealt the Olympia's games site a mortal blow. In this century too, Christians settled in Olympia and the atelier of the famous sculptor Pheidias, which had not been completely destroyed by the earthquakes, was converted into a Christian church. Then the rivers Alpheios and Kladeos completed the destruction of the site by inundating the area and covering it with tons of mud. [59] The Games of Olympia expired. In the reign of the Roman Emperor Claudius (AD 51–54), the people of Antioch had secured permission to stage competitions modelled on those of Olympia. [60] Regrettably, however, the competitions of Antioch, annual athletic events at which athletes competed for an olive wreath, also suffered the fate of Olympia when the Byzantine Emperor Justinus banned them in AD 520. [61]

The Modern Revival of the Games and their Financiers

The idea for the revival of the ancient Games of Greece, as is well known, emerged in the mid-nineteenth century when Evagelos Zappas (see Figure 2), a Greek landowner who became very rich in Romania, [62] offered to finance the revival of the games. Zappas notified King Otto of his intention in 1856. The king delegated the matter to the distinguished scholar Alexander Rizos Rangaves, the Foreign Minister. [63] Rangaves regarded sport as a luxury and advocated that efforts to ensure national progress should focus primarily on the development of industry, which at the time left a lot to be desired in comparison with industrial development elsewhere in Europe. Sport for him was not priority. Industrial exhibitions were regarded as more important, with athletic events simply held during the exhibitions to amuse visitors. [64] Zappas accepted this with the proviso that athletic events were guaranteed. Thus, by a royal decree in August 1858, Zappas's donation to the Greek government was assured and industrial exhibitions and athletic events under the name 'Olympia' were sanctioned. [65] The Committee for the Promotion of National Industry, which had been constituted in 1837, [66] was entrusted with the arrangements. [67]

The first 'Olympia' took place in 1859 at Athens's Loudovikou Square. A short-distance race, the *diavlos*, a long-distance race, the *dolichos*, discus and javelin throwing, a log jump, horse races and wrestling were included. Athletes from all over Greece travelled to Athens to be involved in the competitions and the presence of the royal family, members of government and local authorities gave the games official recognition. Despite the best of intentions, however, the games were not successful and the Greek government took no further interest in the promotion of this athletic innovation. [68]

In 1865 Zappas died. Before his death he left his immense fortune to his cousin, Constantine Zappas, providing that the continuity of the games would be secured and that the Greek government would be the legatee of his fortune after Constantine Zappas's death. [69] The Committee of the Olympia was constituted immediately and approved by royal decree in 1865. [70] The committee was entrusted with handling the Zappas fortune, the construction of an exhibition building and the restoration of the ancient Panathenaikon Stadium to host the Olympia Games. In 1869 the committee unanimously decided that it was a suitable time for the resumption of the athletic events. The second Olympia occurred in 1870. [71]

Figure 2 Evagelos Zappas

Five years later, Athens held the third Olympia, which, due to inadequate preparation, was unsuccessful. In the meantime, a new gymnasium was financed by the Olympia Committee in 1874 for the training and preparation of the athletes involved in the Olympia Games. The gymnasium was under the direction of Ioannes Phokianos, the man who dominated physical education in Greece in the late nineteenth century. [72] In 1888, although the Zappeion Mansion, an imposing building designed for Olympia exhibitions, was completed, the committee was hesitant about staging the fourth Olympia due to financial difficulties. For this reason, Phokianos took the initiative and staged athletic events at the Central Gymnasium of Athens on 30 April and 12 May 1889. This was the last time the Athens Olympia saw the light of day. [73] The Romanian government, for unknown reasons, put serious obstacles in the way of the transfer of Zappas's liquidated fortune from Romania to Greece. Therefore, the Olympia Committee, which had spent a large amount of money on the construction of the Zappeion Mansion, found itself in the unfortunate position of having no money. [74] Although the Olympia Games expired, Zappas was immortalized in history as the first sponsor of the modern Olympics.

As is also well known, the 1894 Athletic Congress in Paris ensured the revival of the modern Olympic Games. Athens was to host them in 1896. [75] At the end of the nineteenth century, Greece's financial position was bad. Half the national income was needed to pay off large loans from foreign banks. As a result, Charilaos Trikoupes, the Prime Minister, had declared the nation bankrupt in 1893 and for this reason he opposed the 1896 games in Athens. [76] Greece had no great interest in modern sport, was without sports facilities and in consequence, was unprepared for an international athletic event. [77] Nonetheless, and despite the difficulties, the decision to go ahead with the 1896 Olympics was made. To secure the necessary funds, the organizing committee suggested that Greeks who were living abroad should be requested to financially support the games. The lack of a modern stadium was one of the most crucial problems the committee faced. For want of a better solution, the ancient Panathenaikon Stadium had to fit the bill, with the proviso that extensive alterations should be made to it. Anastasios Metaxas, a talented Greek architect, undertook the task. The original excavation records of the German archaeologist Ernst Ziller in 1893 became the basis for the adjustments to the stadium. During Ziller's excavations the track of the ancient stadium was discovered and four marble busts of Hermes were unearthed. [78] Initially, the stadium consisted of two high embankments that faced each other on opposite sides of a long, narrow track. In no time at all, the stadium took on an impressive look replete with gleaming marble. Two large ancient stones shaped like human figures, which were excavated during the restoration work, were placed on each turning of the track to evoke memories of the past. [79] Where marble could not be used, white painted wood was used effectively to complete the tiers. Metaxas also restored some of the impressive columns that had decorated the ancient stadium, as well as the Propylaea, the majestic gate. His work endured. Through the first half of the twentieth century, although the stadium could not meet all the increasing requirements of modern sport, it was host to numerous sports events with its setting and decor attracting the admiration of the spectators. [80]

George Averof, a deep-pocketed Greek businessman, was essential to the successful restoration. Early in April 1895, Timoleon Philemon, secretary of the organizing committee of the games and a keen supporter of modern sport, visited Alexandria in Egypt, where a Greek community flourished, with the purpose of persuading the wealthy Greeks there to finance the games. Philemon discussed with Averof, president of the Greek community in Alexandria, the financing of the Panathenaikon Stadium's restoration. [81] Born in Epirus, Averof (see Figure 3) had moved to Alexandria and acquired great wealth. In Alexandria, he was a respected figure. He had provided the Greek community with a high school, a college for girls and a hospital for the poor. Averof responded positively to the appeal for financial support. Initially, he offered the sum of 585,000 drachmas (about 1,135 pounds sterling in today's prices). Later he provided more money when the expenditure on repairs exceeded the initial estimate. In total, Averof donated 920,000 drachmas (about 1,785 pounds sterling) to the organizing committee – a huge donation for the time. [82] In gratitude, his statue was placed at the entrance of the Panathenaikon Stadium. The unveiling ceremony was held on the eve of the games (24 March 1896) in the presence of Prince Constantine, heir to the Greek throne. Timoleon Philemon commended the donor, pointing out

Figure 3 George Averof

that only thanks to his generosity had the dream of a re-established Olympics come true. [83] Greece did not overlook Averof's beneficence. It presented him with a memorial medal on which the Panathenaikon Stadium was depicted in relief as well as with a silver crown. [84] On 5 October 1896, at a moving ceremony in the Hall of the Patriarchate in Alexandria, Philemon offered Averof the medal and the crown. Three years later, the great Greek benefactor died. Before he died, he willed one-third of his fortune to the Greek government for the building of a warship to be named after him. [85]

Other Greeks living abroad also responded positively to the appeal for financial support. The largest amounts were donated by the Greeks of Egypt and Constantinople. The games were also financed by anonymous Greek citizens, members of trade and sectional unions, municipalities and communes, athletic and military clubs and religious societies. Enthusiastic about the revival of the ancient games, they rallied to support them. [86] Individual and group generosity had its reward. The games, after a lapse of centuries, had revived in the place they were born.

Modern Sponsors and the Olympic Movement

Sponsorship, then, was essential for the re-establishment and early success in Greece of the modern Olympic Games. Whatever the ideals of amateur fellowship in amateur engagement may have been, the games needed facilities, which were provided by individual donors and various well-intentioned groups. It is certainly true that there was not the overt commercial motivation that was to be the case in the second half of the twentieth century. This later development is not the central theme of this chapter and can be briefly covered in order to complete the story of sponsorship continuity that has characterized both the ancient and modern Olympic Games.

In the twentieth century, the games speedily evolved and increasingly became an exceedingly costly event. As a result, the individuals who had initially financed and encouraged the revival of the ancient games were eventually replaced by major companies. In their role as sponsors, they established 'Olympic sponsorship', a trade relationship between the International Olympic Committee (IOC) and sponsors. This took time to develop. The Olympic movement experienced financial difficulties for most of the early decades of its new life. Those who succeeded de Coubertin as presidents of the Olympic Committee repeatedly called attention to a lack of income. [87] Modern sponsors appeared at the Stockholm Olympic Games in 1912, when Swedish companies funded the organizing committee with a view to securing exclusive photographic coverage of the games. Another company set up weighing machines at the venue and charged for their use. Eight years later, in Antwerp, a contract under which the sponsors were entitled to advertise their products in the games' leaflet allowed the organizing committee to obtain money for the games. Advertising placards were placed in the stadium in the 1924 Paris Olympics the first and last time. The Olympic Committee barred advertising immediately after the games. [88] However, precedent for commercial sponsorship was now established. Thus, in the 1928 Amsterdam Olympics, beer companies were allowed to place refreshment stands in the recreation grounds and the games' brochure again included advertising material. [89] The organizing committee of the 1932 games in Los Angeles went one step further and made a large profit by selling the buildings of the Olympic village to individuals and companies. [90]

The big breakthrough in commercial sponsorship, of course, took place in the second half of the twentieth century thanks to television rights. It will be recalled, however, that it was the 1936 Berlin games when television made its first appearance. German television attempted to transmit blurry images of the games within a radius of two miles from the stadium. Although the undertaking was experimental, television coverage of the games had taken its first, if faltering, steps. [91] Sponsors had effectively contributed to the improvement of the Olympic Committee's finances, but the money obtained could not cover the increasing expense. Remuneration from the payment for television coverage of the games, it was hoped, was the answer. Thus at the 1948 London Olympics, a contract was agreed between the organizing committee and BBC for coverage of the event. However, the BBC could not meet the olympic committee's charges due to financial difficulties consequent upon the Second World War. [92] Eventually, the Olympic Games proved to be an attractive global television show and the Olympic Committee exploited the situation. There were still difficulties to be overcome. In Melbourne in 1956, for example, television representatives argued that the games should be covered as news and therefore without payment. The committee of the games, however, saw them as entertainment and demanded that the payment should be commensurate with entertainment value of the opening ceremony and the athletic events. Since there was no precedent, the organizing committee permitted coverage of the games without specific charges. In return, the television representatives offered a small sum of money to the committee's treasurer. [93] Some time later, Avery Brundage, as the IOC's president, initiated rules for television coverage as a recreational spectacle with appropriate remuneration. At the 1960 Squaw Valley and Rome Games, not only television but also a large number of company sponsors financed the organizing committee and provided the athletes with food, perfume and soap. [94]

Thus, by the second half of the twentieth century, the games appeared to have secured a stable income. This favourable development stimulated the IOC to create, in 1961, a committee to provide the sports communities of poor nations in Africa and Asia with economic support. The Committee of International Olympic Assistance came into being. Ten years later, this committee merged with a sister organization that had been founded by the Permanent General Assembly of National Olympic Committees to create 'Olympic Solidarity', an organization empowered to handle part of the income from television rights. [95] Sponsorship increased at the 1964 Tokyo Olympic Games, which were transmitted throughout the world by satellite, when many companies financed the event. In addition, the advertisement of a new brand of cigarette under the name 'Olympia' yielded considerable profits. [96] By the mid-1970s, the greatest part the IOC's expenses were covered by the sale of television rights. Although the profits from television rose to impressive heights in the 1980s, they produced only half of the IOC's income. The other half derived from the 'product licence'. [97]

In 1983, driven by the desire for economic self-sufficiency in order to keep the games free from political influence, the Committee for New Sources of Funding was created. [98] Gradually, large companies offered the IOC, the national Olympic committees and the organizing committees large amounts of money to advertise their products side by side with the famous five-ring symbol created by de Coubertin in 1914. Thus the Olympic Committee was able to cover the costs of numerous activities. The 1984 Olympics in Los Angeles marked a new era for the Olympic sponsorship. [99] International rules were set up to establish the rights and obligations of sponsors. Representatives of company sponsors met the Olympic Committee to discuss a reduction in the number of sponsors and an effective means of protecting the Olympic emblem from uncontrolled exploitation. [100] From a limited number of sponsors, who offered substantial remuneration for the use of the Olympic symbol, the organizing committee of the Seoul Olympics in 1988 obtained considerable sums of money. [101] A similarly small but wealthy number of commercial sponsors financed the 1992 Barcelona Olympics, while four years later Atlanta got prodigious amount of money from sponsorship and the sale of television rights. [102] Sponsors and television ensured the 2000 Sydney games' success, while the construction of new sporting buildings was financed by the state budget, a form of state sponsorship. [103]

The organizing committee covered most of its expenses from sponsorship for the 2004 Olympics in Athens. Athens aspired to turn the 2004 games into an attractive forum for athletes from all over the world, to pursue the Olympic spirit and to promote a great urban transformation that would improve the quality of life of the city. [104] Once more, in an effort to control excessive commercialization but also to secure the necessary finances to ensure a successful games, the Olympic organizing committee favoured a limited number of company-sponsors. The National Sponsorship Programme was established, which embraced various categories of financers, sponsors, suppliers and the like. [105] In the final analysis, in the twentieth century, the Olympic Games increasingly gained popularity throughout the world and linked sport with commerce, in an effort paradoxically to generate moral attitudes and a peaceful world. Certainly, the financiers of athletic and cultural events in ancient times and those munificent donors who encouraged and supported the revival of the modern Olympics are a thing of the past. Modern sponsors nowadays aspire to profits. However, one common link with the past is sponsorship, which has been constant in the history of the Olympics-past and present.

This article begins with Greece and ends with Greece. At one level it deals *inter alia* with the continuity of sponsorship in sport from classical times to modern times. The Olympic (and other) Games of the ancient world required sponsorship; the Olympic Games of the contemporary world require sponsorship. At another level it confronts the elementary fact that enthusiastic amateur participation has not been enough in the history of the Olympic Games in the Greece of the past and in the present. Sponsorship has changed in nature over time. This much is clear. But within change continuity has remained. Political sponsorship was a feature of the ancient Olympics; it is still a feature of the modern Olympics. Beijing will make this clearer than ever! Change has made its profound mark on sponsorship. It was once mostly characterized by the generosity of the wealthy for a variety of reasons; it is now mostly characterized by the commercialization of cooperation for a single reason. Thus Olympic sponsorship has been constant in history. Now, however, for better or worse, it is very different from what it was. Greece of the past pre-Christian era and the present 'post-Christian' era has provided the symmetrical means of demonstrating this and permitting the closing of an analytical circle.

Notes

[1]　Thanks are due to Professor J.A. Mangan for this title.

[2]　In ancient Greece, the word tribe (*phyle*) meant 'seed'. The word for sex (*phylon*) meant 'species'. See *Historia tou Hellinikou Ethnous: Archaikos Hellinismos* ['History of the Greek Nation: Archaic Hellenism'], II (Athens: Ekdotiki Athinon, 1971, 2000), p.35. In ancient Athens, three *trittys* (the word *trittys* meant 'a third'), one from each of the three regions of Attica, that is, from the *asty*, the *mesogeia* and the *paralia* were united to form one tribe. The ten tribes that were finally formed carried out the public functions of the political and social life of Athens. Each of the ten tribes was assigned an Attic hero to be the mythical ancestor and patron, whose name the tribe henceforth bore, and cults in honour of its hero were established for each tribe. Each tribe contained a cross-section of the whole of Attica, since every region was represented in it. The regional differences could be settled at the tribal meetings. See M. Ostwald, 'The Reform of the Athenian State by Cleisthenes', in J. Boardman and N.G.L. Hammond (eds.), *The Cambridge Ancient History, VI: Persia, Greece and the Western Mediterranean 525 to 479 BC* (Cambridge: Cambridge University Press, 1997), p.316.

[3]　*Historia tou Hellinikou Ethnous: Klassikos Hellinismos* ['History of the Greek Nation: Classic Hellenism'] (Athens: Ekdotiki Athinon, 1972, 2000), III, pp.362–5.

[4]　Ibid., pp.97–8.

[5]　Ibid., p.98. It is possible that the institution of *leitourgeia* had been established in other Greek cities too, but more information about it is still in obscurity. The same institution was also consolidated in Egypt in the reign of Ptolemies and in Rome. See 'Leitourgeia', *Papyros Larousse Britannica*, XXXVIII (Athens: Papyros, 1989), p.50.

[6]　*Historia: Klassikos Hellinismos*, p.98; *Historia: Archaikos Hellinismos*, p.266.

[7]　M.I. Finlay and H.W. Pleket, *The Olympic Games: the First Thousand Years* (New York: The Viking Press, 1976), p.100.

[8]　Y. Touratsoglou, 'The Political and Social Character of the Competitions of Antiquity', in Ministry of Culture (ed.), *Hellada, Athlitismos, Politismos* ['Greece, Sport, Culture'] (Athens: Cosmo Press, 1988), pp.17–20.

[9]　*Historia: Klassikos Hellinismos*, p.559.

[10]　Ibid., pp.559–60.

[11]　Ibid., p.331; Th. Giannakis, 'To Panathinaiko Stadio' ['The Panathenaikon Stadium'], in G. Theodorakopoulos (ed.), *Panathinaikon Stadium: A 2300 Years Long History* (Athens: Central Organizing Committee of the 6th World Championship in Sport 'Athens 97', 1997), p.4.

[12]　The length of the *dromos* was about a *stadion*, a unit of length that lent its name to the whole construction. See A. Kokkou, 'To Panathinaiko Stadio' ['The Panathinaikon Stadium'], in Ministry of Culture and Benakes Museum (eds.), *To Pneuma kai to Soma. He Anaviossi tes Olympiakes Ideas 19os–20os Aionas* ['The Mind and the Body. The Revival of the Olympic Idea, 19th–20th Century'] (Athens: Rachel Misdrachi-Kapon, 1989), p.41.

[13]　S. Ulrich, *Cult, Sport and Ancient Festival* (Princeton, NJ: Markus Wiener Publishers, 2000), pp.96–7.

[14]　N. Gialoures, 'To Iero tes Olympias' ['The Sanctuary of Olympia'], in G. Christopoulos (ed.), *Oi Olympiakoi Agones sten Archaia Hellada* ['The Olympic Games in Ancient Greece'] (Athens: Ekdotiki Athinon, 1982), p.99.

[15]　Ibid.

[16]　The Macedonians increasingly began emerge from their isolation from the eighth century BC onwards. The Macedonian realm flourished in the reigns of Kings Amyntas, Philip II and Alexander the Great (fourth century BC). See 'Macedonia in History', in G. Christopoulos

and J. Bastias (eds.), *Macedonia: History and Politics* (Athens: Ekdotiki Athinon, 1991), p.8.

[17] N. Gialoures, 'Katagoge kai Historia' ['Origin and History'], in Christopoulos, *Oi Olympiakoi Agones*, p.87; Ulrich, *Cult, Sport*, p.99. It was the first time that a building in the round under the name *tholos*, which till then had been constructed to host only cult ceremonies, was erected to be reminiscent of the royal family. Circular buildings, under the name *tholoi*, were modelled on old Hellenic architectural principles. From the fourth century BC onwards, this style prevailed in Greece. In this century, three magnificent round edifices were erected at Delphi, Epidaurus and Olympia. Here, the architects masterly adapted the exterior colonnade to the round construction whose fascinating decoration inspired admiration. By contrast with the round buildings at Delphi and Epidaurus, which did duty as temples, the Philippeion at Olympia was constructed to only lodge the golden statues of the Macedonian royal family. See *Historia: Klassikos Hellinismos*, pp.287–8.

[18] Ulrich, *Cult, Sport*, pp.99–100.

[19] Ibid., p.100.

[20] Ibid.

[21] Ibid., pp.101–3.

[22] *Historia tou Hellinikou Ethnous: Hellinistiki Epochi* ['History of the Greek Nation: Hellenistic Era'], V (Athens: Ekdotiki Athinon, 1974), p.146.

[23] *Historia tou Hellinikou Ethnous: Hellinismos kai Romi* ['History of the Greek Nation. Hellenism and Rome'], VI (Athens: Ekdotiki Athinon, 1976, 2000), p.491.

[24] Ibid.

[25] V. Kyrkos, 'He Poreia tou Athletismou sta Hellinistika kai Romaika Chronia ['The Evolution of Athleticism in the Hellenistic and Roman Era'], in Christopoulos, *Oi Olympiakoi Agones*, p.282.

[26] In the Roman period, the pan-Hellenic games were divided into two major categories. Somewhat less prestigious were the games known as *themides* or *agones thematitai*, at which the winners were given a prize of money (*thema*). Such competitions were staged annually, biennially or every four or eight years. The second category included the 'sacred' or 'sacred crown' games and entitled the winners to a 'sacred' crown, which was dedicated to the gods. 'Sacred crown' games were held at two- or four-year intervals, with the most eminent occurring every four years. Despite some differences, *thematitai* and 'sacred crown' games corresponded in many ways. Both lasted several days; their comparable promise of glory and money attracted professional athletes, mainly from guilds of athletes and regional contestants; both included equestrian events, foot races and wrestling as well music, drama and poetic contests; finally, both the 'sacred crown' and *thematitai* competitions had to meet with the emperor's approval. See M.T. Boatwright, *Hadrian and the Cities of the Roman Empire* (Princeton NJ: Princeton University Press, 2000), pp.94–5.

[27] Finlay and Pleket, *The Olympic Games*, pp.109–10.

[28] *Historia: Hellinismos kai Romi*, p.484.

[29] Ibid., pp.491–2.

[30] Kyrkos, 'He Poreia tou Athletismou', p.284.

[31] Ibid.

[32] *Historia: Hellinismos kai Romi*, p.484.

[33] Kyrkos, 'He Poreia tou Athletismou', p.284.

[34] Ibid., p.112.

[35] Ulrich, *Cult, Sport*, pp.104–5.

[36] *Historia: Klassikos Hellinismos*, p.289.

[37] Ulrich, *Cult, Sport*, pp.104–5.

[38] Ibid., p.114.

[39] Ibid.

[40] Kyrkos, 'He Poreia tou Athletismou', pp.284–85; *Historia: Hellinismos kai Romi*, p.488. The distinguished members of the unions were honoured, after their death, with statues or busts placed in the gymnasium. From the first century AD onwards, there is evidence that professional athletic unions were founded in many cities of the Roman Empire financially supported by the Roman emperor. The Emperors Marcus Antonius, Claudius and Vespasian offered privileges to active members of the athletic unions including exemption from military service. In gratitude, *inter alia*, the athletic unions were named after the emperor. These unions, modelled on professional and religious societies of the time, elected their administrative members from veteran athletes and gave their head a 'sacred' title. See *Historia: Hellinismos kai Romi*, p.488.

[41] N. Gialoures, 'To Iero tes Olympias' ['The Sanctuary of Olympia'], in Christopoulos, *Oi Olympiakoi Agones*, pp.102–3; S. Ulrich, *Cult, Sport*, pp.114–16.

[42] Prompted by the honour and flattery extended by the emissaries of the games in Greece, Nero commenced his trip to Greece. He departed probably in September AD 66. To enable him to compete in all the major games, the four-yearly events were rescheduled (and in several cases repeated) to create a probable grand-touring sequence, where Nero first appeared at the Actia and then at the Pythia, Isthmian, Nemean and Olympia festivals before returning to perform a second time at the first three contests. The traditional content of some of the festivals was altered, with tragic acting introduced to the Isthmian of Corinth and a musical contest interpolated into the Olympia. Having ordered that as many inhabitants as possible be present in the market place at Corinth during the Isthmian festival there in November AD 67, he publicly proclaimed the liberation of the entire province of Achaia, granting it a degree of governmental autonomy and freedom from Roman taxation. Nero's tour was valuable as a calculated act of diplomacy. The 'sacred games' had long been a vitally important element of Greek civic life and both their number and their role grew significantly during the imperial period, providing a vital focus on national identity, the communication and sharing of experience. Moreover, it had been an acknowledged imperial policy to encourage games in the East as a means of spreading largesse and fostering local support. Nero's activity could be viewed simply as an extension of Roman interest and participation in these festivities. See R. Beacham, *Spectacle Entertainments of Early Imperial Rome* (New Haven, CT, and London: Yale University Press, 1999), pp.246–8.

[43] Ulrich, *Cult, Sport*, p.117.

[44] Ibid., pp.119–20.

[45] Ibid., p.120. During recent excavations a bronze inscription containing the names of the winners of the AD 385 Olympics was brought to light. Prior to this discovery, inscriptions with names of winners evidenced involvement in the games up to AD 267. See Kyrkos, 'He Poreia tou Athletismou', p.285.

[46] Boatwright, *Hadrian*, pp.144–5.

[47] Ibid., pp.100–1. It is important to note that in about AD 134 Hadrian transferred the headquarters of the 'ecumenical' guild of the 'Dionysus' artists, hitherto located in the Greek East to Rome, and accorded permission to the 'synod of athletes and sacred winners' to establish its own headquarter in the Roman capital. As a result, Rome became the athletic hub of the known world, and in appreciation of the benefaction several athletic guilds throughout the Roman Empire added the epithet 'Hadrianian' to their names. See Boatwright, *Hadrian*, p.103.

[48] Ibid., p.127.

[49] Ibid., p.209.

[50] *Historia: Hellinismos kai Romi*, p.488.

[51] Ibid., pp.468–70.

[52] Ulrich, *Cult, Sport*, p.106.

[53] Ibid., pp.106–8.

[54] Kl. Paleologos, 'He Organosse ton Agonon' ['The Stage of the Games'] in Christopoulos, *Oi Olympiakoi Agones*, p.109; S. Ulrich, *Cult, Sport*, p.108.

[55] Gialoures, 'To Iero tes Olympias', p.102; *Historia: Hellinismos kai Romi*, pp.469–70.

[56] M. Andronikos, 'He Symvoli tou Athletismou sten Agogi ton Neon' ['The Contribution of Sport to the Education of the Young'], in Christopoulos, *Oi Olympiakoi Agones*, pp.64–5.

[57] A. Kokkou, *To Stadion*, p.41; *Historia: Hellinismos kai Romi*, pp.468–70. In the course of time, the Panathenaikon Stadium became an arena for gladiators and battles against wild animals, while during the Frankish occupation of Athens the stadium, in the early thirteenth century, was host to tournaments. From the fifteenth century AD onwards, when the Ottomans occupied Greece, it fell into disrepair. Finally, in 1778, the materials of the marble bridge over the Ilissos River that offered access to the stadium were used by the Turks for the construction of a wall. See Giannakis, 'To Panathinaiko Stadio', pp.4–5.

[58] Gialoures, 'To Iero tes Olympias', p.103.

[59] Ibid.

[60] *Historia: Hellinismos kai Romi*, p.492.

[61] Ibid.

[62] Zappas gained great wealth in Romania through real estate business.

[63] Zappas was born in a village in Epirus, Northern Greece, in 1800. In 1831 he emigrated to Bucharest (Romania), where he became one of the wealthiest landowners. A poem written by the Greek poet Alexandros Soutsos (1803–63), inspired Zappas and urged him to finance the revival of the games. Soutsos is regarded as the earliest supporter of the idea of the games' revival. His ideas were expressed in a poem published in the newspaper *Helios* in 1833, just a few years after the emergence of Greece as a modern state: P. Manitakes, *100 Chronia Neoellinikou Athlitismou: 1830–1930* ['A Hundred Years of Modern Greek Athleticism: 1830–1930'] (Athens: Hellenic Amateur Athletic Association, 1962), p.13.

[64] Manitakes, p.13; D.C. Young, 'Modern Greece and the Origins of the Modern Olympic Games', in W. Coulson and H. Kyrieleis (eds.), *Proceedings of an International Symposium on the Olympic Games* (Athens: Lucy Braggiotti Publications, 1992), pp.175–84.

[65] 'About the Establishment of the Olympia', Royal Decree, 28 August 1858, *Official Gazette*, I, 38 (Athens: National Printing Office, 1837), pp.251–52.

[66] 'About the Constitution of a Twelve-member Committee under the Name Committee for the Promotion of National Industry', Royal Decree, 9 February 1837, *Official Gazette*, I, 5 (Athens: National Printing Office, 1837), pp.6–9.

[67] 'About *100 Chronia Neoellinikou Athlitismou*, the Establishment of the Olympia', p.252.

[68] Manitakes, *100 Chronia Neoellinikou Athlitismou*, pp.14–15.

[69] 'Zappa's Will', 31 August 1865, *Official Gazette*, I, 42 (Athens: National Printing Office, 1865), pp.274–7.

[70] 'About the Definite Constitution of the Olympia Committee the Committee of the Legacy, Royal Decree, 31 August 1865, *Official Gazette*, I, 42 (Athens: National Printing Office, 1865), p.274.

[71] *Royal Decrees, Circulars, Evagele Zappas' Will and the Regulation of the Olympia for the Year 1870* (Athens: National Printing Office, 1869), p.8.

[72] Manitakes, *100 Chronia Neoellinikou Athlitismou*, pp.21–4.

[73] Ibid., pp.22–3.

[74] Ibid., p.24.

[75] A. Tarassouleas, *Helliniki Symetochi stes Sychrones Olympiades* ['Greek Involvement in Modern Olympiads'] (Athens: A. Tarassouleas, 1990), p.13.

[76] A. Vakalapoulos, *Nea Helliniki Historia: 1204–1985* ['Modern Greek History: 1204–1985'] (Thessaloniki: Vanias, 1999), pp.319–20.

[77] Pierre de Coubertin, 'The Olympic Games of 1896', in Norbert Muller (ed.), *Pierre de Coubertin 1863–1937: Olympism – Selected Writings* (Lausanne: International Olympic Committee, 2000), p.350.

[78] P. Mylonas, *Peri Stadiou* ['About the Stadium'] (Athens: N. Deledemetris, 1952), pp.1–25.

[79] De Coubertin, *Olympism*, p.351.

[80] Ibid.

[81] B. Tselika, *Olympiakoi Agones 1896: To Photographiko Album tou Albert Mayer* ['The 1896 Olympic Games: The Photo Album of Albert Mayer'] (Athens: Exantas, 1996), pp.10–12.

[82] Ibid., p.36. Averof also financed the Athens Polytechnic School, the Military Academy and the Juvenile Prisons of Athens.

[83] E. Spathari, *To Olympiako Pneuma* ['The Olympic Spirit'] (Athens: Adam, 1992), pp.321–2.

[84] N. Polites, *Olympiakoi Agones tou 1896 opos ten Ezessan tote oi Hellenes kai oi Xenoi* ['The 1896 Olympic Games as they were seen by the Greeks and the Foreigners'] (Patra: Achaikes Ekdosses, 1996), p.31.

[85] Ibid., p.31.

[86] Tselika, *Olympiakoi Agones 1896*, p.11.

[87] R.K. Barney, 'American Olympic Commercialization: A Boon for Olympism', in International Olympic Academy (ed.), *Triakoste Trete Diethnes Synodos* ['The 33rd International Session'] (Athens: International Olympic Committee, 1993), pp.132–3.

[88] D.S. Likman, 'Marketing – Sponsors and the Olympic Spirit', in International Olympic Academy (ed.), *Triakoste Ogdoe Diethnes Synodos* ['The 38th International Session'] (Athens: International Olympic Committee, 1999), pp.84–5.

[89] Tarassouleas, *Helliniki Symetochi*, pp.109–13.

[90] Ibid., pp.121–3.

[91] M. Payne, 'Sponsorship and Marketing of the Atlanta Olympic Games', in International Olympic Academy (ed.), *Triakoste Evdome Diethnes Synodos* ['The 37th International Session'] (Athens: International Olympic Committee, 1998), p.68.

[92] Likman, 'Marketing', p.85.

[93] Barney, 'American Olympic Commercialization', p.133.

[94] Barney, 'American Olympic Commercialization', pp.133–4; Likman, 'Marketing', p.85.

[95] N. Girard-Savoy, 'Olympiaki Allilegye ['Olympic Solidarity'], in International Olympic Academy (ed.), *Triakoste Enate Diethnes Synodos* ['The 39th International Session'] (Athens: International Olympic Committee, 2000), pp.177–8.

[96] Likman, 'Marketing', p.85.

[97] Barney, 'American Olympic Commercialization', pp.134–5.

[98] Likman, 'Marketing', pp.86–7.

[99] Payne, 'Sponsorship and Marketing', p.66. The sponsors were now divided into categories. The sponsors were divided into big sponsors, the suppliers of the games, and those who were entitled to utilize the Olympic symbol for advertising purposes.

[100] Likman, 'Marketing', p.87.

[101] S.P. Kang, 'Local and Universal Dimensions of the Olympic Games', in *39th International Session*, pp.121–33.

[102] C.H. Battle, 'Skepses pano stous Olympiakous Agones tes Ekatondaetias tes Atlanta ['Thoughts about the Olympic Games in Atlanta on the Century Anniversary'], in *37th International Session*, pp.176–82.

[103] P.W. Coles, 'He Diorganosse ton Olympiakon Agonon tou Sidney in 2000' ['The Stage of the 2000 Olympic Games in Sidney]', in *38th International Session*, pp.66–7.

[104] 'Sponsors', *Athens 2004 Olympic News*, IV (2003), 15–6.

[105] Ibid., 17–8.

Maharajas and Cricket: Self, State, Province and Nation

Boria Majumdar

Cricket was much more than just another game to the Victorians. Indeed, they glorified it as a perfect system of ethics and morals, which embodied all that was most noble in the Anglo-Saxon character. They prized it as a national symbol, perhaps because – so far as they could tell – it was an exclusively English creation unsullied by Oriental and European influences. In an extremely xenophobic age, the Victorians came to regard cricket as further proof of their moral and cultural supremacy. [1]

From the earliest years of British settlement in India, cricket was nurtured by leading public figures, military commanders, educators and journalists. Consequently, it was natural for men of status and affluence in India, i.e. the princes or maharajas, to take up this alien sport. Maharaja patronage of sport was an established practice in India by the middle of the eighteenth century. As Ann Morrow points out in her book *The Maharajas of India*, sport was thought to be an important way of 'sweating the sex' out of the other ranks. The British upper classes loved big-game hunting, which was a symbol of status, the criterion being the number of animals one shot. In colonial India, sports such as big-game hunting became a short cut to being a gentleman, drawing the maharajas into it. [2] It was their way of proving their credentials to their peers. In fact, as Rosalind O'Hanlon has shown, hunting was an integral part of the Indian aristocratic tradition from the early decades of the eighteenth century. 'Manly qualities', she argues, were displayed in very direct and physical ways: in the splendour of men's physiques, the dazzle of equipage, the grim efficiency of their weapons and the magnificence of their fighting animals. Here, allies, troops, patrons and rivals continually weighed and judged, challenged and affirmed each other's possession of the manly qualities and competence deemed essential in the successful ruler, ally, military commander and warrior. [3]

The maharajas also took to polo from the 1870s. In fact, the Hindu princes were at the forefront of the revival of polo. Armed with equestrian kills and with enormous resources at their disposal, the maharajas took the polo-playing world by storm. The princely houses of Patiala, Jaipur, Jodhpur, Hyderabad, Kishangarh, Alwar, Bhopal, Kashmir and Bikaner were the leading patrons of the sport in colonial India. [4]

Some of the rajas patronized wrestlers. Famous among the patrons were the maharajas of Patiala, Jodhpur and Datia. The Raja of Datia patronized Aziz Pehlwan, father of Gama, one of the best-known wrestlers in Indian history. The Maharaja of Patiala was another major patron and arranged a bout between Gama and Zbysco, two well-known wrestlers in contemporary India, in 1928. In Bengal, the Maharaja of Cooch Behar was a leading patron of *kushti* [5] and it was under his patronage that the world wrestling competition was held in Calcutta in 1892.

Other sports that received royal patronage were horse racing and golf. Maharaja Krishnaraja Wodeyar started horse racing in Mysore and races were held during the birthday celebrations of the maharaja, attracting among others a large number of British officers. Kashmir was the golfing Mecca of India from the late nineteenth century. Golf began in Kashmir when Colonel Neville Chamberlain prepared a six-hole course in 1890–1. In 1901, the Maharaja of Kashmir donated land at Gulmarg for laying out a golf course, which became known as the Upper Golf Course. In 1915 a nine-hole course, known as 'Rabbits Course' was built.

It was natural that the maharajas would take to promoting cricket in the course of time. The reasons behind cricket patronage by the maharajas were, however, much more complex, some of which have not been discussed in existing studies on Indian cricket. For some aristocrats, cricket was a tool of social mobility; for others it was a means of challenging the British masters by defeating them on their own turf. For some others, however, much more than achieving social mobility by emulating the colonizers, it was a means to further other ambitions, to gain economic stability and political power over their rivals.

The roots of cricket patronage by the Maharajas can often be traced back to the peer rivalries that dominated princely life in early-twentieth-century India. It was to outdo his sworn rival, the Maharaja of Cooch Behar, that Jagadindranarayan Ray, the Maharaja of Natore, patronized cricketers from across the country, disregarding social taboos. [6] Such aristocratic patronage, rooted in political and commercial considerations, played a significant role in making cricket 'representative' in colonial India, an aspect of the game ignored in existing studies on the subject.

This article, by detailing the nature of cricket patronage by the Maharaja of Natore, will analyse some of the complex reasons behind cricket promotion by aristocrats in colonial India. While existing studies on the subject have dealt with princely investment in cricket, the complex reasons for such involvement have only been partially analysed.

Patronage Rooted in Peer Rivalries

Yet it seemed to be the nature of Indian cricket that it should sprout briefly here and there, and then die away again. ..The best case in point was Calcutta. Before the first war, the Maharaja Nripendra Narayan of Cooch Behar had maintained at his own expense no less than three cricket teams. ... With the help of two Sussex professionals, Joe Vine and George Cox, and later Frank Tarrant, the Cooch Behar XI more than held their own with the Calcutta Cricket Club at Eden Gardens ... even with the powerful Jamnagar Jodhpur combination captained by the Jam Saheb himself and including A.C. Maclaren. Local Calcutta and Bengali cricket prospered tremendously as a result, but in 1911 the Maharaja died in England ... and Calcutta by the early 1920s had simply ceased to be an important centre of Indian cricket. [7]

The lead of Cooch Behar was followed in Bengal by a Zamindari estate, Natore, which formed a team around 1906. The Raja recruited extensively and his team included some of the leading players of Bombay, such as P. Vithal, J.S. Warden and P. Shivram, and K. Seshachari of Madras. Cricket patronage at Natore, for reasons, which are not entirely clear, did not last for many years. [8]

In contrast to these views, the following analysis will demonstrate that a decline in cricket patronage in Bengal cannot be linked to the premature death of the Maharaja of Cooch Behar in 1911. [9] Bengal cricket continued to be a significant presence in the country until the early 1930s, though patronage by royal families declined after 1914. Even after Cooch Behar had ceased to be a patron of cricket, the Maharaja of Natore could have continued, and was in a position to continue, earlier policies of patronage. [10] Yet he had given up promoting cricket, forcing Cashman to declare that the reasons why Natore ceased to be a major patron of cricket 'remain unclear'. [11] The truth, as the following narrative will demonstrate, is that the Maharaja of Natore had started promoting cricket to challenge his arch-rival, the Maharaja of Cooch Behar. With the premature death of his rival, he lost his incentive and by the second decade of the twentieth century shifted his interests to promoting the development of Bengali literature. [12]

The Maharaja of Natore's initiative may be traced back to the year 1900. [13] It was soon after the Maharaja of Cooch Behar had formed his own team, hiring English professionals as coaches, that Jagadindranarayan Ray of Natore decided to form a cricket team of his own. He was determined to improve upon the performances of the Cooch Behar side. To fulfil his ambition, he purchased 45 acres of land at Bondel Road near Old Ballygunge in South Calcutta, converting it into a cricket field by the turn of the century. [14] The maharaja also erected a pavilion in his private cricket ground at Old Ballygunge, one that had all the necessary facilities for players. By his own admission, he had taken to cricket patronage having observed that the Maharaja of Cooch Behar's efforts weren't proving effective:

> To improve the standard of cricket in Bengal, the Maharaja of Cooch Behar, Shri Nripendra Krishna Bhup Bahadur, had undertaken a series of steps. He had recruited professional coaches from England together with professional European players from all parts of India to play for his team. He also arranged regular matches wherein his team could get valuable practice by playing against local and provincial sides of the country. However, because of a strong European presence in his team, whether his efforts contributed to improving the standard of native cricket in Bengal remained unclear. [15]

Similar sentiments were expressed by Hemchandra Ray, commenting on cricket patronage by the Maharaja of Natore:

> At the time when the Natore team dominated Bengal cricket, the Maharaja of Cooch Behar had also formed a quality cricket team. However, we, Bengalis, could not rejoice at the victories of the Cooch Behar side. This was because Bengalis were a marginal presence in the Cooch Behar team and hence the credit for these victories went to the European players of the team. [16]

It was in response to this 'defect' that Jagadindranarayan Ray decided to form a cricket team consisting of Indians only and to this extent his involvement in the game can be seen as part of a nationalist enterprise. To develop Bengali/Indian cricket, he invited Saradaranjan Ray, [17] the father of Bengal cricket, to join him as coach of his team, recruiting players of merit from all parts of the country. [18] The duo had initially planned to take over the Town Club, the best-known native cricket club in late-nineteenth-century Bengal, [19] but after much discord with the officials of the club over financial matters, abandoned the idea. [20] Jagadindranarayan, who had been a leading patron of the Town Club since 1895, left the institution at the turn of the century to form his own Natore team. Saradaranjan and his two brothers, Muktidaranjan and Kuladaranjan, joined him in his new role as Bengal's foremost cricket patron. [21]

To fulfil his ambition, Jagadindranarayan spared no pains, evident from his efforts to save the life of Srishchandra Ray, an aspiring young cricketer of the province. [22] Having observed Srishchandra's talent, Jagadindranarayan adopted him, paying all his expenses from the Natore treasury. The boy came from a poor family; his father was a clerk at the Natore court. Elated at the raja's interest in grooming his son, his father allowed Srishchandra to be brought over to the royal palace at a very young age. [23] Jagadindranarayan made no distinction between his own son, Prince Victor, and Srishchandra, giving them equal opportunity to master the game. However, Srishchandra soon fell ill and despite all attempts by the maharaja to save him, died within a week. This episode, as Ramakanta Bhattacharya asserts, had a devastating effect on the Maharaja:

His family members were surprised at the loss the Maharaja felt at Srishchandra's death. Failing to recuperate with this tragedy in Calcutta, Jagadindranarayan left for Bolpur, Shantiniketan, soon after. Having spent a month at Shantiniketan, he returned to Calcutta. Even Srishchandra's parents were amazed at the way Jagadindranarayan had mourned the loss of their son. [24]

His determination to promote cricket among the rank and file is also evident from episodes surrounding the inclusion of Mani Das in the Natore side and Kaladhan Mukherjee in the Bengal team that toured Rawlapindi in 1911. [25] Kaladhan Mukherjee was the younger brother of Bidhubhusan Mukherjee, Bengal's leading batsman in the early twentieth century. [26] As far as Mani Das was concerned, the maharaja rated him very highly and included him in his team, ignoring opposition from upper echelons of Bengali society. This was a rare honour for a person of low caste and justly made him apprehensive. However, the maharaja showed confidence in the youngster, instructing Mani Das to open the batting against the touring Gwalior side. [27] Jagadindranarayan described this episode in his memoirs, asserting:

> Among the current lot of Bengali players, Mani Das is one of the very best. I had sent him to open the batting against Gwalior. He wasn't willing to open and was afraid of performing poorly in front of his more illustrious teammates. Noting this apprehension I called him and said, 'We are Bengalis. In a predominantly Bengali cricket team it is the duty of the Bengalis to take the lead.' Upon hearing this, he touched my feet to take my blessings and went out to the middle to play an innings that proved invaluable for the team in the end. [28]

Kaladhan Mukherjee was in prime form during the 1912/13 season, and was a prolific scorer for the Bengali schools against their Anglo Indian counterparts. [29] Yet he was not included in the Bengal touring team, a decision that made the selectors extremely unpopular with the maharaja. Having failed to provide a just explanation on why they had left him out, the selectors incurred the maharaja's wrath: peeved at the unfair treatment meted out to talented Bengali players, he decided to undertake the organization of tours to all parts of the country. To this end, he hired leading professional cricketers from western India Baloo, Semper, Vithal and Ganpat, forming one of the best cricket combinations in colonial India. These tours were a characteristic feature of Bengali cricket in the first decade of the twentieth century. [30]

Cricket as Nationalist Enterprise

While taking on one of his peers, the Maharaja of Cooch Behar, the Maharaja of Natore was also trying to fulfil his other ambition: that of defeating the English at their own game. Existing studies of princely patronage have assumed that all princes saw cricket as a means of associating with the ruling British. [31] This view ignores the evidence of native princes' determination to set up cricket teams comprising of Indians only, an initiative deriving from the belief that this was the only means of challenging the British. The Maharaja of Natore was an ardent nationalist, having been an active member of the Indian National Congress for some years. [32] Soon after turning 18, he became president of the Natore Political Association at the request of Surendranath Banerjee. [33] In 1894, he joined Banerjee [34] and Anandamohan Bose [35] as a member of the Rajshahi municipality. [36] After the partition of Bengal in 1905, he was a key figure in the anti-partition movement, delivering a famous speech against the partition at the Calcutta Town Hall. [37] That his nationalist credentials were well known is evident from the following testimony by Charuchandra Mitra:

> Prior to him, no other member of the royal family, either in Natore or in other families of the state, had actively supported the nationalist agenda. This was because they wished to be close to the ruling classes. It was to break this tradition that the Maharaja of Natore had joined the National Congress and had actively advocated the demands raised by the nationalists. This was best evident during his speech at the Town Hall in protest against the partition of Bengal. [38]

However, he differed from the nationalists in his modes of resistance. Until 1914, he used the cricket field to challenge the English, after this time investing in the evolution of the vernacular press. That he was to a large extent successful in rousing nationalist sensibilities among his subjects is evident from contemporary accounts:

> Whenever the Natore XI defeated the European teams of Calcutta, our chests swelled with pride. Before the formation of the Natore XI, we, Indians, were losers on most occasions. But with the formation of the Natore XI, Maharaj Jagadindranarayan turned the tables on the English. Whether it is a fault of ours or not, we do not regard games as something simple, rather we are affected by the results of these encounters. This is because this is the only arena where we are allowed to compete on even terms with the English. The English have always ridiculed us as 'effete'. It is on the sporting field that we may counter such false allegations. This is why we justifiably perceive a victory on the sporting field as a 'national victory' against the British. Though the English mock us for our perceptions, it is evident that whenever they lose to us, they are filled with rage and humiliation. Thus, whatever is said on this count, that the Natore XI stimulated nationalist instincts among the youth is doubtless. This is a great achievement and has given the Maharaja immortality. [39]

The Maharaja's advocacy of cricket to mount resistance against colonial rule proved effective because he had also appropriated the virtues of cricket, namely, fair play and a sporting spirit. These traits were in evidence when the Natore side played against Presidency College [40] at Natore Park. In this match, the college team was bowled out for a small total against the fancied Natore bowling line-up, comprising Palwankar Baloo and H.L. Semper. [41] However, the college struck back, removing the frontline Natore batsmen cheaply. With eight wickets down, Natore were still 20 runs in arrears. At this moment, one of the batsmen played with skill, taking the Natore side close to victory. Controversy arose when he had hit a ball hard and thought that it had crossed the boundary ropes. In reality, it had not, and when the fielder retrieved the ball and threw it to the keeper, the batsman was found short of his crease. [42] As a result, the umpire declared him 'run out'. The Natore team, with the maharaja the only batsman remaining, protested that the other umpire had signalled a boundary, arguing that the decision was unfair. When everyone hoped that the maharaja, fearing he would have to bat in failing light against fast bowlers, would intervene on behalf of the batsman, Jagadindranarayan surprised everyone by declaring that the umpire's decision was final and the batter was out. Jagadin-dranarayan also came out to bat, but with little time remaining the game was declared drawn. He was angry with the members of his side for the trouble they had raised and rebuked them sternly, proving his adherence to the ideals of fair play. [43]

On another occasion, when the Natore team was playing against the lawyers of the High Court, the umpire wrongly adjudged a Natore batsman out. The batsman had hit the ball to the bowler, who had failed to stop it. When the ball hit the stumps on the other end, the umpire, thinking that the ball had hit the bowler's hand on the way, declared the batsman 'run out'. [44] The bowler, Purna Ray, [45] went up to the umpire requesting him to reverse his decision. The maharaja, however, intervened, saying that it was against the norms of the game and that the batsman was out. The umpire, scared by the fact that he had given a wrong decision was made to relax by the maharaja, who assured him that it was only human to make mistakes. [46]

The maharaja, so deeply involved in the game, had given up on cricket patronage after 1914, a couple of years after the death of Nripendra Narayan, the Maharaja of Cooch Behar. Panchanan Niyogi, commenting on the maharaja's move to develop literary activity in Bengali declared in the early 1920s that 'In recent times, the Maharaja was so deeply involved in promoting the cause of the Bangiya Sahitya Parishad that he was unable to concentrate on promoting cricket as he had done a few years back'. [47] Rakhaldas Bandopadhyay, commenting on the Maharaja's activities expressed similar views:

> Prior to his interest in stimulating the development of literary activities in Bengali, the Maharaja of Natore was actively involved in promoting cricket. So much so that he had hired professional cricketers from all parts of the country to strengthen his team. These men, recruited by the Maharaja, always lived in his palace. They, fearing what would happen to them if the Maharaja gave up his patronage of cricket, opposed his shift to promoting vernacular literature and his eagerness to be the editor of the *Manasi* magazine. [48]

His giving up on cricket patronage, a game he dearly loved, soon after the death of the Maharaja of Cooch Behar points to the contention that Jagadindranarayan had started promoting cricket to take on his rival.

Finally, it is worth mentioning that cricket patronage by Natore followed a similar trajectory as that by Cooch Behar, raising a suspicion that behind cricket promotion laid a deep-seated desire on the part of the patrons to dent each other's pride. As the Maharaja of Cooch Behar had established his own cricket ground at Woodlands, in South Calcutta, it was essential for Jagadindranarayan to have his own ground, despite the huge expenditure. He had spent more than 100,000 rupees in forming his own ground at Old Ballygunge, an investment that had almost depleted the Natore treasury.

The Legacy

In bringing to light the complex reasons behind cricket/sports patronage by the maharajas, some other extremely significant findings come to the fore. The maharajas, aiming to form quality cricket teams, ignored caste, creed and economic prejudices when recruiting players of merit, making cricket a representative sport in colonial India. Players from diverse economic and cultural backgrounds in colonial India had made their way to the highest rungs of fame – Palwankar Baloo, Palwankar Vithal, H.L. Semper, Lala Amarnath, Amir Elahi and DD Hindlekar, [49] to name but a few. Though the captains of the touring Indian teams – the Maharaja of Patiala in 1911, the Maharaja of Porbander in 1932, the Maharajkumar of Vizianagram in 1936 and Iftikar Ali Khan Pataudi in 1946 – were men from aristocratic families, the leading players in their teams – Palwankar Baloo in 1911, Mohammed Nissar and Amar Singh in 1932, Lala Amarnath in 1936 – were men of humble origins, from economically underprivileged lower-caste backgrounds. Their careers demonstrate that by the early years of the twentieth century prowess in cricket had come to symbolize a ladder for social mobility among the relatively underprivileged. With mastery of the game holding before them prospects of association with, and opportunities to draw benefits from, the ruling elite, cricket was already being looked on as an attractive career option.

Further, contrary to what has been argued in Indian historical writing, it is evident that the maharajas, to fulfil their ambitions and to safeguard their economic needs, had often allied themselves with the nationalists. The Maharaja of Natore promoted cricket in collaboration with Bengali middle-class patrons, Saradaranjan Ray and his brothers. The alliance between the middle classes and the princely patrons, the nationalists and the maharajas, has received scant attention in existing works on Indian history. The Maharaja of Natore's covert agenda of challenging the colonial masters clearly has a nationalist flavour. Such initiatives indicate that not all princes were collaborators of the Raj, as has often been argued, and not all of them took to cricket promotion to associate with the British. From the close of the nineteenth century, some patrons employed cricket and football for furthering nationalist objectives – instances that complicate existing histories of sport in India. This was often the case in Bengal, unlike in Bombay, where there are limited evidences to link the game with the nationalist project, [50] proving that a social history of Indian cricket cannot be written without looking at specific local and regional contexts.

Notes

[1] Keith Sandiford, *Cricket and the Victorians* (London and Aldershot: Scolar Press, 1994), p.1.

[2] Ann Morrow, *The Maharajas of India* (London: Grafton Books, 1986); also see Joanne Punzo Waghorne, *The Rajah's Magic Clothes* (University Park, PA: Penn State University Press, 1994).

[3] Rosalind O'Hanlon, 'Issues of Masculinity in North Indian history: The Bangash Nawabs of Farrukhabad', *Indian Journal of Gender Studies*, 4, 1 (1997).

[4] For details see; Patrick Mcdevitt, 'The King of Sports: Polo in Victorian and Edwardian India', *International Journal of the History of Sport*, 20, 1 (2003).

[5] Indigenous term for wrestling.

[6] In his memoirs, the Maharaja of Natore mentions that the cricket team formed by the Maharaja of Cooch Behar hardly contributed to the improvement of indigenous cricket in Bengal. This was because the Cooch Behar team was composed of British and European players. To remedy this deficiency and ensure an improvement in Indian cricketing standards, the Maharaja of Natore decided to recruit Indian players from all parts of the country. His covert intention in doing this, it may be surmised, was to prove that he was a greater patriot than his Cooch Behar counterpart.

[7] Edward Docker, *History of Indian Cricket* (Delhi: Macmillan, 1976), pp.8–9.

[8] Richard Cashman, *Patrons, Players and the Crowd* (Calcutta: Orient Longman, 1979), pp.39–40.

[9] There was much more to cricket patronage in Bengal than promotion by the Maharajas of Natore and Cooch Behar. The 1910s and 1920s were the glorious years of cricket in colonial Bengal.

[10] This is evident from the huge benefactions the maharaja made in the 1920s for the development of the Bangiya Sahitya Parishad, the best-known literary association in colonial Bengal. For details see Jagadindranath Roy and Prabhatkumar Mukhopadhyay (eds.), *Manasi o Marmabani* (Calcutta, 1925–26).

[11] Cashman, *Patrons, Players and the Crowd*, p.39.

[12] Rakhaldas Bandopadhyaya, 'Smriti Tarpan' in Roy and Mukhopadhyay, *Manasi o Marmabani*, pp.618–19.

[13] Roy and Mukhopadhyay, *Manasi o Marmabani*, pp.525–7.

[14] Ibid.

[15] Charuchandra Mitra, 'Smarane', in Roy and Mukhopadhyay, *Manasi o Marmabani*, pp.575–9.

[16] Hemendrakumar Ray, 'Swargiya Maharaj' in Roy and Mukhopadhyay, *Manasi o Marmabani*, pp.552–4.

[17] A leading intellectual of his time, he was Principal of Vidyasagar College between 1909 and 1925.

[18] Roy and Mukhopadhyay, *Manasi o Marmabani*, pp.575–9.

[19] Saradaranjan founded the Town Club in 1884. The club was the first Bengali team to play against the European Calcutta Cricket Club. This match between the Town Club and the Calcutta Cricket Club was an annual affair from 1895 onwards.

[20] Roy and Mukhopadhyay, *Manasi o Marmabani*, p.580.

[21] Ibid.

[22] Ramakanta Bhattacharya, 'Maharaja Jagadindranath' in Roy and Mukhopadhyay, *Manasi o Marmabani*, pp.561–8.

[23] Ibid.

[24] Ibid.

[25] Ibid., pp.575–9.

[26] He was the first Bengali batsman to score a century against the Calcutta Cricket club at the Eden Gardens in 1907. He was also selected to tour England as part of the Maharaja of Patiala's side but did not tour, fearing excommunication by his caste.

[27] Roy and Mukhopadhyay, *Manasi o Marmabani*, p.580.

[28] Ibid.

[29] Saradaranjan took the lead in organizing a series of matches between the Bengali and Anglo-Indian schools in 1912. A third team, the European schools, joined in 1913, making it a triangular contest.

[30] In one of these tours to Patiala, the Natore team led by the Maharaja defeated the Patiala side, rated to be the best cricket team in colonial India.

[31] Docker, *History of Indian Cricket*; Cashman, *Patrons, Players and the Crowd*; and Mihir Bose, *History of Indian Cricket* (London: Andre Deutsch, 1990) have all argued on these lines.

[32] Roy and Mukhopadhyay, *Manasi o Marmabani*, pp.525–7.

[33] Ibid.

[34] A nationalist leader of the time, Banerjee formed the Indian Association, which merged with the Indian National Congress in 1886and was author of *A Nation in Making*.

[35] Bengali nationalist leader, active during the Swadeshi movement, 1905–8.

[36] Roy and Mukhopadhyay, *Manasi o Marmabani*, pp.525–7.

[37] Ibid., p.576.

[38] Ibid.

[39] Roy and Mukhopadhyay, *Manasi o Marmabani*, pp.552–4.

[40] One of the oldest educational institutions of Bengal. Formed as the Hindu College in 1817, it was renamed the Presidency College in 1855.

[41] Purna Ray, 'Krirakhetre Jagadindranath' in Roy and Mukhopadhyay, *Manasi o Marmabani*, pp.585–8.

[42] If a ball crosses the boundary rope four runs are awarded to the batting side and the ball becomes a dead ball. A batsman cannot be run out after the ball becomes dead.

[43] Roy and Mukhopadhyay, *Manasi o Marmabani*, pp.585–8.

[44] Under the laws of cricket if a ball touches the bowler's hand on its way to the stumps and if the batsman is still out of his crease, he is declared 'run out'. It is perhaps one of the most unfortunate ways of getting out.

[45] He had excelled that season. On another occasion, Ray had smashed the Natore bowling attack to all corners of the park, earning praise from the maharaja.

[46] Ray, 'Krirakhetre Jagadindranath'.

[47] Panchanan Niyogi, 'Jagadindranath Smriti', in Roy and Mukhopadhyay, *Manasi o Marmabani*, pp.555–60.

[48] Bandopadhyaya, 'Smriti Tarpan'.

[49] Baloo, Vithal and Semper were economically underprivileged men from the lower castes, Amarnath the son of a farmer and Amir Elahi the son of a butcher. Faced with severe financial crisis, Elahi had to bowl in local matches for the payment of one rupee. Hindlekar, India's wicketkeeper on the 1936 tour of England, came from to a modest Bombay family and died for lack of medical treatment in 1949.

[50] The struggle between polo and cricket in 1880s Bombay, dealt with in detail by Shapoorjee Sorabjee in his monograph, *Polo vs. Cricket* (Bombay, 1897) and reproduced by Mihir Bose and Ramachandra Guha, is one such instance.

The Political Significance of Sport: An Asian Case Study – Sport, Japanese Colonial Policy and Korean National Resistance, 1910–1945

Gwang Ok

We need to describe the Korean experience under Japanese colonial rule in order to understand the motivation behind the rise of nationalist sport and the role of sport in Korea as an instrument of both domination and resistance.

It is often said by historians that the annexation of Korea by Japan in 1910 was an incident in a larger pattern of imperialism. Japan needed to occupy the peninsula to ensure its progress through the Asian continent. Young-hill Kang wrote about the moment of annexation vividly in his autobiography, *The Grass Roof*:

> All treaties were annulled and Korea was publicly annexed. ... When the news reached the grass roof in Song-Dune-Chi, my father turned a dark red and would not even open his mouth. My uncle, *pak-sa* became suddenly very old, and he shrivelled and fainted in his own room. My crazy-poet uncle sat staring straight ahead of him until far into the night. [1]

Japanese imperialism in Korea was a unique colonial policy. M.R. Peattie has written of contrasting approaches towards colonialism. One involves an exclusionist notion based on cultural and ethnic dissimilarities and the other is an integrationalist notion based on cultural and ethnic similarities. He has argued that the Japanese embraced the worst and most contradictory assumptions of both patterns in its relations to the colonized of Korea. [2] Thus its uniqueness.

The Japanese term *Nikkan heigô* means 'amalgamation of Japan and Korea'. [3] After the March First Movement in 1919, nine years after the annexation, the Japanese premier Hara Kei announced that the Japanese government would treat Koreans in all respects in the same way as the Japanese. [4] Koreans were never the equals of the Japanese during the colonial period. Brutal and savage discrimination characterized the entire period. Ultimately, the Japanese government in Korea was militaristic in nature and action. Of the eight governors-general, seven were army generals and the other was a naval admiral. One Japanese historian, Shakuo Shunjo, frankly admitted in *A History of Korean Annexation*, published in Tokyo in 1926, that 'the entire Korean peninsula was turned into a military camp'. [5]

The actual relationship between Korea and Japan in this period has been revealed in Korea, but *not* in Japan. This actuality should not go unrevealed. We will see what happened in this article; we will discover how Japan ruled Korea and how Koreans reacted against this rule during the colonial period between 1910 and 1945.

Japanese Colonial Policy, 1905–45

The Japanese penetration of Korea became a reality after the fateful Ulsa Treaty of 22 August 1905 [6] between the two nations. The Japanese colonization of Korea was a stepping-stone for Japan's Asian continental expansion. As already made clear, when Japan annexed Korea, it imposed military rule. Koreans lost their freedom. [7] Thousands of Koreans had to leave their homeland to work for the recovery of its independence abroad or to work in Japan in various types of colonial slavery such as enforced military service and as comfort women. This harsh imperialism had been signalled as early as in 1876 by the unequal and ruthless Treaty of Ganghwa. [8] The eventual full colonialism lasted from 1910 to 1945.

An evaluation of the Japanese colonial policy in Korea by Andrew C. Nahm offers a generally accepted view: it was cruel and highly exploitative; it was discriminatory against Koreans; it involved material exploitation; it failed to lay any foundation for progressive modernization; it failed to convert the Korean people to the Japanese way of life. Furthermore, it gave rise to a strong sense of national identity and to a bitter anti-Japanese hostility. [9]

The Japanese exploited both human and natural 'material' in order to further the economic development of Japan. To this end the Japanese fully utilized the Koreans. Ironically, the Japanese called Korea at the time 'a thriving land'. [10] This was an arrogant imperialistic point of view. In fact, it 'thrived' less than intended. Attempts for it to 'thrive' in Japanese terms were vigorously rejected by the Koreans. In the long term, colonization was less than fully successful due, in large measure, to strong resistance by patriotic Koreans.

After the Russo-Japanese War of 1904 and 1905, Japanese power in East Asia was stronger than ever. Japan confidently forced Korea to be a Japanese protectorate in 1905 and eventually occupied it. In August 1910, Korea was annexed and had to reorganize its governmental system based on Japanese advice. The Prime Minister, Wan-yong Yi, signed the treaty of annexation and the last king of Korea, King Sunjong, announced the annexation to the people on August 29, 1910. The Korean dynasty, which had survived for 518 years, ended with the treaty. As shall be discussed shortly, annexation greatly affected the direction of Korean nationalism in the early twentieth century. [11] Nahm has described Japanese colonial rule in Korea as characterized by three periods. The first, from 1910 to 1919, was the period of total oppression. The second period, from 1919 to 1931, was the period of awakening resistance to colonial rule. The final period, from 1931 to August 1945, was the period of attempted Japanization. [12]

The first governor-general, Terauchi Masatake (1852–1919), [13] in office from 1910 to 1919, firmly implemented orthodox Japanese aims. He insisted that there was a natural relationship between the Korean and the Japanese. He noted historical and cultural ties between the two nations, and attempted the assimilation of the Korean people into Japanese society and culture. However, the relationship was always one of Japanese superiority and Korean inferiority. Terauchi suspended the publication of all Korean newspapers, disbanded political organizations and prohibited public gatherings of all types. With the countryside pacified and opposition in the cities stifled, Terauchi was in position to finish constructing the political institutions of the colonial state, a process begun during the Residency-General period (a colonial government by a military general) of 1910 and 1919. [14]

Japanese rule in Korea was rooted in past political and economic opportunities. In fact, Japan had obtained tacit international approval for designs on the Korean peninsula as far back as 1876. [15] Japan began to strengthen its strategic and economic ties with the peninsula through wars with China (1894–5) and Russia (1904–5). Moreover, the forming of the Anglo-Japanese Alliance (1902) [16] and the signing of a memorandum of understanding with the United States (Taft-Katsura Memorandum, 1905) [17] allowed Japan to eventually secure its domination in Korea. The annexation of Korea was already predicated, therefore, on earlier actions; it was formalized in the eyes of the world and in practice in 1910. [18]

At the beginning of the annexation period, the governor-generalship consisted of a secretariat and five departments: general affairs, internal affairs, finance, agriculture-commerce-industry and justice. There were six bureaux of the secretariat: police, investigation, railway, monopoly, communication and land survey. In 1912, agricultural-commerce-industry was divided into two departments, agriculture-forestry and production. [19] An independent department of security, separate from the secretariat, was also established later, in 1917.

Importantly, also in 1917, a new criminal law was created and a law concerning *political* criminals was announced in April 1919 after the March First Movement of 1919. [20] To run these departments and bureaux, from 1910 to 1937, senior colonial officials totalled 87,552. Initially the Japanese numbered 52,270 and Koreans numbered 35,282. In total by 1937, those who worked for the colonial government amounted to 246,000 Japanese and 63,000 Koreans. It was a significant imbalance. Most senior colonial officials were Japanese. Occasionally, a few Koreans were appointed as provincial governors. A few Koreans were also engaged as county superintendents after 1919. Koreans were mostly appointed as chiefs in districts and villages. [21] No official was elected. In total, around 42 per cent of Japanese residents in Korea were directly or indirectly involved in the colonial government of the Korea. [22]

During the first decade from 1910 to 1919, the Japanese colonial government ruled Korea absolutely, politically, economically and culturally. Despite pious statements about 'equality', Koreans were repressed. The aim appears to have been the subjugation of the people by means of a military dictatorship. [23] This is often called the 'dark period' of the colonial period in Korea. Incidentally, the later tone of the Japanese Empire in Asia was actually set in Korea. The first governor, General Terauchi Masatake, set the tone in Korea when he warned that if he met any resistance, he would whip offenders with scorpions. [24] Japan banned political organizations and the right of assembly. Only innocuous journals, newspapers, religious bulletins and youth magazines were permitted during the period. Major Korean publications, including the respected *Korean Daily News* (*Taehan Maeil Shinbo*, 1905–10), were prohibited. Every publication allowed the right to survive was censored by the Japanese government. [25] Moreover, all Korean textbooks in schools were banned and hundreds of private schools were closed. [26]

The Korean loss of press freedom was graphically described by a Japanese reporter from *Tokyo Nichi Nichi Shimbun* on 2 October 1910: 'Newspapers were checked one by one; controls on companies were exercised to an extreme, unsatisfactory companies being destroyed one after the other. Reporters and writers were at their wit's end, gasping. If one grumbled, he would be arrested. ... I felt as if I were in hell.' [27]

During the second period, between 1919 and 1931, with Japan still confidently in control but somewhat concerned by Korean recalcitrance, Japan announced a new Imperial Rescript with the avowed intention of bringing about reconciliation between the two nations. As already noted, the official policy of the colonial government was based on an alleged principle of non-differentiation between the two countries. These changes of Japanese colonial policy were strongly influenced by the March First Movement of 1919, which was a massive national unarmed protest movement against both the harsh colonial policy and blatant discrimination. Japanese officials now realized that their covert colonial policy, total oppression and appropriation, was less than successful. The Koreans' resistance was unexpected and massive. In response, according to a new ordinance of December 1920, Koreans became eligible for certain positions at work. Pay became equalized with Japanese employees. However, there was still differentiation in bonus payments. Furthermore, a new more humane civil code was proclaimed, and a more lenient family registration law came into effect on 1 July 1923. [28]

The second governor-general, Saitô Makoto, permitted Koreans to publish newspapers in Korean in January 1920. Several newspapers resulted. Among them were the *Dong-a Ilbo* (Oriental Daily), run by a group of nationalists, and *Choseon Ilbo* (Korean Daily). The *Jung-ang Ilbo* (Central Daily) was later established in Seoul in November 1926. However, all of them were continuously censored by the police and if they contained any anti-Japanese material, they were suspended. [29]

During this period, the colonial government organized the Committee for Compilation of Korean History and published a History of Korea in December 1922. Its contents, containing many inaccuracies and misrepresentations, were to legitimize Japanese colonialism in Korea both before and after 1905. [30] In essence, therefore, there was an easing of repressive control in this second period but mostly it was cosmetic. Firm control was still maintained.

The third period of the Japanese colonial policy was called 'the critical times'. All the policies during this time were intended to serve general Japanese military aggression. The first governor-general of this period, Ugaki Kazushige (June 1931–August 1936) launched his policy for Korea to support the Japanese military empire with his slogan 'unity in spirit and increase in production'. In fact, there was no option for Japan, since the policy of the assimilation of two nations was urgently needed for the colonial government to contribute to the Sino-Japanese War of 1937. Minami Jirô, the governor-general of the second administration in this period (August 1936–May 1942), preached Japanese integrationist theory relentlessly to the Koreans in order to obtain his urgent military materials for the war. When the Sino-Japanese War became a long-term war, Japan transformed Korea into a military supply base for the war. Minami established a new army special volunteers regulation in accordance with the Imperial Ordinance No.95 of 22 February 1938. From then on, progressively, military training centres for the army special volunteers were established throughout Korea. This arrangement remained in place until 1943, when the military conscription system was introduced. Between 1938 and 1939, 15,294 Korean youths were forced to 'volunteer'. When military conscription was applied to Korea, about 214,000 Korean youths were given physical examinations and 25,000 were inducted into active military service in 1944. In 1944, a navy special volunteer system was introduced and at this time about 3,000 Koreans were inducted into the Navy. [31]

The colonial government also began to mobilize Korean labour from 1939. Koreans were sent to work in Korea and Japan, and later they were sent to the Pacific, to Asia or wherever the Japanese were fighting. Furthermore, thousands of Korean women were forcedly sent to war areas to 'comfort' Japanese soldiers. [32]

In this the last phase of Japanese colonial policy, Japan's aim was to force Korea to assist Japan in pursuit of its war objectives. This caused great resentment in Korea. Between 1940 and 1945, some 5,600 Koreans were arrested as 'thought criminals' or as undesirable or rebellious individuals. [33] Colonial oppression ended only when the Japanese mainland was attacked by American atomic bombers on 6 August 1945. Japan surrendered and Korea was liberated at 12.00 p.m. on 15 August 1945.

It is time now to consider more fully the nature of Korean resistance to Japanese control in the colonial period.

Korean Resistance during the Japanese Colonial Period: 1905–45

The independence movement in Korea was, in some regards, like the movement in India. It was mostly non-violent, except for the Koreans in China and Manchuria, who were supported by the Communist military. [34] However, Robert T. Oliver has concluded that, unlike India, Korean resistance lacked coherence, unity and sustained continuity and was less successful. He suggested one significant reason: 'For one thing, Japan was not England. Nothing like the All-India Congress Party was possible in colonized Korea.' [35] Perhaps Korean resistance was far from successful, but it was successful enough to plant the seed of Koreanism and to stimulate a refusal to capitulate without protest.

Before the Japanese annexation of 1910, Emperor Kojong had tried to enlist foreign support for Korea's sovereign independence by sending the special envoys Sangseol Yi, Jun Yi and Wiyong Yi to the second International Peace Conference held in June 1907 in the Hague. Unhappily, the world in the early twentieth century did not respond to Korea. Koreans had to rely on themselves. There were various kinds of Korean national resistance against Eastern imperialism. The 'Righteous Army' (*Euibyeong*) movement was the most aggressive, but there were less violent independence movements. Resistance occurred throughout the whole country right through the Japanese occupation, and national resistance was vigorously maintained nationwide during the whole of the Japanese colonial period. [36] Moreover, Korean independence armies fought against Japanese military troops located in foreign countries, especially in China and Russia under the command of the Provisional Government, which was established by Korean nationalists in Shanghai in April 1919. [37]

After the governmental system was set up by the Japanese following the Protectorate Treaty of 1905, the Korean Army was completely disbanded except for a small unit of palace guards. Many from the disbanded army created the Righteous Army [38] In 1907, the Righteous Army became a serious challenge to Japan's 'indirect' rule of Korea. By then the Japanese government in Korea had demobilized the whole of the Korean army, including even the units of the royal bodyguard. Some of the Righteous Army refused to surrender. They were eventually totally defeated by Japanese army. According to Japanese records, 17,600 Korean guerrillas were killed by the Japanese military and police in the fighting between 1906 and 1910. [39] Table 1 shows the extent of the resistance of the Righteous Army between 1907 and 1911.

The defeat of the insurgents was inevitable. The Righteous Army was armed only with old matchlocks, swords and spears. Among its leaders were radicals who were in

Table 1

The Resistance of the 'Righteous Army' against Japanese Aggressors

Year	Number of battles	Number of volunteers
1907 (August–December)	323	44,116
1908	1,452	69,832
1909	898	25,763
1910	147	1,891
1911 (January–June)	33	216

Source: Jeong-myong Kim, *Chosun Dongnip Undong I* ['Korean Independence Movement I'] (Tokyo: Weonseobang, 1967), p.131.

favour of modernization and conservatives who were against modernization. Anti-Japanese resistance brought them together. [40] A stalwart defender of Confucian orthodoxy and former minister, Ikhyeon Choe (1833–1906) [41] led a Righteous Army group in Jeolla province in early 1906. He was arrested and exiled to the Japanese island of Tsushima. Choe refused food and starved himself to death in 1906. Jongsik Min, a modernizer and former minister, led the army in Chungcheong province and Dol-seok Sin, also a modernizer, organized the army in Gyeongsang province.

In the winter of 1907, Righteous Army groups from 13 provinces under the command of its leader, Inyeong Yi (1867–1909) were ordered to attack the Japanese forces in Seoul. The Korean forces were outgunned and outmanoeuvred. In the face of modern Japanese military power, the Righteous Army had to use hit-and-run guerrilla tactics. The Koreans continued their resistance even after 1910 along the border between Korea and Manchuria under the name of *Gwangbokgun* (the Independent Army). [42]

The non-violent independence movements involved literature, education and religion. Thus this moment in Korean history is called the 'Korean Risorgimento'. [43] However, 'although Japanese rule stimulated Korean national identity and political consciousness, the very success of its co-optive political control policies exacerbated internal cleavages among Korean independence fighters. Such contradictory effects have left a mixed legacy among Koreans to this day.' [44]

Despite the fact that the Japanese suppressed political organizations and the press, Korean intellectuals did not easily give up their opposition to the Japanese policy of Korean cultural destruction. Si-gyeong Ju standardized the Korean language and carried forward his commitment to the Korean language even under ferocious Japanese suppression, thus laying the groundwork for the emergence of a Korean language movement in the 1920s. Gwangsu Lee wrote a novel, *Mujeong* ('The Heartless', 1917) that established the respectability of the modern novel in Korea. In journalism, the magazines *Sonyeon* ('Youth', 1907–11) and *Cheong-chun* ('Young Years', 1914–18) offered forums for Western literature, social commentary, history and literary experimentation. [45] In these ways both the Korean language and culture and Western influences and contacts were kept alive.

As already made clear, various independence movements, such as the Righteous Army movement, the Society for the Restoration of the Korean Nation and the League for the Restoration of National Authority existed during the first Japanese colonial period, 1910–19. And the New People's Society (*Shinminhoe*), founded in 1907, which was organized by Chang-ho An (1878–1938), an independence movement leader, should be added to the list. It continued its fight for freedom beyond Korea as branches of Seungman Lee's United States-based Korean National Association (*Gungminhoe*). In 1913, a women's association, the Pine and Bamboo Society, was established under the leadership of Shin-deok Hwang (1898–1933) to promote female patriotism. Thousands of Koreans who belonged to those societies resisted Japanese colonial rule, and many of them were arrested and some eventually killed. By way of example, in 1919 some 700 Koreans suspected of involvement in the assassination of Governor-General Terauchi (1852–1919) were arrested. Among them were over a hundred Christian leaders. However, patriotism was not stifled. National independence movements flourished more strongly than ever after the great nationwide mass demonstration, the March First Independence Movement in 1919. This movement signified the beginning of a new struggle for Korean independence inside and outside Korea. Thus the 1920s saw a cooperative movement which resulted in a Korean Provisional Government established in the French concession of Shanghai on 18 September 1919. Its constituents were representatives of Korean groups in Manchuria, Siberia and China. The first president was the veteran nationalist Seungman Lee (1875–1965). [46] Koreans in Siberia also organized communist and socialist groups between 1918 and 1919. Lenin, however, did not regard such Korean groups as part of the Comintern, because they were exiled parties from their homeland. Thus Korean communist groups from Siberia, Shanghai and Tokyo organized a new underground Korean Communist Party in Seoul in April 1925.

After 1927, the New Foundations Society (*Shinganhoe*), which was made up of both nationalists and socialists, played a significant role on the domestic front, especially from 1927 to about 1931. This society aimed to achieve a new integration of the national liberation movement front. Shinganhoe had three principles: 'to promote political and economic awakening, to strengthen national solidarity, and to disavow any form of opportunism'. [47] This group, however, was eventually dissolved, a victim of its own disunity and the intense attention of the Japanese police. [48]

Students played an active part in dissent. A large-scale student protest took place in 1929 on commuter trains in Gwangju, South Jeolla Province. The students were strongly against the Japanese colonial discriminatory policy. ProtestS continued in 1930; 54,000 students from 194 schools participated in this movement. It was the largest movement since the March First Movement, and was wholly comprised of students. Many were arrested, imprisoned and killed by the Japanese imperial police.

After the March First Movement, however, some Koreans were not afraid of the Japanese police and often vigorously confronted them. [49]

In the 1930s, the independence movement was characterized by an attempt to create a nation state. Its leaders aimed to establish a unified nation. They formed political parties and organizations in order to confront the Japanese imperialists. The movements of the 1930s were divided between China, Manchuria and Korea. In 1931, Shinganhoe, as noted above, was dissolved because of internal disunion. Between 1935 and 1941 Korean resistance against Japanese imperialism was largely carried on by groups outside Korea. The groups organized parties to achieve independence. There was the North-east Anti-Japanese United Army (*Tongbuk Hang-il Yeon-gun*), led by Kim Ilseong, who later became the leader of North Korea. This party was based on support from Koreans in Manchuria; Kim Ku's national party, the United Association of Movements for the Revival of Korea (*Han-guk Gwangbok Undong Danche Yeonhaphoe*) cooperated with the Chinese Nationalist Government (*Kuomintang*) in Chungching; and Seungman Lee, who later became the first president of South Korea, had American backing. [50] After 1935, some of the Korean Communists joined the Chinese Communist Party and reached Mao Tse-tung's Yenan headquarters in northern China. Later they organized a Korean Independence League and also a small Korean Volunteer Army of several hundred men which fought against the Japanese until independence came in 1945. [51] On the domestic front, the National Foundation League was not only a unified body of left and right but also formed ties with overseas fronts. Eventually, the Korean independence movement faced a Japanese Empire which spread into Manchuria, northern China and then deep into China in the 1930s. [52] By the late 1930s the common conviction shared by the far-flung members of the different Korean independence movements was the conviction that only the military defeat of Imperial Japan would bring freedom to Korea. [53]

Having set the nationalist political scene, now it is time to consider in some detail the context in which nationalist (and other) sport developed during the period of Japanese colonial rule, 1910–19. The analysis will discuss features influencing this development, notably the practice of colonialism, the development of nationalism and the associated inexorable move towards modernity. It is important to appreciate that sport was used as an instrument of both colonialism and anti-colonialism.

Japanese policy in Korea shared common characteristics with colonialism in other countries. [54] In particular, it recognized the importance of education as a means of socializing the population and instilling in it an orientation to colonial rule. Education, however, at this time also served both the aims of Korean and Western missionary ideals. Japan therefore sought to change the curriculum, including the sports curriculum. The colonial policy, however, was not inflexible. To win goodwill it reacted to and, to a certain extent, adapted to Korean attitudes and responses. Japan recognized the potential of sport both for the development of imperial subservience and the creation of Korean nationalism. It tried hard to weaken the latter and to strengthen the former.

Sport in Korea: An Introduction

Some Korean intellectuals [55] in the early twentieth century, who advocated an open-door policy, insisted on the acceptance of Western culture as the necessary means to achieve the modernization of the country. They specifically advocated sport as a means of building a healthy, powerful and modern Korea. They believed that in a highly competitive world only the fittest survived. As already stated, due to Japanese ambitions, Korea was confronted with the danger of losing its national identity. One way to remedy the damaging situation and fight back was to build up physical prowess as well as public morale through sport. Consequently, by 1910, influential segments of Korean society launched physical education programmes in modern Western-type schools and athletics meetings for communities. This embryonic stage of modern sport in Korea set the tone for the general direction of sports development. The bulk of physical instructors, at this time, were former army officers of the late Chosun dynasty. They were antagonistic towards Japanese colonialism and strongly nationalistic. Their attitudes were reflected in their instruction. They inculcated nationalism into the young and, at the same time, inspired the public with patriotism by means of sport. Sports activities were held in schools and in the wider community. They helped Koreans develop a strong sense of solidarity and thus promoted corporate unity. [56]

One form of Christianity, Roman Catholicism, had been introduced to Korea well before the late nineteenth century. Severe persecutions accompanied Catholicism and continued until Korea opened its doors to the Western world. After Japanese colonization there was a rapid growth of Christianity. In Table 2, we can see the rapid increase of Christianity in Korean society during the colonial period. Its increase was much more rapid than that of the population. [57]

If Christians remained a small section of the population as a whole, they were influential. During the first phase of the Japanese colonial period, 1910–19, it was extremely difficult for Christians because of Japanese oppression. As discussed earlier, the Japanese tried to 'absorb' the Koreans during the period of colonization. Western

Table 2
Increase of Christian Population, 1912–38

Year	Roman Catholics	Protestants	Population of Korean Peninsula
1912	78,850		
1914		86,000	15,508,872
1934	147,476		
1936		168,477	
1938			22,800,647

Christianity was an obstacle to this policy. [58] Therefore Japanese officialdom considered that Christianity had to be removed from Korean society. In fact, however, this ambition never succeeded throughout the entire occupation. And in fact Christianity, as we shall see, provided a tool in the form of modern sport for Korean nationalists.

The Japanese, for their part, attempted to control both education and sport in education. Their aim was to turn Koreans into Japanese. Mould the young and thus mould future adults is an old approach in imperialism. Thus the Japanese did not sit idly by and watch helplessly the development of nationalistic tendencies in Korean sport. The Resident-General's office banned military-style gymnastics and the mass drill that resembled military training, restricted general participation in sport and then curbed the frequency and size of athletics meetings. Furthermore, as Korean resistance against Japanese aggression gradually developed, the Japanese instituted 'government by bayonet' and tried to stamp out all resistance movements. One of the first repressive measures of the Japanese was the dismissal of the physical instructors who had served in the Korean army, on the grounds of inappropriate qualifications. They were suspected correctly of promoting nationalistic sentiments in the schools and in society. The awakening Korea did not let the Japanese rulers have their way unchallenged, and consequently there ensued increasing friction between Japanese and Korean. [59]

At the same time, the Japanese authorities changed physical education itself from a group activity to individualistic gymnastics that emphasized individual technique. This was designed to undermine 'team spirit' among Koreans. [60] Moreover, the governor-general's office closely monitored and controlled all sporting events. These were allowed to take place only under strict supervision. More importantly, Korean schools were deprived of autonomy in the field of physical education and the colonial government dictated what was to be taught and what was not to be taught.

In spite of, or indeed because of, the heavy-handed oppression of the Japanese colonial government, the Korean people's interest and participation in modern sport steadily increased. As already noted, it became a form of national protest. Koreans now revived their traditional sports such as *Ssi-rum* (Korean traditional wrestling), Korean-style wrestling and archery, and thereby tried to stress the longevity of national identity as well as to maintain national self-respect through indigenous as well as modern sport.

On 1 March 1919, as already made clear, a nationwide movement of resistance ignited. The same day marked the beginning of a new era in the sports history of Korea. There developed conscientious efforts to unify various sports movements combining all different groups into one national organization. It also meant that Korean sport reached a mature stage in which Koreans were ready for a single umbrella organization to provide a unified and purposeful leadership. In compliance with such a timely spirit, in 1919 there emerged the Korean Sports Federation – under the aegis, however, of Japanese officialdom!

The Development of Modern Sport in Modern Schools and Colonial Education

As already stated, after Japan annexed Korea in 1910 it forced Koreans to accept its military control. Japanese colonial policy from 1910 to 1919 aimed at the Japanization of Korean society by repressing national consciousness and culture. In this brutal early stage of colonial policy, Japan oppressed Koreans ruthlessly. In this process, Japanese imperial education played an important role. Dr Horace H. Underwood (1890–1951), who was professor of psychology at Gyeongsin College (Chosun Christian College) in Korea from 1934 to 1941, once described modern Korean education under the Japanese as follows: 'It was now the scene of many experiments in ... *assimilation*'. [61]

Japanese colonial education during the first decade aimed to produce useful workers, to develop the economy and to educate Koreans in Japanese culture and language. It was a tool for transmitting Japanese cultural and political values and to justify colonial rule in Korea. A significant educational ordinance was announced by the Japanese government in Korea on 23 August 1911 as the 229th Imperial Command. It stated:

> Article 1: Education for Koreans in Chosun shall be given in accordance with this ordinance. ... The date of putting this ordinance into force shall be determined by the Governor-General of Chosun. The common schools, high schools and girls' high schools which have existed hitherto will be recognized as common schools, high schools and girls' high schools established in compliance with this ordinance; also agricultural schools, commercial schools and industrial supplementary schools which have existed hitherto will be recognized as agricultural schools, commercial schools and elementary industrial schools established in accordance with this ordinance. Concerning those schools existing at the time of the enforcement of this ordinance, irrespective of its provisions, the Governor-General of Chosun may make or take necessary arrangements or measures. [62]

Japanese efforts to control the educational system in Korea, in fact, had begun earlier in the protectorate period, in 1906. In a series of ordinances promulgated after 1906, the Japanese established government control of textbooks and the curriculum in public schools. After 1910, codes regulating all public and private schools were unified. The tight regulation of private schools was significant because after 1906 private schools, operated by Korean nationalists and foreign missionaries, had encouraged intellectual freedom and had provided a cover for political activity. In consequence, because of Japanese regulation, the numbers of private and mission schools were reduced. In 1907 missionaries ran 508 primary schools, 22 high schools and two theological colleges; by 1917 only 34 missionary schools remained.

After the Japanese governor-general announced the 1911 Education Ordinance, a further ordinance followed, on 20 October 1911 concerning common schools [63]: a General Government Edict. [64] Summarized, it is as follows:

1. common schools (*Botong Hakgyo*) were established for primary education; they aimed to educate children in health and the Japanese language, to inculcate virtue and to teach general knowledge;
2. the schools provided a four-year course. There could be exceptions but only in accordance with local circumstances;
3. the entrance level was at age eight or over;
4. the subjects were ethics, Japanese language, Korean-Chinese language, arithmetic, science, singing, gymnastics, painting, manual training (for boys), handicraft (for girls), primary level economics and agriculture. [65]

There were three different types of common schools: government (under Japanese control), public and private. The numbers of common schools between 1911 and 1919 decreased. There was, however, an increase of government and public schools. For instance, in 1911, there were two government, 234 public and 70 private schools (mission schools and schools operated by Korean nationalists). In 1913, there were two government, 366 public and 20 private schools; in 1915, there were two government, 410 public and 17 private schools; in 1919, there were two government, 535 public and 33 private schools.

The secondary school was called *Botong Hakgyo* (the higher common school). It also had a four-year course (three years for girls): 'No provision or plan existed for raising the grade of the lower schools or for providing a University for Korea. This situation was maintained until the 1920s.' [66] The situation in the period from 1910 to 1919 was of particular importance. The Japanese government revised the educational ordinance on 20 October 1911, especially for boys' secondary schools. It changed the name to secondary school for boys and revised its regulation under Government Edict No.111: [67]

1. Educational aim: the secondary school for boys taught boys to develop their character and practical knowledge for life;
2. the period: a four year course;
3. the entrance level: boys over years old or common school graduates were eligible to enter;
4. the subjects: ethics, Japanese, Korean-Chinese, history, geography, mathematics, medicine, business, law, writing, painting, singing, gymnastics, English (only in veterinary studies).

The Japanese government also established government secondary schools throughout the nation between 1911 and 1919. Furthermore, according to Government Edict No.187, some subjects were added, such as chemistry, legal economic studies, foreign languages (English, German and French) and educational studies for desirable or appropriate student teachers. The establishment of the higher common schools is given in Table 3.

The Japanese government also established higher common schools [68] for girls (see Table 4), such as the Kyeongseong Girls' Higher Common School (its name was changed from Hanseong Girls' Higher Common School in September 1911) and Pyeongyang Girls' Higher Common School in 1914. Girls' schools had domestic training, music and handicraft as well as the basic subjects discussed earlier. These schools were regulated in accordance with Government Edict No.188, which was drawn up specifically for the girls' higher common schools in December 1919. [69] Gymnastics was also typical of the girls higher common schools.

The colonial government issued regulations for higher education in 1915. Subsequently, there were several colleges: Kyeonsung Joensu College, Kyeonseong Medical College and Kyeongseong Engineering College in April 1916. In 1918, Suwon Agricultural College was established. The 1915 regulations for the colleges were as follows:

1. educational aim: to educate at a higher level of studies;
2. the period of study: three or four years;

Table 3
The Establishment of Boys' Higher Common Schools, 1910–19

Types	Year								
School	1911	1912	1913	1914	1915	1916	1917	1918	1919
Gov.	2	2	2	2	2	3	3	4	5
Pub.									
Priv.	1	1	2	2	2	4	6	6	7
Total	3	3	4	4	4	7	9	10	12

Gov: government schools; Pub: public schools; Priv: private schools.
Source: *Dae 11 and 13, the Annual Statistics of the Japanese General Government* (General Government in Korea, 1924), p. 2.

Table 4
The Establishment of Girls' Higher Common Schools, 1911–19

Types	Year								
	1911	1912	1913	1914	1915	1916	1917	1918	1919
Gov.	1	1	1	2	2	2	2	2	2
Pub.									
Priv.	1	2	2	2	2	2	2	4	4
Total	2	3	3	4	4	4	4	6	6

3. entrance level: for those who have graduated from higher common schools at the age of or over;
4. the subjects: Japanese ethics, professional studies and finally, gymnastics. Gymnastics were an essential physical education component in schools under the Japanese. As stated earlier, team games were not popular with the Japanese. They were dangerous; they promoted nationalism. Gymnastics on the other hand was individualistic and developed strong bodies for military purposes. However, the Japanese encouraged certain kinds of team (war) games. These will be discussed briefly later.

Now it is time to examine the role of the mission schools and the YMCA in promoting resistance through sport and education.

Missionary Education, the YMCA and Sport, 1910–19

After Korea had opened its doors to the world, Western missionaries were involved in the development of modern education. It is important to explore this missionary work during the first period of Japanese colonial rule from 1910 to 1919.

For missionaries, evangelization was important. A large number of Bible classes enrolled students throughout the country. A report in 1907 identifies 191 local classes in Pyeongyang which had over 10,000 students. [70] The classes were held for both men and women. The women were also taught hygiene, sanitation and child care. When a missionary arrived in a village for the class, the women of the village arranged a programme for the day. They gathered to pray and to sing. The sessions lasted sometimes until evening. The first classes targeted women, but classes for men were held later. [71]

P.L. Gillett [72] arrived in Korea to work for the YMCA in late 1901. In fact, the Korean YMCA was formally created on 28 October 1903. Although the American committee offered funds to establish the organization and sent missionaries such as John Wanamaker and John D. Rockefeller, the Koreans themselves were keen to be responsible for its establishment. A Korean member of the Independence Party, Heung-taek Hyeon, [73] was the owner of the land first given to the association.

Frank Brockman (1867–1944) [74] arrived in 1905 and George Gregg, [75] the founder of the Industrial School, also came to work for the YMCA in 1906. Later Lloyd H. Snyder [76] came to Korea to teach English and general education at the YMCA. Snyder was appointed as director at the Department of Industry, which included education and industry, in 1915. [77] In 1906, the Physical Education Committee of the YMCA was formed. The best Korean athletes came to the YMCA because that was where the best instructors were. In 1907, three buildings, financed by funds from America, were completed. These buildings became important meeting places for political organizations as well as for sport. In 1916, P.Y. Barnhart arrived to work for the junior department and athletics. Also in 1916, an indoor gymnasium was built, and basketball and volleyball were promoted, especially as winter sports.

The YMCA was the only institution among mission schools which engaged in general physical education during the period. [78] Although all schools had drill exercises in this period, the YMCA strongly emphasized general physical education. Its emphasis eventually influenced schools. H.H. Underwood stated in *Modern Education in Korea*: 'General classes in physical education with indoor and outdoor programmes now enrolled between 700 and 1,000 in addition to the special classes which have supplied the teachers of physical education to many of the schools in Korea.' [79] The Boy Scout movement and the Christian Citizenship Training Programme were also set up by the YMCA, [80] first in Seoul and then in other cities. Furthermore, the radical effects of the world student movement within the YMCA international organization were felt in Korea. Even as late as the 1980s, progressive reforms continued to be an important part of the YMCA youth group's agenda. Indeed, the Christian student movement is still intensely involved in promoting positive social change in modern Korean society. One early influential outcome was a four-year secondary school course founded by the YMCA in 1907. In the school, there were three grades of English classes, two grades of Japanese classes and industrial classes as its daytime classes. There were night school classes in English, Chinese, Japanese and music, including a working boys' night school. [81]

The YMCA came to Korea at a critical time. After Japan's victory over China in the Sino-Japanese War, the Korean peninsula was eyed hungrily by Japan and Russia, but Japanese control, as stated earlier, came about following Japan's victory in the Russo-Japanese War. Furthermore, an agreement in 1905 between President Theodore Roosevelt and Japan conceded Korea to Japanese control and confirmed US hegemony over the Philippines. Because of these foreign actions, various indigenous political organizations were formed to fight for Korean independence. These organizations comprised a new intellectual class that was much influenced by Western bourgeois thought and groups such as the YMCA. This was because the YMCA reached out to the Korean elite. Western sport was as yet not popular with the general public. YMCAs became established throughout the country and of course, as has already been made clear, promoted Western sport, among other things. This was appreciated by the elitists. Physical education, as already noted, was fully appreciated as an important part of the nationalist curriculum. There were baseball and athletics and, in addition, tennis, basketball, volleyball, skating, football and various other games. [82] More importantly, however, the YMCAs were meeting places for the nationalists. The Japanese did not interfere with their activities, clubs and meetings since they were American, not Korean.

Korean Reaction to the Japanese Physical Education Programme, 1910–19

Colonial education was symbolized by the restriction of the private schools. This is clear from the announcement of the Revision of Regulation for Private Schools by the Governor-General in 1915:

Our educational purpose is not only to development the intelligence and morality of the people, but to plant a national spirit of allegiance to the Japanese empire … the efforts of missionaries should be restricted to pure evangelism and education in Korea should be totally in the hand of the Governor-General. [83]

Korean education in Japanese hands became colonial education. The earlier nationalistic character of modern education received a setback. The nature of school sport was changed. At the time of the Japanese annexation of Korea, sport in school had been modernized, mainly due to Western foreign teachers in schools. [84] It now changed crucially to militaristic sport that aimed – by means of gymnastics and 'war games' – to ensure Japanese martial purposes.

Hak-rae Lee [85] found clear evidence of the change in Korean sport at this time. Lee noted that physical education was now controlled by the Japanese government. The aim was to create a new curriculum. [86] The physical education curriculum changed in accordance with the announcement of the physical education curriculum on 10 June 1914 as Edict No.27 of the Governor-General:

The importance of physical education does not need to be mentioned. However, in the past its curricula in schools were not formulated. Therefore, here we enact the curriculum of physical education. Every school should adhere to this curriculum for physical education. Every school should create appropriate courses, considering the circumstances of the area, the facilities of each school, its gender character and levels of developments of mind and body of the pupil. [87]

The *Chejo Kyowoen Kangsup Hwoe* ('Short Course for Teachers of Physical Education'), established in 1914 by the Governor-General's Department of Education, was further responsible for a sea-change in Korean modern sport. Now pupils and teachers were centrally controlled.

Thus programmes of physical education for both teachers and pupils were now centralized and physical education made uniform in all schools. Japan, however, was not concerned with genuine physical education for general well-being. As with other aspects of Japanese colonial policy, physical education was used to achieve the Japanization of Koreans. Physical education during this time makes this very clear. Firstly, the drill, previously present with the purpose of instilling patriotic confidence through fitness, changed in character. It became blatant Japanese military training. It included shooting, skirmishing, surprise attacks, drilling by companies and gun drill. In essence, Japan intended to introduce military training under the guise of physical education as a means of expanding the supply of men for the Japanese Army.

Secondly, team games were permitted, but they were mostly 'war games' and were divided into two groups: Western competitive games and militaristic action games. There was flag raising, flag transmitting and so forth. Competitive games did include those played before annexation. The Japanese, to an extent, adapted to Korean interests to make them more amenable to Japanese intentions. Modern Western sports such as baseball, basketball and football, therefore, remained in the curricula of physical education in schools. However amenability was not always achieved.

Football was especially popular. Boys could play it almost anywhere. And through football boys could indirectly express their feelings about Japanese colonialism. Songs in support of their own football teams were various and partisan, and obliquely patriotic. Consider the following example from the match between Kangjin Primary School and Haenam Primary School:

Kangjin youth are as hard as granite,
Haenam youth are as soft as pumpkin,
Play, play Kangjin youth,
Play, play Kangjin team! [88]

Understandably, therefore, in Japanese-controlled schools, baseball was played more often than football. One observer recounted: 'It was rather strange that I had never seen the students of the Japanese primary school (called *sho-gak-go*) playing football. I don't recall a single incident in which the Japanese schoolboys played football. Instead, they always played baseball.' [89]

Finally, also in these schools there were traditional games such as *dotaerang, wagwon, jiri* and *daehwanamja*. They were all Japanese traditional games; Korean traditional games were proscribed. There is no better illustration of the naked attempt at the Japanization of Korean youth sport.

Conclusion

In the early twentieth century, Korean society began to appreciate that Western culture could act as a positive means of necessary change. Later, Western sport helped Korean society develop a sense of solidarity in the face of Japanese oppression. It became one of several ways of promoting and sustaining patriotism. Thus Western missionaries' involvement in modernization was seen as an obstacle to Japanese colonial ambitions. For this reason Japan actively but not successfully pursued the removal of Christianity from Korean society. A nationalistically awakened Korea challenged the 'Japanization' policy, despite heavy-handed oppression, by *inter alia* involving itself in Western religious activities, modern education and physical activities. For the Japanese, paradoxically, these physical activities, suitably adapted under Japanese rule, became part of their policy of assimilation. Japan recognized the significance of modern sport in shaping Korean society and in promoting a spirit of independence among Koreans and the Japanese sports policy, in response, was to attempt to ensure the establishment of a Japanese militaristic infrastructure. In short, Western and Eastern imperialism both impacted on Korean sport. Thus early Western missionaries' educational initiatives and later thwarted Japanese intentions both contributed to the evolution of modern sport in Korea.

Notes

[1] Young-hill Kang, *The Grass Roof* (New York: C. Scribner's Sons, 1931), p.167.

[2] M.R. Peattie, 'Introduction' in R.H. Myers and M. R. Peattie (eds.), *The Japanese Colonial Empire 1895–1945* (Princeton, NJ, and New York: Princeton University Press, 1984), pp.14–15. See also M.R. Peattie, 'Japanese Attitudes toward Colonialism, 1895–1945' in the same volume.

[3] Robert T. Oliver, *A History of the Korean People in Modern Times* (Newark, NJ, and London: University of Delaware Press and Associated University Presses, 1993), pp.111–12.

[4] Ibid.

[5] Shakuo Shunjo, *A History of Korean Annexation* (Tokyo: Chosun and Manchu, 1926), p.100.

[6] The Ulsa Treaty was concluded by Japanese force in November 1905. After the treaty, Japan launched the Resident-General Administration in Korea in March 1906. Ito Hirobumi was appointed as the first Resident-General. See Myeon-hoe Do, Chang-gil Kang, Yun-sang Lee, Ik-han Kim, and Kyeong-seok Im (eds.), *Iljae Sikmin Tongchi Yeon-gu I: 1905–1919* ['A Study of Japanese Colonial Policy I: 1905–1919'], Han-guk Jeonsin Munhwa Yeon-gu-weon Pyeon (Seoul: Baesan Seodang, 1999), p.15.

[7] Andrew C. Nahm (ed.), *Korea Under Japanese Colonial Rule: Studies of the Policy and Techniques of Japanese Colonialism* (Seoul: Western Michigan University Press, 1973), p.9.

[8] The Treaty of Ganghwa of 26 February 1876, incorporating 12 articles, was signed in July. By the treaty, Korea had to open up Busan and the other two ports within 12 months. In addition, Japan was allowed to map the Korean coastline. It was a totally unequal treaty and revealed Japan's sinister designs on South East Asia.

[9] Nahm, *Korea Under Japanese Colonial Rule*, p.12.

[10] Ibid., p.224.

[11] Carter J. Eckert (ed.), *Korea: Old and New A History* (Seoul: Iljogak, 1990), p.254.

[12] Andrew C. Nahm, *Korea Tradition and Transformation: A History of the Korean People* (Seoul: Hollym, 1988), p.224.

[13] He was charged with the first governor-generalship of Korea from 1910 to 1919. He was a Japanese army general before he became the governor-general of Korea. His imperial duties were to take charge of the Japanese Army and to control Korea. Thus he implemented the policy to control Korea and to build an imperial military base in Korea. Subsequently he became prime minister of Japan in 1916 and played a major role in Japanese imperialism in Pacific Asia: Taek-bu Jeon, *Han-guk Gidok-gyo Cheongnyeonhoi Undongsa* ['The History of Independence Movement of YMCA in Korea'] (Seoul: Beomusa, 1994), pp.163–224.

[14] Eckert, *Korea: Old and New*, p.256.

[15] On 20 September 1875, the Unyo (a Japanese military ship) arrived at a small strategic position between Ganghwa and Youngjong Islands. Korean soldiers fired warning shots. The Japanese prepared for combat and next day they attacked Ganghwa Island and killed 33 and wounded 16 Korean soldiers. After this, the Japanese moved on Dongrae, near Busan (southern strategic port of Korea), where a group of Japanese troops landed and fought with Korean troops. The following year, a Japanese force landed at Kapkot, Ganghwa Island on 16 January 1876, fully equipped for combat. Japan now had a chance to force Korea to become 'open'.

[16] A British foreign policy, it arose from the Russian interest in British influence in China. Both Britain and Japan agreed that if either party was involved in a war, the other would remain neutral, but in the event of one ally being attacked by two or more powers, one would help the other.

[17] The Taft-Katsura Memorandum confirmed that Japan would not harbour any aggressive designs on the Philippines and Roosevelt traded Korea for the Philippines through this memorandum with Japan. Japan now required that Korea entered into no foreign treaties without the consent of Japan as the logical result of the Russo-Japanese War: T. Dennett, 'President Roosevelt's Secret Pact with Japan', *The Current History Magazine*, 21 (October 1924), 15–18.

[18] Eckert, *Korea: Old and New*, p.255.

[19] Mainly rice.

[20] Nahm, *Korea Tradition and Transformation*, p.225.

[21] Ibid., p.226.

[22] Eckert, *Korea: Old and New*, pp.257–8.

[23] Oliver, *A History of the Korean People*, p.114.

[24] Ibid.

[25] Eckert, *Korea: Old and New*, p.260.

[26] Nahm, *Korea Tradition and Transformation*, p.229.

[27] *Tokyo Nichi Nichi Shimbun* (Tokyo Daily Newspaper), 2 Oct. 1910.

[28] Nahm, *Korea Tradition and Transformation*, p.228.

[29] Ibid., pp.230–4.

[30] Ibid.

[31] Ibid.

[32] Miyada Setzko, trans. Hyeong-rang Lee, *Chosun Minjung-gwa Hwangminhwa Jeongchaek* ['The People of Chosun and the Policy for Imperial Subjects'] (Seoul: Iljogak, 1997), pp.29–56.

[33] Ibid.

[34] Oliver, *A History of the Korean People*, p.124.

[35] Ibid.

[36] Peter H. Lee (ed.), *Source Book of Korean Civilization* (New York: Columbia University Press, 1996), p.402.

[37] *Euibyeong* can be translated as 'voluntary soldiers', 'fighters for justice' or 'partisan militia'. The *euibyeong*'s military bases were in China, Russia and Korea. The *euibyeong*'s military independence movement was more vigorous and better organized after Japanese colonization in 1910. There was also the *Chosun Kuk-kweon Hoebokdan* (Korean Army for National Independence) which was organized in Daegu in Korea in 1915. The CKH attacked the Japanese police force in 1919 in several incidents. *Bungno Gunjeonseo* (The North Route Corps) was founded in Manchuria in 1919 where about one million Koreans lived. Weon-bong Kim coordinated the *Uihyeoldan* (Righteous Bloody Corps) and Ku Kim organized *Aegukdan* (the Patriotic Corps). They were small resistance groups. In 1930, these two groups attacked the *Dongyang Cheoksik Jusik Hoesa* (Oriental Development Company), which was the largest Japanese imperial company in Korea (established there in 1908), and attempted to assassinate the Japanese Emperor 1932. *Chosun Dongnip-gun* (Chosun Independence Army), which was led by General Jwa-jin Kim, defeated a Japanese army division at Quingshanli and Fengwudong in Jilin in northern Manchuria in 1920. There was also a left-wing corps, *Kungminbu* (the People's Army), founded in Manchuria in 1929, and it joined with the Chinese First Route Army to attack the Japanese armies in the Manchuria region in 1933. Dae-yeol Ku, 'The Chientao Incident (1920) and Britain', *Transactions of the Royal Asiatic Society* (Korea Branch, Seoul), 55 (1980), 1–34.

[38] The term, in fact, was first used for private organizations of patriotic volunteers in the Japanese invasion in the 1590s. Furthermore, there was also a 'Righteous Army' movement after the assassination of Queen Min (1851–95), the last Queen of Korea in 1895.

[39] Eckert, *Korea: Old and New*, p.256.

[40] Lee, *Source Book of Korean Civilization*, p.403.

[41] He gave the king five reasons why Korea should not open its door to the world under Japanese duress, when the government made the Kanghwa Treaty of 1876 with Japan. He sent it to the king for careful consideration. The document's name was *Cheokhwa Uiso*: 'This treaty, the result of Japan and Japanese aggressive ambition which underpins it. ... The Japanese have only greed, ... they have the morality of wild animals. We cannot live with wild animals.' Tae-

seop Byoen, *Hanguksa Tongron* ['The Brief History of Korea'] (Seoul: Samyeongsa, 1993), pp.414–15.

[42] Lee, *Source Book of Korean Civilization*, p.404.

[43] Nahm, *Korea Under Japanese Colonial Rule*, p.10.

[44] Eckert, *Korea: Old and New A History*, p.255.

[45] Ibid., p.264.

[46] Also known as Syngman Rhee. He later became the first president of South Korea after independence in 1945. He had been imprisoned for seven years when the Japanese-Korean government suppressed the Independence Club in 1898. After his release, he studied at Harvard University and received a doctorate from Princeton in 1910. On his return, he was involved in the national independence movement. See Seung-keun Rhee, 'Evolution of Korean Nationalism I: The Political Views of Syngman Rhee', *Korea Observer*, 4, 4 (1975), 395–404.

[47] Ki-baik Lee, *A New History of Korea*, trans Edward W. Wagner with Edward J. Shultz (Cambridge, MA: Harvard University Press, 1984), p.362.

[48] David Rees, *A Short History of Modern Korea* (London: Ham Publishing, 1988), p.68.

[49] Gi-san Han, Jeong-hak Kim, Seong-ui Park and Ju-hwan Oh (eds.), *Iljeui Munhwa Chimtalsa* ['Japanese Cultural Invasion'], (Seoul: Muneumsa, 1996), pp.88–94.

[50] Takashi Hatada and Warren W. Smith (eds.), *A History of Korea* (Santa Barbara, CA: ABC-Clio, 1969), p.54.

[51] Rees, *A Short History of Modern Korea*, p.68.

[52] Ibid.

[53] Ibid.

[54] Gi-wook Shin and Michael Robinson (eds.), 'Introduction: Rethinking Colonial Korea', in Gi-wook Shin and Michael Robinson (eds.), *Colonial Modernity in Korea* (Cambridge, MA and London: Harvard University Asia Centre, 1999), pp.1–18.

[55] This group of intellectuals organized political parties such as the *Gaehwadang* (Enlightenment Party) and the *Jinbodang* (Progressive Party). The leading members of the group included Ok-kyun Kim (1851–1894), Young-hyo Park (1861–1939), Young-sik Hong (1855–1884), Kwang-beom Seo (1859–?) and Chae-pil Seo (1864–1951). They supported King Kojong's attempts at modernization. They also insisted that Korea needed to develop diplomatic relations with Western countries. In 1884, they led the Kapsin Coup, which raised the issue of Korea's modern transformation. Yong-ho Choe, 'The Kapsin Coup of 1884: A Reassessment', *Journal of Korean Studies*, 6 (1982), pp.105–24; Yong-ha Shin, 'The Coup d'Etat of 1884 and the Pukchong Army of the Progressive Party', *Korea Journal*, 13, 22 (1993), pp.5–16; Ki-suk Shin, 'International Relations with Respect to the Coup d'Etat of 1884', *Korea Journal*, 24, 12 (1984), 22–37.

[56] See Gang-woo Lee, 'Han-guk Sports-ui Ji-bae Ideologi-jeok Gineung-e Gwang-han Yeon-gu' ['A Study on Ideological Function in Korean Sport'] (Ph.D. thesis, Seoul: Seonggyungwan University, 1993), *passim*.

[57] Kenneth Scott Latourette, *A History of the Expansion of Christianity*, Vol. VII: *Advance Through Storm* (London: Eyre & Spottiswoode, 1947), p.401.

[58] Ibid., pp.401–2.

[59] Hak-rae Lee, *Hanguk Gundae Chaeyuksa Yeon-gu* ['A Study of Modern Sport in Korea'] (Seoul: Jisiksaneupsa, 1990), p.307.

[60] Ibid., p.308.

[61] H.H. Underwood, *Modern Education in Korea* (New York: International Press, 1926), p.1.

[62] Ibid., pp.302–4.

[63] General Government Edict No.110.

[64] Jae-choel Jung, *Iljae ui Daehangukmin Shikminjy Gyoyuk Jeongchaeksa* ['History of Japanese Colonial Policy on Korean Education'] (Seoul: Iljisa, 1985), p.325.

170   *G. Ok*

[65] Young-wu Kim and Joung-man Pee, *Choishin Hanguk Kyoyuksa Youngu* ['New History of Korean Education'] (Seoul: Kyoyuk Gwahaksa, 1995), p.336.

[66] Underwood, *Modern Education in Korea*, p.42.

[67] *Mae-il Shinbo* (the Daily Newspaper), 1809 (27 Oct. 1911).

[68] The higher common school was equivalent of the secondary school.

[69] Japanese General Government Edict No.2196 (5 Dec. 1919).

[70] Horace G. Underwood, *The Call of Korea* (London: Revell, 1908), p.111.

[71] Underwood, *Modern Education in Korea*, p.31.

[72] He was transferred to China in 1913.

[73] He was born in 1859 in Seoul. He was an attendant of Yeong-ik Min, who headed a mission to the United States in July 1883, and he wrote his tragic memory of Japanese oppression. His personal story was used as the source for *The Tragedy of Korea* by Fred A. McKenzie. He was also involved in establishment of the *Dongnip Hyeophoe* (Society for Independence) in August 1876. See *Seoul YMCA Undongsa 1903–1993* ['History of Seoul YMCA'] (Seoul: Nochulpan, 1993), p.123; Fred A. McKenzie, *The Tragedy of Korea* (London: Hodder & Stoughton, 1908).

[74] He was born in Virginia and was appointed as the secretary for China of the US YMCA from 1898 to 1900. He worked as the vice-secretary of the International YMCA between 1915 and 1924. He worked as the joint Secretary for Korea of the US YMCA from 1908 to 1922. *Seoul YMCA Undongsa 1903–1993*, pp.83 and 531.

[75] He was from Canada and his background was commerce and education. He was the principal of the Hartford Commerce School and was also an expert in industrial education on the New York YMCA International Committee before he went to Korea as an educational superintendent at the Seoul YMCA in 1906. *Seoul YMCA Undongsa 1903–1993*, p.100.

[76] He left the YMCA in 1914.

[77] *Seoul YMCA Undongsa 1903–1993*, p.513.

[78] Lee, *Hanguk Gundae Chaeyuksa Yeon-gu*, p.152.

[79] Ibid.

[80] Ibid.

[81] Ibid., p.92.

[82] Ibid., p.188.

[83] Ibid., pp.90–1.

[84] Ibid.

[85] He is a well-known Korean sports historian and currently a professor in the department of physical education at Hanyang University in Korea. He has published 14 books and 30 articles, mostly on Korean sports history. He has contributed to sport's advance as a sports historian, sports innovator and sports ambassador. He played an important part in the creation of the single Korean team uniting the North and South Koreans for the 2000 Sydney Olympics. He became the general manager of the united Korean athletes at the Sydney Olympics. His two respected books on Korean sports history are *Hanguk Gundae Chaeyuksa Yeon-gu* ['A Study of Modern Sport in Korea'] and *Han-guk Cheyuk Baeknyeonsa* ['One Hundred Years of Korean Sports History'] (Seoul: Han-guk Cheyuk Hak-hoe, 2000).

[86] Lee, *Han-guk Cheyuk Baek-nyeonsa*, 2000.

[87] Official gazette of the Governor-General, 10 June 1914, 2–8.

[88] Byong-kuk Kim, 'World Cup and Korean-American', New Horizon, *Korea Times*, 21 Nov. 2002.

[89] Ibid.

Sport as a Political Tool: Tanzania and the Liberation of Africa

Hamad S. Ndee

Throughout the 1950s Tanzania (then Tanganyika) was engaged in the liberation struggle, a struggle that saw the country become independent from British trusteeship in 1961. Soon after gaining her independence, Tanganyika became Tanzania under the leadership of Julius Kambarage Nyerere, and committed itself to the liberation of the whole of Africa. This involved liberating those countries which were still under colonial rule and bringing about political change in those countries under oppressive governments. In particular, Tanzania set out to influence political change in apartheid South Africa and in the white-minority-ruled Southern Rhodesia. As will be illustrated below, Tanzania also attempted cultural liberation.

To attain the goal of the political liberation of Africa, Tanzania adopted various strategies ranging from direct military involvement, aiding freedom fighters, to vigorously supporting punitive measures passed by international organizations such as the United Nations (UN) and the former Organization of African Unity (OAU), now the African Union (AU). These measures took the form of economic sanctions and isolation and were aimed particularly at 'forcing' political change in South Africa or Southern Rhodesia. Other Tanzanian strategies included diplomatic liaison within those international organizations. One other strategy, explored in this article, by which Tanzania exploited, and exploits, opposition to oppression in Africa has been, and is, the use of international sport. As will be made clear in due course, Tanzania used sport as an aid to independence but more significantly to achieve political goals in southern Africa.

Regarding the diffusion of modern sport in Africa and the question of cultural imperialism, Allan Guttmann once wrote that 'although Peter Rummelt and other critics of the destruction of indigenous African sports by the European colonial powers are unquestionably right about the suppression of indigenous sports, they have probably not done enough to acknowledge the ways in which Africans have adapted modern sports to their own needs'. [1] Such needs relate to the politics of both colonial Tanganyika and independent Tanzania.

It is well known that during colonialism, especially during the years of the struggle for independence, the colonial government restricted public rallies and similar large group gatherings by the indigenous population through fear of political agitation. Sports gatherings, however, were unaffected, and such meetings provided 'secure' venues for members of (sometimes underground) political parties to discuss liberation strategies. In the mid 1950s, the Young Africans Sports Club of Dar es Salaam provided covert forums for members of the Tanganyika African National Union (TANU) to hold political meetings. [2] Eventually, TANU led Tanganyika to independence. For the obvious reason – the 'secret' nature of the meetings – the minutes of such meetings, if they were taken, are hard to find. However, consideration of the relationship between the Young Africans Sports Club and TANU demonstrates how the indigenous people used sport to achieve national political goals.

The history of Young Africans Sports Club goes back to the mid 1920s, when Africans began to take a real interest in football, following the formation of the Dar es Salaam League. [3] It was about this time that the club was formed. Records are hazy as to the exact date of its formation. There are many different stories told about the origin of the club. However, the arguably most authentic one goes back to 1926. [4] Some time that year, a group of youths gathered in a 'playing field' at a place called Jangwani and formed a football team, which they called 'Jangwani'. [5] When they started, these boys did not have even the most basic equipment such as the football itself. Instead they banded rags together to make a 'ball'. Rags are still used today by children in place of footballs in the less privileged areas of Tanzania.

The club adopted different names at different times. In 1926, it started as Jangwani Club; later, it changed its name to Navigation Sports Club, [6] then to Taliana Sports Club, and then to New Youngs Sports Club. In 1935, the Young Africans Sports Club was born. It later changed its name to Yanga Sports Club. While the club was still called New Youngs, a number of players are said to have left it and formed what is believed to have been the nucleus of the present Simba (formerly Sunderland) Sports Club. Observers of the evolution of football in the country consider this split to be the beginning of the traditional sporting rivalry which now exists between the present two football club giants in the country, Yanga (formerly Young Africans Sports Club) and Simba.

Parallel to the evolution of Young Africans Sports Club, on the Islands of Zanzibar the Wananchi Sports Club, which was to play a significant role in the politics of Tanzania, was formed in the 1930s. The exact date of its formation is not known; *Wananchi* is the Swahili for 'citizens'. The club had close historical links with the Afro-Shirazi Party (ASP), [7] the party that formed the revolutionary government on the islands following the popular political revolution of 11–12 January 1964. [8] Indeed, Wananchi and the ASP became so close that Wananchi and ASP were in effect the same thing – in order to join Wananchi one had to join the ASP. [9] The interdependent cooperation between the two dates back to the 1930s, the formative years of nationalist movements on the islands, with Wananchi providing a façade behind which the ASP discussed political issues. [10]

In 1937, a sporting relationship began between the Young Africans Sports Club and the Wananchi Sports Club. The relationship developed into what came to be known as 'cultural exchanges' between Dar es Salaam and Zanzibar. These exchanges involved alternate annual sports visits during the Easter Holidays and *Eid* celebrations. Initially, these visits were bilateral and involved mainly football teams. Over time, the activities expanded and included not only other sports but also other sports groups, thus acquiring a wider cultural dimension and so establishing popular annual cultural festivals between the islands and the mainland. These festivals reached their political height in the mid-1970s, apparently due to the call by the TANU party to give sport the 'same status' as other development projects. This point will be fully considered later. Sport was also seen as one way of strengthening the political union between Tanganyika and Zanzibar. Today these festivals are legendary.

The bilateral relationship between the Young Africans and Wananchi sports clubs had far-reaching political implications. In 1970, Young Africans announced that the club would build a clubhouse at Jangwani, but the club did not have enough money. It is intriguing to note how the scheme was 'politically handled' by the leaders of TANU, and particularly by those of the ASP, thus illustrating the role of the club in the politics of the country. The Zanzibar Revolutionary Council, the supreme legislative body of Zanzibar, approved a contribution of two million Tanzanian shillings from the Wananchi Sports Club finances towards the project. This amount covered half the total cost of building the clubhouse. Undoubtedly this was a significant contribution. Over and above this major contribution, the top political leadership of the islands' Revolutionary Council is known to have embarked on numerous fund-raising campaigns to help Young Africans build the clubhouse. The then secretary-general of the ASP, Thabit Kombo, inaugurated the construction of the Young Africans' clubhouse and the then first President of Tanzania, Julius Kambarage Nyerere, who was also the president of TANU, inspected the finished product. This involvement of such top leaders of the country in a way further demonstrates the close connection between Young Africans and Wananchi and the ASP and TANU.

The financial contribution by the ASP towards the construction of the Young Africans' clubhouse and the involvement of the top leadership of the ASP and TANU in the welfare of the club may justifiably be interpreted as the country's political will to promote sport for a variety of reasons: to maintain and develop the physical abilities and fitness of the citizens; to promote a sense of identity, belonging and unity among citizens; to safeguard public order; and to emphasize values and orientations consistent with the overall political ideology within the community or society. [11] But there was more to it than that. Both sports clubs had played an important role in the activities of the two political parties in their struggle for independence for their respective countries. It is thus reasonable to state that the involvement of the country's top leadership in the affairs of the two sports clubs was a reward for past services, and in addition, was aimed at bonding to them, for further use, the affiliates who had been useful to them in the past. After all, participants and spectators were potential voters who could be and were subjected to political indoctrination. One immediate result was the expansion and consolidation of membership. Furthermore, Wananchi members were automatically members of the ASP on the islands. Correspondingly, the majority of the members of the Young Africans Sports Club were members of the ruling party, TANU, on mainland Tanzania. [12] Undoubtedly, it was because of such an inseparable historical connection between the two sports clubs and nationalist movements that sport was considered an important and useful tool for not only liberation but also for the retention of political power after independence as well as for influencing various national and international political goals.

Nationally, it was seen as an effective medium for communicating national policies to the masses and a means of helping to validate the changing values of society in independent Tanzania. Governments can use sport to shape the values of citizens. The underlying assumption is that ideally success is based on discipline, loyalty and the ability to keep working in the face of suffering and pain. Discipline, loyalty and determination to work are but some of the values emphasized in Tanzania's policy of self-reliant socialism. Sport can be used to promote these values and to shape the orientations that people use to explain what happens in the rest of their lives. Moreover, given the popularity of a sport such as soccer, any team representing a specific group has the potential for bringing people together and creating emotional unity among group members. For example, when a soccer club represents a nation in a major international tournament, it seems that for the moment differences in religion, level of education and social status are forgotten among the team fans. Thus sport can create a temporary sense of togetherness and there are those in the governments who see this as an important reason for supporting sport.

There is, of course, something else to be considered, namely that the extent to which sport effectively serves as a tool for policy implementation of course depends largely on the degree of state control of the sport itself: 'The greater the regime's control of sports, the greater their potential use in policy implementation.' [13] In Tanzania attempts have been made to gain this control and they have been incorporated into major policy changes.

Policy Changes in Tanzania and the Use of Sport in Policy Implementation

As mentioned above, in 1961 Tanzania became independent. Julius Kambarage Nyerere became the first prime minister and first president of the republic set up in 1962. Nyerere had a clear if idiosyncratic vision for his new nation. He set about transforming its political traditions. In this process he was supported by, among others, Rashidi Kawawa, (Vice President) and Oscar Kambona [14] (Minister of Foreign Affairs) – the initial political clique. It took a little time. Nyerere set a new course for the new nation. This was reflected in the two major policy changes that occurred in 1965 and 1967. These were milestones in national development. They involved the overhaul of the country's political system, which in turn, profoundly affected all other systems.

In July 1965, mainland [15] Tanzania declared that it had become a one-party state and that TANU, the ruling party, was the only political party allowed in the country. [16] For the next quarter of a century, TANU (later *Chama Cha Mapinduzi*, or CCM) enjoyed absolute supremacy and directed all major political, social, economic and educational policies in the country. In its general conference, held at Arusha, on 26–29 January 1967, [17] TANU decided that Tanzania would pursue socialism. This was another crucial policy change for the country. What became known as the Arusha Declaration was proclaimed on 5 February 1967. The essence of this declaration was a commitment to the principles of self-reliant socialism, which became the keystone for all future developments. The Arusha Declaration gave the TANU government even greater control over many aspects of society, including sport, in order to facilitate socialist development.

The most comprehensive attempts to bring sport under government control, in line with the Arusha Declaration, were contained in two major pieces of legislation, enacted between 1967 and 1971. The National Sports Council Act No.12 of 1967 established the National Sports Council (NSC) to oversee all sports activities in the country. [18] Article 4.1(a) of the act reads: 'The function of the Council shall be to develop, promote and *control* all forms of amateur sports on a national basis', and article 4.1(c) states that 'The function of the Council shall be to *approve* international and national sports competitions and festivals organised by national and other associations'. [19] It is clear from the two clauses that the TANU government was determined not only to monitor the development of sport in the country but also to exercise control over all external sports contacts. The NSC (Amendment) Act No.6 of 1971 gave the NSC even more control over sports organizations. [20] It gave the council responsibility for the registration of all sports organizations in the country and empowered it to refuse registration and dissolve any of them at any time if necessary.

The intention of the NSC Act of 1971 was to give the government yet more control over both sports organizations and sportsmen in order to complete the process of moulding disciplined sportsmen, and by extension, disciplined socialist Tanzanians. Launching the act, the Minister of Sports declared: 'We will be able to discipline them now. We could not do so before because we were legally tied up. We asked some associations to make some changes in their administration but they refused. They knew there was nothing we could do.' [21] Such statements of authority are clear indications of the government's intentions to establish total control over sports activities in the country.

There are several basic assumptions that can be made about the government's keenness to control sport. At the outset of independence, the new government recognized the importance of, oddly, foreign games in the implementation of various policies – liberation, propagation of national unity and conservation of national culture. [22] In addition, there was the TANU government's anxiety to establish control over all sections of the population in its bid to cultivate the new social values and attitudes embedded in the country's newly declared 'socialist path' to national development. Control over a dynamic force, such as the enthusiasts of a popular sport like football, was an important political step towards establishing control over one influential section of the population. A brief reflection on some major events that occurred in the late 1960s and early 1970s involving the Football Association of Tanzania (FAT) and the government will help explain why the government wanted to establish control over sports organizations. By 1971 it was felt that, despite the establishment of the NSC to strengthen the organizational links between the government and sport, control over some sports organizations, particularly of football, was slipping, and thus undermining effective policy implementation due to these organizations' 'indiscipline'.

Discipline may be defined as 'the acceptance of, or submission to, authority and control'. [23] For individuals this is tantamount to organizational control at group level. Certainly, the presence of 'indiscipline' indicates the inability of authority to control behaviour and such control is crucial for the implementation of most policies, especially the then newly instituted Tanzanian policy of socialism and self-reliance.

In 1967, the TANU party newspaper alleged that the Football Association of Tanzania was, among other things, incompetent, inefficient and incapable of managing its funds, in a description of the 'chaotic affairs' of the association. [24] Later, the government took the drastic measure of sacking the entire FAT leadership and appointing a caretaker committee. Other corrective measures included the fine 'screening' of aspirants for the various posts in the FAT in future elections in order to bring about what one influential politician called 'Party superiority in sports ... to make the Party strong enough to be in a position to issue orders to [sports] clubs'. [25] The 'screening' process required first and foremost that the candidate had to be a member of TANU or one of the organizations affiliated to it.

The TANU government was also concerned, in the 1960s and 1970s, about the intensity of feeling for football, which was seen as turning 'sports rivalry into hostility and sports hooliganism, thus interfering with the discipline of citizens', [26] and by extension the unity of the nation. For example, in 1968, the opening match of the National Football League between the country's two most popular teams, Young

Africans and Sunderland, had to be abandoned in the early minutes of the game because of fighting. The players, egged on by the spectators, challenged the referee's authority and attacked him. [27] The incident was blamed on a lack of discipline on the part of the players and the spectators as well as on the failure of the FAT to control the players. This incident, and indeed similar ones that followed, were strongly condemned by the party and the government. They lamented that 'indiscipline has taken the place of soccer rules and that abuses, indifference and blows have taken the place of the language of football players', [28] and this could not be tolerated.

Other important domestic policy objectives that Tanzania sought to achieve through adapted sports were the building of social national unity and the inculcation of sound communal attitudes. Notably, since the Arusha Declaration of 1967, Tanzania's primary objective had been the promotion of appropriate communal attitudes and the suppression of divisive individualism. [29] That is, groups were to come before individuals in any acquisition of wealth or status. Sports competitions and sports clubs were seen as ways of bringing people together and, therefore, had the capacity to build new civic bonds between people through joint participation in competitions and joint membership in clubs. Sport, through team work and effort, was seen as having the potential to unify rural and urban areas, the mainland and the islands and the other different sections of the population.

Undoubtedly, it was with such objectives in mind that at its 15th annual conference, held in Dar es Salaam from 18 to 29 September 1971, TANU passed a resolution that required the government apparatus to engage in the development of sport at the grassroots level. At the national level, all sports organizations that existed by then were reorganized and new ones were formed. Sub-councils were established at regional, district and divisional level to coordinate, promote and control all forms of (amateur) [30] sports in their respective areas. And, at its sixteenth conference in 1973, TANU adopted yet another resolution that elevated sport to the status of 'an important sector in the life of the nation'. Thus sport was to be assigned the same status as other developmental projects. Consequently, the resolution called upon all government departments and parastatal organizations to promote sport in their respective places. Following this call by the party, a kind of sports 'pandemic' swept the country. Numerous organizational initiatives were taken by both the central government and its departments and the parastatal organizations to promote sport extensively at all levels.

The central government, through the administrative hierarchy of the NSC, directed all the regional, district and divisional administrative units to engage people in sports activities in their areas. It also appointed regional and district sports officers to ensure implementation. In response, the wards, divisions, districts and regions hurriedly and ambitiously began to organize sports groups, mainly football teams, but without the necessary infrastructure, basic equipment or expertise. The different ministries and parastatal organizations, for their part, cooperated and together they founded the Inter-Ministerial and Parastatal National Championships. Today these games attract and bring together large numbers of sportsmen and sportswomen from all over the country.

However, although sport had the potential to enhance national integration and promote unity, it remained capable of producing division. Although membership in sports clubs may unite people, it often does so at a sub-national group level, which may distract members from allegiance to the nation. The internal club controversy, the Young African crisis of 1975/76, must certainly have posed a problem for the propagation of national loyalties. [31] The controversy began with the club's defeat in an international match in mid-1975. The team's coach, who was a Zairian national, firstly blamed the defeat on the players' lack of discipline. He then attacked the club's executive and accused them of misappropriating club funds, which he claimed had deprived the players of the necessary resources for adequate preparation. As a direct consequence of his allegations, a dispute erupted, factions developed and the players refused to play any further matches, including those arranged by the party to celebrate some national events. This infuriated the TANU government. As the crisis deepened the police were called in and they suspended the club's meetings indefinitely and dismissed the club officials. But the crisis continued. Eventually, the government issued a statement charging two of the officials with the serious offence of conspiracy against the TANU government. The statement claimed that 'foreign subversive elements' were using the crisis to divide people and that the two officials were actually agents of those foreign elements. [32] The two officials, however, were not formally prosecuted, but were banned from participating further in sports affairs. They appear to have been useful scapegoats.

The Young Africans crisis was an extreme case. However, it offers an opportunity to examine the government's determination to gain control over sport. Following the Young Africans dispute, a series of yet further legal measures were taken. In the first instance, the government issued a directive dismissing, with immediate effect, the Young Africans' coach. Then it ordered the expulsion of the Guinean coach of the other most popular club in the country, Sunderland Sports Club. Finally, in an unprecedented move, the government banned all foreigners from coaching, claiming that they were the source of the controversies in sport in the country and that they were foreign elements who wanted to use sport to destabilize the country. [33] The government also issued directives requiring all clubs to demonstrate patriotism and nationalism. It recommended that clubs with foreign names should adopt indigenous ones in order to conform with the nation's pledge to promote nationalistic sentiments in its bid to create a new, independent and socialist Tanzania. The Young Africans Sports Club and Sunderland Sports Club responded almost immediately and changed their names to Yanga Sports Club and Simba Sports Club respectively. Many other clubs that had foreign names followed suit and acquired indigenous names. Whether this was done voluntarily or under pressure of the threat of dissolution is hard to know. Today, the majority of the sports clubs in the country bear indigenous names.

It is not only at home but also abroad that Tanzanian sport has been enmeshed in politics. As will be made evident, Tanzania has regularly denied its athletes participation in international competitions as a means of implementing foreign policy. Indeed, as one observer has noted, 'Tanzania used this control with some considerable skill'. [34] Many examples could be given of this, but perhaps the most important one involved the isolation of the then white minority regimes in southern Africa (South Africa and Rhodesia) in the 1960s and 1970s. To this end, among other things, Tanzania used boycotts or threats of boycotts of the Olympic Games.

Tanzania, the Olympic Games and Opposition to Oppression in Africa

Tanzania participated in the Olympic Games, as an independent country, for the first time in 1964. South Africa was excluded from these Olympics but Rhodesia participated under the British flag. Undoubtedly, because Tanzania was a newcomer to this arena, it did not play any significant role in the exclusion of South Africa then, but was to play a significant role in South Africa's exclusion from the Olympics that followed.

Tanzania's position on South Africa's participation in the 1968 Mexico Olympics is contained in the TANU statement of May 1967:

> As long as South Africa adheres to its principle of apartheid in sport, it cannot be allowed to take part in international tournaments. ... Because South Africa insists on categorising some sportsmen as human athletes and others as sub-human, she should not be allowed to pollute the Olympic atmosphere. ... It must be hoped that other members will be persuaded to this line of thinking so that pressure against South Africa's obnoxious policy of apartheid may gain further momentum. [35]

In February, 1968 the International Olympic Committee (IOC) decided to allow South Africa to participate in the Mexico Olympics. Tanzania reacted strongly and took the lead in challenging the IOC's decision. It accused the IOC of double standards and of what the government's newspaper, *The Nationalist,* called 'European racialism'. [36] Tanzania then withdrew her application for participation, but reapplied some months later when the IOC reversed its decision and excluded South Africa from the games. Tanzania then participated in the 1968 Olympics. The Mexican government, apparently basing its decision on the United Nations resolution on Rhodesia, successfully and legally barred Rhodesia from their Olympics. [37] As a result, Rhodesia sought admission to the 1972 Olympic Games in Munich under the '1964 conditions' when she was allowed to participate in that year's Tokyo Olympics under the British flag. But in 1965, under the leadership of a white man, Ian Smith, Rhodesia had unilaterally declared independence from Britain under what was known as the '1965 Unilateral Declaration of Independence' (UDI). Rhodesia's decision to now participate as a British colony was interpreted by the IOC and some African countries as a repudiation of the declaration and, therefore, to be encouraged. The IOC decided to admit Rhodesia to the games and the leadership of the Supreme Council for Sport in Africa (SCSA) – the coordinating body for sport in Africa – concurred. This sparked yet another strong objection from Tanzania. It accused the SCSA of failing to adhere to the 1972 decision of the Organization of African Unity (OAU) and denounced the IOC for countenancing racism, and subsequently withdrew from participation. [38] Some African countries joined the Tanzanian-led boycott of the games. Others did not. Eventually, the then Secretary-General of the UN intervened and pointed out to the German government that the admission of Rhodesia to the games would violate the UN resolution on Rhodesia. Just a few days before the games were to start, the IOC reversed its decision and barred Rhodesia. The author remembers, [39] as a participant, how quickly Tanzania had to send her team to Munich, how difficult the journey was (it took over 36 hours – Dar es Salaam–Nairobi–London–Dusseldorf by air; Dusseldorf–Cologne by train; Cologne–Munich by air) and the devastating effect all this had on the performance of the Tanzanian athletes at the games. For example, some of the boxers had to weigh in at 5.00 a.m., having only arrived in Munich at 1.00 that morning, for competition that evening. Although many of them had fasted throughout the journey, some failed to meet the weight requirements in their respective categories and thus were disqualified without ever reaching the ring. Those who did qualify to fight were so tired and weak that not one of them managed to progress to the second round. Nonetheless, a political point had been scored on the part of Tanzania in the international arena.

In summary, Tanzania sought to actively cut off sports contacts with South Africa and Rhodesia in order to speed up the end of minority white rule: 'The isolation of South Africa and Rhodesia required only the negative ability to block participation, and the TANU government was able to exercise such control.' [40] Tanzania played an important role in keeping these regimes from participation in the Olympics. Its relative success in the implementation of the policy of isolating South Africa and Rhodesia, however, was not due to the quality of the athletes that the government threatened to withdraw but rather the skill with which Tanzania managed to gain support from, and built solidarity with, other countries. [41]

Finally, in 1976, Tanzania led the boycott, mostly by African countries, of the Montreal Olympics over New Zealand's participation in the games. As may be recalled, New Zealand's National Party government 'sanctioned' sporting ties with apartheid South Africa, and this was unacceptable to many African countries; hence the boycott.

Tanzania, Sport and Pan-Africanism

Tanzania has been positive as well as negative in linking sport with international politics. The country has also used sport in her attempts to propagate the idea of Pan-Africanism and promote unity among independent African countries. In theory, regional sports competitions such as the East and Central Africa Challenge Cup, the All Africa Cup of Nations and the All Africa Games, in which Tanzania was a prominent and enthusiastic member, may be considered forums for bringing Africans together in harmony. In reality, however, what was happening on the sports fields – involving both players and spectators – was largely independent of the kind of political relations that Pan-Africanist politicians sought to establish. More often than not, for example, competitions on the football pitches created frictions that rendered African unity an illusion. Numerous examples of such frictions exist but are far too many and too complicated for examination in this article. However, two examples may be mentioned in passing to illustrate the point.

A major protest resulted from the African Cup match in Cairo in October 1974 between Sunderland of Tanzania and Mehalla of Egypt, when Sunderland alleged that its players had been threatened with knives and pistols during the match. The prime target was Sunderland's goalkeeper, who was considered one of the best goalkeepers on the continent, and who, some Egyptians thought, 'narrowed the chances of Mehalla to advance in the tournament' [42] It took some time before the 'political tension' between Tanzania and Egypt that resulted from this incident was 'eased' at an OAU summit.

Perhaps the most striking example, however, involved a football match, in 1975, between the Young Africans Sports Club and a visiting team from Mozambique. The two countries were very close politically and had just initiated sports contacts following Mozambique's independence in July 1975. The match was intended to mark the successful inauguration of these contacts, but unfortunately the game had to be abandoned before full time because of fighting. The incident, which cast doubt on the value of any further matches between the two countries, prompted the government's *Daily News* to observe that 'for African countries ... sports bring us closer together', then to ask 'how could things go so wrong between such close countries?' [43] As it turned out, very few matches were played between the two countries for some years after.

It is clear from the above that Tanzania has adopted and adapted modern sport to its own political needs – among them implementation of both domestic and foreign policy objectives. Effective use of sport for policy implementation has required strict control. This has had positive and negative aspects – attempts to patriotically mould the behaviour of individuals, and attempts to block individuals and organizations from engaging in sports activities. [44] The TANU government has had little difficulty in asserting negative control over both individual athletes and sports organizations in the implementation of policy objectives, particularly foreign ones. However, domestic positive control, as has been seen, is another matter; resources have not matched the ideals.

Although the TANU government has used modern sport for the implementation of both domestic and foreign policy objectives, there has been concern, especially among politicians, that foreign sports are replacing indigenous ones. The existence of such concerns may be traced back to the time of independence in the 1960s. The feeling was then that the spread of modern Western sport during the colonial era and the popularity of this sport before and after independence compromised the nation's own indigenous sports culture.

At the outset of independence, some organizational adjustments were made that involved the creation of a national body responsible for national culture. A sector for this culture was created under the Special Act of Parliament No.48 of 1962, leading to the formation of the Ministry of National Culture and Youth. [45] For the last four decades, presumably to improve implementation or because of the problems of implementation, this culture sector culture has been moved over ten times – from the original ministry to, among others, the Prime Minister's Office, and finally to the present Ministry of Education and Culture. [46]

It was not until 1975 that the government took significant steps aimed specifically at the restoration of indigenous culture. It attempted to revive and promote those indigenous games considered to have been popular among the tribes before the coming of the Europeans. A National Association of Traditional Games (abbreviated in Swahili to CHAMIJATA) was formed. Four sports were chosen to form the basis of this association – *bao*, [47] wrestling, (traditional0 spear throwing and archery. These games were considered to be widely representative of the national culture as many tribes in the country practised them. The first National Championships in Traditional Games were held in Dodoma in 1975. For the next few years, the championships were held, in rotation, at different regional capitals in the country. The participation, however, remained poor year after year. For example, less than half of the regions were represented at the inaugural games. [48] A few years later the championships collapsed.

The obvious reasons for the discontinuation of the championships included lack of facilities, resources and expertise. In my opinion, [49] there was also the technical difficulty of a lack of national norms for playing the chosen 'games', and this made them less than appealing across the 20 regions. For example, although wrestling was (and still is) common among many tribes in the country, different rules, techniques and tactics apply to contests in the various tribes. Therefore it was difficult either to adopt any one set of norms or to set national ones – nor indeed was there the will, expertise or resources to do so. Consequently the National Championships in Traditional Games never attracted many regions, as evidenced by the poor attendance from the start and subsequent dwindling participation. The essence of the games remained localized – that is, they were practised in the different regions and districts according to the norms of the respective places. While CHAMIJATA still exists to this day, since the cessation of the national championships it appears to have little or no function.

A government policy document on sport was issued in 1995. [50] One of its aims is to promote research into indigenous games in order to revive and develop them. [51] In the preface to this document, the then Minister of Education and Culture commented:

Although modern sport has helped the country gain recognition on the international arena, it has done so at the expense of the national heritage. The most damaging development is that the growth of modern sport has resulted in the indigenous games being disregarded and neglected to an extent that most of them are now extinct, and this has made our nation look like a nation without a cultural identity. [52]

What effects the implementation of this new policy will have on the revival of indigenous sports remains to be seen.

Conclusion: Adoption, Adaptation and Modernization

Adoption, adaptation and modernization symbolize the introduction of modern sport into the Tanganyika Territory, the spread of modern sport in Tanganyika, and the eventual use of modern sport in the process of modernizing Tanzania.

Colonial administrators and the armed forces constituted the earliest principal disseminators of this modernizing agent. And while sports clubs may be seen as the major channels through which modern sport, mainly football, was diffused, the flourishing of the National Football League and the various football cup competitions may be considered as the clearest manifestations of the growth of modern sport in the country.

A. Guttmann once wrote:

> The adoption by one group of a game popular among another is only partly the result of recognising the intrinsic properties of the game. In the long run, a modern sport like soccer may become so thoroughly naturalised that the borrowers feel that it is their game, an expression of their unique national character ... in which the intrinsic ludic properties are jumbled together with cultural associations. [53]

There is not enough evidence to suggest that football in Tanzania is thoroughly naturalized, although some Tanzanians may feel that it expresses their national character. But certainly some aspects of football – competition, 'national building' and national image improvement – are integrated into the cultural fabric of Tanzania's society and as such, football commands support as a national game. This support, however, is based on the popularity of the game rather than anything else. For example, during the FAT crisis of the 1970s, when the government newspaper complained about the FAT 'bringing the *national game* to its lowest ebb', the newspaper was clearly referring to what it had earlier singled out as *Tanzania's major and most popular sport*. Undoubtedly, it is this popularity of football that inspired Tanzanian leaders to adopt modern sport as a political medium, a means of national bonding and an instrument of modernization.

Both TANU and the ASP used the Young Africans and Wananchi Sports Clubs' meetings to chart liberation strategies during their respective struggles for independence. After independence had been achieved, the leaders of the newly independent states saw sport as a valuable means of communicating political messages to particular groups, such as sports enthusiasts. The Young Africans and Wananchi were also pioneers of the now legendary annual sports festivals between the Tanzania mainland and Zanzibar. From the humble beginnings of a bilateral sports contact between two clubs, a mass cultural bonanza on a national scale developed. However, for many people a love of sport more than anything else seemed to have been the driving force behind the festivals, despite the party's wish to use them to strengthen the political union between the mainlanders and the Zanzibaris.

In contemporary Tanzania, many functions may be ascribed to sport. Some of these functions have been discussed earlier in the chapter as illustrations of the use of sport in the process of liberation, nationalism and Pan-Africanism, particularly in accordance with the then country's ideology of socialism and self-reliance, adopted in the 1960s.

On the domestic policy front, the TANU government made several attempts and adopted different measures to gain overall control of both sports organizations and individuals – players and fans – as an act of policy implementation. It also wanted to pave the way for the further implementation of other policy aspects. The control of sports organizations was sought through the organizing body of the most popular game in the country, football. The FAT was under constant criticism from both the government and the ruling party for gross incompetence. The public, in addition, frequently blamed the association for 'not producing a winning team' for quite some time. The government adopted managerial and organizational strategies in order to gain an 'upper hand' and then tried to use this advantage to improve the image and the working ability of the FAT. It sacked officers, screened candidates for office and adopted more controlled legislation. Disappointedly for the government of the day, not much control was achieved despite all these measures. Indeed the government appeared to be able to impose only negative control over both sports organizations and individuals. As a result, Tanzania's efforts to use sport to mould communal behaviour and produce disciplined socialist Tanzanians failed miserably.

National integration was at the heart of Tanzania's efforts to build a socialist state. As sports competitions often led to heightened hostility among players and fans, with sports fields turning into 'battlefields', not much progress was made towards this objective. Furthermore, the split between Dar es Salaam and other parts of the country may have been exacerbated by the favoured position of sports in the capital, thus creating 'social distances' between the urban and rural populations.

With only limited control of organizations, players and fans at home, major difficulties also confronted Tanzania in its endeavour to promote African unity through sport. Very little was achieved in this particular aspect of foreign policy. For example, where sports competitions were expected to harmonize relations between countries, the same competitions often created hostility. Sometimes these competitions did not even take place, thus diminishing further the chances of improving relations through such contacts. The underlying difficulties may also be attributed to the fact that what happened on the sports field was usually independent of or unrelated to the political relations between those countries involved.

Tanzania has had more success in the international politics of sport. The country, in collaboration with other countries, in its bid to fight apartheid, used boycotts of the Olympic Games to successfully isolate South Africa and Rhodesia from the international arena. Its influential involvement was well summarized by D.E. McHenry in 'The Use of Sport in Policy Implementation: the Case of Tanzania':

> Tanzania bitterly attacked the International Olympic Committee when it appeared that South Africa would be allowed to compete in the 1968 Olympic Games; she vigorously criticised the Supreme Council for Sport in Africa when it accepted Rhodesian participation in the 1972 Games; and she was one of the first to withdraw from the 1976 Games because of New Zealand's participation. [54]

Although there was support for the government's use of sport in the implementation of various national policy objectives, it was felt by many that modern sport unacceptably displaced indigenous games. The government, through the Ministry of National Culture and Youth, the formation of CHAMIJATA and the adoption of the 1995 sports policy, made various attempts to rectify the situation. However, as yet, no real progress has been made.

The choices available to Tanzania in her pursuit of cultural self-assertion through sport are an acceptance of the adoption of modernity, the restoration of tradition or a combination of tradition and modernity. In many respects, the reality is that modern sport is an integral part of the process of modernization in Tanzania. But it is a complex reality: 'on the one hand, it helps to push the process forward and influences the norms and values of the participants and the society as a whole; and on the other hand, the process of modernization is itself moulded by the traditional norms and values'. [55] However, in terms of widespread modernization there is a major problem. In Tanzania, many of the infrastructures built during colonial times have not been maintained and have fallen into disuse. Westernization is continuing to take place, but essentially without effective modernization, and bureaucracies modelled on Western experience are becoming more and more corrupt. In short, although specialized and differentiated organizations have been created, new efficient structures have not yet been fully institutionalized and established to cater for them.

As far as the restoration of traditional or indigenous 'games' is concerned, it is fair to say that even if the collapse of modern structures leave less complicated ones intact this will not necessarily lead to a complete return to traditional forms. In all probability, the efforts to revive traditional 'games' will not result in the restoration of the traditional sports culture. Mainly because, to do this successfully, traditional structures of consciousness will have to be simultaneously revived, and this is virtually impossible.

To sum up, a restoration of the traditional sports culture is unlikely, while at the same time, the modernization of the country, *inter alia*, by adopting *in toto* a modern sports culture is ambitious. Both cultures, however, offer potential values and hopefully they can be combined and expressed in Tanzania's own modern cultural evolution through sport in the future. On the whole, sport is pursued and valued in the modern global village not only as an end in itself, but also because it represents a complex of meanings in connection with cultural restoration, modernization and assertion. And there is one glimmer of light in a dark tunnel: as the characteristics of modern sport culture are similar all over the world, this surely will assist the eventual integration of Tanzania into the 'global village of sport', on balance to her advantage with eventual beneficial congruency for resources, facilities, participation and performance. Politicians, in the interest of their own prestige, will try to see to that.

Notes

[1] A. Guttmann, 'Our Former Colonial Masters: The Diffusion of Sports and the Question of Cultural Imperialism' (unpublished), p.56.

[2] H. Konde, *Young Africans: Story of Champions of Soccer* (Dar es Salaam: Printpak, 1974), p.4.

[3] In Tanzania the term 'football' strictly means 'soccer'. Thus the term 'football' is used throughout this article to mean soccer.

[4] Konde, *Young Africans*, p.4.

[5] Ibid., p.4.

[6] The formation of Jangwani aroused the interest of many workers of the then East African Cargo Handling Services (EACHS) at the port of Dar es Salaam, who enthusiastically supported the team. Eventually many players of the club came from the EACHS. Probably that is why the club changed its name to Navigation. However, when they were working at the port the players of Navigation Club came into contact with some Italians and learned from them that the Italians were good football players. That may explain why the club adopted the name 'Taliana' after playing as Navigation for sometime. See Konde, *Young Africans*, *passim*.

[7] The Afro-Shirazi Party was a union of the African Association and Shirazi Party concluded on 5 February 1957. Back in 1934, indigenous African Zanzibaris formed the African Association. But in 1938 a Shirazi Association, with the majority of the members coming from the second largest island of Pemba, broke away from it. In 1957, apparently due to the political changes that were taking place on the isles, the Shirazi Association rejoined the African Association to form the Afro-Shirazi Party. For detailed discussion of this see J. Iliffe, 'Tanzania Under German and British Rule' in B.A. Ogot and J.A. Kieran (eds.), *Zamani: A Study of East African History* (Nairobi: East African Publishing House, 1968), pp.308–10.

[8] Zanzibar became a British Protectorate in November 1890. On 10 December 1963 the British granted independence to Zanzibar but left power in the hands of the Sultan, an Arab. This was unacceptable to the majority indigenous African people. A month later, the dynasty of the Sultans was overthrown and the ASP established a revolutionary government. For the background to the African revolution in Zanzibar see H. Haroub Othman, 'Zanzibar's Political History: The Past Haunting the Present?', Centre for Development Research Working Papers, No.93.8 (Copenhagen: CDR, 1993), *passim*. See also Iliffe, 'Tanzania Under German and British Rule', pp.290–311.

[9] Konde, *Young Africans*, p.7.

[10] For detailed discussion of the emergence and growth of the nationalist movements in the 1940s and 1950s, both in Tanganyika and on the isles of Zanzibar, and the use of the meetings of sports and dancing clubs for political purposes, see J. Iliffe, *A Modern History of Tanganyika*, African Studies Series 25, Newcastle upon Tyne (Cambridge: Cambridge University Press, 1979), Chapter 13. See Konde, *Young Africans*, *passim*.

[11] J.J. Coakley, *Sport in Society, Issues and Controversies* (St Louis, MO: Times Mirror/Mosby College Publishing, 1990), p.303.

[12] Konde, *Young Africans*, p.7.

[13] D.E. McHenry, 'The Use of Sports in Policy Implementation: The Case of Tanzania', *Journal of Modern African Studies*, 8, 2 (1980), 239.

[14] He later disagreed with the principles of the Arusha Declaration and fled the country in 1967. He returned in the 1990s.

[15] In Zanzibar, except for the ASP, the activities of all other political parties were suspended following the 1964 revolution. The Zanzibar Revolutionary Council became the supreme legislative body on the islands.

[16] In theory, Tanzania was a one-party state. In practice, however, two main parties operated, TANU in mainland and ASP on the islands. TANU and ASP united in 1977 and formed the revolutionary party *Chama Cha Mapinduzi* (CCM).

[17] 'The Arusha Declaration and TANU's Policy on Socialism and Self-Reliance', The Arusha Declaration, 1967.

[18] United Republic of Tanzania, National Sports Council Act, No.12 of 1967.

[19] Ibid., p.3.

[20] See National Sports Council of Tanzania (Amendment) Act, No.6 of 1971, Section 28: Sports Association Regulations, *passim*.

[21] McHenry, D. E., (1980), 'The Use of Sports', 240.

[22] Jamhuri ya Muungano wa Tanzania (The United Republic of Tanzania), Wizara ya Elimu na Utamaduni: Sera ya Maendeleo ya Michezo (Ministry of Education and Culture: Policy of Sports Development) (Dar es Salaam: Government Printers, 1995), iv.

[23] McHenry, 'The Use of Sports', 242.

[24] *The Nationalist*, 7 Oct. 1967, 4. Also see McHenry, 'The Use of Sports', 240.

[25] McHenry, 'The Use of Sports', 240. Also see *The Daily News*, 21 Nov. 1975, 1.

[26] McHenry, 'The Use of Sports', 242. See also *The Nationalist*, 13 April 1968, 4.

[27] *The Nationalist*, 13 April 13, 1968, 4.

[28] Ibid.

[29] 'The Arusha Declaration'.

[30] Although some forms of professional boxing existed since the early 1980s, professional sports were officially allowed in Tanzania in 1995. See Jamhuri ya Muungano wa Tanzania, 'Wizara ya Elimu na Utamaduni', 33.

[31] The author remembers the crisis as it unfolded day by day as it was widely reported in the media and the resultant political, social and cultural implications of this crisis. See also *The Daly News*, 24 Sept. 1975, 8; 26 Sept. 1975, 8; 29 Sept. 1975, 8; and 1 Oct. 1975, 14.

[32] See *The Daily News*, 24 Sept. 1975, 8; 26 Sept. 1975, 8; 29 Sept. 1975, 8; and 1 Oct. 1975, 14.

[33] The author recalls the angry tone of the government. See also *The Daily News*, 24 Sept. 1975, 8; 26 Sept. 1975, 8; and 29 Sept. 1975, 8.

[34] McHenry, 'The Use of Sports', 240.

[35] Ibid., 245. See also *The Nationalist*, 6 May 1967, 4.

[36] *Sunday News*, 14 Feb. 1968, 4.

[37] *The Nationalist*, 25 April 1968, 4.

[38] See McHenry, 'The Use of Sports', 246. Also *The Daily News*, 21 Aug. 1972, 1.

[39] The author was one of the members of Tanzania's athletic team to the games.

[40] McHenry, 'The Use of Sports', 255.

[41] Ibid., 248.

[42] *The Daily News*, 28 Oct. 1974, 8. See also McHenry, 'The Use of Sports', 249.

[43] See McHenry, 'The Use of Sports', 249. See also *The Daily News*, 25 July 1975, 16.

[44] *The Daily News*, 25 July 1975, 16.

[45] P.M. Sarungi, 'Sera ya Maendeleo ya Michezo' ['Policy of Sports Development'], Jamuhur: ya Muungano wa Tanzania (The United Republic of Tanzania), Wizara ya Elimu na Utamaduni:

Sera ya Maendeleo ya Michezo (Ministry of Education and Culture: Policy of Sports Development) (Dar es Salaam, Government Printers, 1995).

[46] Ibid.

[47] *Bao* is a sedentary game played by two people by moving pellets around a 12-hole board. The holes are arranged in rows of six. The game is played all over Africa but is known by different names such *Wari* in North and West Africa, *Solo* in Southern Africa and *Bao* in Eastern Africa.

[48] As a sports officer from the host region in 1975, the author was involved in the organization of the first championships and therefore has first hand information on this point. A future descending trend was confirmed by the National Chairman of CHAMIJATA, E. Sulus, in an interview held in February 1997.

[49] As a sports officer in the Dodoma region between 1976 and 1979, the author was directly involved in the preparation of the region's team for the Traditional Games, the preparation of the championships and all that was involved. Based on this experience he has an informed basis for this opinion.

[50] See Sarungi, 'Sera ya Maendeleo ya Michezo'.

[51] Ibid., 8.

[52] Ibid., 2.

[53] Guttmann, 'Our Former Colonial Masters', p.49.

[54] McHenry, 'The Use of Sports,' 255.

[55] Ibid., 130.

Celluloid Soccer: The Peculiarities of Soccer in Bengali Cinema

Sharmistha Gooptu

I

This essay tries to understand the uneasy relationship between sport and Indian cinema through a study of soccer as it figures in Bengali popular cinema. [1] Of course, it needs to be mentioned at the outset that the uneasy relationship between sport and cinema that I have explored in this essay has been in the process of transformation in recent times with a growing dynamic 'inter-textuality' between cricket and popular Hindi cinema. [2] However, cricket remains an exception on account of its commercialism, which makes it part of an integrated glamour industry in contemporary India, and most other sports have remained marginal to Indian cinema. In the case of Bengal, this marginality of sport in popular cinema is most striking in the case of soccer, a game that is broadly identified with the Bengali middle classes, [3] as against cricket, contemporary India's most popular sport, which is still identified as elitist by sections of the Bengali intelligentsia. Through a study of three Bengali films, this essay identifies some of the problematic elements of the Bengali identification with soccer, which in turn helps to understand the uneasy relationship between soccer and Bengali cinema. The particular connotations of soccer in the three films discussed here will reveal a society's curiously ambiguous relationship with a sport that is commonly acknowledged to be one of its leading passions.

Soccer has occupied a special place in Bengali life since the turn of the nineteenth century, when Bengalis, often accused of effeminacy [4] by the British, took up European sports such as football and cricket to prove their masculine prowess to their colonial masters. With the historic victory of the Bengali club Mohan Bagan against the East Yorkshire Regiment in 1911, [5] soccer firmly established itself in the collective psyche of Bengal, and had emerged as a career option by the 1950s. The Bengali passion for soccer, documented and commented upon by many observers, has been the subject of popular fiction [6] and has, to a lesser extent, been featured in Bengali popular cinema. While there are several Bengali films that have bits of soccer, it is noteworthy that there are only a handful of films that have plots centring on the game, or that at least feature the game as a key element. [7]

For this essay, I have picked out three such films, which, to my mind, are significant to this study both because of the relatively significant element of soccer in the plot and also because they carry those undercurrents that help to identify the peculiarities of Bengali society's relationship with the sport. These films, *Dhanni Meye* ('Sporty Girl!', 1971), *Saheb* (1981) and *Aashray* ('Refuge', 2000) could all be called family dramas, though the first is a comedy while the second is a more serious film dealing with the plight of a young footballer from a modest middle-class family. The third best fits the classification of family drama and has all the mish-mash of elements that are typical of contemporary mainstream Bengali cinema, namely, romance, slapstick comedy, melodrama, stylized fight sequences and dance numbers.

II

A popular comedy, *Dhanni Meye* is full of impossible situations that crop up around the final match of a local soccer tournament. The tournament is funded by the leading landholding family of Harbhanga, a village close to the city of Calcutta, the prize being the Nyangteshwar Challenge Shield, named after the father of the current lord, Gobardhan, who has pledged to retain the shield for the third time in a row. Gobardhan is the head of an extended family which supports, among others, Manasa, Gobardhan's orphaned niece, a spirited young girl who frequently gets into trouble for teasing other villagers. She is a liability for the family, which would be only too glad to get rid of this extra mouth that they have to feed. The other leading players in the film are Kali Dutta, a Calcutta-based businessman, his wife and younger brother Bagala. Kali had been a soccer player in his youth, and has built up his own amateur soccer team, led by his brother, which qualifies for the final of the Nyangteshwar Shield hosted by Gobardhan. The drama begins with the visitors defeating the home team by a slapping margin of 12 goals to one. Determined to return the insult, one way or another, Gobardhan invites Bagala, the captain of the visiting team and the highest scorer, to his house, and forcibly marries off Manasa, the troublemaker, expecting that she will make life miserable for those in her new home. There follows a succession of dramatic moments, with Kali Dutta refusing to accept the new member of the family, though Bagala falls in love with his wife. Eventually a humiliated Manasa returns to her village around the same time that Kali Dutta decides to send his team back to Harbhanga village for a rerun of the final match, since the shield had been left behind in the chaos of the previous visit. Though Gobardhan arranges to hire some professional players from Calcutta to play for his team, these men are frightened away by Manasa, who wants her husband to have a fair chance. This time, too, the visiting team scores a victory, and Kali marches to the house of his foe, Gobardhan, at the head of a large group of followers to claim the shield. Upon reaching the house, however, he learns that Gobardhan and his wife have been beating their young niece for siding with the enemies. Kali is won over, and steps in to rescue Manasa, declaring that Gobardhan is welcome to retain the shield since he had got the true prize, a dedicated girl like Manasa to grace his home. The visiting team departs with a bride instead of the trophy!

On a more serious note, *Saheb* tells the story an aspiring footballer, who is forced to give up his career to support his family. Saheb, played by newcomer Tapas Paul, is a boy from a middle-class family of modest means, and is the youngest of four brothers with a younger sister who is soon to be married. Though a good footballer, Saheb has been a disappointment to his family, and particularly his ageing father, for repeatedly failing in his qualifying examinations, which would have got him a degree entitling him to white-collar employment, like his brothers. His is a typical Bengali middle-class family, which values academic excellence and considers sport to be a waste of time – unless, of course, sporting prowess has proved to be economically rewarding in some way. Because of his poor academic record, Saheb is branded as a useless boy and is ill-treated by most family members. His only hope is that if recruited by a leading club he would be able to secure regular employment on the basis of his professional standing – an established practice in India since the 1950s. Still struggling to enter the professional circuit, Saheb suffers from an inferiority complex for being economically dependent on his brothers and for not being able to share the family's responsibilities. Foremost among the family's concerns is the impending marriage of Saheb's younger sister, for which they need a large sum of money, and the only option seems to be the mortgaging of the family home. To save the house, and his father from humiliation, Saheb decides to sell a kidney to fund his sister's wedding. He responds to an insertion in a local newspaper by a business magnate whose son is in dire need for a kidney transplant. Unknown to his family, he makes the decision to go through with the operation, knowing well that though he would be able to lead a normal life, he would never be able to play football again if he has only one kidney. When his family gets to know it is already too late, and the film closes with his father and eldest sister-in-law at his bedside. For Saheb, however, this is depicted to be a victory, for though he has lost his career, he has succeeded in fulfilling his responsibility to his family. It is also suggested that though he can never be a professional footballer, he will be economically independent. In an earlier scene, Saheb had asked Sinha, the businessman who had bought his kidney if he could let him have a job in one of his offices once he recovered, and the response had implied an affirmative. In fact, the Hindi version of the same film, by the same director, does more than just suggesting a happy ending. The film closes with a transformed, well-dressed Saheb walking out of an office complex, briefcase in hand, with a contented smile on his face. In the end, therefore, the sportsman's tragedy is minimized and all seems to be well so long as he has been successful in fulfilling his social commitments and securing a degree of economic stability, even if it is at the cost of the sport itself.

Unlike *Dhanni Meye* and *Saheb*, which were both distinctive by way of plot, *Aashray* is a run-of-the-mill entertainer, with soccer thrown in to add flavour to a weak script. The leading protagonist Sudhangshu, played by leading Bengali actor Prasenjit Chatterjee, is a young man who belongs to an affluent middle-class family. His father, a doctor, and other members of the family, with the exception of his mother, are antagonized by his opting for a career in sport instead of one of the conventionally respectable professions such as medicine or law. Sudhangshu, however, experiences none of the trauma that Saheb goes through. He is soon recruited by the East Bengal club, a front-ranking soccer body of Bengal since the 1920s. He receives a handsome signing-on fee, and is offered a secure job as part of the remuneration package. Around this point in the film, there are guest appearances by two leading figures in Indian football, P.K. Banerjee and Subhas Bhaumik. Both Banerjee and Bhaumik had been ace footballers in the 1950s and 1970s and subsequently established themselves as two of the best coaches of Indian football. The plot thus far builds up expectations about a climax centring on the game. However, from this point onwards, the soccer element in the film simply fizzles out, with family drama and the romantic aspect assuming centre stage. It is significant to note here that the family's disapproval of Sudhangshu, which had centred on his opting for a career in sport, gets diverted to their opposition of his amorous association with a girl whose antecedents are looked upon as potentially damaging for the family's reputation and social standing. With Sudhangshu securing economic stability, his career as a footballer ceases to be an issue in the film, and other aspects, such as his relationship with his mother and his romantic involvement, become the propellers.

In effect, in both *Saheb* and *Aashray* the sport itself is minimized once the respective protagonists have fulfilled their social commitments. In Saheb's case, this fulfilment comes through his sacrificing of his career to support his family; for Sudhangshu, it is through establishing his worth to his family by securing economic independence through his recruitment into a leading club. In *Saheb*, Saheb and his friends, passionate sportsmen, also look upon the sport as a passport to economic stability, not simply through a lucrative sporting career, but because of the prospect of securing a steady job which would be a security for life, even after their sporting careers are over. Thus, in a scene where Saheb and his friends are taking a bus home the day before the results of their bachelors' qualifying examination are to be declared, a friend tells Saheb that he is lucky to be a good player, for even if he does not pass the exam he will surely get a good job through his soccer connection. Again, it is suggested that Saheb's father, though disapproving of his son's neglect of academics, would have been less critical had Saheb been able to secure some sort of steady employment through his soccer. In one scene he says with regret that he has heard that the corporate sector is keen to employ 'strikers', 'stoppers' or 'linkmen' but that goalkeepers like Saheb have little prospect. Similarly, in *Aashray* Sudhangshu's recruitment by a leading club is all the more welcome because it gets him a secure job, which will outlast his career as a soccer player. In *Dhanni Meye*, on the other hand, while the soccer tournament and the rivalries centring on it remain in the forefront until the end of the film, the sport simply becomes a trope for generating the most absurd situations. Most significantly, Kali Dutta, who had lost his sleep over the prized shield, comes away from Harbhanga village giving it up, declaring that the prize looses its worth when pitted against the prospect of his brother winning a bride such as Manasa. In the end, therefore, sport is subordinated to other aspects of the social fabric.

Some other observations, however, need to be made before we can identify a common strand in these films, which would provide an insight into the overall dynamics of soccer in Bengali society. It is significant that although in all three films most characters that represent the larger society are disapproving of the game, certain key figures most symbolic of familial authority in Indian society are supportive of characters such as Saheb and Sudhangshu. Though Saheb's father is critical, his eldest sister-in-law, who is like a mother to him, is supportive. In the absence of Saheb's biological mother, she is the mother-figure in the extended family, and her defence of Saheb against criticisms by other family members, and her sympathetic stance carries distinct weight, given the mother's hallowed status in Indian society. At the same time, Saheb's father, it is indicated, was a football fan in his younger days, and in one instance, after Saheb is selected to play for the university side, he exudes quiet pride, expressing the desire to see Saheb play in the next match. Similarly, although Sudhangshu's father disapproves of his son's choice of career, his mother is encouraging and supportive. Further, Saheb and Sudhangshu, though characters that are contrary to the popular Bengali notion of ideal youth, are sympathetically depicted. Much of the criticism against these characters comes from those family members who are portrayed as mean, selfish and conceited, or simply misguided. On the other hand, those that are supportive, such as Saheb's sister-in-law or Sudhangshu's mother, are figured as generous and balanced individuals, notwith-standing the fact that the criticisms made against Saheb or Sudhangshu are the most natural under the given circumstances. Saheb's family, as depicted in the film, is the archetypal Bengali middle-class joint-family of the time, which like most such families is haunted by the unemployment problem in contemporary West Bengal. Unemployment among middle-class Bengali youth had been a mounting social issue since the 1930s, becoming endemic in the 1950s and 1960s. With a bachelor's degree being the basic requirement for respectable white-collar employment, most middle-class families aimed to somehow push their wards through college, expecting them to augment the family's resources once they had secured steady employment. Accordingly, the expectations of Saheb's family, who want him to somehow secure his bachelor's degree so that he can contribute to the family's income, and their criticisms of him for repeatedly failing in his exams and for spending his time playing football, are not out of proportion. This is more so because soccer was a very limited avenue, and only a handful managed to secure steady employment on the basis of their professional standing. Moreover, such jobs were of the lower levels in any sector, and most graduates would be on a higher pay-scale than semi-professional soccer players without the same academic qualifications. Accordingly, the depiction of Saheb's family members as one-dimensional selfish individuals amounts to the presentation of a skewed perspective. On the other hand, despite the absurdities surrounding the tournament in *Dhanni Meye*, the underlying tone is one of indulgence towards the leading characters, and their passion for the sport – both Kali Dutta and Gobardhan are lovable eccentrics. Evidently, therefore, though sport is challenged by other priorities, and might eventually lose ground, the underlying tone in these films is one of indulgence for the sport and its players. For this is a sport that is considered the Bengali's special forte, and the following lines from a catchy song in *Dhanni Meye* pithily capture the essence of the Bengali romance with soccer:

> King of all sports, you are the Bengalis' favourite, football. What sweetness there is in that name – football. ... The English have taken flight after a rule of two hundred and fifty years. Today they are a toothless lion with neither force nor guile. But the truth remains that they were the ones who taught us football. Because of them the names Mohun Bagan and East Bengal have become immortal.

The Bengali identification with soccer, imbued with nationalist sentiments from the colonial past, and a sense of self-worth based on the performances of clubs such as Mohun Bagan and East Bengal thus finds its place in popular culture. Football being identified as the sport that is closest to the Bengali heart, the leading protagonists of the film are characterized as essentially Bengali in manner and habits. Kali Dutta has retained his 'Bengaliness' through his preference of clothes, food, his regular regimen and, of course, his passion for soccer. Kali's 'Bengaliness', as manifested in his passion for soccer, stands in contrast to the hybrid culture of other characters in the film. Naffar, a business associate of Kali, and his fashionable wife are caricatures of the much-ridiculed Westernized Bengali elite of the time and have a craze for cricket, commonly identified as a senseless elite indulgence by the bulk of contemporary Bengali society. At the same time, soccer is closely identified as 'non-elitist' and associated with a democratic perspective. In *Dhanni Meye*, Kali Dutta tells an associate that though a successful businessman, he had risen from modest roots. His father was a poor schoolteacher, and Kali himself had risen to eminence through his prowess in soccer, which had got him a steady job and economic affluence. For men like Kali Dutta, or aspiring footballers like Saheb, soccer is symbolic of a democratic society, with equal opportunities for those of modest means. Again, in *Aashray*, though Sudhangshu is born into an affluent, elite household, he takes up a sport that is commonly identified as a social leveller. Through several other associations, he is portrayed a democratic individual – he is closer to his mother's family, who are middle-class people of more modest means, and befriends and falls in love with a girl from an underprivileged background. In fact, throughout the film, the chief dissatisfaction of his father and other members of the household concerns his intimacy with social elements below their own class, with football being a primary object of contention. In one instance, Sudhangshu's father grumbles that he would not have been quite so dissatisfied had his son taken up cricket or tennis, two games commonly identified as elitist, because of their expensive nature. Thus the footballer, whatever his social station, is depicted as someone close to his roots, and to the mass of Bengali society.

Given these social connotations, and the commonly affirmed Bengali passion for soccer, one wonders why there has been such marginal depiction of the sport in Bengali cinema. As noted at the beginning of this essay, there are just a handful of Bengali films that deal with soccer to any reasonable extent, and, as discussed above, here too the sport itself is compromised in favour of other priorities, with the sport element simply fizzling out at various points during the latter halves of the films. Yet given certain aspects of the history of soccer and cinema in Bengal, there should have been a more potent relationship between these two pillars of twentieth-century Bengali culture.

III

Soccer began to be played in Bengal from the 1870s, but it was after Mohun Bagan's historic win of 1911 that the sport really acquired popularity. [8] By the 1930s it was the most popular game of the Bengali middle classes, and was adequately politicized by regional ethnic rivalries. [9] The game was part of film culture as early as 1912, when Madan Theatres Ltd, the leading film company of contemporary Bengal, filmed the first-round match of the IFA Shield between Mohun Bagan and the Calcutta Football Club. [10] According to the *Indian Cinematograph Year Book* of 1938, between 1920 and 1936, various leading film companies of contemporary Bengal, such as Madan Theatres Ltd, Aurora Cinema Company, Radha Films and Kali Films, had filmed several soccer tournaments, including a number of the Indian Football Association's Shield finals, as short films. [11] These short films were in the nature of 'attractions' to the film-going public, a bonus over and above advertised feature films, in the same league as footage of the Calcutta races or the Kumbha Mela, a sensational gathering of pilgrims organized every 12 years in northern India. Such films as the IFA Shield matches or the one entitled 'Football Play by Marwari Men', [12] however, remained on the fringes of film culture, the stuff of the marginal genre of short films, even though the sport itself had become an integral aspect of Bengali society. For though sport was definitely valued for its character-building qualities, [13] it seems that there remained an unresolved tension between the very physicality of sport and the intellectual connotations of cinema as they evolved in Bengal from the about the second decade of the twentieth century.

From the middle of the 1920s, with the educated middle class's growing involvement with cinema, there had been a stream of writing in the Bengali popular press about the need to distinguish Bengali cinema from the run-of-the mill entertainers being churned out in other parts of the country, most notably Bombay, the leading centre of film production in the country. The bulk of the films churned out by Bombay were a mish-mash of action, drama and sexual content, and were dismissed by Bengali intellectuals as *Khel*, literally meaning 'mere play' and implying light or cheap entertainment. The swashbuckling action genres of the 1920s and 1930s, though immensely popular, were viewed as mindless entertainment by the Bengali intelligentsia, stuff suitable only for the lower classes. [14] Interestingly, therefore, while the playing field itself was becoming increasingly important in the lives of the educated middle classes, who were increasingly drawn to European sports such as cricket and soccer during the 1920s and 1930s, the contemporary action genres of cinema were being dismissed as 'mere play' by members of the same social group(s). 'Play' as epitomized by the physicality of the action genres, was viewed as antithetical to the intellectual and aesthetic potential of cinema, a medium that was most closely associated with literature and the fine arts. Many contemporary writers agreed that in order for cinema to become respectable and acquire currency among the educated classes, Bengali filmmakers should draw upon Bengali literature, the hallmark of high culture in Bengali society. By the mid-1930s, literariness had become a hallmark of what was to be considered good cinema in Bengal, and it is reasonable to assume that cinema's intellectual connotations ensured its distance from sport, notwithstanding the growing Bengali identification with soccer.

At the same time, with left ideology becoming popular in Bengal from the 1940s, cinema was emerging as a medium for political expression, and by the 1970s, Bengali cinema was a significant mouthpiece for leftist intellectuals. Throughout this period, Bengali cinema, not only the art/avant-garde genres but also the more popular variety, retained its distance from the formulaic mainstream cinema produced by Bombay and the southern-language cinemas, through a self-conscious elitism manifested in literariness and political content, its greater realism, naturalistic performances and largely muted sexuality. For most Bengalis, their cinema was an elevated brand of entertainment, often contrasted with the crassness of Bombay cinema [15] – an idea which, it seems, remained unreconciled with notions of the 'mere physicality' of sport.

At the same time, soccer was characterized by a violent fan culture [16] and carried the connotations of rowdiness – unlike cricket, which was popularly accepted as a gentleman's game. While cricket had a rising female viewership from the 1950s, the football field was considered totally unsuitable for respectable women, and soccer, though a passion in Bengali society, never found a stable following among Bengali women. Accordingly, it is understandable that mainstream Bengali cinema, which had its strongest base among middle-class women, stayed away from the game, and certain scenes involving the two leading female characters in *Dhanni Meye* are an apt commentary to the effect. While Kali Dutta's wife, Snehalata, the respectable middle-class housewife is totally unenthused by football, and often rather upset by her husband's craze for the game, Manasa, who is often referred to as 'a wild girl', is the only female spectator of the first match. Perched on a tree, she enjoys the game with the men of the village, a stance radically reversed during the later match, when she is transformed into a demure woman following marriage. During this match, the only time she is seen on the field is when she dutifully comes up to the sidelines to offer a drink to her brother-in-law, Kali Dutta. Of course, there has been a much-celebrated tradition of Bengali women providing inspirational support from behind the scenes, and both *Saheb* and *Aashray* seem to draw upon this lore through the key roles ascribed to two female protagonists, Saheb's sister-in-law and Sudhangshu's mother. However, in both cases, the significance of these characters is more on account of their nurturing actions, and their indulgence of their wards against projected misguided opposition by other family members, and not on account of their encouragement of the sport per se.

From the above analysis, one would begin to comprehend why the early genre of short films based on footage from important sporting encounters failed to make an impact on the mainstream genres of the feature film. Though soccer became a Bengali passion, it remained a marginal component of Bengali cinema. Mainstream Bengali cinema, which has popularly been identified as 'middle-class' (as against Bombay cinema, which, in Bengal, has often been labelled as a subculture suitable for the lower classes) developed at best a tepid relationship with another pillar of Bengali culture that has been identified as a forte of the middle classes. On the few occasions that soccer did feature as a significant element in mainstream cinema, it was in the relatively marginal genre of comedy, as the backdrop for a host of absurd situations (*Dhanni Meye, Mohun Baganer Meye, East Bengaler Chele*). At the same time, its initial centrality in the plot was given over to other priorities in all the three films discussed above – a replication of its marginalization in cinema by other aspects of Bengali culture.

Acknowledgements

I would like to thank Boria Majumdar and Kaushik Bandyopadhayay for their very helpful opinions and insights.

Notes

[1] In this essay, the terms 'soccer' and 'football' have been interchangeably used.
[2] For a discussion, see Sharmishtha Gooptu, 'Mixing Magic', *Sahara Time*, 11 Sept. 2004.
[3] A generic term commonly used to describe a cross-section of the Bengali middle class is *bhadralok*, literally meaning 'respectable person(s)'. It is important to note that the *bhadralok* status is not defined by economic standing, so that one may be poor and yet be considered *bhadro(lok)*, or genteel, so long as one sports an investment in a distinct ethos of life that sets one apart from the rustic masses.

[4] For an instructive discussion on the British construction of Bengali effeminacy and the Bengali response to this charge through a physical culture movement in the third quarter of the nineteenth century, see John Roselli, 'The Self Image of Effeteness: Physical Education and Nationalism in Nineteenth Century Bengal', *Past and Present* (February 1980), pp.121–48.

[5] The first-ever Indian club to achieve this feat, Mohun Bagan's victory raised the status of soccer overnight from a mere entertainment pursuit to a cultural weapon to fight the colonial masters, and beating them on the football field increasingly came to be viewed as a victory of nationalism.

[6] The Bengali passion for soccer finds eloquent expression in the writings of Bengali sports writers, journalists and novelists such as Paresh Nandi, Rakhal Bhattachrayya, Moti Nandy, Jayanta Dutta, Shantipriya Bandyopadhyay, Rupak Saha and Manas Chakraborty.

[7] Bengali films that have soccer as key element of the plot are *Dhanni Meye, Mohun Baganer Meye, Saheb, East Bengaler Chhele* and *Aashray*.

[8] For a recent consideration on the significance of the Shield victory in contemporary Bengali society, see Kausik Bandyopadhyay, '1911 in Retrospect: A Revisionist Perspective on a Famous Indian Sporting Victory', in J.A. Mangan and Boria Majumdar (eds.), *Sport in South Asian Society: Past and Present* (*International Journal of the History of Sport*, 21, 3–4) (London and Portland, OR: Frank Cass, 2004).

[9] Politicization of soccer through ethnic conflict found prolific expression in the rivalry between Mohun Bagan and East Bengal, the most popular clubs of Bengal since the 1930s. For a discussion, see Paul Dimeo, '"Team Loyalty Splits the City into Two": Football, Ethnicity and Rivalry in Calcutta', in G. Armstrong and R. Giulianotti (eds.), *Fear and Loathing in World Football* (Oxford: Berg, 2001).

[10] This was the first football match in India to be filmed. It may be noted here that one or two Mohun Bagan goals that had been disallowed on the plea of 'offside' in that match were, going by the film, not so. This allows us an insight into the discriminatory practices against native teams in European sports such as soccer. For details see *Mohun Bagan Platinum Jubilee Souvenir* (Calcutta: Mohun Bagan AC, 1964), p.29.

[11] B.D. Bharucha (ed.), *Indian Cinematograph Year Book, 1938* (The Motion Picture Society of India, 1938), pp.183–204.

[12] The Marwaris are a business community of western India, who had migrated to Bengal in large numbers during the late nineteenth and early twentieth century.

[13] Sport's utmost value as a tool of character-building has been written about at length by J.A. Mangan in trying to explain the seminal importance of sport and athleticism as an imperial/moral tool in colonial society. See J.A. Mangan, *The and Imperialism: Aspects of the Diffusion of an Ideal* (London and Portland, OR: Frank Cass, 1998). Also see, J.A. Mangan, 'Soccer as Moral Training: Missionary Intentions and Imperial Legacies', in Paul Dimeo and James Mills (eds.), *Soccer in South Asia: Empire, Nation and Diaspora* (London and Portland, OR: Frank Cass, 2001), pp.41–56.

[14] For a derogatory reference in this vein see Basu, 'Deshi Film Sambandhe Du Char Katha', *Bioscope*, 27 (1930), 9–10.

[15] Bengali film journals and magazines of the period between the 1950s through to the 1980s – *Roopmancha, Chitravas, Chitrabikshan, Anandalok* and so on – are replete with discussions on the mindlessness of popular Hindi cinema.

[16] Violence in Indian soccer has a long history, which reached a climax on 16 August 1980, when 16 fans were killed during the local derby between Mohun Bagan and East Bengal. What started as a small feud gradually escalated into full-scale violence among fans, resulting in one of the worst tragedies of Indian soccer. As a mark of respect for the martyrs, 16 August is celebrated as blood donation day.

Sedentary Games and the Nationalist Project: A Silent History

Nirbed Ray and Projit Bihari Mukharji

It has been argued that in colonial India there were two distinct domains of power, in which the idioms and metaphors of authority were completely different from one another. This distinction is further said to be symptomatic of the failure of the Indian bourgeoisie to speak for the entire Indian nation. The only relationship between the two domains was, or so it is alleged, one merely of domination and subordination. [1] Our contention is that though this might largely be true for situations of violent insurrectionary politics, such as peasant uprisings, our study of sedentary games allows us to read other modalities in relating the two domains. While this does not flatten out the obvious hierarchies of power that underwrote the distinction itself, it does try to eke out the alternative ways in which the two domains interacted with each other.

Sedentary games are especially useful as a counterpoint, since they are perhaps as far removed as possible from the violence of insurrections. Furthermore, unlike field games, a significant number of these games are played indoors, thus often necessitating the access of the players to the interiors of homes. This last facet of sedentary games allows them to throw in the stark distinctions drawn between the *ghor* and the *bohir*. [2] These distinctions are not only a spatial matrix that underwrites hierarchies of gender but indeed touch the very heart of the nationalist project. For both temporally as well as culturally, nationalisms are a marriage of opposites: a relatively modern phenomenon, each of them allege an archaic antiquity;

a member of the modern comity of nations, each proclaims uniqueness of its national characteristics. Narratives of the nation are thus marked out by a perceived and acknowledged inferiority in terms of an universal world standard while at the same time vociferously asserting the national community's potential to bridge this gap and attain the universal standard. Thus while on the one hand accepting post-Enlightenment rationality as an index of self-evaluation, it is also deeply romantic in attempting to reach an unity of experience at the level of the folk, which it creatively re-fashions at the level of the classical, by both giving it a standard form and bequeathing it a hoary past. [3]

Orientalism and Nationalism: The Play of Identity and Difference

Though the tradition of trying to collect and write about the sedentary games of India began early in the career of colonialism in India, and Sir William Jones, the pre-eminent Orientalist and founder of the Asiatic Society, himself wrote a piece on the Indian game of chess, [4] yet the interest among Indian authors seems to have taken a long time to mature. It was only in the twentieth century that one finds a spate of essays on various sedentary games of India by Indian intellectuals. Scholars such as Professor Hem Chandra Das Gupta, Dr Charu Chandra Das Gupta, Haraprasad Shastri, Jatindra Mohan Datta wrote extensively on the subject. If this interest was indeed merely a derivative interest born out of proximity with the British Orientalists, one would have expected much more writing between 1790, when Jones's piece appeared, and 1895, when Haraprasad Shastri's pieces appeared. Yet there were none, but between Shastri's piece and 1942, there were more than 20 pieces that appeared in the journal of the Asiatic Society and in the *Calcutta Review*. The conspicuous absence in these forums is particularly important, and even if further research does throw up texts on sedentary games in the intermediate period, an answer would still be needed as to why such texts were unavailable in forums so conspicuous for their connections to the corridors of power. From their very inception, they were forums that sought to catalogue and unravel histories of culturally distinct groups with one eye towards the pressing need for the purposes of governmental control. This might easily be gleaned from even a cursory glance at the careers of some of the more important authors to write on sedentary games. Sir William Jones, for example, was a judge of the Supreme Court at Calcutta; Captain Hiram Cox, the man who wrote on Burmese chess, was a British Resident at the Burmese court. Among the Indians, Prof. Hem Chandra Das Gupta was not only professor of geology at the Presidency College but also instrumental in the establishment of the Geological, Mining and Metallurgical Society and the Geological Institute, and in 1928 was elected president of the Geological Session of the Indian Science Congress. Jatindra Mohan Datta, another enthusiastic collector and writer on sedentary games, was a politician and served as Secretary of the Hindu Mahasabha for a long time. These exemplary cases, we hope, clearly bring out the proximity of authors writing on sedentary games to governmental power. [5] While the British authors were important members of the colonial bureaucracy, the Indians were close to nationalist politics. This is especially significant, as we seek to argue here that despite the failure of the Indian bourgeoisie to forge a common idiom with the rising tide of nationalism, there was definitely an attempt to appropriate, classify and hegemonize the cultural idioms, not only of vertical segments but also horizontal segments of the cultural space. After all the first steps towards the construction of the strident German national identity that was to have such disastrous impact on the history of the twentieth century started with the Brothers Grimm collecting folktales from the region. [6]

The Chequered Board: Sedentary Games and Playing Cultures

First, we seek to unravel the stratifications within which cultural practices in general, and sedentary games in particular, were enmeshed. For it is only after we establish the segmented nature of this field of study that we might undertake to attempt to read the ways in which these stratifications were related to one another.

The first segmentation, as was to be expected, took place horizontally, viz. from one place to another. An essay in the March 1923 issue of the *Calcutta Review*, for instance, details dice games found in the Punjab. Hem Chandra Das Gupta also speaks of dice games in the Jubbulpore region in 1924. Also Jatindra Mohan's pieces on variations over shorter distances within Bengal, such as the Basirhat region, or Lower Bengal, point out the geographical segmentation that was prevalent in a era before the dawn of globalization or mass-marketed sedentary games. The geographic provenance of these games were also important, since they were an important means of preserving folk memory, and the narratives around these games were created and articulated by marshalling metaphors deeply embedded in their local contexts. Take for instance the game of *Mangal-Pata* played in the Bikrampur region around Dhaka in Eastern Bengal (now Bangladesh). Describing the game in the *Quarterly Journal of the Bangiya Shahitya Parishad*, 1314 BS (1907), Binodeshwar Das Gupta writes [7] that

> the name is derived from the word 'Mughal-Pathan', in a number of places it is still called 'Mughal-Pathan' instead of 'Mangal Pata'. The story of the battle between the Mughals and the Pathans, for the control of Bengal, is still fresh in popular memory even in the most remote of villages in Bengal. It is perhaps to preserve the memory of this battle that the game was invented.

Though the author does not comment on it, one might even be so daring as to eke out a subtle shift in the very corruption of the original name. That 'Mughal-Pathan' is slowly changed to 'Mangal-Pata', which literally means the Holy Board, in the Bikrampur region, which after all was a region that produced a disproportionately high number of Bengali upper-caste Hindu *Bhadraloks*; a demographic group that played a significant part in the communalization of Bengali politics in the decades to come, might well be a significant pointer to subtle and long-drawn-out changes affecting the region. Similarly Hem Chandra Das Gupta's article [8] in the *Asiatic Society Journal* on the game of *Pretoas* played in western Bihar, is similarly connected to the local cultural milieu. [9] The name is believed to have been derived from the word *prêt*, a species of ghosts specifically connected with the region. Similarly Sunder Lal Hora's description of games such as *Lam Turki* and *Sipahi Kat* being played in the Teesta Valley is also significant. [10] While the former name clearly refers to some sort of a Turkish ancestry for the game, the latter, literally meaning 'slaughtering the soldier' [11] is also a reference to battles of yore waged in the region. The region saw a lot of troop movement during the Mughal attempts to subjugate north-eastern India, and was the site of bloody guerrilla ambushes on the Mughal troops. Even place names such as Mughalkata ('slaughter the Mughal') dot the place, and though Dr Hora has not left us any hints, it is a fair enough conjecture that the games too were created out of this collective social imaginary. In fact, the lack of local details and narratives around these games is noteworthy, since it is symptomatic of the inner tensions of the nationalist project. While cataloguing and collecting elements of local cultures, the nationalists were constrained to see them as variants of an original unity and were distrustful of giving them any autonomy. As Ernst Gellner, detailing the project of nationalism, says:

> [it] is, essentially, the general imposition of high culture on society, whose previously low cultures had taken up the lives of the majority, and in some cases the totality. ... It is the establishment of an anonymous, impersonal society, with mutually substitutable atomized individuals, held together above all by a shared culture of this kind, in place of a previous complex structure of local groups, sustained by folk cultures reproduced locally and idiosyncratically by the micro-groups themselves. [12]

There are other ways too in which the locality impinges upon the game. A rather curious example of this are the following comments of Dr Hora about the game *Pretoa*:

> I have incidentally collected two superstitious beliefs connected with this game. If young boys indulge too much in playing this game, the elderly people warn them that there will be a heavy downpour and consequently a deluge. The second belief is that if this game is played too much, then the cereals will become dear and consequently there will be famine. I have no doubt that both of these beliefs are meant to dissuade young boys from spending too much time on these games instead of attending to their regular work of cultivation. I am further informed that this particular game ... is usually played during the rainy season when the agriculturists have more leisure from the care of their crops. [13]

Contrapuntally, Binodeshwar Das Gupta, writing of the Bikrampur region, informs us that since the region is especially prone to floods, during the monsoon season the prevalence of sedentary games actually declines. As the eastern Bengal region is broken up into a number of small islets by the floods, and it becomes difficult for people to meet each other, sedentary games give way to *baich*, which is the local variant of the boat race. Thus clearly it is the relatively drier monsoons in western Bihar and the heavy monsoons of riverine east Bengal that regulate both the temporalities as well the mythologies surrounding these games.

To turn now from the geographical segmentation to the social one, we hear Dr Hora commenting once again that he had collected his games from a 'old man engaged as a cooly to help [him] collect zoological samples' and helped by the watchman of the PWD (Public Works Department) Rest House at Kalijhora; the rules were later verified by Dr Hora's friend Dr Raj from the coolies of Kalimpong. [14] Similarly Jatindra Mohan Datta speaks of a 'new and rare type of Mughal-Pathan' found near Belghurriah (Belghoria) and Dakhineswar and states that 'Muhammadan masons, who appear to be descendants of Hindu converts and mostly have Hindu names, play the game'. [15] Again, Irving Finkel comments on the game of Aasha played exclusively by the Cochini Jews. [16] These are but a few instances; yet they clearly bring out that apart from a geographical or horizontal differentiation, there was clearly a vertical segmentation whereby different groups, based on class, caste or religion, often had their distinctive sedentary games. The point that we are seeking to make here is that sedentary games, like all other cultural products and artefacts, were keenly enmeshed in cultural motifs and memories that were irreducibly local in both a geographical as well as a sociological sense, and may indeed in themselves be an interesting text to read, in order to get a glimpse into the technologies and the tropes through which social memory was created, constructed and changed over time. The difficulty in pursuing such an approach, though, is that the project that monitored the collection of these games was premised on a denial of these local exigencies. By stressing similarities and ignoring differences, the authors sought to portray their collection as 'variants', 'degenerations' and so on. To them the more important question was the witch-hunt of paternity, of lineage, rather than the plurality of invention and innovation. Just as earlier Orientalists such as Jones or Hiram Cox had debated about whether Indian or Chinese or European chess was the original, so did Das Gupta, Datta and Hora keep on trying to find the standard form of the game and then trace the deviances. Jatindra Mohan Datta for instance writes:

> At Titagarh, some thirteen miles north of Calcutta, the population is heterogeneous and consists mainly of mill-hands coming from United Provinces, Bihar, Orissa, and Madras. There we have found several degenerate [17] forms of *Challis Ghutia* played by men and boys, some of whom are born there and some come from their native districts in UP and Madras. [18]

Clearly the terms of human lineage and cultural lineage are here represented allegorically and within the trope of 'degeneracy' rather than 'novelty' or 'invention'. The tropology is not unique to the representation of games alone, from the debates over caste precedence that are to be found in the census reports of late colonial India, to volumes such as Risley's *Tribes and Castes of Bengal*; from the models of comparative philology and linguistics to the discussions of Aryan race theorists and scholars of 'Ancient Indian Sciences', we find it everywhere. The belief that a homogenized originary moment is later degenerated into pluralized shadows of the former glory is persistent in all these writings – of course just as all of India itself is a degeneracy of its age-old ancient glory! Further, one might be so bold as to suggest that Datta's own involvement with the Hindu revivalism of the Mahasabha, corroborates our reading, for the Mahasabha movement was indeed premised upon the faith in a an ancient and glorious Hindu past that needed to be revived.

There is also for that matter a segmentation premised on gender. Binodeshwar Das Gupta, for instance, informs us of a game called *dosh-pnochish*, a game played almost exclusively by women of the Bikrampur region. Or that 'of late', perhaps again as a consequence of the rising tide of Brahmanical patriarchy in the region, women have been turning away from local sedentary games such as *Baghbondi* and *Pait-Pait* and turning towards localized card games.

Uniting the Strands: A Hidden History of Nationalism

In the writings on sedentary games we thus find a nationalist project at work. A project that shared much of its impetus with an earlier Orientalist project to codify, classify and 'know' the Orient. Yet it also had significant differences from this earlier project. One of the major differences was that while the older British scholars depended on textual corroboration, the Indian scholars showed little interest in sniffing out ancient textual references to their games. Jones, for example, writes that 'I cannot find any account in the classical writings of the Brahmans. It is indeed, confidently asserted, that Sanscrit books on Chess exist in this country, and, if they can be procured at Benares, they will assuredly be sent to us.' [19] He further goes on to cite references from Firdausi and Jam and also makes a point of choosing only learned Brahmans, Radhacant and Jagannath, as his interlocutors and informants on the issue. Similarly Hiram Cox mentions the *Amaracosha* as a source of information on the Burma chess that he describes and the *Bhawishya Puran* as a source for 'Indian' chess. Or indeed H.G. Raverty who mentions the works of the Kashmiri authors Ratnakara and Rudrarata as well as Abu Rihan al Beruni. In turn the Indian authors, as we have seen, have depended solely on the testimony of coolies, villagers and the occasional 'gentleman', but never on textual sources. In fact, so much so that the only exception to the rule of not citing textual references, Jatindra Mohan, while writing of a game found in Assam, actually premises his excursion by the phrase 'though perhaps not strictly pertinent, we would like draw the attention of the reader to the fact that sedentary games were popular in the time of Emperor Akbar'. [20] Clearly, then, even when the stray textual reference was dug up, it was seen not to be 'strictly pertinent' but merely as an additional piece of information. In part, this is due to the difference in their aspirations. While the British Orientalists sought to retrieve a temporally distant India, the new breed of Indian scholars sought to posit an experiential unity of the subcontinent. Both were united in their search for a glorious and united people of India, but while the former saw the present as irremediably plural and united only by the British sword, the latter sought to prove an empathetic and cultural unity that was to be articulated by the new Indian bourgeoisie as its sole and only representative. At its heart, then, it was a question of agency. Partha Chatterjee, comparing the problematic of nationalism and Orientalism, states that 'the problematic in nationalist thought is exactly the reverse of that of Orientalism. That is to say, the object in nationalist thought is still the Oriental. ... Only he is not passive, non-participating.' [21] Hence the Orientalist abolishes the living Oriental as merely a tout or conduit to track down the lost texts of a past which can safely be granted a voice by virtue of the fact that it is after all dead. The reading of the text is after all a gesture in which the active agency rests not with any really living 'Oriental' but rather with the Western scholar, whose voice like that of a ventriloquist speaks for the text. Whereas the nationalist project, despite its mistrust towards the 'coolies' whose memory must not only be depicted as a 'degeneracy' but indeed continually and severally verified by others, is still constrained to see them as participants in the nation.

Recent scholars have commented on the failure of the nationalist project, since there was never one nation, but rather several nations within the Indian polity. Be that as it may, our study here is interested in the attempts to forge that non-existent unity into a reality. Detailing the need to collect such narratives, Dr Hora writes: 'Before discussing the wider significance of the various games now being played in India, it seems desirable to record all the different types that are prevalent at the present time and to study the variations undergone by them during the distribution from place to place in this country.' [22] Thus not only was the model of dispersal, the branching out of one united family, clearly outlined, but a need was asserted to preserve and record the variations. It is noteworthy that this model has no space for non-linear evolutionary strategies, for instance games may have travelled in both directions, have been hybridized with others, cross-hatched between earlier and later forms of the same game and so on. Yet the model adopted by Hora and his compatriots could accommodate only the linear dispersal from one unified moment of origin into a pluralized set of 'variants', which again in the hands of ultra-nationalists such as Datta could easily become 'degeneracies'. Further Dr Hora goes on to assert that

> The present generation of educated people is almost ignorant of these local games, while the illiterate masses are also taking more and more interest in imported games for their amusement. The old games are thus dying out, and it is important to record the things which another generation may rarely, if ever, see.

Hence we find the typical anxiety of the Western-educated elite over losing their heritage, and the need to record at least some part of it for their progeny. Also significant here is that the 'illiterate masses' are seen as the last repository of what is already lost to the elite. Frantz Fanon had commented upon the way the 'white' establishment appropriated and appreciated jazz music when they needed to integrate 'black' labour power into their exploitative structure; could the elite's nostalgic turn towards the masses be a similar strategy? Whether it was or not is definitely a question that requires further research, but what is indubitable is that the relationship we see expressed in these narratives between the elite 'domain' and the subaltern 'domain' are clearly not premised on the *danda*; there are clearly other forms of relating the two domains than domination and subordination.

Notes

[1] For a brilliant recent reiteration of this position see Dipesh Chakrabarty, 'A Small History of Subaltern Studies', *Habitations of Modernity: Essays in the Wake of Subaltern Studies* (Delhi: Permanent Black, 2002).

[2] Scholars such as Partha Chatterjee have taken this distinction between the *ghor* (indoors) and *bohir* (outdoors) as being symptomatic of the peculiar split that defined the split or double consciousness of the colonized elite. While the domain of the outdoors was an area where 'Western' influence and institutions were freely adopted; the domain of the *ghor* was largely sought to be kept free of such influences.

[3] For a fascinating discussion on the issue see Partha Chatterjee, 'Nationalism as a Problem in the History of Political Ideas,' in *Nationalist Thought and the Colonial World: A Derivative Discourse* (Delhi: Oxford University Press, 1986). Also see Homi K. Bhabha, *The Nation as Narrative* (London: Routledge, 1994).

[4] Sir William Jones, 'On the Indian Game of Chess,' *The Asiatik Researches*, II (1790), 159–65.

[5] In fact the list is in a sense interminable, for one only has to pick up any random copy of the *Asiatic Society Journal* or the *Calcutta Review* and go through not merely people writing on 'sedentary games' but its contributors at large to be able to perceive the proximity of the authors to the powers that were.

[6] Students of 'nationalism', such as Eric Hobsbawm, Ernest Gellner and Benedict Anderson have commented on how one of the first moves in the constructions of nationalisms is the forging of alternate 'great traditions' from a number of 'little' or folk traditions. Of course there are serious differences between the three above-mentioned authors as regards the conceptualization of this process itself, yet that there is a process that creatively appropriates elements of folk traditions and forges a classical culture from such raw material is pretty much a consensus amongst them; what is in dispute is the extent.

[7] Binodeshwar Das Gupta, article in the *Quarterly Journal of the Bangiya Shahitya Parishad*, 14 (1314 BS [1907]).

[8] In an interesting reflection of the material world, the spiritual world also had regional, caste and communal differences. In eastern India there are different species of ghosts such as the *Mamdos*, who are ghosts of Muslims, *Prets*, who are usually dead Bihari coolies, *Brohmodottis*, who are Brahmins and so on.

[9] Hem Chandra Das Gupta, 'On a Type of Sedentary Game known as Pretoa', JL-1931-NS:XXVII.

[10] Dr Sunder Lal Hora, 'Sedentary Games of India', JL-1933-NS:XXIX, pp.5–11.

[11] In fact though the word *Sipahi* in Hindi designates soldier, it is derived from the Turkish word *Spahi*, which specifically designated cavalrymen.

[12] Ernest Gellner, *Nations and Nationalism* (Oxford: Basil Blackwell, 1983), p.57.

[13] Dr Sunder Lal Hora, 'A Note on the Sedentary Game known as Pretoa', JL-1931-NS: XXVII, pp.211–12.

[14] Hora, 'Sedentary Games'.

[15] Jatindra Mohan Datta, 'A New and Rare Type of Mughal-Pathan found near Calcutta,' Jl-1938-3S: IV(L), pp.283–4.

[16] Irving L. Finkel, 'An Introduction', in Nirbed Ray and Amitabha Ghosh (eds.), *Sedentary Games of India* (Calcutta: The Asiatic Society, 1999).

[17] Author's own emphasis.

[18] Jatindra Mohan Datta, '*Challis-Ghutia* and Its Degenerate Variants,' JL-1939-35: V(L), p.259.

[19] Sir William Jones, 'On the Indian Game of Chess,' The Asiatic Researches, II (1970).

[20] Jatindra Mohan Datta, '*Bagh-Chal* at Kamakhya,' JL-1939-3S: V(L), p.259.

[21] Chatterjee, 'Nationalism as a Problem', p.38.

[22] Dr Sunder Lal Hora, 'Sedentary Games in India'.

Sports History in India: Prospects and Problems

Kausik Bandyopadhyay

And across the globe, sport is now too important to be left in the hands of sportsmen and women. More and more, it is the property of the 'People' in their various manifestations as politicians, entrepreneurs, educationists, commercialists, publicists, and, not least, academics. [1]

As such the history of sport gives a unique insight into the way a society changes and impacts on other societies it comes into contact with and, conversely, the way those societies react back upon it. [2]

Sport was one of the most important new social practices of the Europe of the late nineteenth and early twentieth centuries, and as such played a central role in the creation of politically and socially cohesive 'invented traditions'. [3]

Introduction

When James Walvin wrote his influential essay 'Sport, Social History and the Historian'· [4] for the first volume of the *British Journal of Sports History* in 1984, he was fully convinced that 'the history of a particular game had an importance which far transcended the game itself' and that 'ultimately, sport could (and perhaps ought to) provide a reflection of wider issues and relationships in society at large'. [5] Yet what seemed difficult for him to reconcile at the time was 'the manifest discrepancy between the undeniable significance of sport in the contemporary world and the refusal of many to accept the importance of sport in its historical setting'. [6] And he mentioned that 'it is vital that the research which will find a place in these pages (of the *British Journal of Sports History*) is able to make an impact beyond the pale of the specialism itself'.[7] For him, the journal's greatest task was to 'overcome that deep and abiding intellectual suspicion which is so commonly manifested towards the very concept of sports history or sports sociology'. [8]

This essay seeks to emphasize a simple truth: that sport in the modern world is a proper subject of study for historians. True, historians have taken an inordinately long time to appreciate its relevance for the lives of both the influential and the insignificant of past communities. [9] Failure to get sport into sharp academic focus may be 'a form of intellectual myopia born of long-established prejudice'. [10] Though sport now has a significant place in Indian life, the study of sport as a serious intellectual discipline, however, remains underdeveloped in India. [11] While the Western academic world in the past two decades has appreciated the relevance of sport in the history of past and present communities, [12] India remains far backward in its appreciation of the role of sport in society. Scholarly literature on the history of sport has been extremely sparse. [13] This essay will attempt to set down the prospects and the problems facing sports history in India at both research and teaching levels.

Academic Writing on Indian Sport: A Historiographical Survey

The first serious academic research by an Indian on sports history was pursued as early as 1988 when Soumen Mitra, a graduate of the Presidency College, Kolkata, and an MA in history from the Calcutta University, submitted an M.Phil. dissertation on the role of soccer in colonial India. [14] Mitra, however, did not continue his academic interests and took up a job in the administrative service in the early 1990s. It was also in the late 1980s that cricket was considered seriously by Indian writers such as Ramachandra Guha, [15] Arjun Appadurai, [16] Mihir Bose [17] and Ashis Nandy. [18] A recent addition to this list is Mario Rodrigues. [19] Very little attention, however, was paid either to historical studies of other sports or to sport in general.

Non-Indian specialists on sport in India have mostly focused on the games introduced by the British during colonial rule. Much of this work has dealt with cricket, since it has become India's de facto national game in recent decades. The works of Edward Docker [20] and Richard Cashman [21] bear testimony to this trend. Some of these studies on colonial Indian sport focus on the colonial introduction of modern sports and explore deeper imperial motives behind it. [22] There have been some essays on football by Tony Mason, [23] and most recently a collection edited by Paul Dimeo and James Mills. [24] Some European scholars have also studied the indigenous sports and games of India. Chief among these are Joseph Alter's works on wrestling and kabaddi. [25] The most recent major Indian contribution to the study of social history of sport has come from the historian, Boria Majumdar. [26] And there are others who promise a better future for India as far as the study of sport is concerned. [27]

Sport in Social History: The Indian Context

Like many other forms of social behaviour, as Walvin rightly noted, sporting activity is largely socially and historically determined. [28] He further pointed out that 'the sports historian and sociologist need to reach beneath the surface, behind the obvious facts of sporting history, if their studies are to be any more than yet another quasi-antiquarianism masquerading as serious social history'. [29] Following Walvin, Boria Majumdar argues that 'a study of sport history is crucial not only for an understanding of the evolution of the sporting heritage of the Indian nation, but for a deeper appreciation of the seemingly unrelated political processes such as nationalism, (and) colonial culture'. [30] The prime purpose in this academic exercise is not the descriptive study of a particular sport, but for what it says about society of a particular period. There have been, as Ramachandra Guha has suggested, two approaches to the Indian history of sport. [31] The first has focused narrowly on its practice, the background of its patrons and players, the evolution of its associations and tournaments, and on how it pays or does not pay for itself. The second approach, which Guha himself prefers, uses sport to illuminate themes of wider interest and relevance: 'It views sport as a *relational idiom*, a sphere of activity that expresses, in concentrated form, the values, prejudices, divisions and unifying symbols of a society'. [32] As he goes on to suggest proficiently, the game of cricket can provide valuable insights into the history of modern India, in particular to the three overarching themes of Indian history: those of race, caste and religion. [33] However, Guha's assertion that the sociology and politics of cricket 'presumes no technical knowledge of the game itself' is not tenable because changes in its rules, rituals and vocabulary are intimately related to, and highly influenced by the politics, culture and economy of the game.

To study sport in the wider perspective of history and culture will help us understand the importance of sport and locate sport within the broader cultural, social, political and economic contexts of colonial and postcolonial South Asian societies. The study of sport as history offers major correctives to our taken-for-granted understanding of the social and economic history of late-nineteenth- and twentieth-century India. For instance, the existing historiography of nationalism, communalism, social conflict, colonial culture and developing economy in India fails to recognize the importance of football as an arena for spontaneous articulation of nationalism, communalism and popular culture [34] or the role cricket has played as a major nationalist, communal and commercial force in the twentieth century. [35]

There has also been an irrational yet popular belief that only the 'committed', the insiders or the practitioners are qualified to pursue sports history. This is certainly a flawed assumption. Personal experience or membership can of course be useful at times in understanding 'certain distinct sensibilities which outsiders could never experience'. [36] But that should never be considered a deciding factor in pursuing academic research on sport. Walvin is again pertinent in his comment:

> (S)uch claims to exclusivity are intellectually crippling and depend ultimately for their *rationale* on the belief that there is, or ought to be, only one particular approach or interpretation of historical experience. It is to be hoped that sports history will avoid such factional fights, although this is not to claim that sporting practitioners have *nothing* to tell us. Far from it. What is quite clear however is that one does not need to be player, spectator or *aficionado* – of any sport – to appreciate its broader social, or historical significance. [37]

Social historians, therefore, should not feel obliged to describe events or matches that they never saw or to engage in discussions on the tactics employed. It is less important for our purposes to understand the genius of Sachin Tendulkar [38] or Diego Maradona [39] than to analyse what sport means and why it matters. Nevertheless, as noted earlier, it can be useful to have a knowledge of the evolution of a game's technicalities, which sometimes exerts important influence on its social history and vice versa.

Socio-historical research on aspects of popular culture in India commonly tends to generalize the regional thrust of particular cultural elements into a national pattern. Sports history to date in India, too, suffers from such sweeping generalizations. For instance, a history of Indian football is often identified with that of Bengal football and the latter with Calcutta football. [40] Cricket in colonial India, in the same way, is understood to be primarily a Bombay-based phenomenon. [41] However, without prior consideration of a sport's local origins, developments and specificities, construction of its wider national history can be a flawed exercise.

Finally, the study of sport in India from the perspective of social history needs to put a strong emphasis on vernacular sources. This has not been true of the past. Furthermore, I work on the assumption that 'historians are made for history and the reverse can not be true' [42] and that a social historian has certain social responsibilities. As S.N. Mukherjee has aptly remarked, 'We should not only concern ourselves with the problems which the man in the street faced in the past, but make them entertaining and instructive for the man in the street today. ... The questions we ask about our past must be related to our present day problems.' [43] Sports historians, in short, have a duty to make people aware of the problems, realities and potentials of sport in our country today, and inform and impress the authorities so as to keep them on the right track toward progress and excellence.

E.H. Carr once made a splendid comment: 'Good historians ... have future in their bones'. [44] Sports history research in India, especially on Indian sport, should not only concern itself with the analytical understanding of specific historical issues, but should offer valuable insights in the light of past historical experience into a better future for sport in India. To achieve this end, it is important to remember what Walvin stated two decades earlier:

> In the determination to establish legitimacy there is the basic danger of overstatement and exaggeration. This, however, is not the most seductive danger, for in seeking to stake out an autonomous historical empire, it is all too easy to wrench sports history from its determining social and economic context. There is no single model upon which the sports historian ought to proceed but in the last resort the viability and even the respectability of sports history must rest upon the quality of the work produced. Unless the traditional canons of historical research and reconstruction are applied to this relatively new field, it will not – and ought not to – gain acceptance. Like sport itself, sports history will ultimately depend on the skills and imagination of its practitioners. [45]

Sports History Research in Contemporary India

The problems faced by a sports historian in India are both frustrating and challenging: frustrating because the 'non-academic' character of sports authorities, personalities and spectators in India makes the task of collecting primary materials hopelessly difficult; challenging not only because researchers have to establish the credibility of this new domain of research by overcoming odds that commonly accompany an under-researched field, but also because they have to confront a conscious, sophisticated exploitation of this under developed state of research by some not-too-learned academic or non-academic writers. The publication of *Soccer in South Asia: Empire, Nation, Diaspora* [46] in 2001 is a case in point. This book should be viewed as a part of the growing concern on the part of the sports historians in the West to give soccer its deserved status as a subject of historical scholarship so long overdue in South Asia. In fact, it pointed the way in this regard for Indians! It contains some excellent essays, especially those by J.A. Mangan and James Mills. But much of the work, which had the potential of becoming a path-breaking contribution towards the study of sport in South Asia, sadly disappoints owing to gross factual errors, [47] omission of the most important primary sources, [48] utter neglect of the vernacular sources [49] and miserable editorial lapses. [50] Moreover, the editors fail to understand that sports journalists, TV commentators and experienced coaches can hardly, save for very few exceptions, make up for academic writers. [51] It had its weaknesses [52] of course, but it was nevertheless an important contribution towards the study of sport in South Asia. It had its virtues – the triadic approach to the study of sport in South Asia recommended by Prof. J.A. Mangan is perhaps the most important of them. [53]

In short, there is a bright side to this story. Prof. Mangan, in his foreword, described the work as 'a stepping stone' that had been put in place and looked to 'more "stones" to be set down', [54] above all by Asians. The voices of Asians *do* need to be heard more fully, as he remarked, not only as contributors to collections but as editors and authors. Partial fulfilment of this request has recently been achieved through the publication of *Sport in Asian and South Society*. [55] More monographs and collections are due for publication. [56] The study of sports history in South Asia is at a taking off stage. [57]

This 'take-off' will be accelerated by the fact that India has already become the first non-European country to have an International Research Centre for Sport, Socialization and Society. [58] The inauguration of the centre established at the department of history in the University of Calcutta, Kolkata, [59] received huge national and regional media coverage in India. [60] The centre is offering an institutional space including a quality research infrastructure to all those interested in sports history. It also has plans to act as an interdisciplinary forum to promote future research in sports studies in general. [61] To make such an ambitious project viable, the Calcutta centre has already started attracting sponsors and funds from private sector. [62] This development will surely be advantageous for Indian studies in the history of sport.

The creation of the centre in Kolkata was followed by meetings with academic publishers in Delhi. The publishing successes of IRCSSS in the West have ensured a very positive response from publishers such as Oxford University Press (India), Yoda Press and Marine Sports of Mumbai. [63] All have expressed a keenness to publish IRCSSS works of relevance to South Asia. Contracts were also offered for specific forthcoming publications and a South Asian series on sport. In addition, Ananda Publishers, Kolkata, agreed to publish the most important IRCSSS works in Bengali. [64]

Teaching Sports History in India: Problems and Prospects

It is high time for Indian historians to include sports studies as an integral part of social history research *and* teaching. Teaching of sports history within the broader discipline of historical studies at both undergraduate and postgraduate level must go hand in hand with research. It will help dispel the erroneous views about the relative unimportance of sport in the shaping of modern Indian society and culture and make students aware of the extent to which entertainment and leisure have a compelling influence on their lives. As important, it will certainly encourage them to pursue research on sports history in future.

At present, however, the teaching of sports history in an Indian university, is not without its difficulties. There have been problems of adjustment for the more senior members of departments regarding this new subject. There are problems regarding the availability of historical material, difficulties finding space in the already crowded history syllabus and so on.

It is relevant here perhaps to provide a glimpse of my own experience of teaching sports history in the North Bengal University's department of history. I started teaching sports history not as a part of social history but as a part of the political history of modern India after 1857. I found it useful to present sport as a novel political tool in the analysis of a redefined relationship between the British and the native princes in the aftermath of the Revolt of 1857. Students showed immense interest and excitement in the early lectures on the importance of sport in the politics of reconciliation in the context of aristocratic reaction in British policy in the post-Revolt period. Later I developed a perspective in tune with J.A. Mangan's widely acclaimed *Games Ethic and Imperialism* in order to impress upon them on the social importance of sport beyond leisure or entertainment by means of a discussion of the significance of public-school sports such as cricket as moral tools of the Empire as well as an essential cultural instruments in the Anglicization of the native aristocracy. Students with modern India as their specialization chose these topics for their seminars with considerable enthusiasm. [65] A few students with Mughal India as their specialization offered as their seminar presentations the games and sports of that age. [66] In case of project papers based on students' fieldwork, I tried to break the mould by suggesting consideration of the nationalist significance of Mohun Bagan's epic IFA Shield football victory of 1911 under my own supervision and an interested colleague of mine. [67]

Despite my efforts to teach sports history at the postgraduate level and to popularize sports history research through students' seminars and projects, it proved to be uphill work. When I set questions for the postgraduate final examinations, those questions on sport were not well received by the moderation board and they never reached the final question papers. [68] The fight to establish the credibility of sports history has continued. In 2002, the postgraduate syllabus in history was drastically revised at North Bengal University, yet sport could not find a place in the social and cultural history of modern India. Instead I was allotted a large portion of social and cultural history and history of Indian nationalism and the nation state as teaching assignments. I responded by offering the students a historical deconstruction of an Indian film *Lagaan*, which blended cricket with nationalism in a novel pattern. The students' response was overwhelmingly positive to the lectures and tutorials that were attended by most who had chosen the topic of nationalism in recent Indian history. [69] In consequence, in the question paper, the moderators have now found reason to include my question on the topic, although my question set on the importance of sport in late-nineteenth-century princely politics was again neglected. Counting on students' positive response as also on the moral support of a few colleagues, I placed before the departmental committee a proposal to introduce 'sports history' at the M.Phil. level. The committee ultimately unanimously agreed to 'the introduction of sports history in the M.Phil. course with potential for external funding' and resolved to 'elevate it to a full-fledged self-financed Diploma Course'. [70] The M.Phil. committee also approved the introduction of sports history as an optional paper in the modern Indian history group from the session 2004/5. [71]

Thus, with hard and sustained effort, the teaching of sports history can be achieved in India. West Bengal has already taken the lead in this regard. Now at least two leading universities in the state have included sport in their postgraduate history curriculum. [72]

Conclusion

This essay has tried to identify a range of realities, problems and prospects associated with sports history in contemporary India and to offer some thoughts on the teaching of, and research into, the subject. J.A. Mangan's much celebrated emphasis on 'a triadic approach' may be recalled here: 'the analytic approach will be multicultural; balance, breadth and depth will be the ambition; completeness of perspective will be the aim'. [73] An invaluable start has been made with the establishment of the IRCSSS in Kolkata. But it will have to cast its net across India to sustain a long-term academic pursuit in sports history. This becomes all the more important with options for publication being opened through both the 'Sport in the Global Society' series of the IRCSSS and reputed Indian publishers. Again, to put it in a more optimistic way after Mangan, 'in the new millennium the East will increasingly come to the West; Eastern voices will speak for themselves; Eastern commentators will advance Western perspectives on Asia'. [74] I will conclude with the suggestion that if Indian historians are to construct an adequate *people's history* of India, especially of contemporary times, they seriously need to consider one of the most integral elements of our popular culture – sport.

Acknowledgements

This essay is a modified and extended version of the paper I presented at an international seminar on 'Sport, Culture and Society in Modern India' held at the Department of History, Calcutta University on 18 September 2003. I would like to thank Prof. J.A. Mangan without whose help, guidance and inspiration this essay could not have been written. I am also grateful to Prof. Arun Bandopadhyay, my supervisor, and Dr Boria Majumdar for their useful comments and criticisms on that paper.

Notes

[1] J.A. Mangan, 'Series Editor's Forward' in Mike Cronin and David Myall (eds.), *Sporting Nationalisms: Identity, Ethnicity, Immigration and Assimilation* (London: Frank Cass, 1998), pp.xi–xii.
[2] Harold Perkin, 'Teaching the Nations How to Play: Sport and Society in the British Empire and Commonwealth' in J.A. Mangan (ed.), *The Cultural Bond: Sport, Empire, Society* (London: Frank Cass, 1992), p.212.
[3] Eric Hobsbawm and Terence Ranger (eds.), *The Invention of Tradition* (Cambridge: Cambridge University Press, 1992), p.283, quoted in J.A. Mangan (ed.), *Pleasure, Profit, Proselytism: British Culture and Sport at Home and Abroad: 1700–1914* (London: Frank Cass, 1988), p.1.
[4] James Walvin, 'Sport, Social History and the Historian', *British Journal of Sports History*, 1, 1 (1984), 5–13.
[5] Ibid., 6.

[6]　Ibid., 13.

[7]　Ibid., 5.

[8]　Ibid.

[9]　J.A. Mangan, 'Introduction' in *Pleasure, Profit, Proselytism*, p.1.

[10]　Ibid.

[11]　Boria Majumdar, 'The Vernacular in Sports History', *Economic and Political Weekly*, XXXVII, 29 (2002), 3069.

[12]　Academic pursuit of sports history in the West began in the 1970s and got concretized in the next decade with the publication of a series of works by a galaxy of social scientists that included such names as J.A. Mangan, Wray Vamplew, Tony Mason, Allen Guttman, Richard Holt and Peter McIntosh. Institutional mechanisms to support their efforts began in 1982 when the British Society of Sports History was founded. Distinguished publishers such as Frank Cass offered active support and launched *The British Journal of Sports History*, which was later transformed into *The International Journal of the History of Sport*. These institutional efforts met with welcome parallels in other Western countries such as Scotland, Finland, Sweden, Denmark, Brazil and the USA. Scholars from Asian countries too such as China, Japan and South Korea as well as Australia were quick to recognize the importance of sports history and joined the venture in right earnest since the early 1990s. Finally, Cass launched three more journals – *Culture, Sport, Society*; *Soccer and Society*; and *European Sports History Review* – and most importantly the 'Sport in the Global Society' series in the late 1990s under the auspices of the International Research Centre for Sport, Socialization and Society instituted at Strathclyde University, Scotland with J.A. Mangan as the executive academic editor. The huge success of all these ventures further point to the current healthy state of sports history in the West.

[13]　However, this does not imply in any way that there is dearth of popular sports histories written in India. Rather, the number of such amateur writings has been increasing by leaps and bounds in the past two or three decades. These histories, mostly produced by journalists, littérateurs and sportsmen themselves, deal with general history of particular games, records and exploits of certain clubs, organizations and players. But these works, although important in their own way, more or less remain in the nature of narratives and are unable to become interpretative or to lead to the formulation of any hypothesis at a more conceptual level. For a recent example, see Jaydeep Basu, *Stories from Indian Football* (New Delhi: UBSPD, 2003).

[14]　The dissertation entitled 'Nationalism, Communalism and Sub-regionalism: A Study of Football in Bengal, 1880–1950' was submitted at the Centre for Historical Studies, Jawaharlal Nehru University. Subsequently, he went on to publish a chapter, 'Babu at Play: Sporting Nationalism in Bengal: A Study of Football in Bengal, 1880–1911' in Nisith Roy and Ranjit Roy (eds.), *Bengal: Yesterday and Today* (Calcutta: Papyrus, 1991).

[15]　Ramachandra Guha, 'Cricket and Politics in Colonial India', *Past and Present*, Nov. 1998; *A Corner of a Foreign Field: The Indian History of a British Sport* (Delhi: Picador, 2002).

[16]　A. Appadurai, 'Playing with Modernity: The Decolonization of Indian Cricket', in C.A. Breckenridge (ed.), *Consuming Modernity: Public Culture in a South Asian World* (Minneapolis, MN: University of Minnesota Press, 1995).

[17]　Mihir Bose, *A History of Indian Cricket* (London: Andre Deutsch, 1990).

[18]　Ashis Nandy, *The Tao of Cricket: On Games of Destiny and the Destiny of Games* (New Delhi: Oxford India Paperbacks, 2000).

[19]　Mario Rodrigues, *Batting for the Empire: A Political Biography of Ranjitsinhji* (New Delhi: Penguin, 2003).

[20]　Edward Docker, *History of Indian Cricket* (Delhi: Macmillan, 1976).

[21]　Richard Cashman, *Patrons, Players and the Crowd* (Calcutta: Orient Longman, 1979).

[22] The most standard text on this interpretation is: J.A. Mangan, *The Games Ethic and Imperialism: Aspects of the Diffusion of an Ideal* (London and Portland, OR: Frank Cass, 1998), especially chapters 5 and 7, pp.122–41, 168–92. Also see Richard Holt, *Sport and the British: A Modern History* (Oxford: Oxford University Press, 1989), pp.203–18; Allen Guttman, *Games and Empires: Modern Sports and Cultural Imperialism* (New York: Columbia University Press, 1994).

[23] Tony Mason, 'Football on the Maidan: Cultural Imperialism in Calcutta', in Mangan, *The Cultural Bond*, pp.142–53.

[24] Paul Dimeo and James Mills, *Soccer in South Asia: Empire, Nation, Diaspora* (London and Portland, OR: Frank Cass, 2001). Worthy scholarly interventions made in the collection include J.A. Mangan, 'Soccer as Moral Training: Missionary Intention and Imperial Legacies', pp.41–56; Paul Dimeo, 'Football and Politics in Bengal: Colonialism, Nationalism and Communalism', pp.57–74; and James Mills, 'Football in Goa: Sport, Politics and the Portuguese in India', pp.75–88.

[25] J.Alter, *The Wrestler's Body: Identity and Ideology in North India* (Berkeley, CA: University of California Press, 1992); '*Kabaddi*, a National Sport of India: The Internationalism of Nationalism and the Foreignness of Indianness', in N.Dyck (ed.), *Games, Sports and Cultures* (Oxford: Berg, 2000).

[26] Boria Majumdar has done his D.Phil., on the social history of Indian cricket, at St John's College, Oxford on a Rhodes scholarship. He is presently the deputy executive academic editor, *The International Journal of the History of Sport*. His most influential writings include *Once Upon A Furore: Lost Pages of Indian Cricket* (New Delhi: Yoda Press, 2004); *Twenty-Two Yards To Freedom: A Social History of Indian Cricket* (New Delhi: Penguin/Viking, 2004); (with Kausik Bandyopadhyay) *Kick-Off to Liberation: A Social History of Indian Football* (New Delhi: Penguin India, forthcoming in 2005); 'The Vernacular'; 'Politics of Leisure in Colonial India – *Lagaan*: Invocaion of Lost History', *Culture, Sport, Society*, 5, 2 (2002); 'Cricket in Colonial India: The Bombay Pentangular, 1892–1946', in J.A. Mangan and Fan Hong (eds.), *Sport in Asian Society: Past and Present* (London and Portland, OR: Frank Cass, 2002); 'The Politics of Soccer in Colonial India, 1930–37: Years of Turmoil', *Soccer and Society*, 3, 1 (2002); 'Kolkata Colonized: Soccer in a Subcontinental "Brazilian Colony"', *Soccer and Society*, 3, 2 (2002); 'Forwards and Backwards: Women's Soccer in Twentieth-Century India', in Fan Hong and J.A. Mangan (eds.), *Soccer, Women, Sexual Liberation: Kicking of a New Era* (London and Portland, OR: Frank Cass, 2003); 'Imperial Tool for Nationalist Resistance: The Games Ethic in Indian History', in J.A. Mangan and Boria Majumdar (eds.), *Sport in South Asian Society: Past and Present* (*International Journal of the History of Sport*, 21, 3–4 (2004). He has also edited, with J.A. Mangan, *The Cricket World Cup: Cultures In Conflict* (London: Routledge, 2004) and *Sport in South Asian Society: Past and Present* (London: Routledge, 2004).

[27] The author is completing his doctorate on the social history of Bengal football in the department of history, University of Calcutta. As for his important publications, see 'Race, Nation and Sport: Footballing Nationalism in Colonial Bengal', *Soccer and Society*, 4, 1 (2003); '1911 in Retrospect: A Revisionist Perspective on a Famous Indian Sporting Victory', in Mangan and Majumdar, *Sport in South Asian Society*; (with J. A. Mangan) 'Imperial and Post-Imperial Congruence: A Challenge to Ideological Simplification', in ibid; (with Boria Majumdar) 'Cricket as Everyday Life: World Cup 2003', *Economic and Political Weekly*, 3–10 April 2004; *Kick-Off to Liberation*.

Besides, a few others have either done or have been pursuing their Ph.D. on sports history/ studies. Among them, mention may be made of Dr Soma Basu, a research fellow in the Asiatic Society, Kolkata, who obtained her Ph.D. on 'Physical Performance and Iron Status of Female Athletes' in the discipline of physiology at Calcutta University, and Suparna Bhattacharya, lecturer in history, Loreto College, who is doing her Ph.D. on 'Women of Bengal in

Sports in the First Half of the Twentieth Century' in the department of history, Jadavpur University.

[28] Walvin, 'Sport, Social History and the Historian', 8.

[29] Ibid.

[30] Majumdar, 'The Vernacular', 3069.

[31] Guha, 'Cricket and Politics', p.157.

[32] Ibid.

[33] Guha deals with these themes in his later publication, *A Corner of a Foreign Field*. For a quite brilliant analysis of these important aspects of Indian history through cricket, *see* Boria Majumdar, 'Cricket in Colonial India, 1850–1947' (Ph.D. dissertation, University of Oxford, 2004), and also his monograph *Twenty-Two Yards to Freedom*.

[34] For an understanding of football's role as such, see Bandyopadhyay, 'Race, Nation and Sport' and '1911 in Retrospect'.

[35] This is made crystal clear in Majumdar, 'Cricket in Colonial India'.

[36] Walvin, 'Sport, Social History and the Historian', 7.

[37] Ibid.

[38] Sachin Tendulkar, the batting maestro of the present Indian cricket team, is considered to be one of the greatest batsmen world cricket has ever produced.

[39] Diego Maradona was the captain of the 1986 World Cup football champions Argentina. Maradona, for his sheer footballing talent, can be compared only to the legendary Brazilian footballer Pele.

[40] Both Soumen Mitra and Paul Dimeo considered Calcutta football to be synonymous with Bengal football and, hence, missed its local character completely.

[41] Even Ramachandra Guha, a most celebrated cricket writer of India, suffers from this flawed understanding in his latest work. For clarification, see Guha, *A Corner of a Foreign Field*. This cliché, however, has been remedied with the publication of Majumdar's *Twenty-Two Yards to Freedom*.

[42] S.N Mukherjee, *Citizen Historian: Explorations in Historiography* (Delhi: Manohar, 1996), p.8.

[43] Ibid.

[44] E.H. Carr, *What is History?* (London: Pelican, 1961), p.108.

[45] Walvin, 'Sport, Social History and the Historian', 13.

[46] Dimeo and Mills, *Soccer in South Asia* (hereafter *SS Asia*).

[47] Such errors are abundant throughout the volume. To give a few examples, Mohun Bagan club, the national club of India, is said to mean 'sweet' (*Mohun*) 'group' (*Bagan*). In reality, it actually means 'beautiful garden'. It derives its name from the Mohun Bagan Villa of north Calcutta where the club was actually founded in 1889. Again East Bengal club, which is supposed to have been founded in 1924 by poor east Bengali refugees, was actually formed in 1920 by respectable East Bengali intelligentsia as a part of their reaction against the ill-treatment and discrimination meted out to them by their west Bengali counterparts in wider social life including sports. Furthermore, it is wrongly mentioned that the Sovabazar club was formed in 1885 and the soccer team of the Presidency College in 1884. The first, in fact, was formed in 1887 while the earliest mention of soccer in at the college goes back to 1879. Then, sweeping generalizations such as 'domestic matches in India in those days [1950s and 1960s] were still limited to 70 minutes and the players were not used to playing full 90 minutes' (p.24) or 'the professionalization of football had begun in the early 1980s' (p.109) make matters worse. While Calcutta League matches were limited to 70 minutes at that time, most of the other tournaments across the country were in tune with international stipulation of 90 minutes. The professionalization of Indian football, on the other hand, has been a feature from only the 1990s, and is still awaiting its much-desired maturity.

[48] The book suffers from a miserable omission of important primary sources. Except for J.A. Mangan's brilliant piece, in most cases, the contributors depend heavily on secondary works and sometimes on not too reliable popular writings available in the newspapers and internet websites.

[49] Unfortunately, most of the writers either ignore or fail to consult tons of vernacular primary sources as well as numerous important popular sporting histories written in the vernacular. Even when vernacular sources are consulted, the exercise is a flawed one. For the much-reported event in the history of Indian soccer, Mohun Bagan's victory of 1911, mention is made of R. Saha's *Ekadashe Surya*. The title of the book is *Ekadashe Suryodaya* meaning 'the sun rises in 1911', hardly conveyed by the error in the book. The book fails to take into account some invaluable sources such as the Mohun Bagan Platinum Jubilee Souvenir, the IFA Golden Jubilee Souvenir, the Mohammadan Sporting Club League Champions Souvenir, the East Bengal Club Golden Jubilee Souvenir, Nagendraprosad Sarvadhikary's two biographies by P.L. Dutt and Sourindra Kumar Ghosh, Paresh Nandy's *Mohun Bagan 1911* and *East Bengal Club: 1920–1970*, ARBI's *Kolkatar Football*, Rupak Saha's *Itihase East Bengal* and so on, not to speak of the massive collections of vernacular newspaper reports and sports magazines.

[50] Editorial lapses, unfortunately, are more serious. The Durand Cup, the oldest tournament in the country, gets two foundation dates thanks to Kapadia (1888) and Dimeo (1886), of whom the former is correct. In his notes, Bill Adams refers to one crore as equal to 10,000. Numerous such lapses only mar the academic value of the publication.

[51] For instance, the articles by Mario Rodrigues, Bill Adams and John Hammond dealing respectively with issues of the game's commercialization and professionalization in the 1990s, the problems and possibilities of the future and talent identification and development have hardly any constructive analysis or original insights to offer. These three chapters, it won't be too drastic to say, only undermine the academic viability of the book. To furnish one specific example, Mario Rodrigues's statement that the policies of liberalization in the Indian economy were initiated by Rajiv Gandhi (p.110) is grossly mistaken since such policies were introduced by Manmohun Singh, the Finance Minister under the P.V. Narsimha Rao Government after Rajiv's death in 1991.

[52] For a critical review of this book, see Kausik Bandyopadhyay, 'Playing Ball', *Biblio – A Review of Books*, VII, 9 and 10 (Sept.–Oct. 2002).

[53] For details, see 'Series Editor's Foreword', *SS Asia*, pp.xi–xiii. This foreword should be a must-read for all future South Asian sports historians.

[54] *SS Asia*, p.xiii.

[55] Mangan and Hong, *Sport in Asian Society*.

[56] Indian sports historians are already in the fray for publication in the 'Sport in the Global Society' series. With Boria Majumdar taking over as joint general editor, this trend will intensify in the future. Already published volumes include Majumdar and Mangan, *The Cricket World Cup* and *Sport in South Asian Society*. Among forthcoming publications, mention may be made of Boria Majumdar and J.A. Mangan (eds.), *Missionaries, Maharajas and Middle Classes*. Volumes are also being planned on sport in Indian society and the social history of Indian football, to be edited or authored exclusively by Indian scholars.

[57] The recently published *Sport in South Asian Society* clearly reflects this take-off. The contributors in the volume are mostly Indian academics and journalists. The list includes, apart from Boria Majumdar and the author himself, Dipesh Chakrabarty, Lawrence A Kimpton (Distinguished Professor of History at the University of Chicago), Jayanta Sengupta (reader in history, Jadavpur University, Kolkata), Sudeshna Banerjee (reader in history, Jadavpur University, Kolkata), Kingshuk Chatterjee (lecturer in history, Scottish Church College, Kolkata), Suparna Bhattacharyya (lecturer in history, Loretto College, Kolkata), Soma Basu (research fellow, Asiatic Society, Kolkata), Sharmishtha Gooptu (Ph.D scholar at the

University of Chicago), Chadrima Chakraborty (Ph.D. scholar at York University, Toronto), Projit B. Mukherji (Felix Fellow and Ph.D. scholar at SOAS); Jishnu Dasgupta (Ph.D student at Calcutta University), Shamya Dasgupta (a senior sports journalist with the *Indian Express*) and Suvam Pal (sports journalist, *Sahara Time*).

[58] The 'Kolkata Centre came off mostly through the initiative of Boria Majumdar, an ex-student of the department and formerly deputy director of IRCSSS, on 17 September 2003 at the department of history, University of Calcutta. Prof. J.A. Mangan, director of IRCSSS, came to Kolkata to inaugurate the centre. The creation was welcomed by the vice-chancellor of the University of Calcuuta, Prof. Ashish Banerjee, pro-vice-chancellor Prof. Suranjan Das, Prof. Bhaskar Chakraborty, director of the Kolkata Centre and the teachers of the department of history at an official opening. It was followed by an international seminar on 'Sport, Culture and Society in Modern India' on 18 September, in which Prof. Mangan himself was the key note speaker.

[59] Asked as to why Kolkata was chosen to be the location of the annex, Prof. Mangan pointed to three main reasons: Boria Majumdar, the former deputy director of IRCSSS was a noted alumnus of the University of Calcutta and instrumental in superbly orchestrating the whole endeavour; the department of history where the centre was set up and the university are both distinguished; and Kolkata is the 'Indian City of Sport'. Interview with J.A. Mangan, 17 Sept. 2003.

[60] Apart from the usual reporting of the event, Prof. Mangan was interviewed by the TV channels NDTV, ESPN Star Sports, Doordarshan, Akash Bangla and Alpha Bangla, by newspapers *Ananda Bazar Patrika*, the *Telegraph*, *Aajkal*, *Pratidin*, *Sahara Time* and the *Times of India*, and by magazines *Outlook*, *Kick Off*, *Khela* and *Unish Kuri*.

[61] Interview with Prof. Bhaskar Chakraborty, director of the IRCSSS Kolkata Centre, 8 Jan. 2004.

[62] It has already attracted two annual research scholarships worth Rs.20000 each for every year from ESPN. Besides this, the centre obtained a consolidated fund of Rs.50000 from local media concerns especially through the help of leading sports journalist Gautam Bhattacharyya.

[63] J.A. Mangan and Boria Majumdar on behalf of IRCSSS met Nitasha Devashar, academic publishing manager, and Manzar Khan, editor-in-chief, Oxford University Press; Thomas Abraham, president, and Diya Kar Hazra, associate editor, Penguin India; Arpita Das and Parul Nayar, joint managing directors of Yoda Press during their visit to Delhi between 28–30 Sept. 2003.

[64] This was agreed at a meeting between Boria Majumdar, the former deputy director of IRCSSS, and the managing director, Subir Datta, and the general manager, Badal Basu of Ananda Publishers.

[65] Mention may be made of two papers in this regard: Bijan Das, 'British Sports and Sporting Princes: A Study in Anglicization of Indian Princes' (MA dissertation, 2001) and Sima Sarcar, 'Princely Light on Cricket: Anglicization of Native Princes through Sport' (MA dissertation, 2001).

[66] Subrata Mallick (MA Part II annual exam, 2000) and Rasmika Tirwa (MA Part II annual exam, 2003) both presented their papers on 'Games and Sports under the Mughals'.

[67] Project papers on sport-related themes submitted under my supervision to date include Aref Sheikh, 'The Cricketing Princes: A Study in their Anglicization' (MA Part II exam, 2001) and Swapan Kumar Pain, 'Nationalist Significance of a Sporting Victory: A Survey of Contemporary Newspaper Reports' (MA Part II exam. 2002). Dr Ratna Roy Sanyal, one of my energetic colleagues in the department showed keen interest in supervising projects on sports history in recent years. Such projects submitted under her supervision include Amrita Kumar Shil, 'The Princes, Public School Sport and the Raj' (MA Part II exam, 2001); Suprakash Bhadra 'Nineteen Eleven: Historiography of a Nationalist Sporting Victory' (MA

Part II Exam, 2002); and Seuli Biswas 'Nineteen Eleven: A Revisionist Perspective' (MA Part II exam, 2004).

[68]   The onus on the paper-setter (the present author) was such that during the moderation of question papers for the MA Part II annual examination 2001, I was called on by the moderation board to show reasons for setting such *out of syllabus* questions and was asked to revise or substitute such questions by relevant ones. Although I agreed to modify the language of a few questions on historiography, I refused to revise or substitute the questions related to sport and left the board with a modest request to choose questions from other options.

[69]   Two papers on the theme ultimately presented by students were: Nibedita Saha, '*Lagaan*: Cultural Resistance and Politics of Sport in Colonial India' (MA Part I exam, 2003) and Rinchen Gyatsho '*Lagaan*: Subalterns, Cricket and the Nation' (MA Part I exam. 2003).

[70]   Departmental committee resolution, department of history, North Bengal University, 25 July 2003.

[71]   Resolution of the M.Phil committee, department of history, North Bengal University, 12 Aug. 2004. It thus becomes the first Indian university to offer such a paper. The course offered in this paper, entitled 'Sport in Modern India' is as follows:

Sport in Modern India

Sport as a theme in Social History: concepts, contours and methodology.

History of Indian Sport: A critique of historiography.

Colonialism and Sport.

'Games Ethic and Imperialism': The Indian context.

Colonial Construction of 'Masculinity' and 'Effeminacy'; Indian response: physical education and nationalism.

Cultural Imperialism, Sport and Nationalism.

Communalism and Sport.

Emerging Issues in Sports History: sport and culture, sport and media, sport and gender, sport and international relations.

Sport in Contemporary India: Role of government and media; Sport, commercialism and professionalism in the age of globalization.

Incidentally, the first examination on the paper was held on 1 Oct. 2004. In the seminar two students chose to deliberate on sports history: Illora Sharma, 'Games Ethic in Action' and Amrita Kumar Shil, 'Sport as Social History: A Critical Overview'.

[72]   Calcutta University included 'sport, colonialism and nationalism' as a module in the special paper on the 'social history of modern India' in its revised curriculum that came into effect from 2003. North Bengal University has also introduced an essay paper from the session 2003/4 in which the same module has been incorporated.

[73]   Mangan, *Sport in South Asia*, p.xiii.

[74]   Ibid.

'For All That Was Good, Noble and True': A Middle Class Martial Icon of Canadian Patriotism and British Imperialism. John Lovell Dashwood, Canada and the Great War

Colm Hickey

The 13th day of the month is traditionally considered unlucky. It certainly proved to be for the newly promoted Major John Lovell Dashwood of the 58th Battalion of the Central Ontario Regiment of the Canadian Expeditionary Force, who was killed in action on Friday 13 April 1917. He was one of 6,000 thousand Canadian soldiers who died in the battle for Vimy Ridge. Although there is little that was especially noteworthy about his death (he was killed clearing a German trench), there is more that is of significance about his life. Dashwood had emigrated from England to Canada shortly before the war He therefore provides an insight into the motives of just one of the many Englishmen who emigrated to Canada and who returned to fight and die in the Great War – a defining moment that helped forge Canadian identity. This chapter considers Dashwood from his schooling in England to his death on Vimy Ridge in France. It sets his final years in context. It argues that Dashwood epitomized the iconic national warrior in the age of muscular Christian imperialism.

Canada, Imperialism and the First World War

When the war broke out Canada was quick declare its allegiance to Britain. Canadian society had been well prepared for imperial sacrifice. J.A. Mangan, among others, has drawn our attention to Lord Meath, [1] who established the very popular and influential Empire Day Movement. [2] Meath had published an influential article 'Have We the Grit of our Forefathers?' in *Essays on Duty and Discipline* [3] in 1910 in which he defined 'grit' as 'the virile spirit which makes light of pain and physical discomfort, and rejoices in the consciousness of victory over adverse circumstances, and which regards the performance of duty, however difficult and distasteful, as one of the supreme virtues of all true men and women'. [4] Sentiments such as these found much favour in Canada. The Ontario Minister of Education, George Ross, [5] about this time declared: 'Empire Day suggests that larger British sentiment which ... now pervades throughout the Empire, and to which Canada has for many years contributed not a little.' [6] Jeff Keshen in *Propaganda and Censorship during Canada's Great War*, writes that:

> In Canada, initial shock was promptly replaced by a sense of exhilaration. Clarion calls were issued. 'Gallant, little' Belgium lay imperilled. In this fight, imperialists claimed, Canadians would finally demonstrate the loyalty, grit and fortitude qualifying the Dominion for a major share in deciding Empire affairs. Citizens would not just be performing God's work in helping destroy a barbaric foe proclaimed many religious leaders, but would also project their nation to a higher plane of conduct since the Great War had clearly infused the multitudes with that Christian spirit of sacrificing on behalf of others. [7]

Keshen helps us understand the motives behind the response of many Canadians to the First World War. A sense of nationhood and a demonstration of Christian sacrifice were powerful impulses which inspired many. The war was seen as an opportunity to demonstrate loyalty to Canada, love of Britain, imperial fealty and martial manhood. As Mark Moss [8] observes:

> For the 'Sons of Empire', the Great War was the culmination of a long tradition not only of Canadian patriotism but of love of English Canada's mother country, Britain. This patriotism was supplemented by a vast array of role models, codes of conduct, and manufactured traditions that young men had to respect if they wished to be seen as upright, steadfast and manly. The pressures to conform in this way came from numerous sources: the family, the church, the school, the various levels of government, the playing field, the press, even the toy shop. The common thread linking these agencies together was the conscious decision to teach impressionable young men what it meant to be a proud representative of Ontario, a good citizen of Canada, a patriot of the Empire, and a manly warrior. There could be no better way to demonstrate such loyalty than to fight for one's country. [9]

Mangan, more than any other scholar, has demonstrated that belief in athleticism as a masculine ideology was eventually widespread throughout empire. [10] His consideration of the potent diffusion of athleticism throughout the empire has encompassed Asia, Africa and America. His work has centred on the education of the elite, a fact he has readily conceded: 'It is to be hoped that, in time, others will repair omissions, reveal fresh facets, add subtlety when required and so augment my early and exploratory efforts. Consideration of the diffusion of this influential ideology is long overdue.' [11] More recent studies have gone some way to meet this request in schools and colleges for the privileged and less privileged throughout the empire. [12] This contribution continues the journey down this overlooked route.

Patriotism, imperialism and militarism were reinforced by a number of Canadian writers in the pre-First World War period, drawing upon the prevailing masculine idealism: 'In order to stand effectively alongside Britain in its various campaigns to spread democracy and other qualities of Anglo-Saxondom, leading Canadian imperialists promoted the need for men of strong bodies and possessing a martial spirit, such as acquired through martial service.' [13] Peter Buitenhuis, in his study of British and North American propaganda and fiction, *The Great War of Words*, suggests that propaganda pamphleteers made use of a 'strain of rhetoric [that] was drawn from the school story (the archetype of which was Kipling's *Stalky and Co*), which had been given mass popular distribution through such organs as the *Boys Own Paper*'. [14] He recognizes that 'These stories promulgate the code of the public-school devotion to games and the spirit of sportsmanship (which was somehow shared by the other ranks, who had never been to public school). It was axiomatic that God was on the side of the good sportsman.' [15]

Leaving aside the fact that Buitenhuis did not seem to know how or why this belief came about, the fact is that he is correct. As Mangan has observed, the games ethic in Canada served contradictory purposes. On the one hand it 'was intended to make a contribution, however insignificant and tangential, to Sir John MacDonald's ambition of imparting solidarity and substance to a flimsy political entity and to make [Canada] an auxiliary Kingdom within the Empire'; on the other hand, it was 'representative however unrecognized and unappreciated, of Henry Bourassa's concern with a concept of nationality which espoused autonomy and rejected assimilation'. [16] Nevertheless, it certainly represented 'sentimental attachment to an old English institution, patriotic emotion, the yearning to keep Canada within the British Empire, the desire to create a leadership class imbued with the ideals of Christian service, the search for an alternative form of education to the state system'. [17]

Furthermore, the ideology was promoted both in England and throughout empire, albeit with greater intensity and more impact in schools, colleges and universities for the wealthy, than for other groups. [18] As Joshua Goldstein [19] reminds us:

> Cultures need to coax and trick soldiers into participating into combat – an extremely difficult challenge – and gender presents a handy means to do so by linking attainment of manhood to performance in battle. In addition, cultures directly mold [*sic*] boys from an early age to suppress emotions in order to function more effectively in battle. This system, supported in various ways by most women, produces man capable of fighting wars, but emotionally impaired. The militarised

masculinity of men who fight wars is reinforced by women's symbolic embodiment of 'normal' life, and by women's witnessing of male bravery. In these ways, gender serves to delineate and separate war from normal life, enabling soldiers both to suspend social norms against killing and to withstand the hell of war. Society's preparation to fight potential wars, however, comes at a high price for all men and women even in times of relative peace.

He explains:

> Being a warrior is an essential component of manhood, forged by male initiation rituals worldwide. 'The warrior, foremost among male archetypes ... has been the epitome of masculinity in many societies.' Common features of 'warrior values' across cultures and time periods are closely linked with concepts of masculinity. Warrior values among young males are widespread in nonstate societies, and underlie the development of an elaborate 'warrior caste' holding high status in many complex societies, such as in medieval Europe and Japan, or twentieth-century Nazi Germany. [20]

Goldstein identifies four common elements that recur in various cultures' conceptions of the warrior's desirable qualities. The first of these is *physical courage*. The warrior enjoys a fight and is prepared to risk wounds or even death. If necessary he will engage superior forces. If death is inevitable he will face it bravely without flinching. The second quality is *endurance*. The warrior can withstand extremes of climate, pain, hunger, thirst and fatigue. He will fight on after defeats and reverses and does not become demoralized. Thirdly, *strength and skill*. The warrior is fit, well trained, disciplined and a shrewd tactician. Finally, *honour*. The warrior is a man of honour who is loyal to his leader and to his comrades. [21] These four qualities provide criteria with which to analyse Dashwood's brief life and death. These, needless to say were the qualities most respected in the Edwardian middle class schools of metropolis and empire. [22]

Beginnings

John Lovell Dashwood was born in 1891 in the small village of Furze Platt near Maidenhead, Berkshire. His father was an auctioneer who had a small business in the town and was sufficiently wealthy to send his son to a newly opened secondary school, Maidenhead Modern, in 1901. Maidenhead had only three schools providing secondary education in the 1890s: Crescent, a day school for the lower middle classes, run by an elderly gentleman, Mr Friene; Maidenhead College, which catered for the professional classes; and a high-class boarding school, Crauford College. Maidenhead Modern was a private venture school. [23] In the words of the school historian:

> several prominent men in the town decided to finance the building of a boys' secondary school. It was incorporated as a limited company on May 19th 1894 and was registered under the title of 'the Maidenhead Commercial School Ltd.' It was

conducted for private profit and was commonly known as the Maidenhead Modern School. [24]

The school was aimed at the sons of businessmen and traders and offered: 'to provide a complete, thoroughly sound and systematic education for boys, preparing them either for the professions or commercial life'. [25] However, the enterprise was not a financial success; in 1906 ownership was passed over to Berkshire County Council, and in 1910 the school moved to a new site, becoming Maidenhead County Boys' School. An excellent pupil in the early years of the school, Dashwood achieved first-class honours in his Senior Oxford Locals examination. His ambition was to be a teacher and he entered Borough Road College on 5 September 1908.

At the turn of the century, education after secondary school for public schoolboys usually meant Oxford and Cambridge. Others aimed lower, at institutions such as Borough Road Teacher Training College. By this time both kinds of institutions were strongly influenced by the now widely pervasive moral ideology of athleticism. [26]

Borough Road College

Arguably, Borough Road College in Isleworth, Middlesex, was at this time the most famous teacher training college in the world. It was certainly one of the oldest, having been founded in 1798 by Joseph Lancaster. [27] By 1908 it was already over 100 years old and in the early twentieth century had an enviable reputation for teaching and sport. [28] As it was one of only two non-denominational colleges for men in England and Wales (the other was in Bangor, North Wales) it made sense for Dashwood, who was a Baptist, to train there. He proved to be an all-rounder. Indoors, his college record noted that Dashwood was 'very clever [with a] good manner'. [29] Outdoors, Dashwood took part in games and rowing. At Borough Road such involvement in sport had major significance. Ever since 1888, when the college appointed P.A. Barnett, [30] a games-playing Oxford graduate, as principal, sport held a pre-eminent position in college life. Oxford and Cambridge were, in the words of Noel Annan, 'little more than finishing schools for public schoolboys'; [31] most public schoolboys revered games above all else at school and university and games success advanced their careers. In his consideration of middle-class education J.A. Mangan has shown that from the 1880s onwards there was a new morality being preached to young public schoolboys and that its exponents 'were moral icons, symbols of a manliness which eventually owed more to rugby or cricket boots then to riding boots and very little to biblical studies, church services or Christian conscience'. [32] Borough Road faithfully subscribed to the belief that stoicism, hardiness and manliness came from games. F.H. Spencer, [33] later to become an inspector of schools in London recalled:

> It was a real co-operative life 'conjoint and collegiate', but in its essentials very like any other college life. Our first winter term was a cold and physically forbidding

time, in the bare comfortless unamenable building. But that mattered little to us. The food, if monotonous and unrefined, was plentiful and good. . . . We played hard at football and ran very successful Soccer and Rugger teams, four of them altogether, and anyone could, and most of us did, kick about at large to our great physical benefit. . . . We were alive, and we were well, and, above all, we were young. Our ideal was the man who was clever, but not too industrious, who worked hard but not long, and was a good fellow and a good athlete. And, indeed, a good half of those in the football and cricket teams were men of brains who did well in the pervading world of examinations, which surrounded but did not dominate most of us.

Games became the axis around which college life revolved. Indeed, the college historian has written that this focus

> hastened the transformation of Borough Road at Isleworth from a prototype of the Victorian residential training college into an institution not unlike a Victorian public school, with a new emphasis on examination success, a prefectorial system and a strong emphasis on health and fitness. . . . Junior staff were selected as much for their athletic prowess as for their academic qualifications and all staff, apart from vice principal Barkby were expected to participate personally in games. [34]

The principal of the college when Dashwood was a student was Arthur Burrell. [35] Burrell was as keen as Barnet about sport. All students took part in compulsory games every afternoon. Burrell once wrote: 'We shall not do our duty unless we see all students taking daily exercise.' [36] Borough Road was not alone in imitating many of the features of the public schools and above all athleticism. Other teacher training colleges enthusiastically embraced the ideology. [37] Writing of the late Victorian enthusiasm of the middle classes for sport, John Lowerson has observed that the ideology created

> a diffusionist model which it is difficult not to accept, one in which the spread is downward and outward from the reformed public schools and their imitators. Whilst the chronology of whole scale dispersal is impossible to establish, the course of the growth seems reasonably clear: public, then grammar schools; older then newer, universities, followed by the metropolitan and provincial clubs in which former public schoolboys played an organisationally if not necessarily numerically dominant role until the ethos was so well established that imitation could run of its own accord. [38]

Of course, as is well known, in this period an obsession with games was not confined to Britain. Anthony Rotundo has argued that competitive sports took on a 'new meaning and heightened importance for northern men' [39] in mid-nineteenth century America as baseball became 'a vehicle for expressing rivalry between towns, neighbourhoods and businesses'. [40] When Dashwood emigrated to North America, in this sense it was home from home!

The fact is that Borough Road was a neo-Spartan institution with an emphasis on fitness and morality through games. It closely resembled the famous Scottish public school Loretto, made famous by Hely Hutchinson Almond. [41] Almond transformed the fortunes of Loretto from a failing private school into one of Scotland's – indeed Britain's – most famous public schools. Almond was obsessed with physical fitness, which he saw as the one of the primary ingredients in education. He established his own educational creed which he called 'Lorettonianism'. 'It consisted an elaborate and systematic programme of health education covering food, clothes, physical exercise, sleep, fresh air and cold baths. … Almond was wedded to the idea of establishing a great new educational ideal.' [42] Almond's ideals, however, were not just confined to mere physical fitness. Rather they were the primary instruments in building '*character*'. His priorities were 'First – Character. Second – Physique. Third – Intelligence. Fourth – Manners. Fifth – Information'. [43] With its emphasis on health through fitness Borough Road was strikingly similar to Loretto. As George Bartle, the college historian, believed:

> It is difficult to overstress the prominent part played by the pursuit of physical fitness in college life. … This was partly due to the contemporary emphasis on the urgent need to improve the health of the nation and the nation's children – a need the Boer War made only too evident. A gymnasium was once again set up in the Speech Room and apparatus such as parallel bars, dumb bells and Indian clubs were installed. All students participated in weekly drill and were regularly weighed and measured, whilst those who presented themselves at first call in athletic costume and 'engaged in vigorous exercise' were exempted from the hour of study before breakfast. Special remedial classes were held for those of defective or underdeveloped physique. … Instruction on the physical health of the children also occupied a place in the college educational syllabus. [44]

No student could have been unaware of the prominent place of games in the moral ethos of the college. This emphasis on fitness, Bartle believed, was not merely a concern with the nation's welfare:

> It reflected also a deep belief in the moral and character training value of games – the public school spirit of '*mens sana in corpore sano*'. … It was a belief which fostered the adventurous and military qualities needed to maintain British rule over a great world empire. It led to the enormous emphasis on sport at Isleworth and the conviction that the best type of student was the clean-cut, manly type who excelled in [*sic*] the sports field as well as in the classroom and the lecture room. [45]

The close similarity to Loretto is abundantly evident. Faced with such physical, educational, emotional and ideological indoctrination, most absorbed this ethos with enthusiasm, with the result that the students became educational missionaries to the lower classes at home and the native 'classes' abroad, taking the games ethic to both with secure commitment. Of course, the ethos was utilitarian as well as idealistic in purpose and consequence. 'The games system,' writes Mangan, 'not only assured control over the children of the middle classes within the schools, in due course it was believed, it also assisted those children in their attempts to control in turn the native "children' of the Empire.' [46]

The belief in the value of games as a useful tool in controlling the far-flung colonies and dominions of Empire was not shared by other European states where, although eventually there was plenty of sport played, it had a different rationale. Fascism, for example, as Jaun J. Linz points out, 'did not appeal to a particular social constituency defined in terms of socio-economic interest, religious institutional loyalty, or ethnic national identity'. [47] Rather it appealed across a broad section of the community. Part of its success was in its use of symbol, ritual and rhetoric, its emphasis on sport and its veneration of muscle rather than intellect.

In many ways, therefore, superficially at least, it does not appear to be very different from the ideology of athleticism promulgated in the English educational system. However, there are some crucial and fundamental differences. Fascism was far more obsessed with militarism and expressed itself in a paramilitary context. It is true that the public schools had cadet corps, but these were more of an adjunct to than a core of athleticism. Secondly, fascism was overtly political while athleticism clearly was not. That is not to say that elements of athleticism were not used by politicians for their own pragmatic ends or that athleticism was not indirectly political. Nevertheless, athleticism can, at its most extreme, be classified as government through games, in the sense that control and order came after the introduction of games, whereas fascism can be seen as games through government, in the sense that games-playing had a martial and overtly political function. Linz explains that fascism comprised 'an appeal to emotion and sentiment, to the love of adventure and heroism, the belief in action rather than words, the exultation of violence, even death'. [48] The same is true, it should be noted, of athleticism and there is another similarity As Mangan reminds us, fascism is a complex phenomenon. He writes of the ideology in the context of Western Europe, South America and South-east Asia that in all cases 'Implementation of belief was promulgated by means of energetic political appeal, by compelling propaganda and by aggressive militarism'. [49] The same could be said of the middle-class imperial militarism of Edwardian England. Mangan concludes that

> Fascism meant various things to various people, and likewise it attracted them for a variety of purposes. In one thing at least there was, however, remarkable congruence. Virtually everywhere, it was the male body that symbolized self-sacrifice. Virtually everywhere it was expendable. Virtually everywhere it was an expendable icon. Virtually everywhere, it was superordinate because it was superior in purpose – the achievement of supremacy. [50]

The notion that games are an antidote to war is considered by Ashley Montague, who concludes that games do not serve as a release valve or an alternative conduit for an individual's aggressive spirit but rather that: 'combative sports ... represent the embodiments of the same theme as war'. [51] While I. Eibl-Eibesfeldt believes: 'Competitive games can in fact divert aggression, but at the same time they train the aggressive system'. [52]

Dashwood was at Borough Road well before fascism was a political ideology, but he experienced directly and indirectly a form of British middle-class militarism, a phenomenon fully discussed by Mangan in various places. [53] Apart from imperial requirements and literature, there was good reason for this Anglo Saxon militarism. There was anxiety about the possibility of war between the great powers throughout the Edwardian era. Britain had to be vigilant. Britain had to be prepared, and Britain's youth had to be ready, able and, above all, willing to offer themselves as sacrificial warriors in an anticipated conflict ahead. It was, after all, what many believed to be their destiny and, indeed, their fate. 'Vigilance was the key word in boys' literature during the years which immediately preceded the Great War, and readers must have realized that they were being exhorted to prepare for the defence of Great Britain.' [54] No doubt Dashwood read period juvenile fiction as a boy; he then studied English at college and would certainly have been exposed to and influenced by the 'military heroism and the martial spirit, service and sacrifice [that] suffused popular poetry'. [55]

It should be recalled that the Victorian upper-middle classes were more than satisfied with the militaristic masculinity they so successfully inculcated in many young public schoolboys. It served the times extremely well. In David Newsome's words, 'Its core of living became so robust and patriotic in its demands that it could be represented in reaching its perfection in a code of dying.' [56] This inculcation was achieved in part by 'rhetoric of jingoistic conceit in poetry, prose and picture' which involved major and minor poets, writers and painters who undertook the cultural indoctrination of the young upper-middle-class male into a chivalric, militaristic manhood, and who depicted brave and cool public-school 'bloods' taking their playing-field courage, determination and confidence onto imperial battlefields in the service of the imperial community. Their image-makers consciously constructed inspirational stereotypes embodying self-sacrificing service personifying natural nobility to justify the grandeur of imperialism. Dashwood inherited this legacy passed, in his case, downwards to middle-middle-class schoolboys such as himself, and indeed to lower-class schoolboys. [57]

After two years at Borough Road, Dashwood graduated from the University of London with a BA in English and French with subsidiary Latin and Maths and took up a post as a teacher of English at Drax Grammar School [58] in Selby in north Yorkshire. He remained there until 1914 when he emigrated to Canada to take up a post as an assistant lecturer in English at Macdonald College, a teacher training college of McGill University in Montreal.

Dashwood's decision to go to Canada places him squarely in the ranks of Englishmen who sought colonial experiences and opportunities for themselves. Patrick Duane has observed that 'Imperial enthusiasms were at their height during the Edwardian years, and this enthusiasm gave the relationship between the Empire and the emigrant new importance'. [59] As an Ontario writer asserted, 'The emigrant is the real custodian of the Empire's future, the living epistle of the only political religion that can preserve British unity throughout the world. By emigration the Empire is made. ... By taking heed of emigration ... the Empire may renew its youth.' [60] Dashwood's decision to emigrate was neither surprising nor uncommon.

He was merely one in a long line of former Borough Road students who capitalized on the imperial games ethic and the opportunities it offered to carve out careers for themselves in the Empire and beyond. [61] T.J. Macnamara, [62] a student at Borough Road from 1880 to 1882, boasted with imperial pride: 'And these are the Borough Roadians, the 'B's'! What fine clean healthy looking lads! What fortunes for themselves and their Empire these lads would make in the Colonies! What a fine company of soldiers thrown away.' [63]

Dashwood both read and contributed to the college magazine, the *B's Hum*. The magazine, edited and produced by the student body, served as an organ of propaganda for the ideals and values of both athleticism and imperialism. Many former students wrote to the editor from far-flung outposts of empire. One who did was Herbert Milnes, who had originally trained at Borough Road from 1893 to 1895. He then taught in Leeds before returning to Borough Road as a lecturer in 1899. In 1906 Milnes resigned from Borough Road to take up the principalship of a teacher training college in Auckland, New Zealand. Milnes was a well-respected 'Old B' (as former students were known) and frequently contributed articles for the magazine. As I have written elsewhere, [64] Milnes epitomized the athletic Borough Road man in imperial action. In his own words,

> As character training is admitted to be our goal, it is interesting to see what effect the play of school games has on it. ... Games undoubtedly have a great effect on character, summed up in the one word 'sportsmanlike' ... they promote social growth and in many and other ways improve one's powers, but when all is said and done, it is learning to 'play the game' and never to hit 'below the belt' that constitute the great values. [65]

Dashwood would have been equally comfortable with the attitude towards education espoused by a host of upper-middle-class educationists, for the games ethic was alive and well in the dominion. As Mangan has shown in *The Games Ethic and Imperialism*, belief in the value of games was commonplace throughout Canada. He quotes Morris Mott who, writing of Manitobans in the nineteenth century, stated that they 'played and promoted manly games, not only because they were certain these activities revealed and nurtured many desirably qualities, but for another reason ... the sense of duty they felt to establish and maintain British culture in their new, still only semi-civilized part of the world' [66] Elsewhere, Mangan has written widely on the notion of manliness in Victorian education both in England and north America. [67] In four sentences he captures the essence of the transformation of manliness in the Victorian age:

> The English concept of manliness changed dramatically in connotation during the Victorian period. To the early Victorians it meant the successful transition from Christian immaturity to maturity demonstrated by earnestness, selflessness and integrity: to the late Victorians it represented neo-Spartan virility as exemplified by stoicism, hardiness and endurance – the pre-eminent virtues of the late Victorian and Edwardian public school. Extrinsic and intrinsic discipline was exemplified

both literally and metaphorically by 'the stiff upper lip'. Headmasters of the Canadian 'public schools' admired the same virtues, enunciated the same pieties and adopted the same means of realization as their English counterparts. [68]

Borough Road College was, therefore, an excellent preparation for Dashwood as he began a new life in Canada. It offered him a view and philosophy of education with which he was familiar and allowed him to do what thousands of English emigrants had done – find personal and career advancement in a new world. And for Dashwood this advancement was to be found at Macdonald College in Montreal.

Macdonald College

Macdonald College owed its foundation to Sir William Macdonald (1831–1917), [69] an emigrant highlander. By 1865 William Mcdonald had become a tobacco merchant and had changed his name to Macdonald. He was knighted by Queen Victoria in 1898. He was greatly interested in educational philanthropy and endowed academic chairs in law, chemistry, agriculture, geology, history and moral philosophy at McGill University in Montreal. Macdonald was also a director of the Bank of Montreal and noticed that the takings of rural banks went up whenever dairy farming was introduced into a district. As a result he set about founding a college for the training of teachers in rural subjects which he established in 1907 as an integral part of McGill University. The purposes of the college were, 'among others',

1. The advancement of education; the carrying on of research work and investigation and the dissemination of knowledge: all with particular reference to the interests and needs of the population in rural districts.
2. The provision of suitable and effective training for teachers, and especially for those whose work will directly affect the education in schools and rural districts.' [70]

The first principal was James Robertson. [71] He was succeeded by Frank C. Harrison, [72] who was principal from 1910 to 1926. Although Harrison was the principal of the college, he had little direct contact with trainee student teachers. Teacher training had begun in 1857 when an English-language college was established in McGill Normal School. Its 1903 inspection by Dr G.H. Locke [73] found that, among other things, the standard of accommodation was unsatisfactory. As Macdonald was in negotiation with McGill University to build a new agricultural college, the time seemed right to amalgamate the teaching college with the new elements of agriculture and household science on a new campus provided by Macdonald. Dr Locke was appointed as the first head of the School for Teachers in 1907. [74] However, his appointment was not a success. Despite being a graduate of Toronto University and associate professor of education at Chicago University (1899–1905), then acting dean (1903–5) as well as an assistant editor (of educational publications) at Ginn and Co. in Boston, his flamboyant and expensive style frequently clashed with the dour and frugal values of Macdonald and he resigned in 1909 to become librarian for the Toronto Municipal Library.

Locke was replaced by S.B. Sinclair, [75] who was head of the School for Teachers until 1913, when he was replaced by Sinclair Laird, [76] who was to hold the post for 36 years until his retirement in 1949. Laird was a Scot who had had an outstanding career as a student at St Andrews University and who had taught in a number of schools and universities in Europe and Canada. Prior to his appointment he had been associate professor of Education at Queen's University, Kingston, Ontario.

Laird was a forceful autocrat. J.S. Cram, editor of *The Macdonald Journal*, the college magazine, described him at the time of his retirement in 1949:

> His vitality seems to fill the space around him and makes him appear larger still, so that many students have been overwhelmed by his mere presence. And his forcefulness is intellectual as well as physical – to stand up to him in an argument is like facing a strongly-wielded sledgehammer. ... He is a man of very deep convictions and the courage to stand behind them: and he has no use for those who quail before him. He likes the ones who stand up and fight, finding them worthy targets for his scathing humour. [77]

Laird clearly found Dashwood a worthy applicant for a post and he was appointed as a lecturer in English in 1914. Yet before he could make any impact as a teacher trainer at the college, the First World War broke out. In 1915 he enlisted in the 58th Battalion of the Central Ontario Regiment of the Canadian Expeditionary Force.

In his *Canadian Essays and Addresses*, [78] published in 1915, Sir William Peterson, [79] vice-chancellor of McGill University, declared:

> I do not object to call myself an imperialist. For to me imperialism is not militarism, or jingoism, or megalomania ... it is the expression of an aspiration which may be cherished in full sympathy with democratic ideals – the aspiration namely, and the desire that for the high and noble purposes of its world wide mission, the British Empire may be able to hold together in all coming time ... we ought to be – and we are – proud of our imperial connection. For we know that in the world as we find it today the strength and prosperity of our united empire affords one of the best guarantees of order and freedom, justice peace and progress ... in their combination in the British Empire they are the highest that has yet been attained in the social and political development of the world. [80]

It was a call to arms. In fact, it had already been answered by university staff and students. McGill University enthusiastically supported the war. Early in the session 1914/15 Harrison recommended the formation of an officer training corps. The president of the Students' Council called a meeting at which the students, almost to a man, joined the corps. It was Harrison himself who 'had been an officer in the pre-war militia [who] commanded the Officers' Training Corps ... and later served as a member of staff of the Khaki College'. [81] J.F. Snell, the college historian and a contemporary of Harrison, described the principal's motive as 'a precautionary measure in view of the insecurity of our position in the Empire and our unpreparedness for defence of our homes'. [82] In the autumn of 1914 and the spring of 1915 a number of staff and students enlisted in the university's own company; the McGill Company of the Princess Patricia's Royal Canadian Light Infantry. Dashwood first joined the Royal Canadian Flying Corps before transferring to the 58th Battalion of the Central Ontario Regiment of the Canadian Expeditionary Force. Thousands of other British-born volunteers also joined up. Patrick Dunae has drawn our attention to the fact that

> British born volunteers were substantially overrepresented in the Canadian Expeditionary Forces. The volunteers were not all from the gentleman class of emigrants, but the gentleman emigrants were well represented. Moreover, whereas many who enlisted in Canada subsequently transferred to British units, a considerable number continued to wear the Maple Leaf throughout the course of the war. [83]

Dashwood and the Great War

Even during his brief period at Macdonald, Dashwood had a significant impact on the student body. A contemporary wrote: 'A large crowd of students and staff assembled to bid him good-bye at the station, but with his characteristic dislike of fuss, he quietly slipped away by another route.' [84] The same writer was in no doubt as to why Dashwood enlisted: 'He left his position of assistant lecturer in English history and Geography to *obey the call of duty*.' [85] He continued: 'The feeling he [Dashwood] left behind in the hearts of all the students and staff was that the college had lost *a real teacher* and a *man*.' [86]

However, Dashwood's career in the corps was relatively short lived [87] and he was transferred to the 58th Battalion Central Ontario Regiment Canadian Light Infantry as a Lewis gun officer with the rank of lieutenant on 2 July 1916. On 20 August, during the battle of the Somme, he was wounded in a German gas attack. By the end of the month the battalion had lost 106 men killed, 298 wounded, 58 shell-shocked and 52 missing since its arrival in France in 1915. [88] Dashwood was hospitalized until January 1917 and rejoined the battalion as the A Company commander on 2 January, having been promoted to the rank of captain. On 20 March he led a trench-raiding party. The raid was a failure, as the party failed either to capture any prisoners or to discover the enemy units they were facing. However, Dashwood displayed exemplary courage by providing covering fire for his retreating troops. He was awarded the Military Cross and promoted to the rank of major.

In April 1917 the battalion was involved in arguably the defining moment in the history of the First World War Canadian forces – the battle for Vimy Ridge. The battle began on 7 April. On Friday 13 April Dashwood, accompanied by Lieutenant Dempsey and a corporal, were surprised by some Germans as they were examining a seemingly deserted trench. In a brief exchange of gunfire Dashwood was killed. His death was greeted with shock by the staff of both Borough Road and Macdonald. At Borough Road, Charles Venning, [89] one of the former tutors, edited a magazine, *The Old B's Roll of Service*, for all current and former students serving in the forces. By 1917 it was in its third edition. Dashwood's death was recorded there. Venning wrote:

> It was Major Walton [90] who first gave me the news. He said only a short time before his death he had tramped in the snow for some miles to have dinner with Dashwood, and he is now indeed thankful that he did so for this was the last happy time they had together. [91]

Venning was sent letters from Dashwood's father written to him by staff and students at Macdonald College. Frank Harrison, the principal of Macdonald College, wrote:

> As you doubtless know we were keeping a place open for your son, and next year it was our intention to make him Head of the English department; a position which would have given him greater opportunity for we recognised the excellent character of his work and his great influence on the students. His death is a noble deed for us all and an inspiration. [92]

Sinclair Laird, head of the school for teachers, wrote: 'He was held in high esteem both for his personal and professional qualities. His work with the students was beyond all praise.' [93] Students, too, were moved by his death. One wrote on behalf of the student body:

> Though we only knew him for a short time when he lectured to us here at College, none of us could ever forget him, for he stood to us for all that was good, noble and true; and the inspirations he gave us through his lectures will last for the rest of our lives. [94]

Venning commented: 'These letters do but bear out what we at Borough had thought and prophesied about him.' [95] These, of course, were conventional elegiac expressions of sadness.

However, whether Dashwood was all the things that his obituarists wrote is beside the point. Canada at war needed its military icons. As M. Moss has observed, 'Traditionally, it was in war that young men displayed their prowess, virility, chivalry and manliness. Warriors were vital to their societies, and thus wielded enormous power and influence.' [96] And elsewhere in a passage of profound relevance, he argues:

> Citizens need myths on which to build a mental construct of a nation. By substituting myth for history, the inconsistencies of the past can be ironed out into a smooth, comprehensible tableau. When translated into myth, historical anguish and experience become simplified and are less likely to give rise to questions and doubt. This is where heroes become especially valuable. The hero embodies the myth, not the history. Flawless, blemish free he represents the greatness of the past.

The national hero is thus held as the definitive illustration of the national man, and heroic individuals usually embody the characteristics that a nation holds dear. Elevating certain individuals above the level of the average citizen gives the latter something to aspire to. When heroes and their deeds are shrouded in a veil of near divinity, they stand as the physical embodiment of the nation. These individuals become essential to the concept of nationhood. Their deeds become frozen into legend, often as a result of their being glorified in print. [97]

Dashwood was a valuable fallen hero for English and Canadian alike. As an idealistic and enthusiastic volunteer, he linked the two imperial training colleges with whom he was associated. Jonathan Vance in *Death So Noble: Meaning, Memory and the First World War*, has argued that there was a conceit in Canadian media after the war

to convey the myth to those people who had not experienced the events themselves and to ensure that a certain version of the war became the intellectual property of all Canadians, not simply those who had lived through 1914–18. In this way, the myth both shaped, and was shaped by, Canadian society in the interwar years; to use Lynn Hunt's terms, the text of the myth configured the context as much as the context created the text. [98]

Dashwood exemplifies the mythological Canadian fallen warrior. Twice promoted and the holder of the Military Cross, he was destined to be one of the dominion's Vimy Ridge 'glorious dead'. He became a symbol of the heroic 'lost generation'. He thus fulfils Goldstein's criteria of many cultures' desirable qualities for a warrior. He had undoubted physical courage, as can be shown through his Military Cross. He had endurance, as can be witnessed by his long period with the 'colours'. He displayed skill in providing covering fire for his men as they returned to their trench after a raiding party. Finally, his decorations for bravery and his promotions demonstrated his sense of honour. His gravestone [99] and those of the 60,000 other fatalities of the Canadian Expeditionary Force are the metaphorical building bricks of a robust, self-confident and self-reliant Canadian nation. Jeff Keshen reminds us that, as recently as 1999, 'two of the country's most prominent historians … selected the Battle of Vimy Ridge as first among twenty-five events that contributed to the formation of modern Canada'. [100] In 1936 a Vimy Pilgrimage was organized and 6,000 Canadians attended the unveiling of the famous Vimy Memorial. The principal speaker was the President of France, Lebrun. He said of the monument that it would remind soldiers that

Here several hundred thousand men from a faraway land spilled their blood to defend their hearth; that they were willing to sacrifice their lives not for the satisfaction of material interests but for the beauty of an ideal and the nobility of a memory; that many of them, faithful to the call of blood recalling the Champlains, the Maisonneuves and the Cavaliers de la Salle, de Montcalm, returned to their ancient motherland to defend and revivify it by mingling with it again. It is a noble and great example. May this magnificent self-sacrifice not be lost for the lessons of the future. May this memorial, a vigilant sentinel in the centre of the fields still echoing with human grief, teach us that more powerful and more profound than community of race and blood there exists a higher solidarity which should always guide the actions of men. [101]

Vance maintains that Vimy Ridge 'is a link constructed upon glorified accounts of Canada's Great War soldiers – accounts first articulated by wartime propagandists. And, to this day, these accounts are still couched in romantic imagery and high diction.' [102] Dashwood's obituaries were among the first illustrations of such accounts.

The story of Dashwood is fragmentary. The schools he attended have incomplete records. Even his death was recorded in the local paper in a perfunctory manner. The *Maidenhead Advertiser* contains the following brief entry:

> News has just been received that Lieutenant J.L. Dashwood of the Canadian Infantry (elder son of Mr. J.L. Dashwood formerly of Maidenhead) who was killed in action on April 13th whilst leading his company at Vimy Ridge, was promoted to Major and awarded the MC for gallantry whilst leading a raid a few days prior to his death. [103]

His imprint on the Borough Road College records is light. And, while there is a memorial to the men of McGill University who died in the war, Dashwood is not there: his contribution was somehow overlooked. However, although the college seems to have momentarily forgotten him, Dashwood did not forget Macdonald College or lose his affection for it, a fact the college belatedly recognized in 1936. At the celebration of the 105th anniversary of the birth of Sir William Macdonald, a hitherto lost verse written by him, was sung. Dashwood reappeared Banquo-like. *The Eastern Times* recorded:

> Macdonald College ... celebrated the 105th anniversary of the birth of its founder, Sir William Macdonald, with a banquet for the whole student body and a concert by the Ottawa Temple Choir. ... An unannounced number was the singing of a song 'Braw Macdonald' which was written by J.L. Dashwood, a former student [*sic*] of the college killed in the war. It had never been sung before.
>
> **Braw Macdonald**
> You may talk to me of Cambridge, with its Gothic soup tureens
> And of German halls of science swept with beer;
> Or of ancient academias where they lived on grapes and greens,
> And incomes of a laurel branch a year.
> You may graduate from heaven or get a Doctorate from Flames,
> And sailed a great airship through the blue,
> But your face is immaterial and your double-barrelled names
> If Macdonald has not christened you anew. [104]

It is period doggerel redolent with well-meaning devotion. It reveals Dashwood as a period sentimentalist; if linguistically limited, then institutionally loyal.

Mangan, in one of his several studies of war and the socialization of the male, has argued that

> Whenever we think of war we dream continually of martial heroes, project them inspirationally and present them continuously as civil icons. ... The warrior is central to the visible existence of the state – and interestingly so incidentally is sport ... the two with the past, the present and the future have been and will be inextricably entwined ... the playing fields in one form or another, have always been the locations for preparation for the battlefield. [105]

Dashwood is a First World War illustration, and writing of the importance of the imperial ideal in both public and state schools – and by extension colleges and universities – Mangan argues that there is 'a shortage of both investigation and information'. He continues:

> Intensive, comprehensive and comparative studies of general attitudes to imperialism within the schools are required; to locate the disseminators and the responses to their dissemination, and to establish the nature and extent of dissent, to discover the ritualistic and symbolic instruments of persuasion, to examine the relationship between the various mechanisms of propaganda and their relative efficacy, to trace the nature of the association between public school and state school in the promulgation of imperial enthusiasm, and to discern the changing nature of school attitudes to imperialism as the twentieth century progressed. [106]

This essay is a modest response to Mangan's call to action. Dashwood was a product of a school and college system that endorsed, promoted and demanded period imperial patriotism. Dashwood and the other Canadian dead were minor iconic heroes who helped consolidate a nation. He, with them, fulfilled the role of the iconic muscular Christian warrior and helped, with them, define Canadian national identity and self-worth.

Notes

[1] Reginald Brabazon, 12th Earl of Meath (1841–1928), was educated at Eton and served in the diplomatic service. Meath held a number of prestigious jobs including vice-president of the Navy League (1909), member of the Executive Council League (1910–14) and president of the Duty and Discipline Movement from 1912 to 1919.

[2] J.A. Mangan, "The Grit of our Forefathers: Invented Traditions Propaganda and Imperialism', in John M. Mackenzie (ed.), *Imperialism and Popular Culture* (Manchester: Manchester University Press, 1986), pp.113–39, p.129. For a consideration of the propagation of imperialism in elementary schools, see P. Horn 'English Elementary Education and the Growth of the Imperial Ideal: 1880–1914', in J.A. Mangan (ed.), *'Benefits Bestowed'? Education and British Imperialism* (Manchester: Manchester University Press, 1988), pp.39–55.

[3] The Rt. Hon the Earl of Meath, *Essays on Duty and Discipline. A Series of Papers on the Training of Children in relation to Social and National Welfare* (London: Cassell, 1910).

[4] Ibid, p.1.

[5] Sir George William Ross (1841–19**) was born near Jain, Ontario. Having originally trained as a teacher, he subsequently became a barrister and politician. He was deeply interested in Canadian education and was president of the Dominion Educational Association.

[6] Quoted in J.A. Mangan, *The Games Ethic and Imperialism: Aspects of the Diffusion of an Ideal* (London: Viking, 1986), p.148.

[7] See also J.M. Bliss, 'The Methodist Church and World War One', in Carl Berger (ed.), *Conscription 1917* (Toronto: University of Toronto Press, 1970), p.53. Jeffrey A. Keshen, *Propaganda and Censorship During Canada's Great War* (Edmonton: University of Alberta Press, 1996), p. 3.

[8] M. Moss, *Manliness and Militarism: Educating Young Boys in Ontario for War* (Toronto: Oxford University Press, 2001).

[9] Ibid, pp.2–3.

[10] See Mangan, *The Games Ethic and Imperialism*, *passim*.

[11] Ibid, p.19.

[12] See J.A. Mangan and Colm Hickey, 'Athleticism in the Service of the Proletariat: Preparation for the English Elementary School and the Extension of Manliness', in *Making European Masculinities: Sport Europe, Gender (European Sports History Review*, 2) (London and Portland, OR: Frank Cass, 2000), pp.112–39, and J.A. Mangan, 'Globalization, the Games Ethic and Imperialism: Further Aspects of the Diffusion of an Ideal', in *Europe, Sport, World: Shaping Global Societies (European Sports History Review*, 3) (London and Portland, OR: Frank Cass, 2001), pp.105–30.

[13] Keshen, *Propaganda*, p.130.

[14] P. Buitenhuis, *The Great War of Words. British, American, and Canadian Propaganda and Fiction, 1914–1933* (Vancouver: University of British Columbia Press, 1987), p.22.

[15] Ibid.

[16] Mangan, *The Games Ethic and Imperialism*, pp.142–3.

[17] J.B. Purdy, 'The English Public School Tradition in Nineteenth-Century Ontario'. in F.H. Armstrong, H.A. Stevenson and J.D. Wilson (eds.), *Aspects of Nineteenth-Century Ontario* (Toronto: University of Toronto Press, 1974), p.239, quoted in Mangan, *The Games Ethic and Imperialism*, pp.143–4. See p.148 for a discussion of the force of feeling for an imperial connotation of Canadian national identity expressed through the symbolic medium of Empire Day.

[18] See J.A. Mangan and Colm Hickey, 'English Elementary Education Revisited and Revised: Drill and Athleticism in Tandem', in *Sport in Europe: Politics, Class, Gender (European Sports History Review*, 1) (London and Portland, OR: Frank Cass, 1999), pp.63–91.

[19] J.S. Goldstein, *War and Gender. How Gender Shapes the War System and Vice Versa* (Cambridge: Cambridge University Press, 2001), p.331.

[20] Ibid, p.266.

[21] Ibid, pp.266–7.

[22] See Mangan, *The Games Ethic and Imperialism*, *passim*.

[23] For a discussion of private venture schools, see Mangan, *Athleticism in the Victorian and Edwardian Public School. The Emergence and Consolidation of an Educational Ideology* (Cambridge: Cambridge University Press 1981), pp.3–5.

[24] D.M. Evans, *One Hundred Not Out. A History of Desborough School* (Maidenhead: the school, 1994), pp.1–2.

[25] *Maidenhead Advertiser*, 22 Aug. 1894.

[26] For evidence of its impact on 'Oxbridge', see J.A. Mangan, 'Oars and the Man: Pleasure and Purpose in Victorian and Edwardian Cambridge', *History of Higher Education Annual*, 4 (1984), *passim*, and J.A. Mangan 'Lamentable Barbarians and Pitiful Sheep: Rhetoric of Protest and Pleasure in Late Victorian and Edwardian Oxbridge', in Tom Winifrith and Cyril Barnet (eds.), *Leisure in Art and Literature* (London: Macmillan, 1992), *passim*. For evidence

of its influence on the training colleges see Colm Hickey, 'Athleticism and the London Training Colleges: The Proletarian Absorption of an Educational Ideology 1870–1920' (unpublished PhD dissertation, University of Strathclyde, 2001), *passim*.

[27] Joseph Lancaster (1778–1838) was one of the foremost educationists of his day. He 'invented' the monitorial system of education whereby older pupils taught younger pupils, meaning that a single teacher could supervise large numbers of children. He established Borough Road College and travelled extensively throughout the world promoting his system. He was killed in a road traffic accident in New York in 1838.

[28] See Hickey, 'Athleticism and the London Training Colleges', *passim*.

[29] Borough Road College Student Register 1907/8, p.88.

[30] P.A. Barnett (1858–1941) was born in London and educated at City of London School and Trinity College, Oxford. He was professor of English at Firth College, Sheffield (1882–8) and principal of Borough Road until 1893, when he joined the inspectorate. He held a number of senior posts in education including Chief Inspector for Teacher Training from 1905 to 1912.

[31] Quoted in Mangan, *Athleticism*, p.122.

[32] J.A. Mangan, '"Muscular, Militaristic and Manly": The British Middle-Class Hero as Moral Messenger', in R. Holt, J.A. Mangan and Pierre Lanfranchi (eds.), *European Heroes: Myth, Identity, Sport* (London and Portland, OR: Frank Cass, 1996), pp.28–47, p.31.

[33] F.H. Spencer (1872–1946) was born in Swindon and educated at the Great Western Railway School. He trained at Borough Road from 1892 to 1894 and taught in Nottingham and London. He was appointed HMI, Technical Branch, South West Lancashire from 1919 to 1922. In 1923 he became Chief Inspector of London Education Committee, a post he held until 1934. See his *An Inspector's Testament* (London: English University Press, 1938), p.138.

[34] G.F. Bartle, 'Staffing Policy at a Victorian Training College', *Victorian Education*, Occasional publication no.2 (1976), 16–23, 20. See also Mangan and Hickey, 'Athleticism in the Service of the Proletariat': pp.112–39.

[35] Arthur Burrell (1859–1946) was educated at Alleyn's College and Wadham College, Oxford. A keen sportsman, he rowed in the college boat for two years. He became assistant master at Bradford Grammar School and stayed there for 20 years, ending up as head of the junior department. He was principal of Borough Road from 1902 to 1912.

[36] *Annual Report, British and Foreign School Society*, 1904, p.62.

[37] See Hickey, 'Athleticism and the London Training Colleges', *passim*.

[38] J. Lowerson, *Sport and the English Middle Classes 1870–1914* (Manchester: Manchester University Press, 1993), p.72.

[39] A.E. Rotundo, *American Manhood: Transformations in Masculinity from the Revolution to the Modern Era* (New York: Basic Books, 1993), p.239.

[40] Ibid, p.244.

[41] Hely Hutchinson Almond (1832–1903) was born in glasgow and studied at the universities of Glasgow and Oxford where he won a Snell scholarship at Balliol College. He drifted into teaching after having been rejected by the Indian Civil Service and became a Mathematics teacher at Loretto school. In 1858 he became second master at Merchiston. He became Headmaster of Loretto in 1862 and transformed it into one of Scotland's leading public schools by the time of his death. See Mangan, *Athleticism*, pp.48–58.

[42] Mangan, *Athleticism*, pp.54–5.

[43] *Loretto Register 1825–1925* (1927), p.xvi.

[44] G.F. Bartle, *A History of Borough Road College* (Kettering: Dalkeith Press, 1976), p.57.

[45] Ibid.

[46] Mangan, 'Muscular, Militaristic and Manly', p.36.

[47] Juan J. Linz, 'Some Notes Towards a Comparative Study of Fascism', in Walter Laqueur, *Fascism: A Reader's Guide* (London: 1976), p.12.

[48] Ibid., p.35.

[49] J.A. Mangan, 'Global Fascism and the Male Body: Ambitions, Similarities and Dissimilarities', in J.A. Mangan (ed.), *Superman Supreme. Fascist Body as Political Icon – Global Fascism* (London and Portland, OR: Frank Cass, 2000), p.4.

[50] Ibid, p.23.

[51] A. Montague, *The Nature of Human Aggression* (Oxford: Oxford University Press, 1976), p.277.

[52] I. Eibl-Eibesfeldt, *The Biology of Peace and War: Men Animals and Aggression* (New York: Viking, 1979), p.236.

[53] See Mangan, 'Muscular, Militaristic and Manly'.

[54] J.A. Mangan, 'Duty Unto Death. English Masculinity and Militarism in the age of New Imperialism', in J.A. Mangan (ed.), *Tribal Identities* (London: Frank Cass), 1990, pp.56–84, p.73.

[55] J. Richards, 'Popular Imperialism and the Image of the Army in Juvenile Literature', in John M. Mackenzie (ed.), *Popular Imperialism and the Military 1850–1950* (Manchester: Manchester University Press), 1992, p.81.

[56] Mangan, 'Muscular, Militaristic and Manly', p.36.

[57] Mangan and Hickey, 'English Elementary Education Revisited and Revised', pp.63–92; J.A. Mangan and Colm Hickey, 'Missing Middle-Class Dimensions: Elementary Schools Imperialism and Athleticism in J.A. Mangan (ed.), *Reformers, Sport Modernizers: Middle-Class Revolutionaries* (*European Sports History* Review, 4) (London and Portland, OR: Frank Cass, 2002), pp.73–90.

[58] Drax Grammar School was founded in 1667through the endowment of Charles Read, a local wealthy merchant.

[59] P. Dunae, *Gentleman Emigrants: From the British Public Schools to the Canadian Frontier* (Vancouver: Douglas and McIntyre), 1981, p.216.

[60] A. Hawkes, 'The Imperial Emigrant and his political Religion,' *Nineteenth Century and After*, 71 (January 1912), 112.

[61] The list of Borough Road men working abroad in the years leading up to the outbreak of the First World War is impressive and included three principals of teacher training colleges, one in the Bahamas, one in New Zealand and one in Vancouver.

[62] T.J. Macnamara (1861–1931) was born in Montreal barracks and educated in England at an elementary school in Exeter before training as a teacher at Borough Road (1880–82). He was the head teacher of a board school in Bristol from 1884 to 1894. He was active in union politics and was editor of *The Schoolmaster* from 1892 to 1907. He became an MP in 1900, rising to the Cabinet with his appointment as Minister of Labour in Lloyd George's government from 1920 to 1922. See R. Betts, *Dr. Macnamara 1861–1931* (Liverpool: Liverpool University Press), 1999.

[63] T.J. Macnamara, 'Training College Student Days', *The New Liberal Review*, VI, 32 (1903), 227–35, 238.

[64] J.A. Mangan and Colm Hickey 'A Pioneer of the Proletariat: Herbert Milnes and the Games Cult in New Zealand', in J.A. Mangan and John Nauright (eds.), *Sport in Australian Society. Past and Present* (London and Portland, OR: Frank Cass, 2000), .pp.31–48.

[65] *Journal of Education*, Sept. 1912, quoted in B. Sutton-Smith, *A History of Child's Play in New Zealand* (Philadelphia, PA: University of Philadelphia Press, 1981), p.198.

[66] Morris Mott, 'The British Protestant Pioneers and the Establishment of Manly Sports in Manitoba, 1870–1886', *Journal of Sports History*, 7, 3 (Winter 1980), 104.

[67] J.A. Mangan and James Walvin (eds.), *Manliness and Morality, Middle-Class Masculinity in Britain and America, 1800–1940* (Manchester: Manchester University Press, 1987).

[68] Mangan, *The Games Ethic and Imperialism*, p.147.

[69] Sir William Macdonald (1831–1917) was born at Glenaladale, Prince Edward Island, in 1831 and was educated at the Central Academy, Charlottetown. He became a wealthy tobacco manufacturer. He was a benefactor to McGill University and founded Macdonald College. He was created a knight bachelor in 1898.

[70] Quoted in J.F. Snell, *Macdonald College of McGill University: A History from 1904–1955* (Montreal: McGill University Press), 1963, p.58.

[71] James Wilson Robertson (1859– 1930) was born in Dunlop, Ayrshire in Scotland and emigrated to Ontario in 1875 to farm. He was professor of dairying in the Ontario Agriculture College from 1886 to 1890, when he was appointed dairy commissioner for Canada. He was principal of Macdonald College from 1905 to 1910. He was awarded a number of honorary degrees: LLD from Queen's University (1903), University of New Brunswick (1904), McGill University (1909) and the degree of DSc from Iowa University. He was made a CMG in 1905.

[72] Frank C. Harrison (1871–1952) was born the son of a British officer, in Gibraltar. He graduated from Ontario Agricultural College in 1892 and studied at the universities of Wisconsin, Berne and Copenhagen before returning to the Agricultural College as its first professor of bacteriology. He was principal of Macdonald College from 1910 to 1926, when he resigned to take the chair in bacteriology in the faculty of medicine at McGill University. He was made emeritus professor on his retirement in 1930. Harrison had an impressive academic pedigree. He was 'a large man, energetic and articulate who was respected as an excellent lecturer and researcher. However, he had a brusque manner of speaking to others which tended to irritate them. ... Perhaps it was due to his boyhood spent in military establishments where it was usual to demand obedience from others. Perhaps too, he suffered when compared to Principal Robertson who had been very popular.' H.R. Nelson, *Macdonald College of McGill University 1907–1988: A Profile of a Campus* (Montreal: Corona, 1989), p.8.

[73] George Herbert Locke (1870–1937) was born in Beamsville, Ontario, and was educated at Victoria College, University of Toronto (BA, 1893; B.Paed., 1896; MA 1895; LLD, 1927).

[74] Macdonald College consisted of the School of Agriculture, the School of Household Science and the School of Teachers. Each school had its own head or Dean. The Dean of the School for Teachers took over the functions of the McGill Normal school. The College had its own principal until 1926. After a gap lasting until 1935 this post was redesignated as that of Vice Principal.

[75] Samuel Bower Sinclair (1855–1933) was born in Ridgetown in western Canada. He was educated at Victoria University (BA, 1889) and the University of Toronto (MA, 1893). He gained his PhD at the University of Chicago in 1901, was vice principal of Ottawa Normal School (19**–1913), and at the Ontario Department of Education, 1913–1933, where he promoted the organization of separate classes for students of above and below average ability.

[76] Sinclair Laird (1884–1954) was born in Montrose, Scotland, and educated at Harris Academy, Dundee, and St Andrews University, where he received his MA in 1906 and his B.Phil. in 1911. He had a brilliant student career, winning medals in three languages, logic and metaphysics, and in education. He took honours in mathematics, political economy, history and moral philosophy. He had taught in several Scottish schools and lectured at St Andrews. He emigrated to Canada and took up a post at Queen's University, Kingston, Ontario. He was created *Officier de l'Instruction Publique* of the French Republic and was awarded honorary degrees by the Universities of Montreal and St Andrews. In addition he received the Order of Scholastic Merit of the Province of Quebec, with the Gold Medal of the

Order and the Diploma of 'Distinguished Merit'. After his retirement in 1949 he served on Montreal Town Council.

[77] Nelson, *Macdonald College*, p.14.

[78] W. Peterson, 'Canada and the Empire', in *Canadian Essays and Addresses* (London, 1915), pp.63–7, quoted in S.F. Frost, *McGill University for the Advancement of Learning*, 2 Vols (Montreal: McGill University Press, 1984), Vol. 2 (1895–1971), pp.95–6.

[79] Sir William. Peterson (1856–1921) was born in Edinburgh and studied at the universities of Edinburgh (BA, 1875), Gottingen and Corpus Christi, Oxford (MA, 1893). He was principal of Dundee College from 1882 to 1895 and vice-chancellor of McGill University 1895–1919.

[80] Frost, *McGill University*, pp.95–6.

[81] Nelson, *Macdonald College*, p.8.

[82] Snell, *Macdonald College*, p.149.

[83] P.A. Dunae, *Gentleman Emigrants*, p.223.

[84] 'Mr. Dashwood's Departure', *Macdonald College Magazine*, VI, 1, 61.

[84] Ibid. (emphasis added).

[86] Ibid. (emphasis added).

[87] Dashwood left the Canadian Royal Flying Corps in 1916. I have not been able to establish why.

[88] K.R. Shackleton, *Second To None: The Fighting 58th Battalion of the Canadian Expeditionary Force* (Toronto: Dundurn Press, 2002), p.77.

[89] Charles William Venning (1883–19**) was born in Hull and attended Crowle St Board School, Hull and the Hull Pupil Teacher Centre. Unusually for an Anglican, he trained at Borough Road College from 1903 to 1905. He was not a strong student academically, being described as 'very nervous' during his practical criticism lesson. He failed physics and English literature. However, he gained his B.Sc. in 1906 and worked at Buckingham Terrace School, Notting Hill, from 1906 to 1908 before being appointed to the staff of Borough Road in 1908.

[90] Percy Walton (1908–10) took his BA at London in 1911.

[91] *Old B's Roll of Service*, 3rd edn (London, 1917), p.22.

[92] Ibid, p.23.

[93] Ibid.

[94] Ibid.

[95] Ibid.

[96] Moss, *Manliness and Militarism*, p.28.

[97] Ibid., p.53.

[98] J. Vance, *Death So Noble. Meaning Memory and the First World War* (Vancouver: University of British Columbia Press, 1997), p.3; Lynn Hunt, 'History beyond Social Theory' in D. Carroll (ed.), *The States of Theory, Art and Critical Discourse* (New York: Columbia University Press, 1990), pp.103–4.

[99] Dashwood is buried in Bois-Carre British Cemetery, Thelus, Pas de Calais. The village of Thelus stands on Vimy Ridge 7 km north of Arras and contains 500 casualties from the 1914–18 war.

[100] Jeff Keshen, 'The Great War Soldier as Nation Builder in Canada and Australia', in B.C. Busch (ed.), *Canada and the Great War. Western Front Association Papers* (Montreal: McGill University Press, 2003), p.3.

[101] Quoted in N. Christie, *For King and Empire. The Canadians at Vimy* (Ottawa: CEF Books, 2002), p.101.

[102] Keshen, 'The Great War Soldier', p.4.

[103] *Maidenhead Advertiser*, 23 May 1917, 6.

[104] *The Eastern Times*, February 1936, in 'McGill University Scrapbook' 8, pp.270–4; 30 Sept. 1935–31 Dec. 1936, p.375.

[105] J.A. Mangan (ed.), 'Epilogue: Continuities', in *Shaping the Superman: Fascist Body as Political Icon – Aryan Fascist* (London and Portland, OR: Frank Cass 1999), p.193.

[106] Mangan, 'The Grit of our Forefathers', p.136.

'Christ and the Imperial Games Fields' in South-Central Africa – Sport and the Scottish Missionaries in Malawi, 1880–1914: Utilitarian Compromise

Markku Hokkanen

This article is a study of Scottish Presbyterian missions and sport in what is now Malawi in the late nineteenth and early twentieth centuries, and discusses the missionaries' use of sport, as well as their physical and industrial education schemes, in the training of African bodies in pursuit of moral and physical health – but above all of Christian character. Furthermore, the article analyses the missionaries' uneasy relationship to indigenous African dancing, and briefly considers modern sport and its imperial associations in the early colonial society in the Shire Highlands.

Drawing its inspiration from J.A. Mangan's pioneering study of English public-school-educated missionaries, this article argues that although the ideology of athleticism was less prominent in the Scottish missionary educational institutions at Blantyre and Livingstonia missions, which emphasized industrial education and manual work in their educational schemes, the Scottish missionaries were important intermediaries for modern sport in Malawi, introducing cricket, rugby, and association football to the area. The Scots, as the English, had their athletic evangelists, who were as enthusiastic in their religious evangelism as British settlers were in their cultural evangelism, introducing imperial sport to British Central Africa during the 1890s.

In the study of missionaries and sport in Africa during the colonial period, a local approach is highly advisable. The missionary organizations and archives from the nineteenth and twentieth centuries onwards are numerous, even if limited to Protestant, never mind British, societies. [1] A consideration of the records of the International Conferences of Protestant Missions held in Edinburgh in 1910 suggests that although there was a general consensus regarding the importance of education of body and mind, [2] physical education and sport were not explicitly discussed in the conference records. Industrial education, in comparison, was an important topic for these missionary authorities. It was seen not only as means for teaching new skills and organizing labour, but also as moral education important for the cultivation of character and manhood. [3] Industrial education could thus be seen as sharing the goals of athleticism [4] and even competing with it. Alexander Hetherwick of the Church of Scotland Mission in Blantyre was especially keen on industrial education, while Revd H.W. Weatherhead, a Church Missionary Society headmaster at the King's School, Budo, was more orthodox. He praised the 'manly and Christian' atmosphere created in the mission boarding schools, although he did not specifically mention the importance of sport. [5]

Hetherwick and Weatherhead, a Scot and an Englishman, might be regarded as representatives of two distinct educational traditions, one emphasizing industrial education and manual work, the other encouraging team games, with both concerned with the character, manliness and the body, in addition to literary education. However, a closer examination of the Scottish missions of Livingstonia and Blantyre, where the industrial tradition seems especially strong, shows that the division was not so stereotypically clear-cut. For his part, Weatherhead had an interest in industrial education too. [6] As will be seen, the Scots were not indifferent to use of games in general education.

To look for connections between missions and sport in Africa, as already noted, it is important to look at events on a local level: individual societies, missionaries and the schools they worked in. This kind of approach, of course, has been pioneered by J.A. Mangan, particularly in his studies of Anglican public-school-educated missionaries and their activities in, for example, King's School in Uganda, Alliance High School in Kenya and Achimota College in the Gold Coast (Ghana). [7] The Scottish Presbyterian missionaries of Blantyre and Livingstonia comprise different, but promising exemplars, not only because they have left a rich archive of local-level sources from the mid-1870s onwards, but also because they provide an interesting comparison to the better-known athleticism-inspired English missionaries.

Sport and Games at Blantyre Mission

The Blantyre Mission of the established Church of Scotland was founded in 1876 in the Shire Highlands, regarded as healthy for Europeans, among the Mang'anja and Yao villages. The mission was not particularly successful in its early years. Lacking an ordained minister and clear leadership, it required constant help from Livingstonia in 1876–9. The missionaries became heavily involved in local politics, assuming legal responsibilities over the Africans at the mission station. After missionaries began exercising corporal punishment and details of Africans flogged and, in one case, even executed, reached Britain, a scandal ensued. One of the missionaries implicated in the 'Blantyre Scandal' was Revd Duff Macdonald, the first minister at the station, who had arrived in 1878. Macdonald had declined responsibility for the political and judicial affairs of the mission, leaving them to the laymen of the station, and although he had not personally taken part in the worst atrocities he was recalled in 1881. Macdonald, an able linguist and scholar, published after his recall *Africana, or the Heart of Heathen Africa* (1882). [8] Macdonald provided, in his narrative of mission work during 1880, an early account of sport and games in Blantyre:

> In finding suitable amusements for our pupils we had at first considerable difficulty. Owing to the heat of the climate, the native children are not so fond of active games as English children are. So long as we took part in a game they played heartily but almost as soon as we ceased, they also gave it up. Each Friday afternoons we had races and gave small prizes. After a time they began to enjoy swings and football, but the favourite game was 'cricket'. We were glad that they showed a special fondness for this game, as it proved a pleasant means of conveying instruction. The calculation of the 'runs' gave them exercise in arithmetic (as we threw aside the Yao notation in favour of the English), and when any one was appointed umpire, he learned to form an opinion for himself and abide by it. Some sturdy bowler would often be heard calling out 'Pray sir!' He meant 'Play sir!' but as the batsman with his bare legs and arms was sometimes in greater danger than his wicket, the formula was allowed to pass, with an occasional laugh... The native technical terms used in this game were amusing. A ball rolled along the ground was termed a 'rat,' while a ball that was overpitched was called a 'bird' (*chijuni*). Soon they learned the value of pitching their balls properly, and a little piece of paper placed to show the spot was called a cricket 'charm'. Again, the umpire, instead of saying that the batsman was out, declared that he was 'dead!' Owing to the great heat, the game was confined to the evening, and I found it a simple means of securing that amount of physical exercise which is indispensable for a preventing a European from becoming a continual martyr to fever. [9]

For the scholarly Macdonald, 'cricket' was a medium of instruction of the mind as well as a recreation and training for the body. Furthermore, it was a pleasant means for missionaries to ward off malarial fevers. Although he believed that African children were generally less active than the English, he explained this in terms of climate rather than 'race' or biology. The example of the players' Yao cricket terminology shows something of how the game took on new, local meanings and interpretations. [10] Macdonald's attitude to this was paternalist amusement. In comparison, later in the colonial period, not a few Europeans felt uneasy seeing 'their' sports and games played differently, or 'wrongly' by the 'natives'. [11] The ethnocentric educational purpose of the activities was in danger of getting lost.

The Blantyre Mission was effectively 'founded again' in 1881, with Revd David Clement Scott in charge. Scott became a legendary missionary, a superb linguist, vocal critic of colonial violence and a passionate defender of many aspects of African culture. [12] During Scott's leadership in the 1880s and 1890s the Blantyre Mission grew as the European presence in the Shire Highlands increased, and with the establishment of the British Central Africa Protectorate in 1891, the mission became part of growing colonial society.

D.C. Scott believed strongly in the 'civilizing' and 'industrial' mission in the British Empire. To him, a missionary should carry both the Gospel and modern culture to Africans, who had an equal right to them. [13] And for Scott modern culture included also modern sport. He was himself a keen sportsman, who had excelled in running in his student days. [14] He continued the practice of cricket among the Blantyre mission school pupils, but proper equipment was needed. In June 1882, just a few months after Scott's arrival, the *Mission Record* published the following request:

> *Could some school now, or family, fond of the sport, give Blantyre a few cricket bats and balls and wickets? ... really good ones, and full sized; for African boys know as well as Scottish lads when a bat or a ball is useless. They are as big, moreover, as are our boys, who like the cricket field, and require to play with the same things. Katunga's son 'slogs' out as freely as any at home, – so says Mr Scott, and he is a good judge of what a cricketer should be. Many of the lads, like Katunga's son, are tall, well-formed, and muscular fellows, and seeing that withal they are well disposed, their play-hours at the proper season could not be better occupied than in the same healthy game in which so many of our boys very properly delight. [15]*

Games were a useful way for a newly arrived, athletic missionary to establish positive contact with the African pupils. Testing of muscle and skill on a cricket field could contribute to or reinforce a notion of physical equality between African and Scottish 'lads', rare during a time when both missionary and imperial propaganda ethnocentrically exaggerated the physical differences between the Europeans and the Africans, to the latter's disadvantage. [16]

After a few months, the pupils of Scott's old school, the Royal High School, Edinburgh, duly 'presented to the Mission an abundant supply of handsome cricket bats, wickets, and balls, in token of their sympathy with Mr Scott, and of their interest in his work of converting the youth of Africa'. [17] A month later, the pupils of Merchiston Castle High School followed suit. [18] These responses illustrate how closely the Blantyre Mission was connected to the Edinburgh upper- and middle-class institutions. It was in such schools that the ideology of athleticism, created in England, was spreading in late-nineteenth-century Scotland, [19] as a form of middle-class cultural imperialism. [20]

By 1883, D.C. Scott reported confidently on extra-curricular aspects of school life in Blantyre. Discipline was well established, pupils were under supervision in dormitories, and cricket was played regularly. This practice was continued throughout the 1880s. [21] It was in this mission boarding school, incidentally, that most of the first African Christians and the future mission staff were educated. [22]

Football was also played in Blantyre with enthusiasm from about 1880 onwards. [23] In 1891, W.A. Scott, the mission doctor and D.C. Scott's younger brother, treated 'slight football injuries such as sprained toes and feet'. Echoing his brother's comments on cricket, he wrote, 'If Scotland feels drawn to Africa, then let Scotch boys know that African boys like their Scotch game as well as they do themselves, and take the knocks ... in the same spirit.' [24] It is not clear from these reports exactly what rules were used in early Blantyre football games. W.A. 'Willie' Scott, who had been very much a 'muscular Christian' student in Edinburgh, was a 'rugger' man himself, however. Scott had excelled at sport at the High School of Edinburgh, being a captain of the rugby football team in his fourth year, and continued his football career at the university. At one point he contemplated quitting football to concentrate on his studies, but rejected the idea after his teammates promised that in order to keep him in the team, no one would 'utter a profane word' in his presence. [25] During his student days, he undertook home mission work in the Greenside parish, holding Sunday evening classes for boys, and from 1884 onwards worked with the University Missionary Association in the Blackfriars Street Mission. [26] There he strove to influence the boys through 'healthy' and 'gentlemanly' sports as well as music. Scott was in charge of the Mission Football Club and organized a flute band to battle against profanity and drunkenness. [27]

Blantyre continued to receive sports equipment including footballs from Scotland, and also from the Anglican Universities' Mission to Central Africa missionaries from Likoma Island. [28] By 1899, the mission had a 'well-trampled football field', in which games were played every evening. It seems that soccer had established itself over rugby as the predominant game by this time. [29] After the mission had received 'a fine football' from Granton Sunday School in 1898, an anonymous missionary with a strong passion for rugby wrote:

> You have but to see the Blantyre Mission teams with their captains, forwards, and backs, keeping rule and keeping time. .... A bugle keeps the time-militaire-barbaric. In native games at ball, the great feature of village boy life, a drum keeps time, as at a dance. One wonders what part of the foot kicks the football if one has no boots. Presumably it is the toeball... If so, one wonders again how it does so undislocatingly. We have tried to introduce 'drop' kick, the kick of all kicks, the kick which makes football football, but apparently punting is going to prevail. We hate punting and Association dunting and shunting and all its associated ways: but apparently Rugby finesse will not take the hold we would like. [30]

The comments suggest some similarities between mission football and local ball games. In both, as in dance, the keeping of time has its place. Adjustment to local usage to promote appeal did not alter the fact that the missionaries believed the British games taught superior order and control. Modern team games were one part of 'civilization' that progressive missionaries such as D.C. Scott had no hesitation in promoting.

Shire Highlands Sports Events, 1890–1900

Following the Scottish tradition, the Blantyre missionaries organized sports and games on Christmas Day and New Year. These games consisted mainly of informal races of various kinds, but in the Domasi station in 1891 a swimming and diving competition was included. [31] New Year's games were arranged also by European settlers, many of whom were Scottish, in the Shire Highlands during the late 1880s and early 1890s. These games became part of the colonial culture of the British Central Africa Protectorate established in 1891. Both Europeans and Africans took part, though it seems that in the larger sports events, a racial demarcation between 'European' and 'native' races was made. In the New Year's games arranged in Mandala, the base for the African Lakes Company and the major European plantation of the Buchanan brothers, Europeans played 'lawn tennis and other sports'. [32] Interestingly, although the missionaries had tennis balls for games with their pupils, [33] there is no evidence of missionaries actually playing lawn tennis with Africans.

The British settlers of the Shire Highlands were eager to declare their identity as imperial subjects through annual sports events. On 24 May 1892, they organized the Queen's Birthday Sports, with separate 'native' and 'European' events. A writer in the Blantyre mission magazine, probably the editor, D.C. Scott, wrote of the event: 'The native events were but poorly contested ... there were very few entries. ... Disappointing it may be to find the native devoid of healthy ambition in contesting the events, but a little fostering may do much to produce trained athletes in Central Africa.' [34]

It seems that the African population of the Shire Highlands was not at all enthusiastic about imperial events in which games celebrated the imperialist's ruler throughout a period of colonial occupation characterized by frequent imperial violence. For the Africans, the only popular event was the tug-of-war. [35]

In 1892, the mission moved the Domasi School Games from Christmas to June, the dry season. Pupils from the Domasi, Blantyre, Mlungusi and Kumjale mission schools attended. A new playground was created, decked round with flags and with tents erected near the winning post. Smaller children had their 'usual races' but the most popular events were tug-of war and the football matches between schools. Blantyre defeated Mlungusi 2–0, a result considered a moral victory for the Mlungusi team, as they had only been playing football for a couple of months. The match between Domasi and Blantyre was won 2–0 by Domasi. [36]

On occasion, the sports events organized by missionaries also attracted older Africans. In Mlanje, the 'Athletic Games' held on New Year's Day 1894 were regarded as particularly successful with both men and women taking part:

> The headmen of the village turned out strong, Yao and Mang'anja; from grizzled haired men and women down to the babe in arms arrived. ... The sports were contested with much spirit, the married women's race, the headmen's race and wrestling were the most eagerly competed. ... After the games there was a feast for the headmen. [37]

The clear purpose of these events was Christian proselytism. In addition to contest and relaxation, the missionaries used the opportunity to promote the establishment of new mission schools in the area.

By 1896, colonial sport in the Shire Highlands had become well established. The 'Blantyre Sports' attracted about a hundred European spectators, perhaps one-third of all Europeans in the protectorate. Events included a cricket match between 'World' and 'Mandala', horse racing and the novelty of a bicycle race, although with only two contestants. A peculiarly colonial sport was the '*machila* race' in which 'teams of able-bodied native carriers are chosen, and the rival teams carry their European round a long course'. [38] This was apparently the only event in which Europeans and Africans participated jointly, though far from equally. Inequality was 'evident' in other things. The editor of *Life and Work* wrote of the 'native races':

> The Native races were excellent, although we have never yet seen here native speed which could equal European. One hears of Arab racing European, and Fenimore Cooper's 'Fleet-foots' certainly held their own with British muscle. These may be only in tale. What seems to us to tell is not so much the size of the muscle or the power of endurance or even build, in all of which the native excels, but in the capacity of putting nerve force, enthusiasm and will into a comparatively little body. The eye gets fire, the nostrils breathe spirit, and the will commands and accomplishes impossibilities. [39]

The writer, in all probability Scott, who was anything but racially discriminatory as a missionary, [40] clearly believed that both racial and cultural factors affected running performance. Basing his thought partly on popular Victorian medico-physiological theory, he believed that European superiority in running was based on nerve force, [41] will power and the culturally fostered enthusiasm for competition which cumulatively made the 'comparatively little' European body ultimately superior to the African, regardless of the excellent build, muscle size, and endurance of the latter.

The following year, the Diamond Jubilee Sports held in Blantyre attracted the largest gathering yet of Europeans in the protectorate, with well over a hundred Europeans in the audience. The size of the African audience was not mentioned, but their being 'most quiet and orderly' was noted with approval. European running races included the 100 yards, quarter-mile and hurdle races. 'It is the best exposition of human life' commented Scott. As well as the European and African events, the Sikhs of the colonial force had their own games celebrating the Jubilee. [42]

The hierarchical nature of colonial society is apparent not only in the occasions considered above, but in the sports events of the plantation and business centre of Mandala. In the Mandala annual sports, held on New Year's Day 1899:

> Each class of native employees at Mandala had its race – cooks, store boys, office boys etc. A new feature was a race for carriers, each competitor being weighted with a truss of calico – an ordinary man's load. Two gangs of eight men competed, every one of whom displayed a most praise-worthy diligence in striving to place his burden at the further end of a 400 yards race. [43]

The missionaries' statements on African participation in the games, as has already been stated, were somewhat contradictory and almost always patronizing. The description of the Christmas games in Blantyre in 1899 is an especially good example of how African sportsmen and audience were perceived by a Scottish missionary:

> The various items in a lengthy programme were fairly well contested. Still, native bashfulness has a good deal to overcome. Sport as sport is a foreign idea in the native mind, and the Homeric Adage as yet forms only a small part of an African sports ground. ... Possibly some of the reluctance to enter the arena is due to the native custom of not applauding the victors so much as of ironically cheering the failures. Somehow the misses seem always more popular than the hits – perhaps a fellow finds expression in this way, and what we take for triumph at the downfall of failure may after all be only an expression of that kindly sympathy which makes the whole world kin. [44]

Whatever their competitive shortcomings, the Africans adjusted to the events and the events to themselves. By the beginning of the twentieth century, the annual Mandala Games held at New Year had, according to the editor of *Life and Work*,

> enriched the native language with a new word. Chaka means originally a year. Because the beginning of the year was associated with the sports at Mandala the word chaka has come to be applied to games or sports of all kind. Any festival gathering at any time of the year is called a chaka. The Agricultural Show last September was dubbed a chaka. Kudia chaka which means literally 'to eat the year' has come to be applied to a feast or party of any kind. [45]

Such details are rare in the missionary publications but offer a glimpse of African perspectives on the missionary and colonial sports activities in the Shire Highlands in the 1890s and 1900s.

Europeans in general, religious and secular elements, were enthusiastic about their sports days and events. The only overt cause for conflict between Scottish missionaries and the more secular settlers surrounding the sports events was the organizing of games on the sabbath, which was completely unacceptable to the Presbyterians. Dr Henry Scott protested strongly after the Zomba Sports Club organized a cricket match on the sabbath in May 1898. He stressed the negative influence this would have on African people: 'with regard to the native population, whatever may be the interpretation of the Sabbath Day elsewhere, the religious teaching predominant throughout this part of the protectorate enforces that public games are not in keeping with the spirit of the Lord's Day'. [46]

But the missionaries' protests were ignored by the settlers in Zomba. The following year they fixed the date for the Queen's Birthday Sports on a Sunday, as if to provoke the missionaries. The editor of *Life and Work*, probably Dr Neil MacVicar, accused the organizers of damaging the religious spirit, obligations and traditions of the colony, and thus endangering its entire Christian character: 'The religious obligation of the Lord's Day lies at the foundation of our national Christian character. To tamper with its sacred institutions is to sap the fabric of our strength.' The writer defended the sabbath as a day of rest and 'thoughtful leisure', as a source of conservation and character improvement. [47]

When a football match was arranged by a local sports club in Blantyre on Sunday, Dr Macvicar complained that

> By so doing it [the Club] could not fail to alienate the sympathies of many who rejoice to see in all such competitions a stimulus to our national pluck and endurance as well as an invaluable source of health in a climate where exercise is a sure preventive of disease. We hope that the next year the club will see fit to depart from this precedent and enable the whole community to join in the celebration of our chief local holiday. [48]

He must have been pleased that the match failed to attract enough players. For the Blantyre missionaries, sport and games were understood to be good for health and character, but only when in their proper place. Both doctors and ministers agreed that a game held on the sabbath was against the teaching of the word of God.

Drill and Team Games at the Overtoun Institution, 1896–1913

In the Livingstonia mission of the Free Church of Scotland, founded in 1875 and funded mainly by wealthy Glasgow businessmen, sport and games were not encouraged until the late 1890s, and then to a considerably less extent than in Blantyre. As noted earlier, some of the leading Blantyre missionaries, notably the Scott brothers, were educated in middle-class Edinburgh schools with introduced English athletic traditions. This explains in part the difference in early attitudes towards sport in Blantyre and Livingstonia. The latter was established by Scottish missionaries with working- or lower middle-class backgrounds and from a different educational tradition. [49] Regarding the education of the body and the development of character, the emphasis on industrial education and work was more prevalent at Livingstonia than at Blantyre and initially left no room for team games. James Henderson, the first headmaster of the Overtoun Institution of Livingstonia, founded in 1894, summarized the general attitude of the pioneer missionary generation led by

Revd Dr Robert Laws thus: 'love of sport is not generally regarded as consistent with missionary service'. [50] There was a notable exception to this: hunting for useful purposes. Henderson was an enthusiastic hunter, who confessed to his fiancée that he probably could not resist the temptation of shooting game on the sabbath if any came his way. [51]

As late as in 1905, a young missionary, T. Cullen Young, lamented that there was 'no football, no cricket, no golf' for missionaries in Livingstonia. However, there was a 'fairly decent' tennis court, and occasional games, stated Young, kept his 'liver going' as well as warded off 'low spirits'. [52] Robert Laws, the leader of the mission and the founder and principal of the institution, believed that a good physique was necessary for well-developed spiritual and mental stature. [53] However, Laws and his close colleague, Dr Walter Elmslie, believed that this was to be achieved through manual work rather than play.

From the early days of the mission, moral education at Livingstonia had been founded on the teaching of the Bible, the base for the 'cultivation of moral powers'. [54] In the station boarding-schools and especially in the institution, the aim was to have the pupils under constant scrutiny to secure their moral well-being. At the institution, located in the highlands, the pupils, many of them from the lake shore, were cut off from their homes except for during the holiday season. There was very little or no spare time, and the pupils were subjected to strict discipline. Some 40 per cent of the students left the institution, or were dismissed, before graduating. [55]

As a remote boarding school with strict discipline, the Overtoun Institution was similar to English public and Scottish private schools. In its initial policies regarding the education of the body, however, it was very different. The institution had a very ambitious curriculum, including theology, philosophy, English, history and mathematics. [56] After Dr Walter Elmslie took charge of the institution during Laws's furlough in 1899, the lack of a physical element in the education seemed to him a shortcoming. He criticized the over-concentration on bookwork in the curriculum.

Furthermore, in January 1900, Elmslie reported cases of 'immoral conduct' and feared there was a 'good deal of secret sin' in the institution. Crowded boys' dormitories, in particular, were seen to be a danger to moral and physical health. Because of a lack of space and warmth, often two or three boys slept in the same bed, which was 'unwise and injurious' for Elmslie, who clearly suspected the conditions fostered homosexual practices. As well as improving conditions and providing separate beds for each pupil, Elmslie believed in hard, productive and profitable manual labour, such as carpentry and gardening, as an effective means of improving moral and physical health. [57] Elmslie and Henderson managed to introduce carpentry work by April 1900. [58] After a few months, Elmslie reported happily that the new arrangement where all pupils concentrated on manual work for three hours in the afternoon, had resulted in the increased 'health and mental vigour of the pupils, not to speak of improved habits, and a new view of manual toil'. [59] All pupils and teachers at the institution took part in building, carpentry, gardening, mat weaving and tailoring as part of their school day; Henderson wrote in his annual report for 1900 that 'The results have been excellent in respect of physique and development of character'. and argued that in this respect Livingstonia could have something to teach to the English public schools, where only occasional tentative attempts at manual training had been made. [60]

The emphasis on manual work as means of improving moral and physical health and well-being highlights the Scottish Presbyterian educational tradition prevalent at Livingstonia. It epitomized the Protestant work ethic and also effectively lessened the cost of education. Elmslie's and Henderson's programme seems very distant from the English public-school tradition with its emphasis on athleticism for, incidentally, the same ends – the cultivation of body, mind, morality and character. In its approach to masculine health, the methods of the institution were in striking contrast to those propagated by Almond of Loretto for the late-nineteenth-century Scottish middle classes. [61] However, gradually, the Overtoun Institution did incorporate sport into its curriculum. The work ethic proved inadequate in itself. Henderson introduced drill to the institution's upper-school curriculum in 1897, for half an hour every Tuesday and Thursday, but at first it was met with little enthusiasm. [62] Eventually, frustrated with the pupils' attitudes towards drill, Henderson threatened them with immediate dismissal from school for any case of absence. He later reported that this threat had worked, especially after a public dismissal of one pupil, and the boys subsequently put on 'a very good exhibition' in the drilling competition. Henderson asserted that drill resulted in increased efficacy in school life:

> Trained as they have now been week after week for five months they are becoming habituated to the orders and fall in mechanically and do most of the movements without thinking. When they are doing work they are marched off to it after the roll call and there is no scattering and waste of time, while in school the saving of time and speaking is enormous. [63]

This assertion, of course, was the same used in the British elementary school for the working classes. Drill was designed to train working class children for future mechanistic occupations in industrial society, while the training for leadership was provided by public-school team games. [64]

By 1897, New Year games were played in Livingstonia, and Henderson chronicled the success of the workers of the Overtoun Institution:

> The sports were well contested. . . . The people are beginning to see the fun, yes and the earnest of games. In the tug of war powerful teams of men from and representing the different villages around here, were matched against one another. They were clothed with only the . . . very short kilt . . . their magnificent muscles were all in view. . . . It was a sight to have made an Ancient Greek wild with enthusiasm, although he might have considered them lacking in nimbleness. More powerful muscle I certainly never saw. We were very proud when the contests were over to find that the winners were the station men. The gardeners and the sawyers

and the carpenters beat all the others. This was I suppose due to their being trained to work together. [65]

Henderson's view was that European influence on the coordination of the working men of the station was significant. It was typical of colonial commentators to praise African muscle [66] but find fault in nimbleness, coordination, and control.

By the opening years of the twentieth century, drill and gymnastics were recognized at the institution as a useful means for ensuring the physical, mental and moral health of the pupils. [67] After Henderson left to take charge of the Lovedale Seminary in South Africa, the teaching at the institution was taken over by Revd D.R. Mackenzie and Peter Kirkwood. They, especially Kirkwood, contributed crucially to the change in education through sport in Livingstonia.

Mackenzie introduced systematic, weekly instruction in gymnastics at the institution in 1902. He fully subscribed to the idea that Christianity 'works physical as well as mental and moral transformation' which he believed was apparent in the 'growing refinement of features among the boys'. [68] Starting with leapfrog, Mackenzie continued with running, leaping, vaulting, and 'all the usual athletic exercises'. The teaching of gymnastics was at first limited to the dry season because of the lack of a building suitable for use as a gymnasium. During 1902, Mackenzie reported the missionaries had 'parallel bars, horizontal bars, and jumping stand, and hope shortly to add Indian clubs and dumb-bells'. Mackenzie hoped also to introduce football and cricket, thinking that 'if we can give to our Amusements a distinctively Christian aspect, it may solve for us beforehand some of the difficulties at home with regard to the relation of sport to religion'. Unfortunately, 'A football came to grief after only a few weeks', and was given up. [69]

The next year, when Mackenzie was doing station work, 'athletics' was dropped from the curriculum, but drill was maintained, and it was included as a formal subject among the 13 comprising the 'normal course' in the institution. Yakobi Sibanda, an ex-trooper distinguished in the Mashonaland campaign, took over the drill instruction, held after school in connection with the Christian Endeavour Society at the institution. [70]

Team games were not part of formal instruction at Livingstonia until 1906, when a young teacher, Peter Kirkwood, was appointed as a Normal School teacher. An active Christian worker, he had graduated from Glasgow University as certified teacher. Before his appointment, he had been a teacher for three years under the Glasgow School Board, at a time when athleticism was gaining increasing prominence in day schools at the 'second city of the Empire'. He arrived at the mission in October 1906, and taught at the institution during 1907–9 and 1910–15. [71] In his first letter to the home committee, Kirkwood stated he was particularly concerned to set an example to his pupils, not so much through words but by action. He believed that the Christian teachers he was training would be 'stamped with the impress' of his character, for better or worse, and pointed to the inconsistency between the gospel of joy and 'gloomy' missionary individuals:

to hear us tell them of a gospel of peace and joy, and then to see us scowl and looking gloomy, or to see us give a passionate gesture, must trouble the boys. One wonders what effect one would have on them if he had truly earned the title of 'sunny saint'.

For Kirkwood, a crucial tool of character training and joyful Christian expression was cricket:

> *The boys are taking to the cricket beautifully. So much has the cricket caught on that the boys of the infant classes may be seen copying their elders by using three sticks for wickets, a piece of box-wood for a bat, and anything from an unripe lemon to a bundle of paper for a ball. For the senior classes the language of the cricket field is English. It is somewhat amusing to hear one of the boys when he has made a bad throw or has missed a catch cry, in the most approved style, 'Sorry.' The hitting of some of the boys is wonderfully clean and strong. Soon we hope to have matches played between the senior classes. Some day two old Africans will meet and talk, not of the hurtling spear and the whirr of the arrow, but of 'that great catch at point,' or 'that neat cut for four' Discipline and true manliness can be taught in the playing field quite different from that of the class-room. By the cricket one seems to get closer to his boys.* [72]

In his first annual report, he wrote:

> Not the least part of our Educational work is the cricket practicing. It is a splendid means of teaching the boys honour and manliness. The boys have taken up cricket keenly and are showing good form. There are some rare fellows among them. One finds great joy in his work here, and that his best for them is so little. [73]

Kirkwood's keen interest in games was apparently appreciated, or at least accepted, by the older staff. In 1907, Kirkwood also taught 'Physical Training and Drill' while the traditional manual training in the afternoon was maintained by Laws and African teachers. However, cricket remained central to Kirkwood's teaching:

> The cricket during the year was a success indeed. The boys took to it enthusiastically, and many of them developed into good all-round players. We had cricket practice thrice during a week, Class IV having an hour by themselves, Class V an hour, and Class VI and VII together for an hour. On Saturday afternoons we had a game for all who turned out. [74]

Before leaving for furlough towards the end of 1908, Kirkwood reported enthusiastically on the sport during the year, after re-introducing football to the institution. Games were now organized according to the season. Classes IV–VII played cricket during the hot season, while in the cold season, Classes VI and VII played football and class V rounders. Kirkwood was especially 'impressed with the football, not only because of the progress the boys made from the kick-and-rush game to a good attempt at combination, but also because of the eager and gentlemanly spirit in which they played. Doubtless so far-off even will show that this training was not in vain.' [75] Throughout the school year, the entire upper school took part in the weekly drill, which was organized with a Scottish military flavour: 'The boys were placed in companies, each of which was put under the command of a boy in Class VII. As at drill they wore a red cloth, kilt-wise, the boys made a goodly show as they marched in company.' [76]

Kirkwood's writings conveyed a sense of imperial mission, in which the games ethic taught in the mission school was expected to bear fruit in missionary fields, colonial enterprise, business and the battlefield. In this he seems to follow closely in the tradition of English public-school-educated imperial missionaries, possibly as an outcome of his own Scottish middle-class education. However, his background and schooling is not clear in the Livingstonia records.

In 1909, 'singing and athletics' were included in the curriculum as one subject. In the absence of Kirkwood, Mr Howie, the agriculturist, and Dr Turner, the doctor, had taken up teaching. Mackenzie confidently reported that 'The value of the singing is too well-known to need a remark, and the athletics are still developing in the boys a spirit of self-reliance and readiness which few natives naturally possess'. [77] Mackenzie was demonstrating an old ethnocentric prejudice in claiming that Africans were 'naturally' passive and lacking in self-reliance. Interestingly, there was no mention of team games during Kirkwood's furlough. However, after his return, Kirkwood reported that it was 'drill and games' as usual. [78]

It seems that Kirkwood was alone in his enthusiasm for games at the institution. By 1912 he felt that the curriculum of the institution was 'too heavy'. Although he did not directly argue for the importance of team games, he gave the impression that the lack of emphasis on games and other subjects valuable for character training had had detrimental effects: 'We of the Normal College staff are here to turn out teachers whose power should be more in their character and ability than their knowledge.' [79] However, the next year, his report was a little more positive. Of the final year students, he singled out an 'XY', who was 'Strenuous in his class-work, strenuous in the games and with a merry and ready laugh.' [80] This pupil clearly matched his ideal of an African graduate.

During 1913, in the afternoons, among gardening and other work, the boys 'measured off, lined, hoed over and rolled the football field, while some of Class VII made the goal posts. Twice during the year they cut the field.' In this way, the industrial training ethic prevalent at Livingstonia was combined with the games ethic. By this time, football seems to have overtaken cricket as the most popular game at the institution. 'The boys made great progress in football, and towards the end of the year could make a good show. The spirit of the games was, as a rule, excellent, and the close contact with the boys in the afternoon was very pleasant,' [81] wrote Kirkwood. This was the last peaceful year in the mission, and during the First World War reporting was scarce. Kirkwood taught at the institution until 1915, when he went on furlough. He never returned to Livingstonia, as he drowned on the way back when his ship was torpedoed in 1918. [82]

Clash of Cultures: Village Dances and the Mission Schools

The Africans had, and held to, their own physical activities for the young (and others). Although organized sport was introduced to the Overtoun Institution during the first decade of the nineteenth century, it seems that the Livingstonia village schools, where the vast majority of pupils studied, offered only book-learning, but no physical education to compete with dancing, which held a central place in traditional African education. This was made clear by T. Cullen Young, a missionary with anthropological aspirations as well as a fondness for sport, in 1912, when he wrote of the challenge dancing presented to the mission schools in Northern Ngoniland. Young reported of 'young men, who, for various reasons, wished to damage our work, to draw our scholars away by introducing during school time the village dance'. This happened 'with a tremendous effect' all over the country, and right in the villages with mission schools. [83]

Young did not regard the Ngoni village dances harmful in themselves, and actually considered them part of a respectable tradition so long as they did not clash with the mission teaching. During the recent years, he wrote, 'it had been an unwritten law that these dances should be reserved for the holiday months and for Saturdays'. Now, however, the dancers directly challenged the missionaries for the education of the young, and Young confessed he had very little to offer in competition. He held that

> This dancing corresponds to our own love of games at home, and it would be sheer nonsense of my part to pretend that our school programme is such as to provide a counterattraction strong enough to expel youth's desire for pleasure and excitement. But for many years the people have been content with the arrangement that leaves ample time for both work and play ... definite antagonism to us has arisen and is capable of drawing great numbers to it. [84]

Young attributed an increased hostility towards missionaries and colonial rule to the rise of hut tax and the spreading ideas of independent African Christianity in the region. [85] Dancing was effectively utilized as an African vehicle of protest and as means for competing for the loyalty of the young under missionary influence. Dancing was a potent way of provoking the missionaries and African converts; the Livingstonia mission had traditionally been extremely critical of African dances. Young was more liberal, however, and in response, organized *ingoma* dances in the cattle kraal at the Loudon mission. [86]

Not all the older-generation Scottish missionaries in Central Africa, however, had condemned African dancing. D.C. Scott, for one, wrote in 1891 of Blantyre school pupils:

> Our children dance beneath the moon as the old fairy tales would have us believe was done in Scotland by beings of some sort. We did not believe these stories until we saw it here with our eyes, and found the material equal to the

best Scotch brownies. The moon however is available ... for about the fourth part of the month; the remaining ... call for labour, games and indoor evening amusement. [87]

However, in his romantic vision combining Scottish mythology and African reality, Scott seems to have been an exceptional missionary. He was careful to check that no 'unseemly' dances took place, [88] while the Blantyre mission condemned certain dances, notably those connected with the rites of passage of the youth.

During the dry season in 1892 the Church of Scotland missionaries at Domasi reported that the mission schoolboys had resisted the chief's personal call to them to attend the *unyago* initiation dance and had rejected the wishes of their parents. It was at that time that missionaries had organized larger sports events for their pupils than before, [89] and it can be argued that they were used in part to attract mission pupils' attention away from the initiation dances. It is unclear what role, if any, the mission games actually played in the schoolboys' decision not to attend the dance. Whatever the motives, the Blantyre missionaries could not speak of any lasting victory over dancing. In October 1892, when the pupils of the Domasi station were trained in the 'mysteries of drill', they reported that the schools had generally suffered because of *unyago* dances. [90]

And, as shown above, the mission schools of the Blantyre mission had organized games, notably cricket and football, in their repertoire from at least the 1890s. The Scots had their initiation rites and the Africans had theirs. However, it was not a simple matter of polarization. Drill could be viewed as mission initiation 'dance', but it was not attractive enough to compete with African dancing. Mackenzie wrote in 1902 that the Overtoun Institution pupils failed to see the point of drill. [91]

In Livingstonia during the early 1900s, some younger missionaries such as Revd Donald Fraser and Dr James Chisholm, who were not wholly condemnatory in their attitudes towards dancing, suggested that acceptable dances should be encouraged and fostered in mission schools to counter the 'obscene' or 'evil' dances. Some of the Overtoun Institution-educated elite such as Charles Domingo eloquently defended dancing. [92] Nevertheless, some of the institution-educated teachers and evangelists continued to maintain that any dance involving both sexes was harmful, [93] and this puritan view was shared by the more inhibited older missionaries.

In January 1908, a conference was held by the Livingstonia licentiates, ruling elders and other leading African Christians in connection with the meeting of the Livingstonia Presbytery. Among the topics discussed was 'Native dances and games'. The conference reached a consensus that 'All good games should be continued, but not to excess'. [94] This seems to constitute a compromise between liberal and puritan views, allowing the definition of what games were 'good' to be decided by the local authorities in kirk sessions and congregations.

The issue did not go away. And compromise remained under consideration. In an article written in 1921, Donald Fraser lamented that the young African Church in Nyasaland had been too extreme in its condemnation of all forms of dancing, and warned that a too puritan attitude could result in negative, joyless religious life. Fraser was careful to make clear that he knew that some dances had 'most obscene tendencies'. He also mentioned the Ngoniland case of the 'healthy and clean' dance, which had become politicized and resulted in the suffering of church and school life. [95] Nevertheless, he made a case for retaining dancing as a central form of African life, as part of Christian culture in Africa, and forcefully asked: 'Why should this natural outlet of African feelings be blocked or made the monopoly of the devil?' Fraser described how a missionary's arrival in a village led to sudden silence:

> Few games are played, no dances take place, people sit about quietly ... that is not pleasant to the soul of a man who responds to the joy of children, and it gives him a narrowed feeling of being nothing more than a preacher, as if the fellowship of manhood were denied him. [96]

Then Fraser painted a joyful picture of the delight of children when he asked them to play: how children danced and played tug-of-war and the adults joined in, instructing the young. With the Christian women of the village, the action was controlled: 'Once or twice in the excitement of the dance actions which are not pretty or pure are attempted, but the girls stop them. These are not allowed to-night. The fun must be as clean as God's moonlight.' After the dancing, Fraser spoke 'on the joy of life that God has given us and how clean the taste of pure sport is. I ask the Christian men and women to guide the evening games, that nothing would be done that Christ would not like to look on.' [97] Fraser concluded that

> unguided dances may be abominable: controlled they may be pure joy. .... We shall be good servants of Africa if we can rescue from foul clutches the treasure of song, fable, dance, and sport which is one of Africa's best possessions, and teach the people how work and recreation are realms over which Christ may rule. [98]

By the time he wrote this, Fraser was an experienced and respected missionary, and confident of writing on a sensitive issue to the home audience. Of course, within the Presbyterian churches, there was a tendency to condemn dancing in Britain as well. [99] For Fraser, the crucial aspect of dancing, as it was for African Christian sport, was control; performed by Christians educated and supervised by the missionaries.

Conclusion

In this contribution, sport in one African colonial society has been studied at the local level, through the archives of one important group of imperial actors. An approach on a local level has its advantages, as already mentioned, namely a focus on detail. As Nicholas Thomas has argued, 'only localized theories and historically specific accounts can provide much insight into the varied articulations of colonizing and counter-colonial representations and practices ... colonialism can only be traced through its plural and particularized expressions.' [100]

On sports fields, the missionaries saw both similarities and differences between Africans and Europeans, yet although their writings convey often a sense of paternal superiority, and firm belief in racial differences, it was also through games such as cricket that some missionaries saw their pupils 'just as Scottish lads', some of whom had considerable talent and potential. In contrast with other European colonists, whose sports events from early on were marked by racial demarcation and celebration of imperial identity and hierarchy, some of the missionaries played earnestly and equally with Africans. To contrast the *machila* race of the Shire Highlands games with a mission-school football match is to illustrate the range of attitudes associated with colonial sports in the region in the 1890s.

However, all the missionary sports, including 'Christianized' dances, were very much about control. When the more progressive missionaries wanted to introduce African Christian dances to combat the challenge presented by African pagan dancing, they were explicit on this point. In the stereotyping of muscular African men in games fields, as has been seen, it was often control and coordination that missionaries believed was lacking and in need of colonial disciplining. 'Uncontrolled' dances were connected to uncontrolled sexuality, a central concern in Victorian missionary thought regarding other cultures, as well as in European racist and ethnocentric prejudices about Africans. Carpentry, drill, team games and 'purified' dances all shared the same objective of regulation of perceived promiscuity. Regulation proved to be a thorny issue. The question of dancing and morality, in particular, divided both the Scottish missionaries and the African Christians.

While throughout the empire sport was widely, and often enthusiastically, accepted as an essential part of missionary education, the relationship between Scottish missionaries and sport was not straightforward. For some missionaries, sport had nothing to do with the missionary enterprise; for others, it was an excellent means of moral education, preservation of health and the training and disciplining of the body. It can be argued with reason that in the education of the body, sport was in part competing with an industrial educational tradition that was central to Scotland and correspondingly both to Blantyre and Livingstonia Missions. Industrial education had other objectives, such as the training of skilled workers and self-reliant craftsmen. However, like games, it aimed at improving skill, coordination, strength, and above all, *control* and discipline of the body. In Blantyre, with its connections to the middle-class Scottish sporting elite strongly influenced by the contemporary English public school, team games were encouraged far earlier and considerably more than in Livingstonia, but by the First World War, team games had been firmly established in the Overtoun Institution too.

In the history of missions and team games, the case of the Scots in Malawi can be regarded as part of a gradually extended complex historical process of cultural diffusion, from England to Scotland to Central Africa. If the Blantyre connections to athleticism and the games ethic can be traced to upper-middle-class schools in

Edinburgh in the 1870s and 1880s, the Overtoun Institution was importantly connected to developments in Glasgow, where in middle-class day schools the curriculum was increasingly broadened to include sport from the 1890s onwards. It can be argued that in this process, English-influenced Scottish promoters of athleticism such as Hely Hutchinson Almond and John Guthrie Kerr, educational 'missionaries to middle classes', eventually indirectly impacted upon Scottish missions in Central Africa. However, this process was not simply 'Anglicization in action', neither in Glasgow nor in Livingstonia. As utilitarian compromise, the combination of literary, practical and physical education in the early-twentieth-century Overtoun Institution can be compared with contemporary Glaswegian middle-class schools, with their distinct 'British' blend of Scottish utilitarian and English athletic education. [101] In Overtoun Institution, the predominant missionary educational programme, formulated by Laws, emphasizing religion, academic attainment, crafts and the Protestant work ethic, gradually accommodated drill and team games advocated by Kirkwood in particular, creating a particular 'blend' of imperial missionary education.

What significance this process had for the African pupils of Livingstonia and Blantyre, and to the wider social and cultural history of education and sport in Malawi, remains beyond the scope of this article. In his analysis of imperial physical education in tropical Africa, Mangan has argued that the English missionaries' enthusiasm for games was not generally shared by their pragmatic African pupils, for whom the literary and technical education offered by the mission schools was considered far more valuable. [102] This may well be the case for the Scottish mission schools too. It is noteworthy that in his detailed memories of mission-school life at Blantyre at the turn of the twentieth century, L.M. Bandawe, who trained as a teacher, does not mention sport or games at all, in contrast to his emphasis on higher education. [103]

However, in time the one game the missionaries imported to Central Africa as part of their cultural baggage that remained and spread on a large scale was association football – not cricket or the rugby favoured by some middle-class Scottish missionaries. It should be noted that by the 1920s at least, the Overtoun Institution-educated teachers of Livingstonia were taking association football to the village schools. Mission pupils were not the only active group in the dissemination of soccer, a process with significant long term consequences for culture and society in South-Central Africa, but they certainly played a part. [104]

In a recent television series on the history of football, a Zambian journalist stated that it was believed that David Livingstone brought the first football to South-Central Africa. This myth perhaps suggests that football has been associated with Livingstone today in part because for many he symbolizes all that was valuable in early exchanges between Africans and Europeans, and because football has been accepted as one of the more beneficial novelties of the colonial era. It is probably impossible to say who brought the first football to the region, but in the case of Malawi and north-eastern Zambia, the two Scottish missions that took their institutional name and religious inspiration from Livingstone were certainly involved in its dissemination, and their motives were as much moral as physical. However, their emphasis on technical and manual education and their partiality to drill demonstrates that English athleticism, so influential as an imperial educational ideology, was adjusted to particular values, not only African but also Scottish, in Africa.

Acknowledgements

I am grateful to Dr Harri Englund and Professor A.C. Ross for their helpful comments on this paper. Any omissions and errors are solely the responsibility of the author.

Notes

[1] D. Arnold and R.A. Bickers, 'Introduction', in R.A. Bickers and R. Seton (eds.), *Missionary Encounters. Sources and Issues* (Richmond: Curzon Press, 1996), pp.4–5; J.A. Mangan, *The Games Ethic and Imperialism* (London and Portland, OR: Frank Cass 1998), p.168.

[2] *World Missionary Conference Edinburgh, 1910: Report of Commission III: Education in relation to the Christianisation of Native Life* (Edinburgh and London, 1910), pp.246–7.

[3] Ibid., pp.187–90 and *passim*.

[4] For a full discussion and analysis of 'athleticism' as potent imperial educational ideology and its origins, see J.A. Mangan, *Athleticism in the Victorian and Edwardian Public School: the emergence and consolidation of an educational ideology* (London and Portland, OR: Frank Cass, 2000). The Cass edition contains a new, extensive introduction. While today athleticism has purely physical connotation in the media, in Victorian and Edwardian usage it signified ideas, feelings and values, particularly regarding moral and character training through team games.

[5] *World Missionary Conference*, pp.187–8. For Weatherhead, see J.A. Mangan, 'Ethics and Ethnocentricity: Imperial Education in British Tropical Africa', in W.J. Baker and J.A. Mangan (eds.), *Sport in Africa. Essays in Social History* (New York: Africana Publishing Company, 1987), pp.146–7, 167–8.

[6] In 1910, for example, the Weatherhead brothers in charge of Budo included woodwork, printwork, building, cultivation and bee keeping in the school programme. Church Missionary Society, *Extracts from the Annual Letters of the Missionaries for the year1910* (London), pp.209–10. Consulted in CMS Archives, Birmingham University Library.

[7] Mangan, 'Ethics and Ethnocentricity'.

[8] The historians' assessment of Macdonald's book has been mixed. For some, it is a valuable historical account of the Shire Highlands of the time, others have stressed it represented Africans in very prejudiced ways. G. Shepperson , 'Introduction' in D. Macdonald, *Africana, or the Heart of Heathen Africa* (London: Dawsons of Pall Mall, 1969), pp.5–11; W.O. Mulwafu, 'The Interface of Christianity and Conservation in Colonial Malawi', *Journal of Religion in Africa*, 34, 3 (2004).

[9] Macdonald, *Africana*, pp.224–5.

[10] This phenomenon is generating increasing scholastic interest particularly in the context of anti-colonial nationalism. In the context of early colonial exchanges between missionaries and Africans in the Shire Highlands, however, it is difficult to see a direct connection between sport and politics. More significant in Macdonald's description is the mention of a

piece of paper as a 'cricket charm', suggesting one local injection of meaning to the imported game. For a recent discussion of Western sport as an instrument of anti-colonialism, see B. Majumdar and J.A. Mangan (eds.), *Sport in South Asian Society: Past and Present* (London: Routledge, 2004), and for the use of Western sport as source of opposition to Eastern imperialism in Korea, see J.A. Mangan and Fan Hong (eds.), *Sport in Asian Society: Past and Present* (Londonand Portland, OR: Frank Cass, 2003).

[11] For a good example of a imperialist resorting to racist ridicule in describing Africans playing European games, see H.L. Duff, *Nyasaland under the Foreign Office* (London: George Bell and Sons, 1903), quoted in A. Werner, *The Natives of British Central Africa* (London: Archibald Constable and Company, 1906), pp.115–16.

[12] A.C. Ross, *Blantyre Mission and the Making of Modern Malawi* (Blantyre: CLAIM 1996), pp.63–8 and *passim*; K.R. Ross, *Gospel Ferment in Malawi: Theological Essays* (Gweru: Mambo Press 1995), pp.107–25.

[13] Ross, *Blantyre Mission*, p.63.

[14] A.H. Charteris, *In Memoriam. David Clement Ruffelle Scott* (Edinburgh, 1907), p.4. Memorial pamphlet in Edinburgh University Centre for the Study of Christianity in Non-Western World library (hereafter CSCNWW), *Nyasaland and Kikuyu*, VI; A. Hetherwick, *The Romance of Blantyre* (London: n.d. [1931]), p.35. Hetherwick claims here that it was partly Scott's 'strong, handsome, muscular frame' that made him 'a leader and a hero' in the eyes of many Africans.

[15] *The Mission Record*, June 1882. CSCNWW, *Nyasaland and Kikuyu*, II.

[16] H.A.C. Cairns, *Prelude to Imperialism. British Reactions to Central African Society 1840–1890* (London: Routledge, 1965), p.101 and *passim*.

[17] *The Mission Record*, Oct. 1882. CSCNWW, *Nyasaland and Kikuyu*, II.

[18] *The Mission Record*, Nov. 1992. CSCN-WW, *Nyasaland and Kikuyu*, II.

[19] R.D. Anderson, 'Sport in the Scottish Universities, 1860–1939', *International Journal of the History of Sport*, 4, 2 (1987), 178. The pioneering Scottish elite school in this respect was Loretto School outside Edinburgh, see Mangan, *Athleticism*; J.A. Mangan, 'Missionaries to the Middle Classes', in H.Holmes (ed.), *Scottish Life and Society. A Compendium of Scottish Ethnology*, Vol.11 (Trowbridge: Tuckwell Press, 2000).

[20] Oxford University played an important part in this process, through the Snell Exhibitions for Scots at Balliol College; see Mangan, *Athleticism*, for its influence on Hely Hutchinson Almond, the legendary nineteenth-century philathletic headmaster of Loretto, but see also J.A. Mangan (ed.), *Pleasure, Profit, Proselytism: British Culture and Sport at Home and Abroad 1700–1914* (London: Frank Cass, 1988) for a discussion of John Guthrie Kerr, a famous Glaswegian headmaster who espoused athleticism. Both Almond and Kerr were Snell Exhibitioners.

[21] Scott, in a letter dated 22 May 1883. Quoted in *The Mission Record*, September 1883, CSCNWW, *Nyasaland and Kikuyu*, II; Scott to Sunday Schools and Families, Nov. 1887 [n.d.], CSCNWW, *Nyasaland and Kikuyu*, II, 59.

[22] Ross, *Blantyre Mission*, p.73.

[23] John McCracken, 'The Urban Experience in Malawi', unpublished chapter. I am grateful for Dr. McCracken for permission to quote this chapter.

[24] Edinburgh University Library Special Collections (hereafter EUL), Mic. P.565, *Life and Work in British Central Africa* (hereafter *LWBCA*).

[25] W.H. Rankine, *A Hero of the Dark Continent* (London and Edinburgh: William Blackwood and Sons, 1896), pp.5–6, 12–13. W.A. Scott was educated at Mr Hunter's private school in Edinburgh, the High School of Edinburgh, and Edinburgh University.

[26] The foreign mission movement in nineteenth-century Britain were paralleled by a wide-ranging movement by various evangelical voluntary societies for the spiritual, physical and

social 'regeneration' of domestic 'savages' , particularly in urban settings. See, for example, C. Brown, *The Social History of Church in Scotland Since 1730* (London: Methuen, 1987); O. Checkland, *Philanthropy in Victorian Scotland. Social Welfare and the Voluntary Principle* (Edinburgh: John Donald, 1980), pp.63–73. Many Scottish medical missionaries, in particular, had experience in the slums of Glasgow and Edinburgh before going to Central Africa. See *The Record of the United Free Church of Scotland,* July 1927, pp.327–9.

[27] Rankine, *A Hero of the Dark Continent,* pp.56–73.

[28] *LWBCA,* Feb. 1895. Among the UMCA missionaries in British Central Africa, soccer was encouraged especially by Arthur Douglas; Mangan, 'Ethics and Ethnocentricity', pp.154–5.

[29] *LWBCA,* July 1899.

[30] *LWBCA,* Feb. 1898. The tone of the letter suggests it was written not by D.C. Scott, but perhaps by one of the mission doctors – Henry Scott or Neil MacVicar, both graduates of Edinburgh where rugby was especially popular. See Anderson, 'Sport in the Scottish Universities', 179–80.

[31] *LWBCA,* Feb. 1891.

[32] *LWBCA,* Jan. 1891.

[33] *LWBCA,* March 1891.

[34] *LWBCA,* June 1892. The identification of anonymous editors of the magazine is based on A.C. Ross's introductory note, EUL Mic. p.565. From its establishment in 1888 to 1898/9, D.C. Scott was the editor of *LWBCA,* followed by Dr. Neil MacVicar (1898/9–1900) and Alexander Hetherwick (1900–1919).

[35] Ibid.

[36] *LWBCA,* Aug. 1892.

[37] *LWBCA,* Feb. 1894. Organizing of races for categories such as 'married women' and 'headmen' is particularly interesting.

[38] *LWBCA,* Nov. and Dec. 1896. In the April of the same year, the annual Military Sport Day at Zomba was attended by one thousand Africans. See L. White, *Magomero. Portrait of an African Village* (Cambridge: Cambridge University Press 1987), p.70.

[39] *LWBCA,* Nov. and Dec. 1896.

[40] Ross, *Gospel Ferment in Malawi,* p.115.

[41] On nerve force in Victorian medical theory, see J. Oppenheim, *Shattered Nerves. Doctors, Patients and Depression in Victorian England* (New York: Oxford University Press 1991), pp.79–109 and *passim.*

[42] *LWBCA,* May, June and July 1897.

[43] *LWBCA,* Jan. 1899.

[44] *LWBCA,* Dec. 1899.

[45] *LWBCA,* Jan.–March 1901. In Malawi, *Chaka* can still mean an annual festival in Chichewa, but a common term for 'sport' is *masawero* from the verb *kusewera,* to play.

[46] *LWBCA,* June 1898.

[47] *LWBCA,* May 1899.

[48] *LWBCA,* July 1899.

[49] McCracken, *Politics and Christianity in Malawi 1875–1940* (Cambridge: Cambridge University Press, 1977), pp.33, 181; P. Forster, *T. Cullen Young: Missionary and Anthropologist* (Hull: Hull University Press, 1989), pp.3–7.

[50] Henderson to Davidson, 6 Feb. 1896. In M.M.S. Ballantyne and R.H.W. Shepherd (eds.), *Forerunners of Modern Malawi. The Early Missionary Adventures of Dr James Henderson 1895–1898* (Lovedale: Lovedale Press, 1968), p.113. Robert Laws was educated in the universities of Aberdeen and Glasgow. He belonged to the generation of students in Aberdeen when organized sports were just about to make their breakthrough. See Anderson, 'Sport in the Scottish Universities', 178–9.

[51] Ballantyne and Shepherd, *Forerunners of Modern Malawi*, p.249. According to Shepherd (p.ix), Henderson had a 'wonderful physique' and he was a legendary marcher during his Nyasaland years.

[52] National Library of Scotland (hereafter NLS), Acc.7548, D71, Letters to the Livingstonia Sub-Committee, 1905, p.82; Young to Daly, 24 Aug. 1905.

[53] *Annual Report for the Livingstonia Mission* (hereafter *Annual Report*), 1903, pp.15–17.

[54] 'Native Education in British Central Africa', *The Aurora*, April 1897, 9–10.

[55] 'The Educational Work at the Institution', *The Aurora*, Aug. 1901, 29–31; McCracken, *Politics and Christianity*, pp.141–2.

[56] For the 1906 educational scheme at the Institution, see NLS, Acc.7548, D71, Letters to Livingstonia Sub-Committee, 1906, pp.39–42; Laws to HM Acting Commissioner, 16 Feb. 1906.

[57] NLS, MS. 7883, 14. Elmslie to Smith, 31 Jan. 1900.

[58] NLS, MS. 7883, 35. Elmslie to Smith, 24 April 1900.

[59] NLS, MS. 7883, 112.Elmslie to Smith, 12 July 1900.

[60] *Annual Report for 1900*, p.11.

[61] Mangan, 'Missionaries to the Middle Classes', pp.416–18.

[62] Ballantyne and Shepherd, *Forerunners of Modern Malawi*, p.116.

[63] Henderson to Davidson, 25 April 1897; Ballantyne and Shepherd, *Forerunners of Modern Malawi*, pp.233–4.

[64] See J.A. Mangan, 'Physical Education as a Ritual Process' in J.A. Mangan (ed.), *Physical Education and Sport: Sociological and Cultural Perspectives, an Introductory Reader* (Oxford: Blackwell, 1973), pp.94–6.

[65] Henderson to Davidson, 25 April 1897; Ballantyne and Shepherd, *Forerunners of Modern Malawi*, p.216.

[66] Already in 1875, during his first journey up the Zambezi, Robert Laws commented with admiration the 'athletic frames and well developed muscles [which] tell of great strength' of African men on the river when in health, but continued that in illness their need for 'the blessings of the gospel' was apparent, linking explicitly bodily health to evangelism. Laws, letter written at the Kongoni mouth of the Zambezi River, Aug. 1875. Aberdeen University Library Special Collections, M/Laws 3/1, Transcripts of letters from Robert Laws.

[67] *Annual Report for 1903*, p.7.

[68] *Annual Report for 1902*, pp.16–19. Curiously, Mackenzie believed that the teaching of (British) history, in particular, was a 'refining' vehicle for his African students.

[69] Ibid., pp.21, 26; Mackenzie to Daly 21 July 1902. NLS, Acc.7548, D70. Letters to the Livingstonia Sub-Committee, 1902, pp.76–7. At this time, unspecified 'games' for girl boarders of Livingstonia were also introduced, but as extracurricular and holiday entertainment. Miss Winifred Knight, a mission teacher, believed they were instrumental in helping the girls to 'rejoice in Christ', complementing teaching in morality and the work ethic.

[70] *Annual Report for 1903*, pp.1–8.

[71] NLS, Acc.7548, D72 and 73, Livingstonia Staff Record Book and Staff Information Book; Mangan, 'Missionaries to the Middle Classes', pp.421–31.

[72] NLS, Acc.7548, D71, Letters to the Livingstonia Sub-Committee, 1907, pp.39–40; Kirkwood to Daly, 7 March 1907.

[73] *Annual Report for 1906*, p.12.

[74] *Annual Report for 1907*, pp.10–12, 18–19.

[75] Ibid.

[76] *Annual Report for 1908*, pp.11–12.

[77] *Annual Report for 1909*, p.7.

[78] *Annual Report for 1911*, p.7.

[79] *Annual Report for 1912*, p.5.

[80] *Annual Report for 1913*, p.4.

[81] Ibid., p.5.

[82] NLS, Acc.7548, D72, Livingstonia Mission Staff Record Book.

[83] *Annual Report for 1912*, p.22.

[84] Ibid.

[85] *Annual Report for1912.*

[86] T.J. Thompson, *Christianity in Northern Malawi. Donald Fraser's Missionary Methods and Ngoni Culture* (Leiden: Brill, 1995), p.153.

[87] *LWBCA*, March 1891.

[88] Ross, *Blantyre Mission*, p.75.

[89] *LWBCA*, Aug. 1892.

[90] *LWBCA*, Oct. 1892.

[91] Mackenzie to Daly, 21 July 1902. NLS, Acc.7548, D70, Letters to the Livingstonia Sub-Committee, 1902, pp.76–7.

[92] McCracken, *Politics and Christianity*, pp.196–7. In Loudon, teacher (later Revd) Charles Chinula organized secret dance sessions at the mission school in 1908. Thompson, *Christianity in Northern Malawi*, p.152.

[93] For an interesting dialogue between Chisholm and African teacher-evangelists on this subject, see NLS, Acc.7548, D70, Letters to the Livingstonia Sub-Committee, 1904, pp.55–6. Chisholm to Daly, 25 Jan.–10 March 1904.

[94] NLS, Acc.7548, D71, Letters to the Livingstonia Sub-Committee, 1908, pp.71–2, Minutes of Livingstonia Presbytery, Jan. 1908.

[95] Donald Fraser, 'The Church and Games in Africa', *International Review of Missions*, X (1921), pp.110–12. Significantly, Fraser fails to mention here that the Ngoni dances were explicitly used to challenge the missionaries and the Christians.

[96] Ibid., pp.113–15.

[97] Ibid., pp.115–17.

[98] Ibid., p.117.

[99] For an example of strong condemnation of dancing, see a book review of 'Dancing Ancient and Modern' in *The Record of the United Free Church of Scotland*, Sept. 1927.

[100] N. Thomas, *Colonialism's Culture: Anthropology, Travel, Government* (Cambridge: Polity Press, 1994), pp.ix, x, quoted in C. Hall (ed.), *Cultures of Empire. Colonizers in Britain and the Empire in the Nineteenth and Twentieth Centuries. A Reader.* (Manchester: Manchester University Press 2000), p.16.

[101] Mangan, 'Missionaries to the Middle Classes', pp.421–31. Perhaps the most distinctive Glaswegian school in this respect was Allan Glen's, headed by John Guthrie Kerr during 1890–1917. J.A. Mangan, 'Catalyst of Change: John Guthrie Kerr and the Adaptation of an Indigenous Scottish Tradition', in J.A. Mangan (ed.), *Pleasure, Profit, Proselytism: British Culture and Sport at Home and Abroad 1700–1914* (London: Frank Cass, 1988).

[102] Mangan, 'Ethics and Ethnocentricity'.

[103] L.M. Bandawe, *Memoirs of a Malawian* (Blantyre: CLAIM, 1971).

[104] *The Record of the United Free Church of Scotland*, May 1924, p.262; McCracken, 'The Urban Experience in Malawi'; J.A. Steytler, *Educational Adaptations with Reference to African Village Schools with Special Reference to Central Nyasaland* (London: Sheldon Press, 1939), p.144. Steytler, a Dutch Reformed Church mission school principal at Mkhoma, observed that soccer was the only European game that had really caught on in Nyasaland by the 1930s, in those communities that could afford a football. Migrant workers, particularly to Rhodesia and South Africa, as well as soldiers in colonial forces, were two other significant groups

disseminating football in early twentieth-century Malawi. I am grateful to Dr. Englund for pointing out the importance of migrant workers, many of whom had mission education. During the period under review, soccer was a predominantly working class game in Scotland, where football professionalism emerged in contrast to amateur athleticism. It is noteworthy that although many early Scottish missionaries to Malawi came from working-class background, they seem not to have taken particularly active part in the dissemination of soccer.

Epilogue: A Fine Example Has Boundless Power

Fan Hong

A fine example has boundless power. – Vladimir Illych Lenin

Professor Mangan is an outstanding scholar. Between 1981 and 2004 he published 32 books; 31 book chapters and 13 articles. Merely two of many accolades: his 1981 *Athleticism in the Victorian and Edwardian Public School* is regarded as both a landmark and a classic. The distinguished Berkeley cultural historian Sheldon Rothblatt wrote in his foreword to the 2001 Frank Cass edition:

> The Mangan prose is witty, spirited and robust – a trademark of his writing in general. And a final if not a last word is that *Athleticism* is a work of good sense. Mangan came not to bury nor to praise public schools but to explain what they were doing and how they did it, intentionally and unintentionally. That is the book's apologia. We can thank all parties for re-issuing a classic! [1]

Mangan's 1987 *From 'Fair Sex' to Feminism: Sport and the Socialization of Women in the Industrial and Post-Industrial Eras* (co-edited with Roberta Park) was 'path breaking' and 'marked ... a watershed in scholarship on women's sport history during the 1980s by focusing substantially upon analysis rather than description'. [2] His research has covered the historical, anthropological, political, sociological and cultural aspects of sport. Phenomenal!

The setting down of simply a small selection of his titles makes the point: *Shaping the Superman: Fascist Body as Political Icon – Aryan Fascism*; *Tribal Identities: Nationalism, Europe, Sport*; *The Games Ethics and Imperialism*; *Reformers, Sport, Modernizers: Middle-Class Revolutionaries*; *Making European Masculinities: Sport, Europe, Gender*; *The Cultural Bond: Sport, Empire, Society* and *Shaping Global Societies: Europe, Sport, World*. His educational works such as *Making Imperial Mentalities: Socialization and British Imperialism* and *The Imperial Curriculum: Racial Image and Education in the British Colonial Experience* should be added to this impressive list.

Professor Mangan is also an innovative, energetic and productive editor. He has been the founding editor and executive academic editor of four international journals: *The International Journal of the History of Sport*; *Sport in Society*; *Soccer and Society*; and the *European Sports History Review*. *The International Journal of the History of Sport* has become the leading journal in the field. In celebration of his contribution to the history of sport, *The International Journal for the History of Sport* dedicated a special issue in 2004 and associated volume to him entitled '*Serious Sport*': *J.A. Mangan's Contribution to the History of Sport*.

There is more. He is also the founding editor and executive editor of the book series 'Sport in the Global Society' – a unique series. It has drawn together many subjects in the expanding study of sport in the global society and provided comprehensiveness and comparison within a single series of some 70 volumes between 1997 and 2004. His vision, ambition, persistence and encouragement has attracted many leading scholars to contribute to the series. Trevor Slack has commented: 'The list of writers involved in "Sport in the Global Society" reads like a *Who's Who* of the socio-cultural study of sport.' [3]

Professor Mangan's role as an editor should never be overlooked, minimized or unappreciated. He remarked to me a little while ago that he felt very tired after 'rewriting the world for so many years'. It was written of the publisher and novelist David Hughes, who died recently, that 'he was frustrated at constantly having to rewrite "the work of men ... who could scarcely string two sentences together" and would sit gazing vacantly over Soho Square bringing up to scratch other men's books when all he wanted to do was be at home plotting his own'. [4] In contrast to David Hughes, Professor Mangan took on his editorial task willingly in the sincere belief that he was advancing an unreasonably neglected subject – the impact of modern sport on the global society – politically, economically, culturally, emotionally and spiritually.

Arguably, however, perhaps his greatest contribution to scholarship will prove to be the selection, nurturing and inspiring of his doctoral and postdoctoral students. His main publisher, Frank Cass, wrote perceptively in his Publisher's Note to the celebratory volume '*Serious Sport*': *J.A. Mangan's Contribution to the History of Sport*:

> The contributors to this collection discuss Tony Mangan's innovative and visionary pursuit of the study of imperialism and sport, and his work on militarism and sport, and on sport and the Victorian social classes, but it is the fulsome tributes from his former students, now themselves established and successful academics, which offer real insight into Tony Mangan the man, the teacher, the guide, philosopher and friend, whose faith in them launched their careers as academics and authors. [5]

As one of Professor Mangan's former students I wholly agree with Frank Cass. Professor Mangan is simply the finest supervisor a research student could hope for. For me it all began on a dark and cold winter day in Glasgow in 1991, when fate led me to his office in Jordanhill. Face to face with the charming but strict professor I was only too aware that it would not be easy. There was a long and difficult linguistic, conceptual and empirical route to travel. In particular, I had to climb a steep linguistic 'track'. In this journey through the landscape of the English language, Professor Mangan was my skilled and sure-footed guide. He supported my every faltering step with the attention to my efforts that every student hopes for. As Professor Mangan's first IRCSSS doctoral student, as I have stated elsewhere in this volume, 'I benefited enormously from his quality of supervision: speedy in response, meticulous in textual scrutiny. He was always available for discussion, continually encouraging and enthusiastic in approach'. [6] I finally completed my journey in Scotland after some tears and much laughter and saw my thesis published as a monograph in his 'Sport in the Global Society' series. It was the icing on the cake.

However, it was not always nose to the grindstone. Studying with Professor Mangan was also enjoyable. One of his qualities was to note and assuage his students' exhaustion. The visits to Ross Priory, the beautiful faculty club on Loch Lomond, remain vivid in my memory. Nor was study with him all culturally one-way traffic: while I learnt to appreciate from him that British policemen did not have the keys to all private houses, he learnt to appreciate that Chinese cooking in China *was* rather different from that in Britain. While I discovered from him that Oxford and Cambridge did not face each other across a meandering stream in the English Midlands, he discovered from me that the Père David's deer at Edinburgh Zoo, was not 'discovered' by the French missionary of that name but had been known to the Chinese for thousands of years! He took the news well. He was always greatly amused, too, when in moments of exasperation at his demanding standards and in a brave Chinese attempt not to lose face, I would forcefully remark that when his 'lot' danced naked in blue paint on the white cliffs at the approach of the Romans, my 'lot' had silk, porcelain, a written language and a sophisticated culture.

My Chinese colleague, Dong Jinxia at IRCSSS, had similar experiences to mine. She was Professor Mangan's doctoral student from 1993 to 2001. She recalls:

> I was delighted when I gained a research place at his centre. However, ... delight was quickly tempered with concern when I discovered just how stony the path ahead was going to be for me. ... I was on my own personal academic 'Long March' on a pathway that climbed up and up and was not only stony but slippery. ... What sustained me was my supervisor's commitment to my success. He backed me – intellectually and spiritually. ... Under Professor Mangan's mentorship, my intellectual competence and my proficiency in English all improved beyond measure. More than this, I learned that determination, perseverance and belief are essential qualities for success. Without any doubt, Professor J.A. Mangan had, and still has, a special influence on my academic career. His lessons are lasting. [7]

Dong Jinxia is now an associate professor at Beijing University and her thesis was also published as a monograph in 'Sport in the Global Society'.

My other Asian colleague at IRCSS, Gwang Ok, came from South Korea. He was Professor Mangan's doctoral student from 1998 to 2003. He met the professor in

Seoul when he was visiting Korean universities. Gwang chose to study sport and politics in Korean society with the professor. He faced the same challenges as we had, linguistically, conceptually and culturally. He has acknowledged that it was Professor Mangan's guidance, support and strength that ensured his success. The chapter he contributes to this book was partially researched during his studies with Professor Mangan. Gwang is now a researcher with the Korean NOC.

I met Henrik Meinander, then a Finnish student, in the mid 1990s at Jordanhill. He was completing his thesis. It was proof-read not only by Professor Mangan but also by his wife Doris, a first-rate proof-reader and first-class linguist. [8] It was later published as a book in Finland. Henrik is now a distinguished professor of history at Helsinki University. In the late 1990s he co-edited a book, *Sport in the Nordic World*, with Professor Mangan. He remembered the summer in 1999 with bemused appreciation, because Professor Mangan did not spend his spare time on the beautiful beach of Santa Barbara – where he was a visiting professor at the University of California – but on the chapters of the book. He corrected, edited and even rewrote some parts of the chapters. The effort was worth it. The book, for the first time, brought Nordic sports studies to the wider English-speaking world. No wonder Henrik has remarked: 'For this the Nordic research community is truly thankful.' [9]

I first heard of Markku Hokkanen, another greatly talented IRCSSS Finnish student, a long time ago but only met him in Bedford in 2003, when we planned this book. I knew he was undertaking the study of Scottish missionaries in Africa. Professor Mangan's work had inspired him from a distance and he wrote to him. Immediately, the professor, with his usual directness, took him under his wing without any hesitation. This clearly had an impact on Markku. When I approached him about a contribution to this book he agreed immediately and was the first person to submit a chapter.

I had dinner with Colm Hickey at Professor Mangan's house when Colm came from London to receive supervision on yet another cold and wet Scottish day in 1993. He was then acting headteacher of a secondary school. During dinner we shared our experience of our supervisor's style: carrot-and-stick. He would praise you when you worked hard and criticize you when you did not. As a part-time student with a heavy workload, Colm knew that it was all too easy to lose sight of his final ambition – a doctorate. He was grateful for the professor's constant encouragement *and* criticism. It kept him, he said, on his toes.

Colm told me a wonderful story. Professor Mangan had not heard from him for some time. The FIFA World Cup was being televised. One day Colm placed his beer on the coffee table beside him, sat himself comfortably in front of the television and waited for the match to start. While he was waiting he opened a letter from Professor Mangan. It read simply: 'Put the beer can down; get off the sofa; switch off the television – and get on with the chapter you promised me!' Colm framed the letter and it now has pride of place on the wall of his study. Colm is now the headteacher of a specialist sports college in London. He is co-author with Professor Mangan of *Missing Men – Soccer Schoolmasters: Pioneering the*

People's Game Across the Globe. It will shortly be published in the series 'Sport in the Global Society'. I am not surprised to read his comment prior to his chapter in this book: 'His [Mangan's] constant encouragement and support while I was completing my thesis is gratefully acknowledged. He is a wonderful mentor and I am proud to call him a friend.' [10]

I met Andrew Ritchie at a conference – in a train. Why in a train? It was part of the conference entertainment. Andrew is both a scholar and a musician: he has played in national and international orchestras. He met Professor Mangan in 1998 when he was doing a one-year M.Phil. at Edinburgh University on his great-great-grandfather, Dr John Ritchie, a politically active Presbyterian minister in mid-nineteenth-century Scotland. However, his passion for cycling led him to contact Professor Mangan. When he saw Andrew's intellectual potential he persuaded him to change his research from Scottish political/ecclesiastical history to sports history. Who can resist Professor Mangan? Andrew now has completed his doctorate dissertation and it will soon be published under the title *Bicycle Racing: Sport, Technology and Modernity, 1867–1903.*

Then there is Hamad Ndee from Africa. He was born and grew up in Tanzania, studied in Moscow for four years for his first degree, went to Norway for his master's degree and then went on to Glasgow for his Ph.D. I believe he can speak at least five languages. He met Professor Mangan in Norway, and then the professor went to Africa on a lecture tour – alone – and came back with Hamad as his doctoral student. Professor Mangan was a wonderful mentor to his African recruit. Hamad has recalled: 'I was fortunate to have been supervised by Professor James Anthony Mangan during my Ph.D. studies. ... His attention to details, his continual patience, his support and his analytical rigour proved to be inestimable supervisory qualities.' [11] Hamad is now head of the department of physical education, sport and culture at the University of Dar es Salaam. I only occasionally receive emails from him, which tell me that he has been 'up country' and 'going round' on teaching practice supervision. I am sure wherever he is in 'the bush' he will never forget his mentor and his friends at IRCSSS.

He too has an illustrative Mangan tale. It happened at the University of Dar es Salaam, where Hamad was at the time a lecturer and Professor Mangan was giving a series of lectures. The professor was staying in a room next to an American scholar, who one day rushed in panic for refuge to Mangan's room, exclaiming that a snake had invaded his bedroom. As he rushed in, Professor Mangan rushed out – for a close look!

How can we all forget Penny Kissoudi, the lively Greek scholar? At a conference in Madrid she approached the professor for his advice on her paper and was so impressed that she ended up as his doctoral student. It is Professor Mangan's determination and encouragement that gave her strength. As she has claimed: 'Due to his excellent supervision and strong support, my ambition to inquire into the politics of sport through the medium of the English language and my desire to work with an inspiring scholar of international reputation have been fulfilled.' [12] Penny has almost completed her English Ph.D. thesis (she has a Ph.D already in Greek!). She is a senior lecturer at the University of Thessalonika.

And finally, and far from least, there is Boria Majumdar. Sufficient to say that it is more than fitting that as a Rhodes Scholar, he will pick up the torch from Professor Mangan who has written so illuminatingly about the Games Ethic in Empire.

These, of course, are merely some of Professor Mangan's students – the ones who have contribute to this Festschrift and whom I have met. They have all learnt from Professor Mangan that determination, persistence and perfection will overcome any obstacles in our future academic odysseys.

A Chinese proverb says that 'a single stone can cause one thousand waves' (*Yishi jiqi qianchenglang*). Professor Mangan, an Englishman, who is both analytical and imaginative, direct and subtle, strict and relaxed, has for decades sent seismic ripples across and beneath the surface of sports studies, with the result that only recently Allen Guttmann, in a personal tribute to him, wrote that 'No one has done more to advance the cause of Sports History'. [13]

In an effort to restore my flagging spirits, Professor Mangan once told me that in his youth at Irish international matches at Lansdowne Road, Dublin, the crowd would sing a song in an effort to revive 'wounded warriors' prone on the pitch. It goes: 'Old soldiers never die, never die, never die / Old soldiers never die, they simply fade away'. When he retired from Strathclyde University, I reminded him of the song. However, I was wrong. Professor Mangan will never fade away. His image remains vivid in his students' memories. Indeed, I suspect he may well prove to be immortal, inspiring new generations of 'soldiers' through those 'soldier students' who have been fortunate enough to have been supervised by him and to have worked with him.

Notes

[1] Sheldon Rothblatt, 'Foreword', in J.A. Mangan, *Athleticism in the Victorian and Edwardian Public School: The Emergence and Consolidation of an Educational Ideology* (London and Portland, OR: Frank Cass, 2001), p.xx.

[2] Debbie Cottrell, 'A Broadening Common Ground in Women's History and Sport History', paper presented at 107th meeting of the American Historical Association, Washington, DC, 1992, cited in Fan Hong, 'Freeing Bodies: Heroines in History', in J.A. Mangan and Fan Hong (eds.), *Freeing the Female Body: Inspectional Icons* (London and Portland, OR: Frank Cass, 2001), p.3.

[3] Trevor Slack, 'Sport in the Global Society: Shaping the Domain of Sport Studies', *The International Journal of the History of Sport*, Special Issue – 'Serious Sport' (2004), 120.

[4] See obituary of David Hughes, *Daily Telegraph*, 13 April 2005, 23.

[5] Frank Cass, 'Foreword', *The International Journal of the History of Sport*, Special Issue – 'Serious Sport' (2004).

[6] See the opening of Fan Hong, Ping Wu and Huan Xiong's contribution to this issue.

[7] See *The International Journal of the History of Sport*, Special Issue – 'Serious Sport' (2004), 142–3.

[8] See Jonathan Manley, 'Editing with J.A. Mangan', *The International Journal of the History of Sport*, Special Issue – 'Serious Sport' (2004), 2.

[9] See the opening to Henrik Meinander's contribution to this issue.

[10] See the opening to Colm Hickey's contribution to this issue.

[11] See the opening to Hamad Ndee's contribution to this issue.

[12] See the opening to Penelope Kissousi's contribution to this issue.

[13] Hand-written tribute on the flyleaf to J.A.Mangan in his personal copy, by the author Allen Guttmann, *Sports: the First Five Millennia* (Amherst and Boston: University of Massachusetts Press, 2004).

Index

Index notes: Tables and illustrations are denoted by page numbers in italics and bold respectively.